Annals of Native America

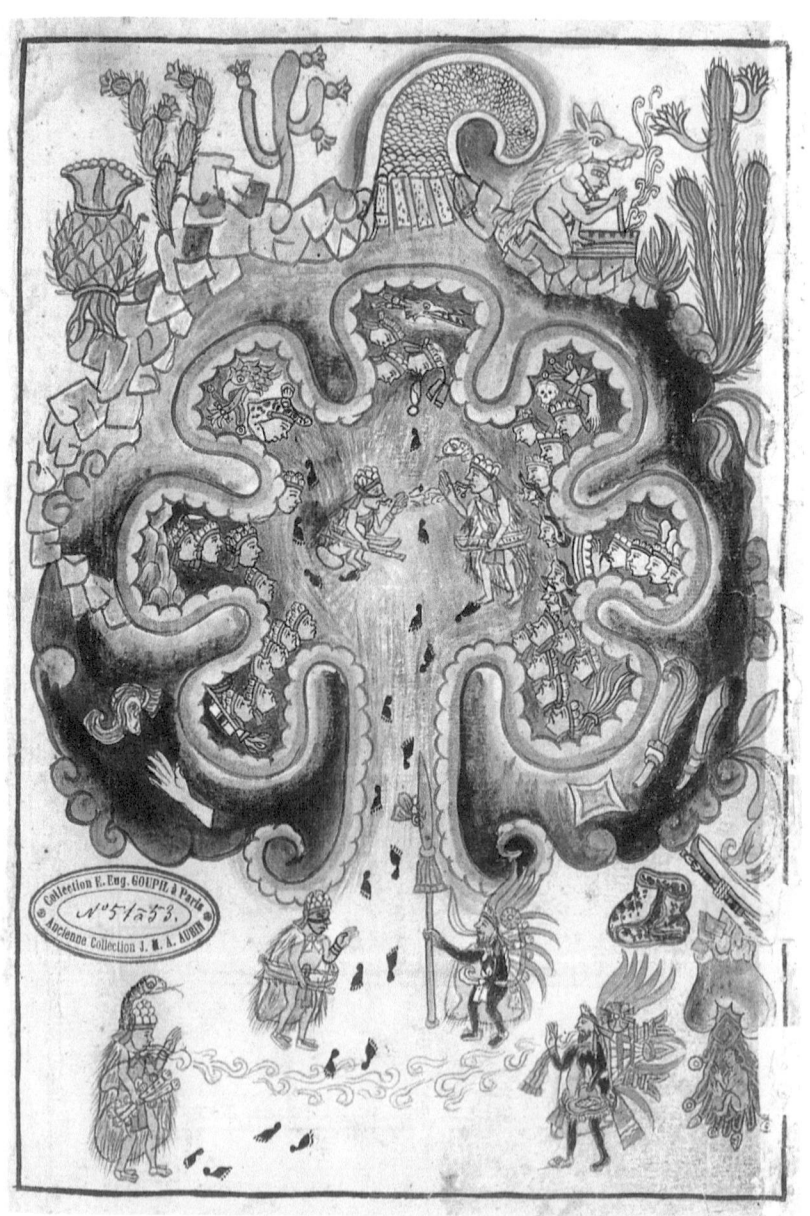

Historia Tolteca Chichimeca, folio 16. The people depart from Chicomoztoc (Seven Caves). Courtesy Bibliothèque Nationale de France.

Annals of Native America

How the Nahuas of Colonial Mexico Kept Their History Alive

CAMILLA TOWNSEND

OXFORD
UNIVERSITY PRESS

Oxford University Press is a department of the University of Oxford. It furthers
the University's objective of excellence in research, scholarship, and education
by publishing worldwide. Oxford is a registered trade mark of Oxford University
Press in the UK and certain other countries.

Published in the United States of America by Oxford University Press
198 Madison Avenue, New York, NY 10016, United States of America.

© Oxford University Press 2017

First issued as an Oxford University Press paperback, 2019

All rights reserved. No part of this publication may be reproduced, stored in
a retrieval system, or transmitted, in any form or by any means, without the
prior permission in writing of Oxford University Press, or as expressly permitted
by law, by license, or under terms agreed with the appropriate reproduction
rights organization. Inquiries concerning reproduction outside the scope of the
above should be sent to the Rights Department, Oxford University Press, at the
address above.

You must not circulate this work in any other form
and you must impose this same condition on any acquirer.

Library of Congress Cataloging-in-Publication Data
Names: Townsend, Camilla, author.
Title: Annals of Native America : how the Nahuas of colonial
Mexico kept their history alive / Camilla Townsend.
Description: New York, NY : Oxford University Press, 2016. |
Includes bibliographical references and index.
Identifiers: LCCN 2016017658 (print) | LCCN 2016027807 (ebook) |
ISBN 9780190628994 (hardcover : alk. paper) | ISBN 9780190055523 (paperback : alk. paper) |
ISBN 9780190629007 (Updf) | ISBN 9780190629014 (Epub)
Subjects: LCSH: Nahuas—History—Sources. | Nahuas—History—Authorship. |
Nahuatl language—History. | Nahuatl literature—History. |
Indians of Mexico—History. | Mexico—Antiquities. | Mexico—History—To 1519. |
Mexico—History—Conquest, 1519–1540.
Classification: LCC F1221.N3 T69 2016 (print) | LCC F1221.N3 (ebook) |
DDC 972/.00497452—dc23
LC record available at https://lccn.loc.gov/2016017658

*Dedicated to the memory
of James Lockhart
and Luis Reyes García*

There is no permanence. Do we build a house to stand forever, do we seal a contract to hold for all time? Do brothers divide an inheritance to keep forever, does the flood-time of rivers endure? It is only the nymph of the dragon-fly who sheds her larva and sees the sun in his glory. From the days of old there is no permanence.

The Epic of Gilgamesh

With sad flower tears [with poet's tears], I the singer set my song in order, remembering the princes who lie shattered, who lie enslaved in the place where all are shorn, they who were lords, who were kings on earth, who lie like withered feathers, like shattered jades. If only this [world] could have been before these princes' eyes: if only they could have seen what is now seen and known on earth.

Cantares Mexicanos

CONTENTS

Acknowledgments   *xi*
Glossary   *xv*

Introduction   1
1. Old Stories in New Letters (1520s–1550s)   17
2. Becoming Conquered (The 1560s)   55
3. Forging Friendship with Franciscans (1560s–1580s)   99
4. The Riches of Twilight (Circa 1600)   141
5. Renaissance in the East (The Seventeenth Century)   175
Epilogue: Postscript from a Golden Age   213

Appendices: The Texts in Nahuatl
   Historia Tolteca Chichimeca   *227*
   Annals of Tlatelolco   *230*
   Annals of Juan Bautista   *233*
   Annals of Tecamachalco   *241*
   Annals of Cuauhtitlan   *246*
   Chimalpahin, Seventh Relation   *252*
   Don Juan Buenaventura Zapata y Mendoza   *254*
Notes   *259*
Bibliography   *301*
Index   *313*

ACKNOWLEDGMENTS

The Nahuas of colonial Mexico who wrote about their history were enmeshed in a network of like-minded fellow travelers. Likewise, I, too, am proud to be part of a scholarly community that somehow is even bigger than the sum of its parts. This book is dedicated to the memory of two giants—James Lockhart and Luis Reyes García—who both recently departed this world, leaving behind friends and former students to carry on their work. I met Jim Lockhart in an advanced Nahuatl seminar that he taught at Yale in the summer of 2002, and from that moment, he helped and guided me in all my studies of Nahuatl documents, including the texts in this volume. He could not have been more generous with his time and energy, and I deeply regret that I did not finish this project while he was still here. Those who knew Jim well will remind me that he would have been unsparing in his criticism as well as warm in his praise; I would have wanted to hear it all. Luis Reyes I never met. By the time I got to Tlaxcala, he was too ill to see me, but he talked with me extensively by telephone. Since then, I have tried to read every word he ever wrote. Without the work of these two men, this book could never have been written.

I also have depended on the funders who made my own work possible. Years ago, the National Endowment for the Humanities and the American Philosophical Society paid for the time off from teaching and the travel that were prerequisites to the writing of what became chapter 5. More recently, the John Simon Guggenheim Memorial Foundation granted me a year-long fellowship that enabled me to draw together the research of many summers in meaningful ways. And in 2014–2015, a sabbatical at Rutgers University rendered it possible for me to finish the writing.

Archivists and librarians in a number of valuable institutions have provided essential help along the way. I give fulsome thanks to the staffs of the Archivo Histórico del Estado de Tlaxcala (AHET), the Bibliothèque Nationale de France (BNF), Mexico's Instituto Nacional de Antropología e Historia (INAH), the John Carter Brown Library (JCBL), the Library of Congress (LC) in Washington, D.C., the New York Public Library (NYPL), Princeton University's Firestone Library, the Princeton Theological Seminary Library, the Thomas J. Watson Library of the Metropolitan Museum of Art, and Sweden's Uppsala University Library.

Colleagues at many institutions were kind enough to invite me to talk about aspects of this work, and the insightful comments and questions I met with were helpful in moving me forward in my thinking or pointing me toward further research I needed to do. I thank the participants in such conversations at Colgate University, the College of New Jersey, Davidson College, De Pauw University, Hartwick College, Nazareth College, New York University, the Ohio State University, Princeton University, Sarah Lawrence, and the University of Utah. I was honored to receive feedback from indigenous language teachers after my address to the Symposium on the Teaching and Learning of Indigenous Languages and Literatures (STLILLA) at Notre Dame in 2011. Colleagues at scholarly conferences also helped me sharpen my thinking. Chapter 1 in particular was the subject of intense scrutiny at the Renaissance Society of America (2014), the American Society of Ethnohistory (2013), and the John Carter Brown Library's conference on Indigenous Literacy in Mesoamerica and the Colonial World (2012). Chapter 5 was discussed at Cambridge University's conference on Indigenous Intellectuals (2010) and the International Conference of Americanists in Mexico City (2009).

Friends and colleagues have encouraged my passionate interest and aided the work in various ways. David Tavárez and Peter Villella went above and beyond the norm and even shared research materials with me. Conversations and exchanges with many other Mesoamericanists (and a few Andeanists) have been invaluable. I thank especially Amber

Brian, Galen Brokaw, Louise Burkhart, Lori Diel, Alan Durston, Lidia Gómez, Rebecca Horn, Michel Launey, Ben Leeming, Dana Leibsohn, Frederick Luciani, Rodrigo Martínez Baracs, Laura Matthew, Kelly McDonough, Leslie Offut, Justyna Olko, Caterina Pizzigoni, Annette Richie, Ethelia Ruiz, Susan Schroeder, Bradley Skopyk, Lisa Sousa, John Sullivan, Michael Swanton, Stephanie Wood, and Yanna Yannakakis. My fellow board members of the *Colonial Latin American Review* have shared their warmth and wisdom with me for many years now; they make me eternally grateful to be part of this field. Over the past decade, my colleagues at Rutgers University have been a delight; I thank them for keeping me on my toes. Two of my students, Jessica Nelson Criales and Tara Malanga, even checked out archives for me in the course of their travels. My friend from Bryn Mawr days, Karen Sullivan, handed me Eric Auerbach's *Mimesis* years ago and told me to read it. Karen has repeatedly opened up to me a vision of what it is I really want to do. I am forever in her debt. Finally, Susan Ferber at Oxford University Press has been the most marvelous editor imaginable and Julia Turner the most terrific project manager; I literally cannot thank them enough.

Last but not least, I thank the companions of my daily life, my husband and two sons. I have learned more in my years with you than I ever could have imagined; you have taught me most of what I know about the nature of the human endeavor. I value that wisdom as much, I hope, as the people I write about once did.

GLOSSARY

These terms may be originally from Nahuatl (N) or Spanish (S). Here follows the usage as seen in Nahuatl texts of the 16th and 17th centuries.

Alcalde (S). First-instance judge who is at the same time a leading member of the indigenous cabildo.

Alcalde Mayor (S). Chief Spanish judicial and administrative official, governing over a large area including several different altepetl.

Alguacil (S). Indigenous constable.

Altepetl (A). Nahuatl term for any state, no matter how large or complex, but most frequently used to refer to a local ethnic state.

Audiencia (S). The high court of New Spain, residing in Mexico City. Often called the Royal Audiencia.

Cabildo (S). A town council in the Spanish style. Used to describe a session of any governing assembly, such as a municipal government or cathedral chapter, but most frequently to refer to the local indigenous council governing their community's internal affairs.

Cacicazgo (S, based on "cacique"). An inherited indigenous rulership, including title and accompanying lands.

Cacique (S, from Arawak). Indigenous ruler, the equivalent of "tlatoani." Eventually, it was used to describe any prominent indigenous person of a noble line.

Calli (N). Literally, house or household. Often an important metaphor for larger bodies, also one of the four rotating names for years.

Calpolli (N). In the central valley, a key constituent part or subdistrict of an altepetl. In the Tlaxcala-Puebla valley, sometimes an inserted or added-on subdistrict of an altepetl.

Cihuapilli (N). Noblewoman, lady, even "queen."

Congregación (S). A resettlement of indigenous people by the Spanish state to achieve greater nucleation, and hence control.

Doctrina (S). Spanish for Christian indoctrination, but used to refer to an indigenous parish.

Don/doña. High title attached to a first name, like "Sir" or "Lady" in English. Applied by Nahuas in this period only to titled nobility from Spain and their own highest-status local indigenous nobility.

Encomienda (S). Grant, nearly always to a Spaniard, of the right to receive tribute and originally labor from an altepetl.

Escribano (S). Notary, clerk. An important position attached to the indigenous cabildo.

Fiscal (S). Chief steward of an indigenous church.

Gobernador (S). Governor and head of the indigenous cabildo. Early on, the position was filled by the tlatoani, but later, elections were held among all noblemen. Sometimes called a "judge-governor."

Guardián (S). The prior of a monastic establishment.

Macehualli (pl. macehualtin) (N). Indigenous commoner.

Marqués (S). Marquess, lord of a border region. Several viceroys bore the title, but when Nahuas used it without a name, they meant either Hernando Cortés or his eldest legitimate son.

Merino (S). Name sometimes given to minor officials within the altepetl government. Seems to have been the equivalent of "tepixqui."

Mestizo (S). Person of mixed Spanish and indigenous descent.

Nahualli (N). A highly complex term, but translatable as "sorcerer" or "shaman" in most documents.

Oficial (S). Generally used to mean craftsman, artisan.

Oidor (S). A sitting judge on the audiencia. Together the oidores formed the council who advised the Viceroy.

Pilli (pl. pipiltin) (N). Indigenous nobleman.

Principal (S). A Spanish term for an indigenous nobleman, often adopted by the pipiltin themselves.

Quauhpilli (N). Literally, an "eagle nobleman." A nobleman by virtue of deeds or merit rather than by virtue of birth.

Real (S). A silver coin worth one-eighth of a peso (hence "Spanish pieces of eight"). Also the word for "royal."

Regidor (S). Councilman, member of the indigenous cabildo.

Rotary labor. Translation of "coatequitl," rotating public labor drafts.

Teccalli (N). Lordly house, containing related nobles, dependents and lands. Among the eastern Nahuas, it was close in meaning to the "calpolli" of the central valley, a key subunit of the altepetl.

Tecpan (N). Literally, "place where the lord is." Originally, the palace or establishment of a local lord. Later, a community house where the indigenous cabildo and other municipal offices resided.

Teniente (S). A term adopted in certain Nahuatl-speaking localities to refer to an assistant to the gobernador who actually handled much of the day-to-day business.

Teopantlaca (N). Literally, "church people." Seems to have been used to refer to people educated as Christians more than to people who attended or worked in a church.

Teuctli (pl. teteuctin) (N). Lord, head of a dynastic household, with lands and followers.

Tlacuilo (N). Painter or writer, sometimes used interchangeably with "escribano."

Tlalli (N). Land.

Tlatoani (N). Literally, "he who speaks." A dynastic ruler of an altepetl, in this book translated as "king." Sometimes applied to a high Spanish authority, such as a viceroy or alcalde mayor.

Tlatoque (N). Plural of "tlatoani." From very early on, used to refer to the councilmen of the cabildo as a unit.

Tollan (N). Often called "Tula" in English, literally meaning "Place of Reeds." A real town in Central Mexico but, in ancient stories, often used to refer to a utopian community of the distant past.

Traza (S). Specifically delineated downtown area in a city governed by Spaniards.

Tomin (S). A coin valued as the equivalent of a real. Often used to refer to any coin or cash.

Virrey (S). Viceroy, highest royal official in New Spain, resident in Mexico City.

Visitador (S). Inspector. These were sent regularly by the Spanish Crown to investigate local government in the Americas in a system of checks and balances.

Annals of Native America

Introduction

In the preconquest communities of central Mexico, the people gathered on certain evenings to celebrate their lives together. Drums beat. Voices rose and fell. Children who were present would remember in later years how the throbbing music stirred their blood, and how the song-poems made their eyes shine with pride and dim with tears, as they reveled in the great deeds of their people and mourned their losses. Sometimes in the wake of the musicians, the history tellers would also perform, one after another stepping forward to tell of this part of the past or that, sometimes with a great painted record to guide them, sometimes with only their own well-trained memories to keep them on course. Together, they brought to life the story of the making of a great mutual commitment, a pact made by the listeners' ancestors—and renewed among the people as they sat together as an audience—to protect their community and its ways against all comers, to bend with changing times, but never break. Life on earth was fleeting, but in remembering the past and renewing promises to posterity, they could render aspects of it eternal.

The Nahuas had long preserved their histories. In the early sixteenth century, when the Spaniards appeared upon the scene, they were the guardians of an already centuries-old tradition known as the *xiuhpohualli* (SHOO-po-wa-lee). The word has tended to be translated as "year count," faintly redolent of a charming primitivism, but it would perhaps better be rendered as "yearly account." Spanish investigators were puzzled by the superabundance of words that sometimes were mentioned instead of *xiuhpohualli*, such as *xiuhtlapohualli, huehuetlatolli, huehuenemiliztlatolli, altepetlacuilolli,* or *huehuenemilizamoxtli*. These Europeans were in some ways wasting their time when they struggled to find minute variations in meaning. Nahuatl is a highly productive and flexible language: new nouns can be constructed with ease, at an individual speaker's will, by stringing other nouns together. There was, however, a significant two-part division within the nomenclature. All the words that were occasionally used can be categorized in one of two ways. On the one hand are the words whose root is either *amoxtli* (the paper on which painting appears) or *-icuiloa* (to write or to paint, the two activities being largely synonymous); on the other hand are the words stemming from a speech act, either *pohua* (to count or give an account, the two possibilities being tightly tied together in usage) or *-itoa* (to utter). The use of words stemming from two different arenas is indicative of the dual nature of history preservation among the Nahuas: there were pictorial texts, and there were oral performances.

The first set of words referred to a custom of painting timelines on long rolls of maguey paper or bark, where the traditional yearly calendar was marked out with well-known glyphs (reed year, flint-knife year, house year, rabbit year, and then again reed year, and so on), and pictographic writing along the line referred to the major events of each period. These writings, like other types of writings (including those organizing religious ceremonies, or tax collection, or landholdings), were called *in tlilli in tlapalli*. Literally, the phrase meant, "the black ink, the colored pigments," but the Nahuas seemed to have meant primarily "the black and the red," the two colors used most often in all their writings. Black ink alone was not understood as a metaphor for writing: it was more likely to be indicative of face painting for war, or markings for sacrifice. Black ink and red taken together, however, became not just a symbol of writing, but the very term for it.

The painted histories were rich texts in their own right. They were able to convey not only lists of subjects but also actions—in other words, a true narrative. They harbored the beginnings of a systematic phonetic orthography. They boasted complex glyphs that cross-referenced each other and sometimes changed each other's meanings when placed in certain pairings, in the same way that two different spoken words, like *in tlilli in tlapalli*, became a third entity when placed together. However, the paintings were never, no matter how complex or beautiful or worthy of attention, the whole story. The audience might crane their necks to see the undulating lines that marked the well-known and sometimes treacherous rivers, or to get a better view of the flaring flames that marked the conquests their grandfathers had made, but even at such visually exciting moments, they were also poised to listen, waiting for the speaker to proceed. The words, the flowing narrations, were the heart of the matter.

The speaker's tone and purport varied, depending on the occasion and the place in the performance—hence the varied terms related to *xiuhpohualli*, perhaps. He might give a litany of ancestors if he was emphasizing continuity, or break out at a certain point and perform a miniature one-man play to illustrate a past political predicament. Sometimes the dialogue was funny and made the people smirk or even laugh outright. Sometimes it was enraging, and when a historical figure asked a certain question, the audience was ready to shout a response. Soon it was another history teller's turn to step forward and represent the perspective of a different lineage or clan. People turned expectantly to hear the alternate view.

Or so it seems to have been.[1] In fact, none of the preconquest pictorials survive, and of course, no one made a secret recording. In reconstructing the Nahuas' methods of preserving their history in an oral arena, scholars have been forced to use indirect evidence of various types. First, a variety of Spanish and indigenous commentators described and even categorized texts and performances. Second, records of court cases heard within the newly established Spanish apparatus occasionally contain descriptions of how the painted records were used, and in one particular case, even lengthy transcriptions of performances. Finally—and most significantly—there exist dozens, even hundreds, of post-conquest histories. As young Nahuas learned the roman alphabet from the friars and took lessons in European-style drawing, they soon recognized the possibilities of using their new accomplishments for purposes other than those originally imagined by their teachers.

Scholars have made excellent progress in their studies of the sixteenth- and early seventeenth-century historical pictorials. Elizabeth Hill Boone and those who have followed in her footsteps have successfully grappled with the ways in which colonial realities shaped the extant texts, as well as with the ways in which they retrospectively illuminate past generations' assumptions and expectations.[2] Significantly less work has been done with what are called the "alphabetic texts."[3] These were most often initially produced when the friars' students, who had become adept at using the roman alphabet to transcribe speech, asked elders in their community to tell them the histories of old and then wrote down whatever they heard in the original Nahuatl. In a few cases, public performances were officially transcribed by order of community elders. These written pieces were subsequently handed on, copied and recopied by interested parties, and often added to as the years passed. Sometimes in later years a young writer held an old pictorial in his hands rather than a written transcription of a performance; then he did his best to reconstruct what a traditional performer would have said, but the results in such cases were usually extremely terse, as he was operating without much knowledge of the glyphs. Possession of these texts was not a clandestine affair—as the possession of old prayers or incantations was[4]—for the Spaniards saw nothing wrong in the people's recording their histories. Yet if it was not a secret activity, it was not exactly a public one, either. Spanish authorities generally knew nothing about it. The keeping of these written histories was not done at their behest, or even with their knowledge. In short, these were not texts being carefully prepared under European tutelage to be sent back to the crowned heads of Europe, like some of the more famous codices;[5] the alphabetic histories that survived to the present day did so in varied and serendipitous ways.

The historical writings were largely in black ink, now faded to brown. A handful of particularly ambitious or talented individuals combined transcriptions of the ancient performances with arresting old-style visual imagery, but most did not. By the end of the sixteenth century, all traces of *in tlapalli*, the bright red ink of former times, had disappeared from the work being produced, even in those cases where black line drawings of calendrical symbols survived. But if the colors were fading, the words of the *xiuhpohualli* were not, at least not yet. Rich sentences and leaner ones, fascinating stories and duller ones, tumbled out upon the pages, as hand after hand copied them out and added to them. Writing without red did not diminish the Nahuas' joy in words.

What did these histories contain? Universally, they clung as tenaciously as they could to the traditional calendar. This was no small feat, for the ancient Nahua calendar was complex.[6] There were two ongoing cycles of time. One was a solar calendar and consisted of eighteen months of twenty days each, plus five blank or unnamed days at the end, for a total of 365 days. The other was a purely ceremonial calendar containing thirteen groupings of twenty days each, for a total of 260. The two wheels of time both reached their starting point at the same moment every fifty-two years. Thus the Nahua symbolic equivalent of a century was a period (or "bundle," as they said) of fifty-two years. The events in the annals were categorized within solar years, probably because a history that was dominated by warfare had to follow rainy seasons and harvests, but the solar years had to be connected to the other calendar to be meaningful, and so they were named in four groupings of thirteen each, to reach the total of fifty-two years (One Reed, Two Flint-knife, Three House, Four Rabbit, Five Reed, Six Flint-knife, Seven House, Eight Rabbit, Nine Reed, Ten Flint-knife, Eleven House, Twelve Rabbit, Thirteen Reed, One Flint-knife, and so on). Some of the later authors may have been aware only of the latter listing, and not its complex origins, but many knew more than this, judging by the frequency with which they referred to the names of the months. They certainly understood that the names of their forebears stemmed from the ceremonial calendar's twenty days signs, and not the solar months. In any case, the use of the fifty-two-year calendar lasted throughout the colonial period, though often authors added the Christian labels for the solar year as well ("1299" or "the year of Our Lord 1519").

The texts' themes were more malleable than the calendrical system they employed, though in this regard, too, they exhibited significant commonality. What they recorded was what was deemed important to the *altepetl* (the ethnic state, the community) of which they were a product. So they primarily included the rise and fall of political authorities, wars and land settlements, epidemics and natural phenomena. However, the altepetl was itself a complex structure, containing at the very least multiple lineages who had chosen generations ago to throw their lot in together, and sometimes even including various sub-altepetls that had come together, each with its own *tlatoani* (ruler, or king) to forge a larger and stronger nation. Thus the performing of history in the old days was almost always in some senses a political act, intended to reify certain alliances, and this pattern continued in the colonial era, when a writer might be attempting, for instance, to underscore a particular traditional alliance or erase it, depending on his present-day concerns. So it was that shifting political and economic realities led to shifting xiuhpohualli, even when texts included some words taken verbatim from other texts. Furthermore, as time passed, less and less was remembered about the significance of certain glyphs, or the meaning of certain references in the alphabetic texts. Gradually the knowledge was lost that a xiuhpohualli should offer the testimony of multiple speakers representing varied lineages; eventually even the inclusion of dialogue became rare. Instead, the writers increasingly chose to include personal experiences or observations as the texts became very specifically theirs.

Given their richness as sources, it at first seems odd that the colonial alphabetic histories have not been studied more assiduously in the recent era, in which indigenous perspectives and voices have been sought after. The explanation itself has a long history. In the eighteenth and nineteenth centuries, when European scholars first saw some of the documents, they noted an interesting resemblance to early medieval European "annals," as the genre is called.[7] That tradition, too, moved forward through time year by year, recounting events that were of interest to the whole community—the births and deaths of rulers, wars, meteorological phenomena, plagues, and so on. To this day, scholars continue to call the indigenous genre in question the "Mexican historical annals" rather than "xiuhpohualli" or some other fitting Nahuatl term, perhaps because relatively few people would feel confident of the pronunciation of a Nahuatl label. The practice has created substantial confusion. Scholars of other specialties have understandably tended to assume that these were histories written under the guidance of the Franciscans in semi-European style, as many other texts produced in that period were. But these histories were in fact written by Nahuas in their own homes, for their own circle of friends and relatives, with their own posterity in mind; they were written in Nahuatl, without gloss or translation, entirely without regard to European interests.

The earlier scholars who looked at the annals not only determined the misleading name by which such texts would henceforth be known, but also largely set the tone for subsequent dealings with them. Some early cultural products of the Nahuas—such as the calendar wheel—were treated with near-reverence by Europeans who, for reasons of their own, were interested in glorifying America's ancient past,[8] but not the annals. The influential nineteenth-century writer William Prescott (he who advertized and rendered permanent the notion of the panicked Montezuma) wrote: "Clumsy as it was, the Aztec picture-writing seems to have been adequate to the demands of the nation, in their imperfect state of civilization.... The few brief sentences [of their histories] were quite long enough for the annals of barbarians." Only the noted Enlightenment scholar Alexander von Humboldt saw that the histories actually exhibited "the greatest method and most astonishing minuteness." His opinion on this was dismissed by others.[9]

Counterintuitively, perhaps, the histories have continued to be marginalized by the very postmodern and multicultural trends that recent generations might have counted on to rescue them from the rigid and judgmental past. Such renowned scholars as Serge Gruzinski and Enrique Florescano have insisted—with some justification, of course—that the very act of converting flexible indigenous performances into fixed texts radically transformed and reduced them. They have argued that their complexity could not be imprisoned within a few frozen fragments without doing irreparable harm, and that attempting to study the results only furthers the processes of colonialism.[10] This is undoubtedly true to some extent. But if modern scholars leave the matter there, secure in their conviction that it would only be imperialistic to study such texts, do they not themselves become party to another kind of imperialism—that which silences? Miguel Leon Portilla, one of the accused, has responded with humor whenever he can. "Such a conclusion is dramatic for those of us who, patiently applying available linguistic and philological resources, have translated some of those texts into European languages. In dealing with them, translating them, or quoting them ... we have not understood what they in fact are. Instead of being testimonies of the ancient Native word, they reflect the forced answers of the vanquished vis-à-vis the imposed attitudes of the invaders and foreign lords...."[11]

There can be no question that the scholarly world of past decades needed to confront the idea that many early indigenous written texts are the products of a painful and traumatic encounter. Yet they are not therefore all to be dismissed as the distorted products of European imaginations and cast aside as somehow unworthy of study. Many are clearly also the products of indigenous imaginations and intended for indigenous audiences. Scholars who study Native American history and culture are increasingly aware of this; the past generation has seen a florescence of revealing scholarship based on such Nahuatl sources.[12] The historical annals are probably the texts most removed from Spanish production or interference, but they have not hitherto generated the dedicated scholarship one might have expected. Even the most sympathetic of souls and most active investigators of the annals have lamented the annals' "repetitiveness" and "disorderliness."[13] In an earlier day, Günter Zimmermann, who spent much of his life studying the work of the most prolific indigenous annalist, Chimalpahin, was so alienated by what he saw as the repetitiveness and disorderliness of his beloved subject's text that he decided to dismantle it and reorganize it himself in his published edition.[14] Only since then has it become clear that the tradition of the xiuhpohualli is necessarily repetitive and disorderly to untrained Western eyes, as it required that multiple speakers each give an account of the same events, and no markers separated their accounts in the alphabetic transcriptions.[15]

In truth, the annals are difficult for outsiders to understand. Their style and format are their very own, and even their Nahuatl may be considered difficult, in the sense that no subject is excluded and the vocabulary is therefore highly variable and occasionally even unique to individual texts. It is necessary to read a great many of them before the broader contours of the genre as well as its remarkable specificities come into focus. Yet they reward the effort: they are inordinately valuable texts, rare in that they were written not only *by* but also *for* indigenous people. For that reason, they are with increasing frequency being marshalled as evidence in scholarly work treating other subjects. This is sometimes problematic, as quoting them without fully understanding their nature sometimes leads to their being misused. Treating them together, for instance, or separately but in no particular order, as if they were sources of one origin, erases the specific historical circumstances that gave rise to them.

This book takes seriously the texts' specificities and cuts away the anonymity in which they have largely been shrouded until now. Because the tradition of the xiuhpohualli was never intended to showcase the artistry of a particular history teller, but rather to commemorate the life of the altepetl as a whole, the names of the speakers were almost never included in the early transcriptions; the expectation of anonymity carried over into the years when other men copied and expanded and wrote segments of their own. The prolific Chimalpahin was one of the very few to mention his own name. Perhaps partly out of respect for the indigenous tradition, scholars have tended to accept the anonymity of the texts. In fact, however, the authors almost always left unintended clues as to their identities within the texts themselves; when these are combined with other clues found in legal documents of the era, it is possible in most cases to deduce authorship, narrowing it down at least to a particular family and sometimes even to a precise individual. Knowing who wrote a text affects readers in concrete ways, in that they understand references that might otherwise elude them; the context of the work's production takes on more of an air of reality and lends itself to comparisons with other moments. In hearing the words of individual artists, rather than the echoing voices of multitudes, readers suddenly come face to face with a group of real and vibrant people, who treasured books and mended quill pens, and who sometimes wrote literature.

In examining each set of annals, this work begins by exploring the life of the writer of a particular text and the context in which he lived before turning to the meaning of the text itself. This book is not a study of Nahua history as found *in* the annals. For that, I refer readers to other excellent works.[16] What I have tried to write here is a history *of* the annals. Who wrote them, and what were the authors' reasons for writing at the time they did? How did they pass down their texts? What were their deepest beliefs, as manifested in their works? Most especially, what notions of history, both their own and the world's, did they uphold, and how did these change?

The answers to these questions are multi-stranded, and will emerge more fully over the pages to come. Briefly, these writers believed in a complex history, in which more than one perspective had to be accounted for. Theirs was a history that prioritized humanity. Although they valued their land, their rivers, and their wealth, the history that mattered most to them was the history of their people, or of the peoples who together constituted their world. It was they who made the land and the water and the jewels matter, not the other way around. And this human history was the story not merely of well-known individuals but of relationships. Primarily, these writers told of alliances and rivalries between communities, both the bonds and rifts largely being constituted through the politics of marriage. Secondarily, they spoke of the relations, sometimes supportive and sometimes tense, between the families who constituted the nobility (*pilli*, plural *pipiltin*) and those who composed the ranks of the commoners (*macehualli*, plural *macehualtin*).

Nahua historians were always concerned with the survival of their people; they dreaded being subsumed in their relations with others. The arrival of the Spaniards made that issue all the more pressing. Their work reveals two profoundly different schools of thought as to the strategies most likely to ensure survival. Most believed deeply in adopting the new without obliterating the old, and they applied this to the writing of history as much as to agriculture or religion. But just as in ages past, there were some individuals who were more aware of feeling anger—or at least something akin to that emotion—in their dealings with the powerful outsiders. They prized a version of their history that they deemed pure and attempted to isolate it from contaminating European influences. Both groups were in many ways much like modern historians. They scouted for sources, read them over the course of years, and often showed a deep understanding of them. They then preserved the knowledge they had gleaned in a form other people could understand, or so they hoped. They used their work to exhort others to hold to certain ideals—most of all, to try to protect their people's future. For they believed passionately that knowledge of the past held the key to their people's future sense of self.

These Nahua historians fit squarely within the world of indigenous intellectuals in early America to whom scholars have been increasingly drawn in the last decade. There has been a florescence of scholarly work treating indigenous authors from colonial South America, Mesoamerica, and North America.[17] The writers of annals certainly belong among their number: they are of central importance, in that they have the capacity to move us forward in our understanding of complex indigenous intellectual traditions as they existed before the arrival of Old World peoples. Probably in the colonial period under consideration in this work some of the Native American writers would have been startled to find themselves presented together; theirs was not an epoch that dwelt on pan-Indian experience. But the work of some of the authors in this book indicates that they would have been pleased at the thought.

***

This book's organization takes its inspiration from an unlikely source: not the work of a Nahuatl scholar, but rather, the work of a scholar dedicated to the study of the West even at its darkest hour. In 1935, the philologist Eric Auerbach was discharged by the Nazi government from his position at the University of Marburg. He went to Istanbul and stayed there for the duration of World War II. Writing *Mimesis* with relatively few books at hand, he began each section with a lengthy quotation from a great classic, then opened his discussion of the words before the reader.[18] He traversed time in an orderly way, and by the end, the reader had learned how the representation of reality had changed—or not changed—in Western literature over the course of centuries, and that, at its core, a greatness in the West's artistry had prevailed over times of horror. Drawing from Auerbach's model, I present segments of texts that readers otherwise might not have access to, and enough information to be able to make sense of the original authors' hopes and intentions.

Each chapter opens with a lengthy segment from a set of annals. The text appears in English, the language of the majority of my intended audience, in the hope that readers may connect directly with the stories found within. Nahuatl speakers and scholars (as well as inquisitive neophytes) can consult the same text in the original Nahuatl in the appendices.[19] The opening pages are followed by a study of the author and his context, then finally by an analysis of the text itself; in the case of two chapters, this pattern is repeated twice. This splicing together of genres (anthology/social history/literary criticism) is unusual, but it seems necessary in this case. With one exception, the texts are available nowhere else in English; with two exceptions, the authorships have not previously been attributed. It would have been impossible to proceed with analyzing the texts without rectifying the other circumstances first: humanizing the authors had to be step one.

One other element that is somewhat unusual requires an explanation. In the analytical sections, I occasionally speak in the first person plural.

This is not a "royal we." I specifically use the word *we* to refer to people alive now, in the early twenty-first century. We moderns, however different we may be in other regards, may find ourselves similarly confused by the assumptions of the past. There were moments in writing, when the evidence was at its thinnest and potential confusion greatest, when I felt that I could do no other than allow for an implicit dialogue with the Nahuas of generations gone.

***

The first chapter is entitled "Old Stories in New Letters (1520s–1550s)." In Central Mexico, the generation in power at the time of the conquest faced repeated crises as the Spaniards arrived and began to attempt to reorganize the political landscape. Such leaders also, however, met with extraordinary opportunities. This chapter follows a remarkable individual, a Cuauhtinchan chief named Chimalpopoca, who later took the name "don Alonso de Castañeda," eventually orchestrating the production of the most beautifully painted set of Nahuatl annals in existence, the *Historia Tolteca Chichimeca*. He saw the ways in which the new roman letters might be put to good use and tried desperately to protect his people's knowledge of the past, apparently foreseeing that the changes occurring might bring social amnesia. His work is also placed in the context of the other great set of annals of his generation, the *Annals of Tlatelolco*. Interestingly, though certain scholars have been worried by the imperialistic tendencies intrinsic to the act of transferring indigenous knowledge to a written page, the Nahua historians themselves were apparently not perturbed by the thought of transitioning to a phonetic system to record their speeches. They seem to have been no more concerned about imperialist overtones than ancient Mediterranean peoples ever were when phoneticism displaced cuneiform writing. They simply seized a useful tool.

The second chapter, "Becoming Conquered," focuses on the decade of the 1560s, pivotal in the experience of the indigenous people of Mexico City. Until then, it might be argued that the urban Nahuas had been treated relatively well by the Spaniards, as they were needed allies in the conquest and governance of other territories, and the Europeans did not yet have enough power to be abusive in their extraction of wealth. All that changed in the 1560s. Exorbitant tribute payments were demanded of them, threatening to change their lifestyles forever. The city's native people wrote histories about their efforts to stem the tide and defend themselves. Their political efforts turned out to be futile, but recording all that they attempted would, they believed, vindicate them in the eyes of posterity. The rich and revealing texts they produced during this time of crisis include the *Codex Aubin,* the *Codex Osuna,* and the *Annals of Juan Bautista.* Through the latter more than any other text, we can learn about Nahua historians' commitment to multivocality and to dialogue. It contains all the linguistic elegance of the works of prior times, but it pertains to a period whose history and politics we can fully understand; it is thus a sort of conceptual Rosetta Stone.

The third chapter, "Forging Friendship with Franciscans (1560–1580s)," examines annals written by two indigenous men, don Mateo Sánchez of Tecamachalco and don Pedro de San Buenaventura of Cuauhtitlan. As some of the friars' earliest native students attained adulthood and became intellectuals in their own right, they found themselves talking to, writing to, and sometimes even arguing with their former mentors. Their works reveal not only their own knowledge, but also their participation in dialogue with Europeans. If sometimes they felt enriched and sometimes bereft, there can be no question that the passage of time and the profundity of their connections with Europeans had changed them. Of course, they had changed the friars as well. But in the end, they seemed uncertain of the future. This segment underscores the positive and negative aspects of indigenous intellectuals' relationships with Europeans: in all times and places, intermediaries who live in close proximity to the powerful both benefit and suffer in subtle ways.

The fourth chapter is entitled "The Riches of Twilight (c. 1600)." By about the year 1600, indigenous intellectuals began to fear that knowledge of the old histories was truly being lost. Their conviction seems to have led to an outpouring of historical writing. Chimalpahin from Chalco, the best-known writer of Nahuatl annals, lived and worked during this period, and a number of other important histories date from this era as well. Chimalpahin did not work anonymously and he produced a large corpus, so it is possible to study him particularly closely. The cosmopolitanism of his vision is breathtaking: he was easily able to fit the history of America's native peoples into his sense of the history of the world. His confidence in his people was matched only by his concern that they were losing their knowledge of their past. It was his mission to prevent that loss. Most remarkably, Chimalpahin got his wish: he kept his people's history alive to an extent that no European ever could have managed. Without his work as a centerpiece, the remaining Nahuatl annals preserved here and there would not be numerous and rich enough to tell us much.

The fifth chapter, "Renaissance in the East (the Seventeenth Century)" homes in on Tlaxcala, just to the east of the Central Basin, where Spanish language and culture were kept at bay longer than in most other places. As a reward for their help in bringing down the Tenochca, the Spaniards made certain promises to the Tlaxcalans which they largely kept for more than a century; few Spaniards settled among them for many years. One result was that knowledge of the tradition of the xiuhpohualli lasted longer here than anywhere else. More than two dozen texts survive from the seventeenth century, among them, most importantly, the work of a fascinating man named don Juan Buenaventura Zapata y Mendoza. He proudly and assertively worked to preserve Nahuatl language and culture; his statements are sometimes almost eerily anticipatory of the ethnic pride movements of later centuries. A young friend of his, don Manuel de los Santos Salazar, an indigenous man who contrary to expectation became a priest, worked tirelessly to preserve don Juan Zapata's work and that of other Nahuas; through him, their texts entered European libraries. There is a kind of irony here: it was the work of Zapata, the annalist most dedicated to maintaining the purity of all things Nahuatl and to living a life relatively isolated from Christian Spaniards, that most directly affected Hispanic historiography, through his young friend don Manuel. This may be somewhat surprising, yet it is hardly the only historical context in which disempowered peoples have found that separatism sometimes helps their voices gather strength.

The epilogue, "Postscript from a Golden Age," closes the history of the Nahua annals in the 1690s. Don Miguel Santos, a remarkable indigenous craftsman, a house builder and head of his lineage, produced the most eloquent and expressive set of Nahuatl annals in existence, now most often called the *Annals of Puebla*. His immediate ancestors were Tlaxcalans who had helped to settle and build the largely Spanish-populated city of Puebla; they had retained their Tlaxcalan heritage, including knowledge of the xiuhpohualli. At the same time, don Miguel was a resident of a lovely Spanish city that had entered its own golden age in the second half of the seventeenth century; its language and customs deeply influenced him. What is most remarkable about the annals he kept is that, on the one hand, his writings demonstrate almost a complete break with the Aztec past, and yet on the other, they prove that on profound levels, Nahua modes of thought about history and life had not changed significantly since the conquest. Both statements are equally true.

Perhaps embedded here we can find what the indigenous historical tradition ultimately reveals about the human condition. The world of these historians was one of evident paradoxes, of survival and loss, persistence and erosion. This is true of the world in which all humans must live, but this book's protagonists lived with these paradoxes in a particularly stark form, and they negotiated them with dignity and even style. Perhaps it was for this reason that they seemed to comprehend the notion of truth as inherently multiple, or of perspective as necessarily variable, when Europeans still did not. Certainly they learned to live with the possibility of erasure, and they managed to do what they could to make it viable for posterity to turn to them later and ask what once was known, what once was seen, during their time on this earth.

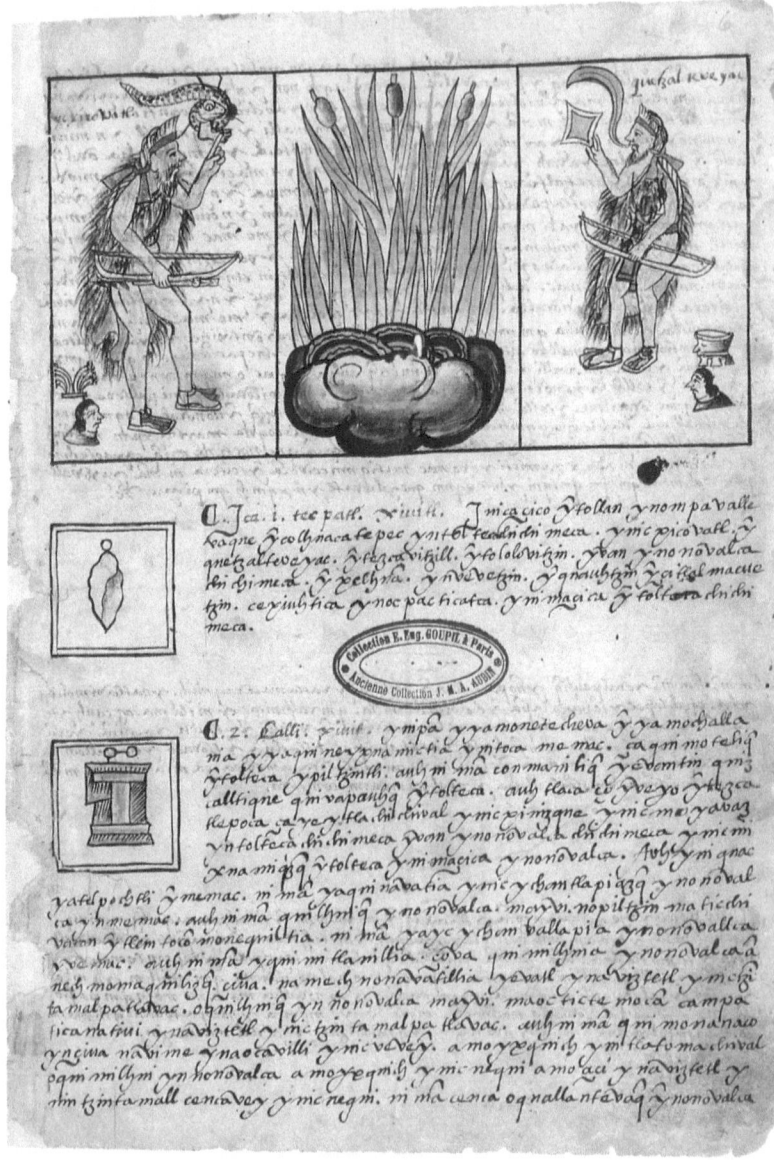

Fig 1.1 Historia Tolteca Chichimeca, folio 2. Years 1 Flint-Knife and 2 House. Courtesy Bibliothèque Nationale de France.

1

Old Stories in New Letters (1520s–1550s)

The early Nahuatl text called the "Historia Tolteca Chichimeca" opens thus:[1]

[F. 1v]
Here are the altepetl that were once the constituents of greater Tollan. Twenty altepetl were the hands and feet [the component subunits], the fellow waters, the fellow mountains [the fellow altepetl] of the Tolteca. Then greater Tollan broke apart, so that each went to seek their own altepetl.

¶ Pantecatli		¶ Nonoualca	
¶ Ytzcuitzoncatli		¶ Cuitlapiltzinca	
¶ Tlematepeua		¶ Aztateca	
¶ Tlequaztepeua		¶ Tzanatepeua	
¶ Tezcatepeua	5	¶ Tetetzincatli	5
¶ Tecollotepeua		¶ Teuhxilcatli	
¶ Tochpaneca		¶ Zacanca	
¶ Cempoualteca		¶ Cuixcoca	
¶ Cuetlaxteca		¶ Quauhchichinolca	
¶ Cozcateca	5	¶ Chiuhnauhteca	5

[F. 2]
[glyph for One Flint Knife]
In the year One Flint Knife they arrived in Tollan. They departed from Colhuacatepec. The Tolteca Chichimeca [who came] were Icxicoatl, Quetzalteueyac, Tezcahuitzil, and Tololohuitzil, and the Nonoualca

Chichimeca were Xelhuan, Huehuetzin, Cuauhtzin and Citlalmacuetzin. For a year the Nonoualca were happy as the complements of the Tolteca Chichimeca [that is, to constitute part of their altepetl].

[glyph for Two House]
In the year Two House there was already friction, there was already discord. The one called Memac [Huemac] caused them to fight. The Tolteca just saw a [stranger] child and they took him for themselves. They raised him, educated him. And of all things, he turned out to be the hueyo [the dedicated servant] of Tezcatlipoca. He was the cause behind the Tolteca Chichimeca and the Nonoualca Chichimeca breaking apart and making war, so that the Nonoualca confronted their complements, the Tolteca. When Memac became a young man, he gave orders that the Nonoualca tend to his home.[2] Then the Nonoualca said to him, "So be it, my lord. May we do what you desire." The Nonoualca came to tend to his home. And then he demanded women of them. He said to the Nonoualca, "You are to give me women. I order that the buttocks be four spans wide."[3] The Nonoualca said to him, "So be it. Let us first seek where we can get one whose buttocks are four spans wide." Then they brought four women who had not yet known sexual pleasure. But in size, they were not enough. He said to the Nonoualca, "They are not of the size I want. Their buttocks are not four spans wide. I want them really big." The Nonoualca left in great anger.

[F. 2v]
At that point he takes[4] the Nonoualca [women] and ties each of them to an obsidian table [for sacrifice]. Then the Nonoualca get really angry and say, "Who is that who mocks us? Perhaps the Toltecs are telling him what to do. Let us go and fight! Where will we catch up with these people who are asking for it?!" And with that the Nonoualca quickly grab arrows, shields and obsidian clubs. Thus do they make war with their complements, the Tolteca, and they kill each other. The Nonoualca get really angry. They do real damage to the Tolteca, Huemac's people. Icxicoatl and Quetzalteueyac [the Toltec leaders] each say, "Why the suffering? For what are the Tolteca being destroyed? Was I the one who started it? Was I the one who sent for the women over whom we're fighting and making war? Let Huemac die! He made us fight." Then the Nonoualca—Xelhuan, Huehuetzin, Cuauhtzin and Citlalmacuetzin—[also each] say, "Don't be angry at me, my lord. Was I the one who did it? Let Huemac die."

And when Huemac heard that the Tolteca and the Nonoualca were making peace, he ran off. The Nonoualca pursued him, shooting him with arrows, shouting and howling like coyotes. They chased him into the cave of Cencalco. As he entered, they went to grab him by the hair and dragged him out. They shot him with arrows. By the mouth of the cave they killed him. As soon as he died, the Nonoualca went to Tollan—Xelhuan, Huehuetzin, and [also the Tolteca leaders] Icxicoatl and Quetzalteueyac. When they got back to Tollan, the Nonoualca gathered together and talked. They said, "Come, listen. What kind of people are we? Perhaps we have done wrong. Perhaps because of it something may happen to our children and grandchildren. Let us go. Let us leave our lands. How will we live, having confronted and made an enemy of Huemac? We should leave the Toltecs behind." Then by night they left. They took all the accoutrements of [the god] Quetzalcoatl, everything that he guarded over.[5]

***

In the wake of the departure of the Nonoualca, the weakened Toltecs also become wanderers. They end up living among the Olmeca Xicallanca and are treated badly. At this point in the drama, where we pick up the story again, the Toltec leaders have hatched a plot and have gone to converse with the Olmeca Xicallanca leaders. Now they have come back to their own settlement.

> [F.11v]
> Icxicouatl, Quetzalteueyac, Tezcauitzil, Tololouitzil and the priest, Cohuenan, greeted the people. They said to the Toltecs, "Listen, o my children, o Toltecs. Does he hear, does he see, our inventor, our creator? We went to place your tears, your weeping [your complaints] before, in front of, the citizens, the householders, the people of the altepetl and the rulers of the Olmeca Xicallanca. The tizacozque and the amapane [Olmeca titles] accept your words [your proposal]. Four days from now, you will celebrate the feast day of their altepetl. They put you in charge of it all. Concentrate on this,[6] my children! May your hands, your feet [the different parts of the group] not fail each other. Make an effort! We went to support you before the world. What will become of us? Here he has placed us, our inventor, our creator. Will we have to hide our faces, our mouths [that is, will we have to die]? What does he say, how does he test us, our inventor, our creator, he who is Everywhere? He knows if we

will be defeated here. What will he dispose? O Tolteca, may you have confidence! Gird yourselves up, take heart![7] May you be satisfied with what we went to say, went to declare to the lords and kings. They accept that we will dance for them. They say, 'Rehearse your songs, lest you be ashamed. You will have brought together the rulers of the Olmeca Xicallanca; you will be the ones who celebrate the feast day.' Listen to what they say [and rehearse with props]. What you are to be careful of is that you not take from them any good weapons. Go and borrow, take as a loan, their weapons. Do not consent to it whenever you are given new ones. Just borrow the old worn-out shields and war clubs, those that are lying fallen somewhere, or that they have thrown away. Listen, whenever they give you a good shield or good club, you will not take it. They will just make it the means of getting something started if you break or hurt something. Now listen, right now, we take nothing from them, we desire nothing from them. We are so mistreated, so put down, that their women throw nextamalli water[8] in our faces and they pen-mark our legs and backs.[9] And who are we that they make us live this way?! Are we dogs?! Do not accept any of the good possessions of the residents. But if they give you old shields or old war clubs, you can fix them up if they are broken somewhere. We will take those, and using them, we will make war. Will the weapons eat us? Or will the Olmeca's shields and clubs eat the Olmeca Xicallanca themselves?!" Then Icxicouatl and Quetzalteueac cry[10] and say, "O my children, o Tolteca, go to it with a will!"

[F. 12]
Then their Tolteca companions answered them, saying to them, "Thank you. We have understood what you, our mothers and fathers [our leaders], have said. What will our inventor and creator dispose? Is it over? Will he hide us, conceal us [that is, cause our death]? Is this the place of our perishing? You have made a good effort. You have girt us up and given us spirit if we were in despair." Then they dispersed and went to do the borrowing, saying to the [Olmeca Xicallanca] residents, "Please lend us your old weapons, some of your old shields and war clubs—not your good equipment—if you gave us that we would break it." /

"What will you do with them? What do you want them for?" they say./

"Listen, we are going to perform for the rulers. It's for when we will dance in the homes, the households, of your altepetl," they say. /

"Maybe you do want our good weapons?" they say./

"No, my child,[11] just your old weapons that lie fallen where you throw out the nextamalli water. Let's fix them up, and with them we will entertain the rulers and lords," they say. /

Then they [the Olmeca Xicallanca] say, "Fine. Here and there our old weapons, our old shields, our old clubs, are lying around. Gather them up. Indeed, we don't even need our new weapons." So then they wander everywhere, looking in the various houses and patios. Wherever they go in where people are, there is eating and drinking going on. The [Olmeca] speak to them. They just belittle them and laugh at them. But they, they prepare themselves.

They were gathering the old weapons—the old cotton armor, the old bows, the old shields and old clubs. They left nothing out in what they gathered. And when they had gotten the things, they went to the various places where they were staying. When they got to their borrowed homes,[12] they really fixed [those weapons] up. They painted the old shields and clubs red and blue and sewed up the old cotton armor.

The sufferings that the Tolteca Chichimeca endured were very great.

***

The old man was blind. When the darkness had come to him, had descended on him, it had blotted out the bright colors of his days, but not his memories. He had seen many things in his fleeting time on earth, for he had played important roles in momentous dramas. He had been a warrior and a chief, a teller of ancient tales and a defender of his people. He was some of these things still, but now he leaned on a younger man as he entered the dusky chamber. He and thirty-two other indigenous noblemen of Cuauhtinchan were gathered in the cabildo hall on this day in 1558 to mark the occasion of the Franciscans' establishment of the new town center, with their monastery at the very heart. Three years before, most of the people had moved here together, abandoning the various tecpan, or noblemen's houses, that still sprinkled the countryside, some now in ruins. Most had not wanted to come, and it had fallen to the nobles to persuade even the most disgruntled to let their resentment dissipate in the wind, lest their troubles become worse.[13]

In the old man's youth, before the Spaniards came and for a long time after, his name had been Chimalpopoca (Smoking Shield, a name often used by warrior kings), and there were undoubtedly still those who thought of him thus.[14] It had been many years, however, since he had used that name on ceremonial occasions like this one. Now he was always don Alonso de Castañeda, bearing the title of *tezcacoacatl*, as the tlatoani of a powerful Cuauhtinchan sub-altepetl and a member of the cabildo or council the Spaniards had asked his people to form. For whatever Chimalpopoca or don Alonso may have mourned in private in that cold season of 1558,[15] he had not come to the great hall to lament the past. He had come to use his people's history to solidify their future. He was there to attempt to guarantee their survival.

He of all people well knew the threats that the passing of time had brought and doubtless would still bring. He had seen great losses in his lifetime and was still wending his way down tangled paths. The very next year, in fact, in 1559, the villagers of Amozoc rejected official policy and refused to move. Mounted Spaniards came. A younger man in don Alonso's social world recorded, "Then by order of the prior [of the Franciscans], fray Francisco de Mendieta, they burned the houses of those who did not want to come. And the roofs fell in."[16] If don Alonso smelled the smoking ruins, then his heart was troubled on that day. For the memories of his childhood and youth were thick with battle and burning buildings. And if there was one great gain in the arrangement he and his peers had made with the Spaniards, it was that the lives of commoners, of the *macehualtin*, were supposed to be free of this kind of suffering ever after. Yet they had not been.

It is important, however, to refrain from making assumptions as to what don Alonso would ultimately have concluded at such a moment. The history he knew was almost entirely a tale of power struggles and reversals of fortune. He himself had even very recently been a skilled narrator of such a past, a highly trained reader of old genealogies and performer of the xiuhpohualli.[17] He could delve knowledgeably into history going back almost two hundred years, to the time of his great-grandfather, Xiuhcozcatl; other men in his circle could weave in and out of stories from the past four hundred years and more. His own family saga reached so far back because the great chiefs in his dynasty tended to rule for decades—as he himself had done. They came to office as young men in their prime, and if they were successful and avoided death in battle and gained the allegiance of many followers, then they ruled until they were very old. Most managed this. But there was one searing exception that loomed large in Chimalpopoca's memory, never allowing him to forget the violence of the years before the Spaniards came. When he was a child, his own father had been killed after only one year of rule. "Here is the reason why it came about . . ." he intoned on history-telling evenings in his older years.[18]

Centuries before, his ancestors had come forth from the northern caves and woods in which they lived at the invitation of the Tolteca Chichimeca who were living in Cholula. They had fought at the Cholulans' side when they were besieged by enemies; thus they had been rewarded with lands just to the east, the hitherto underpopulated and wild hills of Cuauhtinchan, "Home of the Eagles." Yet despite their common history, the lineages of Cuauhtinchan were deeply divided between those (like his) with a longstanding practice of continued intermarriage with Cholula—whose people also spoke primarily Nahuatl—and those with a longstanding practice of intermarriage with Pinome-speaking peoples to the east. The "Nahuapan" had long dominated Cuauhtinchan's history, until the late fourteenth century (the time of his great-grandfather), when the "Pinopan" slyly (or perhaps cleverly, depending on one's point of view) gained the upper hand by bringing in the Mexica on their side. They subsequently abused their power, using it to increase their landholdings. When Chimalpopoca's father, Cotzatzin, had only recently inherited the chieftainship, his figurative "elder brother," the chief of the most powerful Pinome clan, and therefore now the high chief of Cuauhtinchan, invited him to his home. "And the one who went to invite him was named Mocnomatitzin. He was a nobleman. He said, 'My lord king, your elder brother summons you, the tecpanecatl Tozcocolli.'" The honorable Cotzatzin went. "And the murderers were already there." Was the child Chimalpopoca forced to watch, or did he just hear the tale? He commented only that his father was put to the rope, but he described the death of the uncle who accompanied him in detail. "When they cut his breast, they did not take his heart out. They left off quickly. He went into convulsions before dying." Cotzatzin had ruled less than a year, from Three Flint-knife to Four House. His younger brother, Tecuanitzin, took over the rulership and wisely said nothing at all about the lands in Tlaxocopan that Tozcocolle had usurped in the wake of the killings.[19]

Ten years later Tecuanitzin, too, was dead, but not from treachery. In the year Thirteen Rabbit, not long after a failed war with Tlaxcala, the Spaniards arrived. "It was learned that the Castile people had arrived at the shore."[20] The next year, One Reed, the Spaniards formed an alliance with the Tlaxcalans and destroyed Chimalpopoca's beloved city of Cholula, home of his grandmothers, before moving on to Tenochtitlan. Then the dying began, from a foul disease that spread through the lands all around. Over the years, people of successive generations would each in turn experience their own first deadly epidemic. Survivors would later recall the days after they recovered, evoking something of their horror without speaking of it directly. "There was no longer anyone traveling the roads."[21] "The villages round about had no more people. The ones who remained were very few."[22] Several chiefs were among the disappeared, including Tecuanitzin. Chimalpopoca was a man now, and he lived. In this time of trouble, he was installed as chief, as king[23]—as tlatoani, he who speaks on behalf of his people.

A chief of a lineage, however, was not merely an orator. He also went into battle. The Spaniards came soon, in Two Flint-knife, with their Tlaxcalan allies, and all the chiefs round about went to defend themselves. Those of Cuauhtinchan went together with those of Tepeaca, Tecalco, Tecamachalco and Quechollac. "We were defeated (*tipoliuhque*)," said don Alonso tersely, using a form of the verb that implies absolute destruction.[24] "We all withdrew to [the marshlands of] the Atoyac."[25] From there they sent emissaries, and by means of an interpreter, a Nahuatl-speaking woman from the coast whom the Spanish had with them,[26] they were able to arrange the terms of peace: they would deliver tribute to a Spanish overlord—a certain number of beautifully woven textiles, gold pieces, and guajalote birds, as well as four hundred fanegas of corn. They even agreed on an exact measuring unit.[27]

This was a result Chimalpopoca and his people could live with, and they returned to their homes. It turned out that the story was far from finished, however. Within six years the required tribute increased substantially. Soon they were paying tribute to the overlord who was their *encomendero* as well as to the Crown, amounting to twenty-four thousand mantas every four years, plus four thousand fanegas of corn, and sixteen half baskets of beans, eighty of chile, sixteen of chia, sixteen of salt, plus twenty guajolote birds and the services of thirty macehualtin.[28] Don Alonso's family certainly could not claim that they did not understand what was demanded of them: the encomendero to whom they were assigned was Juan Pérez de Arteaga, who had married a Tlaxcalan woman and claimed he had been a sort of apprentice to the woman translator named Malintzin; he spoke good Nahuatl.[29] The tribute was far more than they had ever owed the Mexica, and there were fewer people left to contribute.

They found they were in no position to protest, however. In 1528 or thereabouts, the Franciscans established a church in nearby Tepeaca.[30] They instructed all the local lords to travel there on certain Sundays, when someone visited to say Mass, but at first only a few went. As long as the newcomers stayed in Tepeaca, they could largely be ignored with impunity. The Spaniards' arms were growing longer, however. It was at about this time that Chimalpopoca did in fact decide to accept Christianity and was baptized as don Alonso de Castañeda. His namesake was apparently the Spanish Alonso de Castañeda who arrived from the Caribbean in 1527 in the entourage of the soon-to-be infamous Nuño Beltrán de Guzmán.[31] In 1528, Guzmán was named to preside over the first Audiencia of Mexico, and in 1529, he sent his henchmen—Castañeda and others—out to the surrounding towns, including those in the area of Cuauhtinchan, with a large armed force in order to conscript several thousand indigenous porters and warriors for the campaign he was planning in the west. Perhaps it was Castañeda himself who informed Chimalpopoca and the other Cuauhtinchan chiefs of Spanish law as it was presently being formulated, according to which they would only maintain their hereditary chieftainship and lands if they embraced Christianity.[32] What we know with certainty is that another nobleman from the immediate area later testified that he himself was baptized in 1529[33]; that Chimalpopoca had accepted the Christian name "Alonso" by early 1532[34]; and that his descendants remembered hearing about the late 1520s as the beginning of Christianity in Cuauhtinchan. An elder had said to them, "But no one yet knew what was happening, if it was Sunday or some other day. We were really new at it.... We still didn't know what was going on."[35]

The next year, someone commented, people began to come to the church voluntarily. There was singing. Then the leading men began to be pressured to abandon many of their wives and choose one to marry. Don Alonso's descendants, in the *Libro de Guardianes*, the same text in which they mentioned the arrival of Christianity, brought up the subject of conjugal discord twice, in different contexts,[36] as though it had loomed large in their family history, but they gave no details on so painful a subject. The divisions between their own various mothers and grandmothers were perhaps best forgotten, if indeed they could be while some of the children yet lived.

In any case, there were graver—or at least more public—troubles than these. In the early 1530s, there was another epidemic, and this, combined with the high tribute demands and Guzmán's policy of forced conscription, turned whole villages of people into migrants, and many lands lay fallow. One day, for example, there appeared in Cuauhtinchan two men, Apiancatl and Elohuehue, who were the leaders of a band consisting of nineteen families traveling together—eight Chichimec Nahua families, six Otomí, and five Pinome. "They were suffering people who had come from distant lands." They begged for succor, and the Cuauhtinchan nobles met together and, according to custom, gave them some land in Amozoc in exchange for guarding the road to Tepeaca and doing whatever else might be demanded of them. The newcomers were told to set up a thatch hut where they could honor the Christian god and a priest would come from Tepeaca to bless their endeavor. In the document the group apparently created with the help of a young indigenous scribe, Chimalpopoca used the hybrid name "don Alonso de Castañeda Chimalpopoca." But it would be the last time he gave the latter name in a public record. Near him stood don Tomás Huilacapitzin, chief of the leading Pinome clan. His participation in the land-giving ceremony would be one of his last acts.[37]

Shortly thereafter, don Tomás Huilacapitzin, tlatoani of all Cuauhtinchan, was found to have authorized human sacrifice on a nearby hilltop. Chimalpopoca's descendants, who sometimes insisted that Spanish accusations were mere calumnies, said that it was quite true and spelled out the details.[38] Of course, this Pinome chief was also the son of the man who had murdered Chimalpopoca's father; they had reason to dislike him. Undoubtedly, however, their dislike only freed them from a need to protect his name; it almost certainly did not cause them to make up the story. The details were also recorded by a writer in Tecamachalco who would not have known the principals so personally.[39] And if common sense were not enough to convince us, there is abundant evidence that forms of the old religion were alive and well in the Mexican countryside.[40] Don Alonso, in the book he later supervised the writing of, commented merely that in this year, don Tomás was hanged.[41] The note was written in the same hand but with another pen, inserted almost as an afterthought, a mention of an event that had been repressed in the first telling.

The Franciscans gave orders that the lords of Cuauhtinchan, as well as those of Tecamachalco, Quecholac, Acatzinco, and Tecalco, were all to come to witness the executions in Tepeaca. These men would always remember what they saw. "His body was not quartered, only hanged. His dog, white with black spots, stayed lying there beside his hanged master."[42] Next two other men, probably the priests who had officiated at the old-style ceremony, were hanged and then quartered. Certain other men and women were only shamed in the hot sun. This was the end of the matter in the immediate vicinity, but not elsewhere. Soon rumor had it that the chiefs in the Tetzcoco region were even being asked to hunt down sorcerers making anti-Franciscan statements, dragging them from their caves and turning them over to the law. One *nahualli* (sorcerer) in the case had apparently made himself *persona non grata* among the indigenous rulers as well, having demanded the delivery of women to his cave, like Huemac of old.[43]

Not long after the hangings in the marketplace, the Franciscans told the people of Cuauhtinchan to build a stone church, and they complied. Indeed, don Alonso's people threw themselves into the building of San Juan Cuauhtinchan.[44] Great building projects in honor of divinities had always been points of pride—the last great one had been a temple to Camaxtle, built in the 1490s[45]—and in this case, there was the added zest of competing with Tepeaca, which had once been a subject polity but in recent decades had lorded it over Cuauhtinchan, and now had even become the seat of the powerful Spaniards. This project was different from any that had come before, however. At the behest of the severe fray Juan de Rivas[46] who presided in Tepeaca, the building was shaped not like a pyramid mountain, but like a great cube; yet it was not flat like an ordinary house, for it had a tower reaching to the sky. The people painted the temple's inner walls beautifully with swirling flowers, as they always had done in the past, and with a jaguar and an eagle appearing in symbolically crucial positions, but also making use of some of the Christian iconography to which they had now been exposed.[47]

In the midst of the project, in 1536, the Franciscans told the indigenous lords that they were starting a school for their sons in the country of the Mexica, in Tlatelolco, where the Franciscans had their great monastery. They wanted boys ten to twelve years old. They would be taken to learn many things—not only the meaning of Christianity but also Spanish and Latin, reading, writing, and the illumination of manuscripts. Don Alonso, a young man and new chief in 1520, would have had sons of about that age. Did he entrust any to the Franciscans? It seems more than likely. In their entry for that year, his descendants wrote: "There was founded, created, a school, a *colegio*, where the children of the *tlatoque* of all the altepetl of all the various people here in Nueva España would study."[48] And by the 1540s, someone in don Alonso's kin network learned to write in a beautiful hand that indicated he could only have had a European master as well as many hours of practice.[49] That student gained perfect mastery not only of the roman alphabet and arabic numerals, but also of other accepted conventions—paragraph markers, asterisks, the "&c."—making it seem even less possible that his knowledge was second-hand, or gleaned in grabbed hours with a friar in Tepeaca. Furthermore, someone in don Alonso's circle later displayed a relatively deep knowledge of European events unfolding in the 1530s. We can guess that either this writer or someone well known to him was taught by a devout Spanish Catholic in that decade, for he commented with disgust on the Protestant heresies caused by such things as the "passions and bad example of the English king, Henry the Eighth" and the rebelliousness of the people of Geneva.[50] Later, a son or grandson of don Alonso, don Cristóbal de Castañeda, became a member of the indigenous cabildo, and the first position he agreed to fill was that of clerk (*escribano*).[51] In short, it hardly seems a stretch to think that a son or two of don Alonso Castañeda were among the boys lined up in the dormitory of the Colegio de Santa Cruz one day in 1536, remembered by the friars "each with his ... *petate*, which to the Indians, is the bed of a lord, and each with his little chest and key, to keep his books and clothes."[52]

It is certain that a group of young nobles in Cuauhtinchan soon began to take pride in their alphabetic literacy. The same writer who mentioned Henry VIII in later decades wrote out in Spanish at the start of his book a sentence loaded with double entendre: "Well-born noblemen who do not know their letters have no understanding. They are noble beasts."[53] By the 1550s, a number of the aging chiefs in the region had been taught to sign their names—and don Alonso seems to have been among them, though we cannot be sure. In that same decade, there was open acknowledgment of the tensions that by then had existed for many years between the old-school leaders and the younger men educated by the Franciscans. Young don Felipe de Mendoza, leader of a Pinome lineage, recalled being invited to the home of a young lord of Tepeaca, don Luis de Guzmán, in the early 1540s. Don Luis said to him and the companions he brought, "I invited only you, because we were raised afterwards, we were educated in the church. The grandfathers, the teteuctin and the tlatoque of Cuauhtinchan, many times have worried me with their statements against us, the people of Tepeaca."[54]

In times of stress, old arguments sometimes explode anew. So it was in Cuauhtinchan in the 1540s. Coronado's expedition into the north country and the explosion of the Mixton War in the west caused the conscription of hundreds, possibly thousands, of indigenous people;[55] meanwhile, large tribute payments continued to be demanded of a dwindling population. In 1545, the worst epidemic since that of 1520–1521 broke out. Across Mexico, 800,000 indigenous were said to have died,[56] there could have been no one left alive who had not lost someone beloved. In this context, the lords of Cuauhtinchan responded with rage when the people of Tepeaca attempted to gain title to some of their traditional lands. There had long been tension over a particular area, and some mediation had been attempted, but in March of 1546, don Alonso, together with the heads of three other Cuauhtinchan lineages, decided to travel to Mexico City and lay their case before the Audiencia, or high court.[57] In the old days, there might have been a war. Now the leaders decided to use their sons' new alphabetic literacy and knowledge of the Spanish state to fight another way. Tepeaca's relationship with Cuauhtinchan had been fraught for centuries, as Tepeaca had once been a subservient state, but then in the 1450s had conquered their old overlords and ruled for a generation. On the other hand, much more recently, when the Spaniards had invaded, don Alonso (then Chimalpopoca) had fought for his life side by side with the warriors of Tepeaca. The decision to sue them would have been disorienting on one level, and yet not on another. A classic historical drama with which he was deeply familiar was being enacted here: an important alliance was being broken because in a time of duress, older tensions came to the fore.

In the great city, the travelers made their way to Tlatelolco, where they had old friends or acquaintances—likely dating from the years of their sons' residence at the school—who were willing to testify for them.[58] They soon found they had to spend frightening amounts of money to maintain themselves in the metropole,[59] but they were not going to reverse course now. By August, they had conducted enough legal business to be able to leave the affair in the hands of a Spanish attorney.

The records of the case reveal a glimpse of don Alonso's dominant personality. He was a figure who elicited respect. At the first reference to him, his name appears after that of the leader who was currently serving as the elected *gobernador* (head) of the indigenous cabildo of Cuauhtinchan.[60] After that, however, it is "don Alonso" whom the scribe begins with every time. (The others were soon reduced to "*e otros principales*," "and other noblemen," but he was always named.) It was he who stepped forward and forcefully demanded that the Tepeaca defendants be made to appear, as he and his fellow governors were badly needed at home; he who nodded his assent after statements were read aloud by the court interpreter, Juan Gallegos.[61] It was implicitly he who orchestrated the compelling evidence that what they were asking for was in fact the upholding of a decision made by the Mexica high king in the *ancien régime*, which ultimately ensured their victory.

But if don Alonso proved himself to posterity to have been a leader of men, there must also have been days when he himself felt like a student. This Mexico he was visiting, whatever else it was, was a city of grandeur and a center of power. And here at the beating heart of the empire, in the chambers of the Audiencia, he saw for himself how power was enacted.

As in his world, it was wielded through statements made gravely and with ritualistic language and then commemorated on paper. But he would have noted a significant difference. These decisions were rendered permanent through the medium of a certain kind of writing. It was not the pictographic writing that he knew so well but that younger men in his world could no longer read easily. He was observing alphabetic writings. These were long writings that encoded the human voice. His exact words could be read back to him smoothly and without a hitch. The young people would have assured him that anyone could learn to interpret the letters; they were not the special province of priests who spent decades learning and creating symbols and then took much of their knowledge with them to the grave. If the worst should happen, if a terrible *cocoliztli* (epidemic) were to strike dead all the trained men of the Audiencia court tomorrow, there would still be other men in the world who could read these documents.

It was in this context, in the late 1540s, that don Alonso's lineage undertook a great project, the creating of the magnificent book of history that later generations would label the *Historia Tolteca Chichimeca*.[62] Given what we know about don Alonso and his context, we can only assume that he was at the helm of such a project and that his sons (or other young relatives) executed it. The first page was a complex drawing of a polity done almost entirely in traditional style. On the next page began, in alphabetic writing, the ancient story of the Tolteca Chichimeca people and the dissolution of their twenty-part altepetl. But at the very top was inserted an explanation of a particular part of the preceding drawing. "This *pintura* is of the *tezcacoatl* Cotzatzin, son of the *apanecateuctli* Xiuhcozcatl, from whose line was born don Alonso de Castañeda, he who closes our year-count."[63] And the remainder of the fifty-two-page manuscript tells a story that is ultimately more relevant to don Alonso's family line than to any other,[64] toward the end including the details of his father's death, the exact years of his grandfather's, his father's, and his own accession, and his leading role in the trip to Mexico City.

Given both the internal consistency of the text and its unusual nature, it is clear that it was the result of careful thought and discussion. We know that don Alonso had in his keeping various traditional timelines and genealogies, probably originating before the conquest, because he helped to interpret at least one of each in a remarkable court case that unfolded in August of 1553. (In the litigation, two other Cuauhtinchan sub-altepetl were battling for possession of certain lands, and don Alonso tried to aid in settling the dispute, drawing on his family's knowledge of the past.) In this same period, several of the Pinome lineages were producing beautiful *mapas*, as they are now called, largely preconquest-style paintings that convey ancient religious origin stories at the same time as they represent the travels of those Tolteca Chichimeca who ultimately landed in Cuauhtinchan and delineate numerous family lines in that region.[65] Don Alonso and his family members certainly must have known of such productions and may even have participated in making some.[66] The project they contemplated, however, would not be exactly like any of these works. They would take both traditional timelines and myth-history paintings and make some purposeful adjustments.

In the past, as don Alonso and his family knew, the year-by-year painted timelines of the xiuhpohualli had been used flexibly. An orator did not necessarily simply stand up, hold out his painting, and recite an unchanging text from memory. He might direct attention to certain major features and comment only on them, depending on the point he needed to make. One of the presenters in court in 1553 said, for example, "The first time the Cholulteca came [to settle here] was when the Acolhua came to shoot arrows at [the temple of] Quetzalcoatl, there at the point they came to make war in Cholula. The second time they came was when Teuctlecozauhqui was defeated and the land was abandoned so they came to settle on it...."[67] We can almost see the speaker moving his finger along the timeline, indicating the relevant moments. Don Alonso, together with others, gave a presentation about the reigning Teuhctlecozauhqui in the late 1300s who was brought down by the Pinome; then they made a particular point about the later year in which the Pinomes' allies, the Tlatelolca, were themselves brought down by the Mexica. "This is just what we are pointing out," they said.[68]

Now don Alonso and his family members would combine this style of flexibility with their new knowledge of a phonetic transcription system to create a beautiful and important text, one that they believed posterity would be able to understand in perpetuity. Important events in the story that they wanted to tell would be marked by symbolic glyphs or even whole paintings, next to which would appear full alphabetic transcriptions of what would have been said in an old-style performance.[69] Between these entries, years in which little or nothing of note happened would be marked merely by an alphabetic naming of the year—*ome tochtli* ("Two Rabbit"), for instance—with perhaps the briefest of comments. This would save both space and effort. Likewise, land maps and king lists would in certain important cases be represented by images next to words, but most often simply by lists of towns or people's names. That would be more efficient, for present and future communication, as those who could read the glyphs were fewer with each passing year.

As was typical of the old-style performances, different component parts of a given polity would each have their version presented in turn. First the Nonoualca would become angry and wander away, then the narrative would backtrack to the moment of their departure and follow the now-bereft Tolteca Chichimeca in their wanderings until some of them reached Cholula. Afterward, when the ancestors of the Cuauhtinchantlaca were summoned from their cave to help the Tolteca Chichimeca of Cholula, different breakaway groups would be followed in turn as they settled the surrounding region, culminating with those who actually fought for the Cholulans and received lands in Cuauhtinchan. Even then, the stories of different subgroups would have to be told as they traveled east, finally ending with the events in the lives of those who were the immediate ancestors of don Alonso Castañeda and their close associates.

In traditional performances, more than one speaker declaimed. Indeed, don Alonso brought several speakers with him to the courtroom in 1553. It thus seems highly likely that the young scribes of the family took down the words of more than one elder. It also seems virtually certain that don Alonso himself was a major source. First, the content of the testimony he gave in the courtroom in 1553 is found in very similar form in the *Historia*.[70] That phenomenon, however, might merely indicate that a large group of elders were still living who had recitation knowledge of the old histories; on its own, the similarity of the content reveals little. Perhaps more important, there are elements of the *Historia* that it would have been unlikely that anyone else would have known as well as don Alonso himself—such as what happened in his father's last days, or when his family ceased to farm certain fields. Don Alonso de Castañeda was the kind of person who was accustomed to being consulted and took great pains to get the story right. In the 1553 court case, a scribe recorded that he was shown a visual source, the contents of which he could not vouch for as true with any degree of certainty. "I myself do not know about that," he responded. "They did not speak to me about it [at the time]. I have only heard about it."[71]

It is conceivable that don Alonso himself or some other elder also participated in the work of the paintings and glyphs, but this is conjecture. It does seem that there are at least two hands at work, as certain pages seem profoundly pre-Columbian, but even of that we cannot be sure. Most of the artwork is clearly a product of two styles of education—indigenous and Spanish—purposefully intermingled. Ancient Nahua motifs and styles appear along with human beings sketched just as a Spanish drawing master would have taught, according to European rules of perspective. (The Franciscan friar Motolinía later remarked condescendingly, "Before [we came] they only knew how to paint birds and flowers; if they did a man or horse, it was badly engraved, but now they do it well."[72]) There are whole pages of text that consist of purely alphabetic writing in black ink. Here, it seems, there has disappeared all semblance of the old style of writing, *in tlilli in tlapalli* ("the black, the red"), using colored pigments. And yet the scribe is not entirely ready to let go of the old notions, even on these pages. At the start of each new idea there is a European-style paragraph marker—each one painstakingly painted in red. Each page is thus a vivid embodiment of "the red and the black." And yet on another level it is nothing of the sort.

Scholars have long wondered what don Alonso's specific purposes were in producing such a book. Art historian Dana Leibsohn has perhaps offered the most useful thoughts:

> ... the heuristic metaphor that seems most apt is the creative wager. I thus have come to see the *Historia* as a kind of nervy gamble: this invented form of record-keeping, unlike others known and used nearby, is the one most befitting Pre-Hispanic history; this new way is the one worth entrusting with the virtues of ancient knowledge. What was at stake for don Alonso in his venture, I am reluctant to put too fine a point on.

This unsettles my positivist and authorial impulses, yet we would be mistaken to presume don Alonso wanted just one thing from his history. No one ever does.[73]

Scholars have suggested that the work may have been intended for use in Cuauhtinchan's courtroom dramas. It may have been, but that could not have been its primary purpose. Both its details and its ultimate arguments, though relevant to the ongoing legal maneuvers, move far beyond the territorial dispute with Tepeyaca in the 1540s and the internal Cuauntinchan quarrel of 1553. Another scholar has insightfully suggested that certain lines in Popoloca that were added to the first page ("Come, uncle, seat yourself on the throne ... ") were not merely the absent-minded language exercise of a distracted student of a later era, but rather, the purposeful attempt to script a political investiture ceremony.[74] When we consider that we know don Alonso to have made wandering indigenous groups welcome in his lands in exchange for their allegiance, it begins to seem likely that someone might have wanted to bring such a magnificent book to a public ceremony for use as a ritual object denoting political authority. In general, it seems enough to say that don Alonso, speaker on behalf of his people and steward of their lands, felt compelled to preserve his knowledge of their past in a form their great-grandchildren would understand. He probably knew he could not envision all possible uses for such knowledge in a rapidly changing world. He did not have to foresee all in order to feel that the possibility of utter amnesia—and the resulting powerlessness, the consequent inability to formulate political arguments—was intolerable.

Already in the 1550s there came a great crisis illustrative of the trials that awaited. The Crown, in conjunction with the Franciscan order, turned the town of Cuauhtinchan over to the Dominicans, who had men available for staffing. But the people of Cuautinchan erupted in protest and refused to host them. The greatest source of information on the subsequent events is the friars. Normally the Franciscans are not to be trusted on internal indigenous affairs—especially when they are developing the theme of the overwhelming love the indigenous extended to them as opposed to other orders. In this case, however, Mendieta names some of the noblemen with whom he dealt and gets the names quite right. He then quotes a letter that sounds quintessentially indigenous—one beginning with a rhetorical apology for having caused so much trouble, even to the point of making the Franciscans ill. The indigenous letter writers insisted, says Mendieta, that having grown as accustomed to the Franciscans as they would be to a parent, they could not be expected to change their allegiance now. They then repeated at least twice (and here we cannot fail to be illuminated as to the reason for the strength of their resistance, even if Mendieta did not see it) that they had absolutely no problems with the current arrangement, whereby they regularly visited Tepeaca, but had no friars living in their own town. Indeed, don Alonso's book was perhaps one of many wonderful results of the recent epoch in Cuauhtinchan's history, in which indigenous people were tutored in European ways, but then largely left to their own devices. No wonder they did not want the situation to change.[75]

It was eventually settled that the Franciscans would keep the town, but would have to manage to found a town and monastery there—which they did. A *congregación* of the hamlets ensued, and a great public ceremony was held in 1558. In this case, don Alonso and his peers had perhaps lost their wager, but they had at least managed to retain their connection with the Europeans whom they knew, rather than starting over with others. And to them continuity was of the essence.

In 1564 the Crown began a great reevaluation of the tribute system which would lead to profound changes for the Mexican indigenous.[76] Don Alonso, now an old, blind man, was still alive, and was entered as receiving from his people a weekly tribute of one hen, eighty cacao beans, and the services of four macehualtin.[77] He died sometime in the presumably not-too-distant future, leaving behind his three most precious gifts: the chieftainship, the accompanying lands, and his great book of history. It is probably safe to say that he trusted his descendants to guard his gifts well, since they had been willing to devote so much time and creative energy to their common book project. He undoubtedly exhorted them in true Nahua style. They did not fail him for several generations. In the mid-seventeenth century, a woman who was either a granddaughter or a great-granddaughter still had the three gifts in her keeping.[78]

***

Doña María Ruiz de Castañeda was hardly the only indigenous person of her generation in central Mexico to treasure documents handed down from the years immediately after the conquest. The central basin was full of them. The oldest, not surprisingly, had originated in Tlatelolco, the site of the Franciscan school. Perhaps don Alonso or his sons had even seen some of these writings; the first few pages of the *Libro de Guardianes* bear an uncanny resemblance to some of the material collected by the students of Bernardino de Sahagún in Tlatelolco.[79] Certainly someone penned the words of the *Annals of Tlatelolco* at about the time don Alonso visited the city in the 1540s, and Sahagún (the Colegio's Latin teacher in the 1530s, when the Cuauhtinchan *principes* would have been there) began his great push to start research on a major scale in 1546, the very year of the visit.[80] In the *Annals of Tlatelolco*,[81] the speakers telling the story begin with the most ancient of tales, their ancestors' emergence from the Seven Caves, and then recount the coming of their people to Chapultepec, and tell of the reversals they suffered there:

[F. 8]
The Mexica were at Chapultepec for forty two years. In the forty-third, in the year One Rabbit, they were despoiled. Huitzilihuitl, the Mexica king, was brought to Culhuacan, together with his daughter, Chimalaxochitzin. To Xochimilco were brought the priest Cimatecatl, and Tezcacohuacatl, and Tozpaxoch. To Matlatzinco were brought a number of women. To Cuernavaca were brought Cohuatzontli and some women. To Chalco were brought Huitziltecatl and some women. To Acolhuacan were brought women. To Xaltocan were brought Tepantzin and [his sister] Tezcatlamiahualtzin, who escaped and didn't die, but later came to join their comrades in Culhuacan. To Azcapotzalco were brought women. To Mazahuacan was brought Yaozol, who escaped and came to join the others in Culhuacan. A few more hid in [the swamps of] Acocolco and went to camp out on the islands. After five days had passed, they went to beg at Culhuacan. Eztloocelopan was he [who led the ones] who went to plead. The [Culhuacan] rulers he went to negotiate with were Acxoquauhtli, Coxcoxtli, Chalchiuhtlatonac, and Achitometl. The Mexica elders said to them, "O rulers, o kings, Tenoch sends us, and Iztacchiauhtototl, Ahuexotl and Tenantzin, saying: 'Plead with the rulers of Culhuacan. The common people are suffering, are enduring hardship, those who are still on the islands. Let us perhaps light the fires or sweep [as their servants]. Let us submit to their rulership.'"

The rulers respond, "Where did you go to save yourselves?" "The islands in [the swamps of] Acocolco," they say. Then they address a messenger, saying to him "Go and count how many saved themselves."

He went and saw about forty people. A princess[82] of the Mexica who was pregnant had given birth on an island, and they called the one who was born Axolotl. Now Huitzilihuitl had not yet died [that is, had not yet been sacrificed] when the people came to beg. They asked, "What does he say about it that his macehualtin are arriving? Indeed the ones who hid themselves have already come." At that the woman [his daughter] suddenly began to shout. She said, "Why do we not die? [meaning, "Why don't you sacrifice us?"] Why are they coming to us? Let the lords listen! Why do we not die? Let us ask for chalk and feathers!"[83] The lords heard, and they said, "Ask Huitzilihuitl if he also wants the chalk and the feathers." They [the two prisoners] rubbed charcoal on themselves, as they had grabbed burnt wood [from the fire]. When they had applied the chalk and lime, they killed them on the altar with a tlaauitectli[84] [knife] and a tlequaztli[85] [fire stick]. When they first set fire to the princess, she exclaimed as she wept, she said to those below, "O people of Culhuacan, I go to where [my] god lives. My hair and my nails will all become men!"[86] So also exclaimed Huitzilihuitl. After they died, their blood was washed away.

Then the Mexica came to Culhuacan and established themselves at Tizaapan. The Culhuaque said to them, "Welcome, o Mexica; settle at Tizaapan." But when they had been there ten days, the Culhuaque rulers gave them an order, saying to them, "O Mexica, you must drag in a chinampa, on which a crane will come to stand and a snake who is discolored from sickness will come to lie. You are to come place the chinampa outside the palace." After they had come to give them the orders, the Mexica wept and said, "Woe is us! How will we do it?" Then Huitzilopochtli spoke to them and said,

[F. 8v]

"Don't be afraid. I know how you are to go and drag the chinampa that is over there. I will show you." They were able to do it by dragging the sod in separate pieces. The crane came along standing upon it, and the snake [restored to health][87] lay in the chinampa. The Colhuaque rulers were amazed at it, saying "Who are these Mexica?"

To those who had pulled the chinampa, they gave another task, saying, "O Mexica, the rulers of Colhuacan say you must capture a deer for them, one that has no wounds. Do not break any of its bones. If you do, we will know what we are to do." When the [impossible] orders were given, the Mexica became really sad. Then they went to seek the deer. They wandered everywhere, in Acuezcomac and Chapultepec. They went along making a lot of noise trying to scare up game. In this way they fell in with the [two] Mexica who had been captives in Xaltocan—Tepan and his elder sister, Tezcatlamiahualtzin. They came out from among the reeds where they were hiding. Then they grabbed them. They did not think,[88] "We are [all] Mexica." They acted as if they were game to be hunted. After that they sent word to the rulers of Culhuacan, saying, "Listen, o kings. There is no such deer as the one you want, but we have gone hunting. One male and one female are what we caught." They took their prisoners and they went along making a lot of noise to scare up game. Thus they fell in with a deer who was wandering in the reeds. They chased it. As they had it going toward Culhuacan it got stuck in the mud. That is how it was possible for them to catch it and bundle it up. And that is how the place that is now Mazatlan (Place of the Deer) was given its name. Then they brought the deer before the rulers of Culhuacan. Looking it over, they saw that there was nothing wrong with it anywhere. Then the rulers of Culhuacan questioned the Mexica, saying, "O Mexica, where are your prisoners?" Just then Tepan and Tezcatlamiahual understood the situation, and then they cried and said, "Why, here we are, the Mexica whom they captured." Then they said, "O rulers, indeed we are Mexica, we are the Mexica who were captives in Xaltocan. We ran away." And so were they brought back by the Mexica to be with the others.

When the Mexica were settled in Tizaapan, then they went to plead with the rulers of Culhuacan. They said, "O rulers, we would trouble you, for we want to build just a bit of an earthen altar where you have let us settle." The rulers did not consent. But later Coxcox said to them, "Brothers, you may build it." And later he sent to say, "It's fine. Build it." When the earthen altar was finished, they went again to plead with the rulers. They said to them, "O rulers, our altar is finished. Let us go, so we may find a rabbit or perhaps a snake so that the firewood falls upon it [so that there may be a sacrifice]." The lords came back with, "That's fine, you may go,

[F. 9]

but you must go far, all the way into Xochimilco." No sooner had they left than the rulers of Culhuacan sent word to the Xochimilca. "Xochimilca, here is what you are to do. The Mexica are coming. Do not let one remain [alive]."

The Mexica went along scaring up game with their shouting, and on their way back, the Xochimilca ambushed them. Then they fought. All the Mexica took captives—some took two, some three. Then the Mexica sent people to address the lords of Culhuacan, saying, "O rulers, prisoners were indeed taken. The Xochimilca ran from the Mexica."[89] When the rulers heard this, they were really amazed. "Who are these Mexica?" they said.

When the Mexica built their altar, it was the year Two Reed, and it was also when they began to bind the years (in counts of fifty-two). Later the rulers of Culhuacan said to themselves, "Is it [really] their home where they have built the altar? They must place a heart there [to make it so]." With that they called those who kept their sacred books and ordered them to place a heart at the altar of the Mexica. They placed as a heart [a cache of] excrement, garbage, dust, spindles and [debris carded from] cotton. The Mexica went right away to take back out what they had buried there. They gathered reeds, thorns [used for holy sacrifice], and cypress wood. And they buried the excrement, garbage, dust, and the remains of cotton and feathers that had been in the middle of the patio, saying, "Are these things our home?!"[90] They placed a thatch house over their altar, and they called for the rulers. They didn't come. Only Coxcox came on his own, saying, "I would like to see what the Mexica are up to." When he came the Xochimilca [prisoners] were spread flat [for sacrifice]. Right in the middle of the fire was where they placed them. First [the figure of] Tetztzohualli came down, then Xiuhcoatl. The Xochimilca were set afire, and then they died. Afterwards the Mexica went to hold a celebration the like of which they hadn't had since they came. While the sacrifice was being made, the Mexica and Coxcox heard the sky screaming. At that an eagle came down, alighting on the peak of the temple's thatch house. What he placed there was something like a nest, upon which he stood. When the sacrifice of the Xochimilca was finished, he flew off in the same direction from whence he had descended.

The Mexica dwelt in Culhuacan for twenty years. There they took wives and had children. But in the twentieth year, anger arose, so that people were killed.[91] Those who had taken wives or who had taken husbands [from among the Culhuaque] were killed. They were killed in the year Eight Rabbit ...

***

When don Alonso Chimalpopoca was a boy, he heard no stories of a Hercules, nor any of a Beowulf. By the time he was a man, any such tales likely would have seemed naïve and overblown to him. His was a world of harrowing battles and of heroism, to be sure, but in the landscapes in which he lived and dreamed, there could be no army of One, no figure so powerful he could not be defeated, no person so isolated that he imagined glory only in the singular. The ancient tales known to Chimalpopoca were stories of countless humans mingling and laughing, jeering and fighting on the seething, teeming, living earth. The people spent much of their time reaching out to one another to build alliances, and deciding when and how to break them. They were proud of the connections that they established and deeply knowledgeable about them; their history keepers memorized long lists of allied clans who traveled together, or of marriages contracted for the benefit of both groups and of the children born. The land itself was a loose-woven mantle with the network of connections between people visible upon it. Roads, rivers, and mountains could separate people, but they were also shared features, approached from different angles by different groups, drawing them together in the vibrant world in which they lived.

It was the consciousness of the frequent unplanned rages that broke people asunder, and of the purposeful betrayals, that troubled the storytellers. In the opening lines of don Alonso's *Historia*, the idyllic twenty subunits coexist peacefully only for two sentences; in the third they break apart, each group to seek its own home. When the story is later told in depth, the angst is palpable. Those who have led the charge against their own relations speak openly of their remorse, and of their fear of the future now that the seeds of bitterness have been sown. "What kind of people are we? Perhaps we have done wrong. Perhaps because of it something may happen to our children and grandchildren." No apology will make up for the loss of the many who have fallen in battle. The people feel that they have no choice but to separate themselves from the submerged anger they would otherwise face forever, and they leave under cover of darkness. The rest of Chichimec history will largely consist of these people's searching for land and home, for stability.

In the *Annals of Tlatelolco*, the teller of tales likewise winces at divisions between those who should have been comrades. He speaks of his ancestors, the Mexica, at the moment when they have chosen to submit themselves to Culhua overlords in the wake of a disastrous defeat in battle. They are in the woods attempting to fulfill a hunting task that has been assigned them by their new overlords, and they come across two of their fellows from another lineage, a brother and sister who had been taken prisoner in battle but then escaped. "They did not think, 'We are both Mexica.'" Instead, in their desperation to satisfy the Culhuaque, the hunters decide to bring the two they have found back to Culhuacan and turn them over as prisoners; they do not even tell their old friends that this is their plan, lest they try to escape. Instead, the two are left to face the stunning betrayal when it is made clear to them what has happened before all the Culhuaque rulers. Perhaps unsurprisingly, the Mexica's troubles grow far worse before things get better.

In these tales, alliances are always vulnerable. When they are strong enough to withstand the insidious efforts of outsiders to dismantle them, it is a source of great pride. In a different set of annals from Tlaxcala, in a segment also recorded in the mid-sixteenth century, the narrator fairly purrs when he recounts the efforts of the Huexotzinca to buy the loyalty of the Otomí, over whom the Tlaxcalans ruled. "The Huexotzinca gave the Otomí leather shields, arms, and cloaks. They desired that, when they came to make war on us, the Tlaxcalans would be defeated. They would divide the lands and the macehualtin between themselves and the Otomí. But when the Huexotzinca had communicated this to them, they came here to bring it before the four rulers of Tlaxcala."[92] Apparently, the Tlaxcalans had been justly governing overlords, or at least they acted fairly enough that the Otomí preferred not to take a risk by betting on new masters. And the Tlaxcalans in later years apparently were well aware that retaining Otomí loyalty had been key to their being able to defend themselves against the Huexotzinca. It was their own history that they were writing for their own posterity, yet they did not dream of taking all the credit for their victory, except insofar as they implied that they had been adept at retaining the allegiance of others.

Probably a central element of the decision by the Otomí to stand by the Tlaxcalans consisted of tight kinship ties between the two groups, who had been living as neighbors for many years. Yet it would be foolish to imagine that intermarriage *necessarily* worked as an effective social cement. All alliances were vulnerable, and marriage was the very heart of alliance; by definition it was fraught with tension. In the *Annals of Tlatelolco*, when the Mexica find themselves once again at war with the Culhuaque, those who have married with the enemy become likewise their enemy and face death. And the same phenomenon occurs in don Alonso's *Historia* at one point. "If a man from Cuauhtinchan had married a Totomihua woman, they killed her, because she was Totomihua. If a woman from Cuauhtinchan had married, they killed her husband, because the man was Totomihua. Even if children had been born, they killed them."[93]

In effect, *all* alliances, lasting or not, were ultimately based in kinship ties forged through intermarriage. Alliances between clans were based on degrees of consanguinity, and relationships with tribute-paying vassals solidified through certain kinds of marriages. Political bonds might be articulated in words in public ceremonies and historical performances, but they were not at root formed by language. They were formed, most centrally, through intermarriage and the birth of children, and always in the context of potential warfare. In modern times, when we think of alliances built through intermarriage, we may think of Queen Victoria's rather poorly thought out and ultimately failed strategy of marrying her children into most of the royal households of Europe. Not so don Alonso Chimalpopoca. When he thought of alliances built through intermarriage, he thought of complex formulas into which almost every altepetl in Mexico was tied as a variable. Critically, these formulas existed with the goal not of making a permanent peace, but of organizing power relations and structuring alliances.

In a relationship between equally powerful states, for instance, a king might marry off his sister or daughter to another king on the understanding that her sons—and not those of some other woman in that household—would inherit the chieftainship. In a relationship with a more powerful state, a king might be made to accept the sister or daughter of the more powerful monarch as the mother of his own heirs, whether or not that had been his intention in the past. Or worse yet, his daughter or sister might be taken away to the more powerful state, there to marry and mother an heir to his own kingdom who would be raised with greater loyalty to his father's people than his mother's, though he would later return to his mother's home to govern. In the worst—and most common—scenario of all, known to all macehualtin but likewise many a nobleman, a man's daughters or sisters might be taken away as mere concubines, never to see their home again, with the full knowledge that their children would inherit nothing. This usually was a result of war, but a comparable situation might come about through a strategic effort to prevent a war as well: young women could be given to a potential enemy as a peace offering, or simply encouraged to marry into an enemy altepetl without expectation. Indeed, which category any relationship fell under was determined largely by what the outcome of a real war had recently been, or what the results of a potential war were likely to be. A union's significance might thus change over time as a particular altepetl rose or fell; in the worst, most extreme and memorable cases recorded in the histories, those who married across lines might later find themselves punished as an emblem of their now-hated people. There were therefore subtleties underlying every marriage, especially among the nobility, of which people in Chimalpopoca's time were well aware, though they may often be lost on us today.[94]

In the courtroom in 1553, don Alonso's area of greatest historical expertise seems to have been that of the nature of the marriages contracted by his people over the preceding generations. A companion of his first explained, "Teuctlecozauhqui had many children, women who went to various altepetl; he gave them to them."[95] He specified that the one who was the daughter of the tlatoani of Cuauhquecholan was the royal daughter, *itlazopiltzin*, whose marriage was particularly politically significant; and her fate was detailed elsewhere in the courtroom drama, as well as in the *Historia*. Then the speaker in conjunction with others demonstrated the ramifications in future generations of the marriages of the other daughters as well, in terms of landholdings and political relationships. Don Alonso spoke at one point. "Here are the words of don Alonso about Teuctlecozauhqui, whose daughter he gave to Xiuhtzone in Xonacatepetl. She was named Yztac Illama and from her were born

Couatecatl and his sister Quetzalcuetzin. Tecamecatl [of another lineage] then took Quetzalcuetzin and sired the [Nahuapan] tezcacoacatl Cuaytztzin and he sired the tezcacoacatl don Alonso. And the [Pinopan] xicotencatl Couatecatl sired Yztaccouatzin. And Yztaccouatzin sired the xicotencatl don Felipe."[96] Don Alonso's point was not just to give a genealogical recitation. Things were such, he tells us, that not only in ancient times but also in more recent ones were the relationships between Nahuapan and Pinopan lineages tightly interlinked and the inheritance of land sometimes debatable.

In his great book, however, don Alonso had the writers begin at the beginning, not in more recent times. The narrative starts with the story of the dissolution of the twenty related Tolteca altepetl, and the migration of those who end up in Cholula, and of the troubles they have there. They decide to go seek help from the more distantly related Chichimeca people of the Seven Caves. Then the writers give the story of the people of the Seven Caves, who listen to the messengers, learn their tongue and their ways, and eventually decide to join them. At the culmination of their winding migration, they defeat the enemies of the Cholulans, and then the unity of both groups is rendered visible in marriages between equals. The Cholulan kings give their daughters to the Chichimeca, to go with them to the east and found a new kingdom. The great procession is remembered in such detail it could have taken place only months before:

> Then the Chichimeca set off. [The Cholulan kings] Icxicouatl and Quetzalteueyac accompanied them. And their brothers came along singing, playing drums, timbrels, flutes, conch shells, and other shell horns; they came cheering on the Chichimeca. They left them in front of the houses of Xallapan and Xiuhtopollan. There they said good-bye and returned home. Then the Chichimeca continued on … who had with them the women who had been given to them, the daughters of Icxicouatl and Quetzalteueyac. To Teuhctlecozauhqui they gave a woman from Calmecac named Tepexochillama. To Moquiuix they gave a woman from Tecaman, and the one they gave was named the teuccihuatl Xiuhtlatzin.[97]

In the east the newcomers conquer the lands of the much less powerful locals and establish their homes. One lineage dominates all others.

Kings named for the original Teuctlecozauhqui and queens for his wife Tepexochillama rule for many generations (224 years, they specify). But finally, in the 1390s, their line is unseated by a different lineage working in alliance with the Mexica of Tlatelolco. The illustrations of the battle and its results are among the most remarkable in the volume. The version of the story told in the accompanying written text is one among several that circulated. "The daughter of Teuctlecozauhqui who was called the Tepexochillama was not killed but only taken prisoner. She was taken to Tlatelolco and [their leader] Cuauhtlatoua took her as his wife, and from her was born a [future] tlatoani [of a Cuauhtinchan lineage at Zacauillotlan], Cuauhtomicicuil."[98] (The version given in court in 1553, for example, was even more colorful, noting that Teuctlecozauhqui and his wife were killed on the road back to Tlatelolco.) The prisoner-wife returned to her people twenty years later with her Tlatelolcan-raised son, who had to be incorporated into the polity, now dominated by the victorious Pinopan lineages.[99] In two very different types of marriages, don Alonso's writers have set forth the central elements of their history—the union of their Cholulan and nomadic ancestors, and the origins of Mexica interference in Cuauhtinchan affairs. Infinite complexities stem from these conjugal scenes.

But if they are foundational moments, they are nevertheless not to be taken for granted. Such marriage alliances are contingent; they are a product of struggle, of effort. If the poor princess Chimalaxochitl who was dragged off to Culhuacan had been married to her captor, she might have been an unwilling partner, but it would have been a much sought-after outcome compared to the alternative—rape and/or the cutting stone—reserved for utterly powerless enemies. The primal fissure in don Alonso's *Historia* centers on a holy man in one political subunit demanding more and more tribute from the members of another subunit, culminating in lewd demands for women. Their menfolk can bear with this to a certain point, but they balk when he makes his final power play and cuts the girls' hearts out. Every lord has to recognize how far he can push his vassals; either this one failed to see his limits, or else he came to earth for the express purpose of stirring up trouble.

The ugliness of what this Huemac did, though extreme, was in some senses not unfamiliar to the storyteller's audience. In Chimalpopoca's youth, every captive woman knew that in times of war she faced the possibility of either a forced sexual relationship or sacrifice. Sometimes that choice might offer an opportunity for heroism, just as torture might for male prisoners of war. In the *Annals of Tlatelolco*, the captive daughter of Huitzilihuitl cannot bear it when her people begin to straggle into Culhuacan and see her there. She begs to be sacrificed. Respecting her strength of character, her enemies apply the chalk and lime, bring the knife and the torch. As she dies, the princess taunts them, swearing that one day her people's descendants will rise. "They will all become men!"

Reality was not always so inspiring, however, so the story was not always told this way. In other extant versions, Huitzilihuitl's daughter is a profoundly shamed figure. In one, the Mexica king and his daughter are brought before Coxcox, the king of Culhuacan. "Huitzilihuitl felt great compassion for his daughter, since not even a little [clothing] was on her. He said to the king, 'Grant some little thing to my daughter, o king.' But [the king] said to him, 'I do not consent. She will stay as she is.'"[100] It is easy to feel on behalf of the Mexica princess, who is denied even a vestige of her former dignity; it is tempting to pity the victimized Nonoualca girls, who are told that as their buttocks do not please their new master, they are to die. We must pause, though, with the thought that these were widely beloved stories, well known to audiences of women as well as men. If the women had felt purely demeaned, would the tales have lasted within the most central of historical narratives? Probably not. Might the women who were listening have been laughing at Huemac perhaps, with his ridiculous, over-the-top demands? Or even at the pompous Coxcox, whose uncontrolled hostility might be said to leave the naked girl with the moral high ground? Male tormentors were certainly dangerous—but their egotism might also be funny at times. It was perhaps this very attitude that they felt one had to take toward most of what threatened one's happiness in life. Mockery brought laughter, and laughter was life. Only the very worst periods of all were beyond humor.

In short, the network of alliances formed largely through conjugal unions and not infrequently torn asunder was ubiquitous in the tales of history. But we must not conclude that it was ultimately the point. Of course, as with all art, the point may well have varied in the eyes of varied beholders; but there were nonetheless particular messages that the tellers wanted to convey, moving far beyond connectedness and threats to that connectedness. That all humans were socially intertwined and were wont to rend the delicate fabric almost went without saying. The narrators wanted to express more; they wanted to exhort their listeners to hold to certain ideals, certain hopes and notions of themselves. The taletellers spoke with purpose not of the heroism of an individual (though individuals in the stories were often brave) but of *survival* writ large, the survival of a people into future generations. In their view, that kind of survival did not come easily. They spoke with conviction not of overweening power (though certain figures in the stories did wield power), but of the experience of being an underdog, and of the cleverness that underdogs must evince if their people are to live on through the vicissitudes of life.

Don Alonso's *Historia* is a classic text in this regard. The Tolteca Chichimeca are wanderers without lands of their own. At one point, to keep from starving, they are living as dependents of the Olmeca Xicallanca. They must tend their lands and serve them. They have no power to respond to the insults that are dished out to them. Old adages suffice to communicate that they are regularly demeaned: the women throw nextamalli water—the acidic lime water used to soak maize before grinding it—in their eyes, and others write on their backs when they are not looking. (This is akin to children making rabbit ears behind their classmates' backs in school photos. "There is a saying, 'Pen-mark the backs of others,'" explained an old man in Tlaxcala later in the sixteenth century.[101]) Eventually, the Tolteca leaders can bear it no longer, and working with others, they concoct a plan and execute it. Offering to have their people dance for their masters on the altepetl's upcoming feast day, they create the perfect excuse to collect old, cast-off warrior regalia and broken weapons. The leaders beg the people not to let each other down. They do not say, "Don't let us down." Indeed, they apologize in advance if their leadership proves not to have been effective enough. Instead, they beg the various subgroups to stand by each other, reminding them that though the outcome is to some extent up to the gods, they are the stewards of each other's fate. Working night after night to repair what they have collected, they prepare to make a successful attack on those who have lorded it over them for so long. It is a story that appears, in one version or another, in all of the very oldest sets of Nahuatl annals.[102] It is a great moment, the moment of turning the tables, of making a significant change; the leaders exhort the people and cry the ceremonial tears of all such high occasions. The triumph itself is left to the imagination of the audience. Perhaps it is more powerful that way, not less.

The Mexica give the story of their own specific ancestral underdogs a somewhat different twist. In the 1540s, the writers of the *Annals of Tlatelolco* took down the words of elders, of men who had grown up before the arrival of the Spaniards, in the period when Tenochtitlan's dominance of the central basin was rarely questioned and Tlatelolco constituted a crucial part of that city. It would have been impossible for the storytellers of their generation to have retained the ancient tales of underdogs in an unadulterated form. Everyone knew that the year count would eventually come to the era of Mexica triumph. Yet the old tropes remained in everyone's repertoire; with fewer than fifty years of such power behind them, no one had truly forgotten the past. So the stories they told were those of wandering underdogs, mocked and sacrificed, their women enslaved, their assigned duties well-nigh impossible—yet always swearing that the future would be different, that there would come a day when their tormentors would regret their actions. Even their enemies seem to have some foreknowledge of this. "Who *are* these Mexica?" they ask at every turn.

Interestingly, in the Tlaxcalan rendition, there is yet another twist, that of a people who bend but never break. In their historians' recent memory, they had lived literally surrounded by enemies but had never been conquered by the Mexica. They had had to defend every scrap of land they held, constantly whirling to face newly risen foes, yet they had managed never to succumb to vassalage. They passed down a story of magical arrows that was common to many Nahuas, but their arrows had even more panache than the norm for Chichimec warriors: "They lived carrying their bows and arrows. It is said that they had been sting arrows, fire arrows, arrows that followed people. It is even said that their arrows could seek things out. When they would go hunting, their arrow just went anywhere. If it went along hunting something above, they would see the arrow coming back with an eagle. If their arrow saw nothing above, it came down to fall on something, maybe a puma or ocelot, snake or deer, rabbit or quail. They went along to see what their arrow had brought down."[103] They, too, were pen-marked by the troublesome Olmeca Xicallanca, but the immediate ancestors of the Tlaxcalans chose to avoid them rather than fight them and went to settle upon some distant hills. Right away, their enemies began to spy on them. At this point, the teller of tales would put on a little drama, reading the script in the present tense:

> One named Xiuhtlehuin is ruler of Huexotzinco. He observes that smoke is rising from the top of the hill of Tlaxcala. He sends for someone and says, "Who are they? Go and see who is making smoke on Tlaxcala hill. Go and see if it is due to those Chichimeca from Teoponyauhtlan."
>
> They came to see, and in truth it was them, the Chichimecs, who made the smoke. They were eating a wood duck.[104]

The rich flavor of their meat could nearly drive their enemies mad. However, the delicious flavor of the local wood ducks notwithstanding, the Tlaxcalans' lives were truly hard, for enemies popped up and invaded at every turn. By dint of perseverance they thwarted all and sundry. Finally, not long before the Spaniards came, the Huexotzinca attempted to enlist the aid of the resident Otomí and attacked. One Huexotzincan nobleman tried harder than others to wrest some land from the Tlaxcalans. The outcome was reported almost matter-of-factly. "The Tlaxcalans burned his home. He came to establish his tecpan in Atlauhtzaca, which they prevented."[105]

If the survival of a beleaguered people is nearly always what is at stake, it is worth considering who the enemies are. There is no question that there are troublemakers—instigators of arguments in some cases and would-be conquerors in others. "Huemac was the cause behind the Tolteca Chichimeca and the Nonoualca Chichmeca breaking apart and making war." He clearly did what was best calculated to cause one sub-altepetl to declare war on another. Or in the case of the *Annals of Tlatelolco*, the duplicitous Culhua king, Coxcox, tells the Mexica that they can settle on his lands, but then sets them impossible tasks almost certain to result in death. He tells them they may build their temple, then sends his underlings to undermine their efforts and cause them spiritual agony.

In neither case, however, is such villainy the full story, or even the main line of the drama. The Tolteca and the Nonoualca confront the fact that they have allowed an outsider to sow division between them and they make peace, so that Huemac himself must flee. In the end, the Nonoualca leave on their own initiative. Likewise, Coxcox is forced to cease his efforts to torment the Mexica and make peace when he witnesses with his own eyes the intercession of the gods and the symbolic landing of the eagle. Despite his efforts, twenty years of peace ensue. It is the touchiness of the Mexica themselves that elicits the next round of violence. In each case, the subtext seems to be that events are not really attributable to one person, that the pursuit of such a theme will only be a waste of time. At one point in the courtroom in 1553, don Baltasar López, a close companion of don Alonso's who was head of another lineage, actually said as much about the real situation in which they found themselves, involving distant relatives in a dispute over land: "We really investigated and inquired into the actions of don Juan Yxconauhqui, because it has been said that he is one who just goes around causing fights in the altepetl of Cuauhtinchan and also Tepeaca. But in no way did we find it to be so; it is not true."[106] It was at that point that don Alonso stepped in to try to show that the history of intermarriage in the region was so complex that the inheritance of certain lands was truly debatable.

In the annals, the real danger in life seems not to be that a people will fall into the clutches of an evil villain but rather that they will find themselves without land of their own, without a defensible home. They will thus be forced to serve others, to depend on them and accept their will. They must do this for the sake of the survival of their people, but it is a grinding fate, harder to bear than almost any other, for the human beings in their world love their independence.

They speak of land and home, of course, in the stories of their gods. Modern readers will look for simplicity in this regard at their peril. For in their peregrinations, a people's devotion to a god may shift as they combine forces with another group or suffer a defeat. No one ever says as much explicitly—for disloyalty is anathema—but the people speak to different gods at different times. And the gods, too, are malleable, taking on each other's characteristics in different eras and different places and texts. Tezcatlipoca, for instance, might be a Hermes-like mischievous god, a king of mockery who brings laughter to people's lives, but he is also gifted with world-determining divine speech. Or he may illuminate the origins of a war in his involvement with a rape or a seduction. He may be opposed to the shape-shifting, border-crossing Quetzalcoatl, or be his twin.[107]

Despite such multivalency, each altepetl's primary god was, when all was said and done, at root a symbol of the people and their land, or at least their hope of land. Like other mischievous gods in many a pantheon, Tezcatlipoca desires to destroy the people dedicated to another god. He sends his dedicated servant, Huemac, to make trouble. When the ancient Nonoualca eventually depart, they carefully gather up all their sacred trust, the emblems of their god Quetzalcoatl. All such ancient migrants in all such stories travel with their holy bundles, for in these reside the symbols of their hope of land and home. They trust their god to guide them to wherever they should be. Later, in the worst of moments, the Tolteca Chichimeca ask, "Will our inventor, our creator, let us die here?!" And the answer to all such rhetorical questions, the audience knew well, was a resounding "No!" He was not going to let them die. He was going to help them win, and earn themselves a home.

In the *Annals of Tlatelolco*, Huitzilopochtli gives key advice to his wandering flock of Mexica, helping them to accomplish apparently impossible tasks. "Don't be afraid," he comforts them. "I know how you are to drag the chinampa . . . I will show you." When the people establish a temple and make their first sacrifice, the god sends an eagle to them. He symbolically alights upon a nest at the crest of the roof, and the people's joy knows no bounds. It is a sign that this must be their true home, their land. Even their enemy Coxcox seems to recognize it and ceases to fight them. The people have survived. They have won their land, and with it, their independence.

If only the happy ending were permanent. But as Chimalpopoca and his peers knew well, nothing lasts forever.

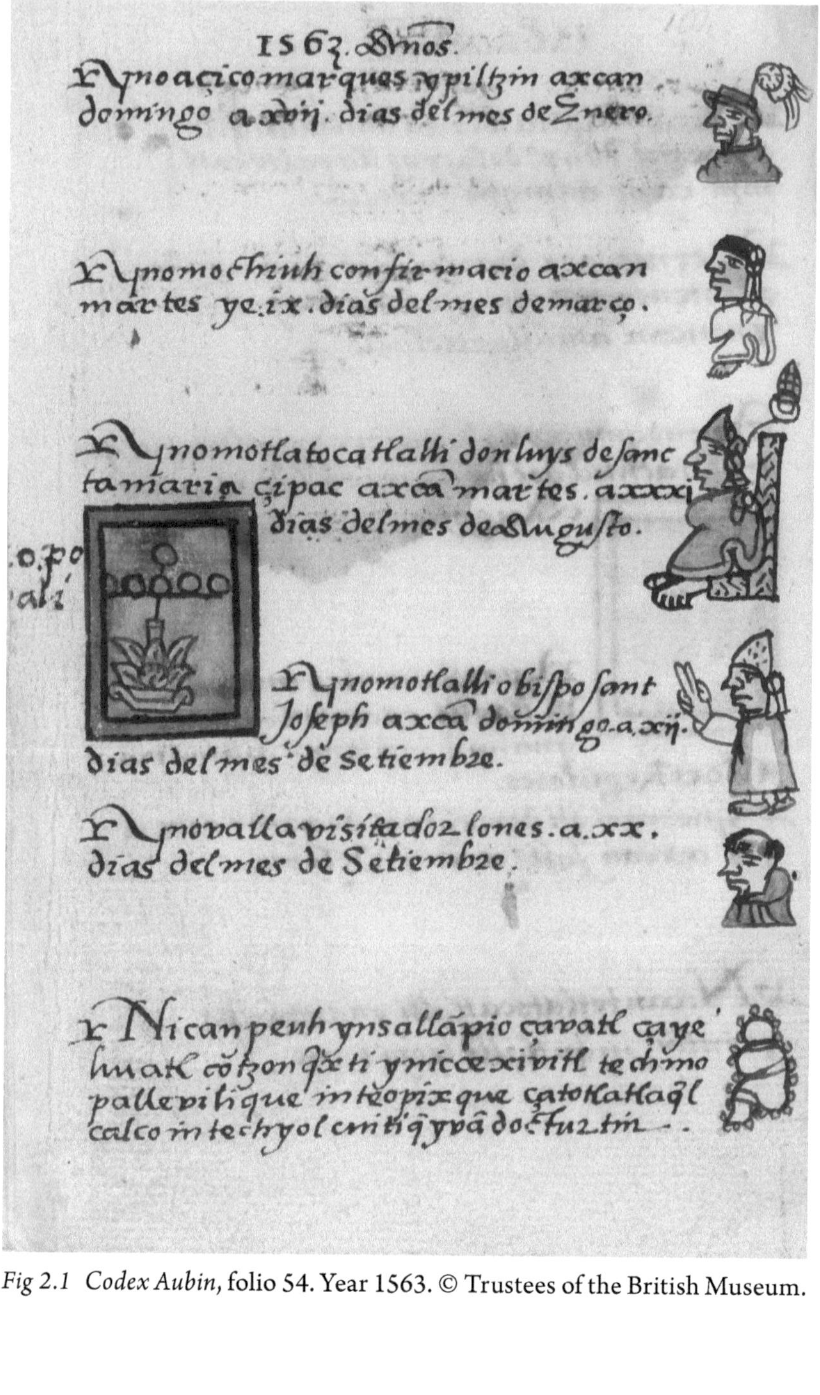

Fig 2.1 Codex Aubin, folio 54. Year 1563. © Trustees of the British Museum.

2

Becoming Conquered (The 1560s)

Decades after the arrival of Hernando Cortés, the Mexica faced the prospect of another kind of conquest. In 1564, tensions over a new head tax to be levied in the City of Mexico reached a fevered pitch. The people wrote about it in what would later be called *The Annals of Juan Bautista*:[1]

[f. 20r]
This day, Tuesday, June 13, 1564, the painters of San Juan [Moyotlan] were addressed. By order of the [indigenous] governor, [the cabildo members] Antonio Tlapaltecatl and Pedro Nicolás set things out for them, went to address them, in the church painters' workshop. They were just getting started with making the painting. When the [officials] got there, they said, "Is it here [at this point in time] that we throw it out, that it passes on, the breath, the words of the altepetl, its exhausting efforts, its sacrifices?" Thus they used to speak, the old-timers.[2] "Perhaps someone is tasking you with something such that in your heart you resist? If you do not obey, you will earn great suffering from the Ipalnemohuani [that is, from God]. The pipiltin are not people who make trouble. They are in the image of our lord. They suffer in the night. They don't eat their little tlamatzohualli [bread] with tranquility, for worrying about how they will bear [care for] the wings, the tail [society's macehualli people]. O artisans, none of you have heard the words of your fathers. Pay attention to your ancestry, from which came forth your artistry. Enter into, think of, your lineage. Otherwise because of your arrogance there will be nothing to be honored, to be renowned. Remember your commitment, your social contract". Etc.

These words were heard by Joan Yaotlaloc, Matheo Xaman, Miguel Tepotzitolloc, Pedro Chimalatl, Francisco Canpolihuiz, Antonio Hueton, Martín Yaotlapan, Miguel Teyol, Martín Cocho, Miguel Xochitl, Miguel

Matlalaca, Francisco Xinmamal, José Xochihua, Cristóbal Cuauhtli, Marcos Cipac, Martín Momauhti, Martín Mixcohuatl, and the aguaciles, Pedro Ahuatzal, Antonio Tezcachimal. "The governor guides and keeps the altepetl for you as it should be. That is why we were sent here."

This day, Tuesday, May 16, 1564, the paint was bought for the church. The paint sellers had come to the church to set out their wares. The paint was bought to make the images of the great retablo. The regidores Francisco Cuauhtli and Antonio Tlapaltecatl bought the paint. Pedro Nicolás was in charge of it. He hurried things along. Martín Josefino was the mayordomo, as he had held the staff for five years.

This day, on Sunday, July 2, 1564, on the feast day of the Visitation, our father, the guardián fray Melchor de Benavente, talked about the tribute. He said, "Yesterday, at dinner time, the visitador sent a message here. He sent a note to summon me. As soon as it struck one o'clock, we went. I brought a few other fathers along. When we got there, he said to me, 'Good, you have come. Here is the reason I sent for you. Since you're here in the altepetl, announce to the indigenous people how they are to pay tribute. A judgment has been made about their obligation to pay tribute. Many times I have summoned the governor, and he doesn't obey me. Not even an alcalde or a regidor comes. What are they about, that nobody has come?'

"When I heard that, I said to him, 'What you are talking about [meaning the amount of tribute asked] is impossible, for where are they to get it? Do they have fields? Do they have lands? You see the situation they are in.'

"Then he said, 'Why will it be impossible? It has been announced; it has been legally set.' Many times I said to him, 'Where will he [the governor] get it, how will he produce it? They do the rotary labor, bring in the hay, and help us with what is done in our homes. They help out everywhere, and with the tithes they help us. Whatever is needed, they do, in order to help us.'

[f. 21v]
"At that he said, 'The [old] duty is being abolished; they are relinquishing it. They shall [henceforth] occupy themselves exclusively with their [cash] tribute: in one year, they gather hay seven times and do rotary labor six times. For one load of hay, they are given half a real. And they

are given twenty bits [cacao grains] when they are hired to carry loads. And when it's cold they are given a [whole] real, and also the twenty bits to drop it off here. If they do the tribute, they end up being paid four reales [in total]. Their [old] tribute is canceled.'

"Then I said to him, 'It will not be possible, o ruler. I know very well that they all are craftsmen. This way they will become somewhat idle[3] and it will destroy their way of life.'

"Then he said, 'The Mexica are really lazy.' So I said, 'That's right. They're really lazy in helping us. When they come the sun is already up, and when they leave it's still light. When we appear, there is no longer anyone there. They have left, because hard labor really is not familiar to them.

[He said,] "Those of the towns around help us, those of Tlacopan, Tetzcoco, Xochimilco. They come very early in the morning and it is already night when they leave, because cultivation [the hard life of the farmer] is known to them."[4]

"Then he showed me the [current] chart. Your tribute is really a lot. Six times you do rotary labor and seven the haying. Then he gave me the [written] judgment. I saw it and read it and was satisfied. It said that if people pay the [new cash] tribute, the tithes will come out of that, and whatever else is necessary will be taken from there. [folio 22] 'Nothing else will be asked of them. They will live just like Spaniards.' After that I greatly rejoiced. I said, 'That's very good.' Your [other] tribute will be nothing. Your various [other] tribute amounts are completely erased. Give the Crown the one peso and three reales. The one peso is your tribute [in effect]. And the three reales are in place of the half fanega of maize [you used to give], and out of it will come the real that goes to your [indigenous] ruler. How will it not be possible for you to manage it? You know how."

When Mass ended, he went inside right away.

Marcos Tlacuilo, Pedro Chachalaca, Francisco Xinmamal and Pedro Nicolás followed him. And the father said to Marcos, "The retablo is to be finished quickly. The provincial sent a letter setting the time for the end of July. At that point he will come, he will come to install the retablo himself, at the time of the lighting of the Assumption. He will come to do it personally." At that Marcos answered him.

He said to him, "Father, how in the world will it be possible to finish quickly? The painters are collecting the hay and doing rotary labor. And the various other duties—they do them all."

Then the father said to him, "Don't you understand what I said about what the visitador has ordered? How will you do the tribute duties? You will leave off the public works and the haying[5] and whatever used to be charged to you for your tecpan [indigenous governorship]. It will all be canceled in view of the one peso, three reales payment, as the visitador told me. You will live just like Spaniards. [f. 22v] And I myself am really happy that the tithe that you used to pay is being completely abolished."

Marcos said, "Very good, father. Then let all the little tribute bosses who assigned the various duties in all the neighborhoods disappear."[6]

Then Pedro de San Nicolás said, "No, Father. The one peso and three reales will be collected as tribute every eighty days [as opposed to once a year]."

When the father heard that, he got really angry. He shoved Nicolás. He said, "He is a [stupid] brute. You are shameless! What do you mean, it will be collected every eighty days? Didn't I read [the document]? Didn't I see it with my own eyes? Did someone else just tell me about it?!"

At that Pedro Chachalaca said, "Father, the Tlaxcalan judges were like thieves when they came; they decreed that a painter who makes a full living would pay two reales, and one who doesn't yet make a full living one real, and also one who earns nothing would likewise pay one real, and a widow half a real. Those devils uniformly set two reales each and one real each, and you could tell they were like thieves when they raised it.[7] Then Nicolás spoke again, "Father, the young men and maids will pay tribute."[8]

And the father said in return, "Calm yourself. They [the young] will not do it on their own. Those who will pay tribute are the widows and widowers. A young man will help his father and a young woman her mother. When they marry they will pay tribute."

Marcos said to the father, "It's really a lot, isn't it, that will all come out of one peso?" And then the father said, "I really don't know. You are the ones who know about that. I'm just [f. 23] asking you to think about things. You might follow what the Tlaxcalans arranged, or make a complaint about it at this time, when it isn't yet being entirely carried out."

Then Nicolás went to speak to the [indigenous] governor in Huehuetlan, where they were having a feast day. He went and said to him, "My lord, the guardián has now spoken about the tribute. He announced it to the people. Marcos was very glad to hear that we would pay tribute that way."[9] But the next day, there was an argument over what Nicolás said. The father guardián again reprimanded Nicolás.

The next day, Monday, July 3, 1564, the regidores were arrested because of the rotary labor duty. Not enough macehualtin came. Seven were arrested: Miguel Teycniuh, Francisco Cuauhtli, Martín Cocolotl, Martín Cozotecatl, Andrés Cohuacuech, Miguel Acxotecatl, and Hipólito de Santa María.

Friday, July 7, 1564 they imposed a definitive sentence for the rotary labor duty, that everybody would do it, [including] all the various craftsmen, and that people would be arrested. Three hundred will be sold off [to labor in various places].[10] There in the palace in the afternoon, they signed the definitive order. They set the tribute on Friday.

Then the [indigenous] alcalde came to the church. He said to the father, fray Pedro, "Father, the rotary labor duty has been judged. All the lords [cabildo members] signed. Then he said to the father, "I am not responsible for it. Can't you [priests] take responsibility to help the common people in some way?[11]

[f. 23v]
This day, Monday, July 10, 1564, began the rotary labor duty. It began harshly there in Santa María Tlaltecayohuacan. The alcalde took care of it himself. He went to people's houses and brought them out. Whoever would say something back was taken to prison.

… This day, Thursday, July 13, 1564, the decision about the tribute was read aloud, when the people of the four quarters gathered together, along with those of the various workshops. People went upstairs to the second floor of the government palace, in the room devoted to justice. It was two o'clock when people assembled. There was a big turnout. A table was placed in the center and three chairs were put around. Then the governor and the alcalde, don Martín Ezmallin, seated themselves, and the eight regidores, and the office-holding pipiltin—Melchor Díaz, Tomás de Aquino, don Lucas Cortés, Martín Cano, don Martín Momauhti, Pedro Nicolás. And two Spaniards seated themselves to the left—Juan Cano and Juan Bautista. The governor spoke right away,

"You have come, here to the altepetl offices. Here is what you are to hear." Then he said to the clerk, Miguel de los Angeles, "Read it," and he read the statement. He spoke these words:

"I, don Luis de Santa María, governor by virtue of his Majesty here in the city of Mexico Tenochtitlan, on January 18, 1564, and we, the alcaldes don Martín de San Juan and don Antonio de Santa María, and the twelve regidores who are responsible for the altepetl, and the leading noblemen, when we heard what the common people would pay in tribute, we consulted among ourselves. We all went before the Audiencia Real, before the lord oidores. We made several appeals, but we could turn nothing around. Nothing more could be done. We met as a cabildo many times so we could discuss it. But nothing at all could be done, as it was already confirmed and verified. It was finally and definitively sentenced yesterday, July 13, in the above-mentioned year of the birth of our lord Jesus Christ." And when he finished his rejecting statement, then Pedro de Santiago read the decree of the sentence, which is given here:

Here in the City of Mexico Tenochtitlan, on February 18, 1564, I, don Luis de Santa María on behalf of his Majesty say what we have been assigned to pay as our tribute, what we are to give to our ruler, the emperor. It has been established for us that we are to pay and contribute 14,260 pesos. Each person will give one peso and four reales, plus half a fanega of maize. Widows and widowers, four reales and a fourth of a fanega. Unmarried young men and women, also four reales and a fourth of a fanega. And if someone doesn't have half a fanega of maize, then you will pay three reales instead, or give wheat. At the time of the harvest, everyone will present and give the maize. And when the tribute is gathered, the governor will divide it up. The Treasurer keeps the royal assets, given regularly to the Emperor's officers [mayordomos]. [f. 25] And from there [the sale of the corn] will come the share of the governor who is responsible for the altepetl, that which belongs to him from the taxation: 6,370 pesos and 4.5 reales. It will be kept in the community [treasury]. The caja will have three pieces [keys]. One the governor will keep, one the alcalde, and one the mayordomo. From there will come the pay of those who keep the altepetl, the governor, the alcaldes, the regidores, and others who are sent out [on tasks], who teach the doctrine in the churches, or who are responsible for some kind of tribute work somewhere. Their share of all of them will come out of there; whatever is needed will come out, perhaps ornaments for the church will be bought with it. No one is to ask the people for anything else. Thus was it set down by the lord oidores, the president [of the Audiencia] and the visitador. And thus was it set by his lordship the viceroy. He sentenced through his provisions and decrees. Thus he set his seal upon it, so that each year we will each owe one peso and four reales. Every four months, we will pay tribute. When the sentence was finished, the governor said, "You have heard the tribute that has been decreed for us. Is it so that we did not do anything on your behalf? It was because it was impossible. In all the time in which we were involved in it, the rulers approved nothing [that we asked for]."

At that, Miguel Teicniuh said, "You heard, you Mexica, you Tenochca, what we are to pay in tribute, as established by our ruler His Majesty? Was it invented here? Did any of the ruling lords establish it here? In all the time we were involved—it is now six months—we talked back in vain. Nothing was possible anymore, we weren't heard. Your governor is here. Is it that he doesn't do anything for you? Does he forget you, does he forget the tail, the wings? What happened in the last six months you have heard here. Now go to warn people, you merinos, make them hear your summons. Go house to house, you who gather the medios [money]." As soon as he finished speaking, people got worked up. The governor said in vain, "Let the instruments be played." People cried out, there was a hubbub. Then people went down shouting. And everyone said, "Where will we get it from?" All the old women cried and got really angry. A person named Huixtopolcatl from Amanalco said, "Who speaks? Is it Tlilancalqui? Is it Quauhnochtli? Is it Ezhuahuacatl?[12] What is happening to the wing [the common people whom society depends on]?" The hubbub got bigger. They went on to say, "Maybe the lords, the rulers who ended up as caretakers of the altepetl, could have made a last gamble [on our behalf]? You come out after you have imposed on us what tribute we are to pay! The rulers should have spoken when the altepetl went to acknowledge defeat. Did Cuauhtemoc gamble anything in the last pass? Did he say anything he wasn't supposed to say?" They said many things. And some said, "Villainy! Bring down Teicniuh and Cocolotl. In all this time that we were bringing complaints, here you are having secret words [with the authorities]. Villain, just come down quietly, Cocolotl." There was even more raging and shouting. And they insulted the governor himself for meddling beyond the time he should rule.[13] Pedro Maceuhqui jumped in, separating people and restraining them. He had his staff of office on his shoulder. Suddenly they grabbed it from him and were going to kill him. They ganged together to kill him. They pulled his shirt off. Just naked was how they left him. They got Juan Cano[14] out. He took out his sword so they would let him go. Otherwise he would have died at the people's hands. And while people were crying out, everybody gathered on the rooftops, the Spaniards' roofs. And some ran about to hear what was happening at the palace, and some ran away. The ones doing business, selling all sorts of things at San Hipólito, at the market, they all came. And all the people in the houses came out, the old women and the old men, the children, the people of the altepetl. People threw stones at the upper floor of the building. They destroyed a floral carving that ran around the wall. Then a Spanish officer came and took out his sword and chased people. The Spaniards and some of the mestizos who were seen there all took out their swords and dispersed people. The women broke through the patio wall on the left side, where people were flung, men and women just climbed over each other so that they fell back and screamed and shouted. Many really got hurt, and they hammered one old woman's face.

[f.26v]
The Spanish officers gathered really fast and pursued people and dispersed them. Right away they took people prisoner. The ones whom they collected they took upstairs and put in the hands of the governor, who beat them. When they were beaten their hands were tied. The Spaniards went to close all the roads everywhere. Everywhere people were seized along the roads. They armed themselves with lances, shields and other weapons . ...

***

Friday morning, May 24, 1565, dawned in silence in the indigenous barrio of San Juan Moyotlan in Mexico City. The neighborhood felt almost flattened with anxiety.[15] The women moved about their household compounds to do the necessary chores more quietly than usual, but in the heavy silence, news of what had happened spread in whispers. Their governor of the royal line, don Luis de Santa María Cipac (or "Alligator"), grandson of Ahuitzotl, had suffered a mental collapse. Perhaps it was this day that gave him the nickname he later bore, Nanacacipac, or "Mushroom Alligator."[16] In the falling darkness of the night, he had armed himself with sword and shield and mounted the stairs to his rooftop. And there for hours in his imagination he battled the enemies who had long surrounded him, before finally leaping to the ground. He was carried inside and tended to; he would live for seven more months before going to another world.[17]

Ten days earlier, on May 14th, there had been an omen. In the morning, a rainbow had surrounded the sun. "Everyone saw it, both we and the Spaniards."[18] Later, a whirling wind had lifted the dirt being excavated in the building of the cathedral and carried it to the sky. The Spaniards in the streets said it was Moctezuma leaving, or else that it was the harbinger of calamity. Some indigenous people who saw the dirt being set back down distinctly recognized in the shifting shapes the figure of Ehecatl, or Wind, whose yawning cavernous mouth led down to the underworld.[19]

In 1565, all residents of the City of Mexico lived with tension. A full generation had elapsed since conquest, and the government of the Crown, long dependent on indigenous middlemen, was growing restive—and more ambitious. Spain now had a greater ability to exert its will, and the indigenous thus had less ability to stave off demands, as don Luis knew only too well. He had been pressured to collect vastly greater tribute, arrested for noncompliance, released, and pressured mercilessly once again. Now the Crown's representatives warily watched not only don Luis and his disgruntled people, but also the early settlers and friars with whom the indigenous had established a sort of alliance, or at least a working relationship; they were ready to strike hard at anyone who attempted to curtail the king's growing power.

It was apparently in these months that some among the heirs of the *tlacuiloque* of old—the indigenous painters and scribes—decided they must do what their grandfathers had always done. They must record the history of this time of crisis. By the time the new year of 1566 was born, they were hard at work. They had begun to collect the statements that would together comprise a great work. Most of them were unacquainted with the old writing. They themselves were *teopantlaca*, men trained in roman letters and Christian iconography. But they could use what they knew to take down all the words that were spoken in these years, just as— some of them remembered—great speeches had once been performed.

What they wrote, what they left for their grandchildren, it turns out, provides a needed piece in the puzzle of what happened in the great crisis that burst open in Mexico in 1566. Traditionally, accounts of the political conflagration that occurred have emphasized one of two narrative arcs: either the sudden death of the viceroy, don Luis de Velasco, in July of 1564, left a power vacuum that bred chaos, or the encomenderos and their heirs, fearing the loss of their wealth as their privileges gradually escheated to the Crown, flocked to the banner of the marqués del Valle, son of Hernando Cortés, who contemplated leading them in rebellion. Whatever the cause, the city was torn apart by plots and counterplots, arrests, torture sessions, executions, and the repeated turning of the tables between factions before peace was finally restored in 1568. The story has always been confusing, to say the least.[20]

In all renditions, historians have been careful to elucidate the complexity of the various sides. People falling under the rubric of "the Crown" may have represented the same set of interests on one level, yet they were each other's rivals for political favor on another. Spaniards living in the colonies were likewise at each other's throats. They might be ambitious settlers, or they might be men of the church. If the former, they might be the sons of conquistadors, or of more recent and less well-endowed arrivals. If the latter, they might be seculars, or members of the orders. If they were friars, they might be Franciscans or Dominicans, and their point of view might shift accordingly. In short, it has long been understood that anyone assuming that "Spanish" interests were the same did so at his or her own peril.

When the Indians have come up at all, their cause has been seen as singular: they have been envisioned as supporting the rebellion purportedly planned by the young Cortés.[21] In fact, their participation was integral to the events that occurred, though perhaps not in the most easily apparent of ways. In their case as in all others, no sense can be made of their role in the story without an understanding of the divisions in their community, divisions based largely on old tlaxilacalli identifications and family lineage, as well as their varied relationships to the different Spanish sectors.[22] The trauma of the decade of the 1560s generated a remarkable paper trail, allowing insight into multiple indigenous points of view. Yet many of these texts, though well known, have been studied in isolation, not only from Spanish sources but even from one another. In the pages of the *Codex Osuna* and its accompanying lawsuit, we have momentary access to the strategizing of the highest nobility—don Luis de Santa María Cipac and his cohort—as well as that of other indigenous lineages who sought to oust the traditional ruling families and replace them.[23] The annals of the *Codex Aubin* are the work of a man who lived in the same barrio as don Luis, San Juan Moyotlan, but who apparently did not often rub shoulders with the powerful.[24] Perhaps most valuably of all, in the document that has come to be known as the *Annals of Juan Bautista*, we have the voluminous words of a group of indigenous artisans, church painters, and scribes who had close connections to both pipiltin (noble families) and macehualtin (commoners). These preserved their own thoughts, as well as many statements that others made in their hearing. They crafted a full work of history, a xiuhpohualli, as they understood the term.

The writers of this extraordinary work hailed largely from the barrio of San Juan Moyotlan. In prior centuries, Tenochtitlan had been founded by closely related migrating bands, each with its own leader (exactly as in Cuauhtinchan's history). In the idealized telling, there had been eight Mexica chiefs leading seven clans or *calpolli* divisions; what is certain is that a number of groups settled the island in four quadrants—Moyotlan in the southwest, Cuepopan in the northwest, Atzacualco in the northeast, and Teopan-Zoquiapan in the southeast. (A fifth group of relatives, also of Mexica descent, the Tlatelolca, settled just to the north of the Tenochca.) Each of the four quarters, and within those each of the calpolli subunits, accepted responsibility for certain duties toward the greater polity. Some duties rotated in perfect symmetry; some were simply assigned differently based on power relations between the segments, which shifted over time. Two of the calpolli of the western half of the island, one from Moyotlan and one from Cuepopan, seem to have been the most powerful and produced political chiefs and war chiefs. Indeed, Moyotlan continued to be associated with matters of administration and political authority through the period of Spanish conquest, even as the number of calpolli multiplied as a result of natural increase and the arrival of new migrants embraced by the Tenochca leadership.[25]

After the Spaniards came, the *traza*, or downtown, was laid out over the former inner sanctum of power in a great rectangle at the central meeting point of the four quarters. The now L-shaped indigenous neighborhoods left surrounding the Spanish center were named San Juan Moyotlan, Santa María Cuepopan, San Sebastián Atzacualco, and San Pablo Teopan. The whole indigenous "doughnut" surrounding the "hole" of the traza was known as San Juan de México, just as the northern segment was Santiago de Tlatelolco. After a few years of relatively chaotic colonial rule, the Spaniards moved toward insisting that the indigenous communities establish cabildos modeled on Spain's municipal governing bodies. The people did not incorporate a perfect replica of the Spanish system—they interpreted some of the positions in their own way and were guided by their own understanding of the role of a tlatoani's council—but they did begin to govern themselves in keeping with European expectations. At first, it was not even clear what the role of the traditional nobility would be. In Mexico City, the first gobernador, or head of the cabildo, was not a member of the royal family, nor was the second. But by 1538, a grandson of Axayacatl was in place as gobernador. He was referred to as "tlatoani" as well, and he governed until he died.[26]

In many ways, the work of the inhabitants of the various quarters of Mexico City remained unchanged from past times. The men continued to labor as they had for many years: although the neighborhoods at the edge of the island maintained chinampas and harvested the lake's flora and fauna, most of the urbanites were not farmers, but rather craftsmen, just as they had long been. The specifics, needless to say, evolved. Aging feather workers no longer trained apprentices; potters sold different styles of vessels; goldsmiths learned new methods. In the past, men from noble families, if they were not high officials themselves, had certainly worked at trades, and they continued to do so, alongside urban macehualtin. The old *tlacuiloque* (painters, writers) had worked closely with the priests and chiefs of the *ancien régime*; undoubtedly a high proportion of them had come from noble families. Certainly the nobility were first in line to send their sons to the schools opened by the Franciscans, where they learned such arts as the writing of roman letters and the illumination of manuscripts, but they were not the only ones who attended.

Unsurprisingly, then, the authors of our *Anales*, who reveal themselves to have been artists and scribes at every turn, seem to have been a collection of men who included both macehualtin and pipiltin; they frequently exhibited sympathy for the ruling families—one, Martín Momauhti, was actually a brother of the governor[27]—but also sometimes skepticism and even alienation. There may have been whole groups of them who came from the same family lineage, but we cannot be certain. For instance, one Cristóbal Cuauhtli, who worked as a scribe for the Franciscans, tells us in the first person that it was he who wrote out some of the words of the text,[28] and a Francisco Cuauhtli—who also at one point speaks in the first person—held office as a regidor in the cabildo at the time and was a patron within his community (buying paints needed for church artwork, for example).[29] It seems very possible—even likely—that these two were related, but we cannot be sure, partly because "Cuauhtli" (or Eagle) was a common indigenous name, and partly because indigenous names applied to individuals and were rarely patronymics. (The annals also tell us, for example, that one Martín Cuauhtli, obviously not a relative of Francisco Cuauhtli, joined some colleagues in bringing suit against the cabildo for wrongful monopoly of power.[30])

There was one man whose speeches were recorded more often than the words of any other, barring only the governor. This was Marcos Cipac, sometimes referred to as Marcos Tlacuiloc. The text implicitly reveals that he was the head of the workshop, for the Spaniards issued orders to the artisans through him. When questioned in 1565, he said that he was fifty-two years old.[31] He was therefore born in 1513 and was eleven in 1524 when Pedro de Gante—whose name appears frequently in the text—founded his original little school at San José de los Naturales. He was thus the perfect age to have attended from the beginning.[32] Bernal Díaz, who was still in Mexico City at midcentury, later wrote that there was an extraordinarily talented indigenous artist named "Marcos Aquino" who worked for the friars and would have been the equal of Michelangelo had he been born in another time and place.[33] Since almost all elite indigenous of this generation, like the governor don Luis Santa María Cipac, had both a Spanish surname and an indigenous name by which they were known to their fellows, it is very likely that Marcos Cipac was the same man as Marcos Aquino. In that case,

Marcos Cipac was a figure who had the confidence that came of being well known not only to the indigenous artisans but also to the city's larger Hispanic community, and the man we come to know in the pages of the *Annals of Juan Bautista* fits that description well.

The artist Marcos Aquino—almost certainly related to Tomás de Aquino, a leading cabildo member in that era[34]—had gained renown in 1555 for painting a beautiful and memorable image of the Virgin of Guadalupe at a chapel in Tepeyac, just north of the city. The chapel was on the site of an old shrine at a spring, dedicated to one or more of the old gods, and indigenous people began to come to see the painting in droves, apparently having rapidly come to believe that the image might be able to work miracles.[35] The men of the church had a heated argument about it at the time, even holding hearings on the question as to whether any of them had actually encouraged what some of them insisted was so "prejudicial to [the souls of] the natives."[36] No one had criticized the talented artist himself, however, whom they specifically referred to as "Marcos, *indio pintor*."[37] Marcos had passed his adulthood in an empowering era for indigenous artists in general—who, for example, could ever forget the sublime experience of descending the steps down into the painted water tank they had produced at the Franciscan church at Tlatelolco?[38]—and he was also someone who had held influence as an individual. No wonder he wanted his words at a time of crisis recorded, and no wonder his colleagues were bent on recording them.

Nor were the artists of San Juan Moyotlan the only residents interested in preserving past and present for posterity. Another man in the same barrio worked long hours at a project of his own. The author of the *Codex Aubin*, as the text is now called, seems to have shown what he produced to numerous members of his community, judging by the number of copies that were eventually made, but he does not seem to have moved in the same circle as the writers of the *Anales*.[39] We cannot be absolutely certain of his name, but it was most likely López, for he mentions the birth of a girl child called "Juana López" in 1567 and, tragically, her death in 1584. Not once in their detailed record did the writers of the *Anales* mention any indigenous person called López, so the author of the *Aubin* was presumably not an officeholder. We cannot be certain what he did for a living, but he was probably a plasterer, as he mentions plastering work frequently and almost never refers to other kinds of craftsmanship.

Without doubt, this man was a great talent: he had mastered not only his trade and the roman letters (as many others had), but he also knew something of the old-style glyphs within the genre of the xiuhpohualli. In his manuscript, he created a beautiful traditional timeline, complete with the old calendar and some artwork reminiscent of work his forefathers would have done. He may once have been a student of Sahagún's, for the images look very similar in style to those produced in Sahagún's earliest years of work with his informants. Next to each year sign, he wrote out alphabetically what it might once have elicited from a speaker. Some of the stories of ancient times he recorded in delicious detail: the beleaguered Mexica not only defeated the Xochimilca when the Culhua king arranged to have them ambushed by them, but they also cut off their enemies' ears—on one side only, lest anyone accuse them of double counting. He recounted the story of the conquest in great detail as well but not along the same lines as the students of Sahagún, nor did he use Sahagún's writing system.[40] This was a man who conceived his own project and carried it to fruition in his own way.

He was interested in the *longue durée* of Mexica history, in their capacity to rise and fall and rise again. He began in the deep past and carried on the project as long as he was able. What happened in the 1560s was of importance to him—as one who would have to manage to pay the new tribute—but he apparently did not imagine himself as somewhat allied to those indigenous families considered to be responsible (whereas some of the authors of the *Annals of Juan Bautista* did). He was therefore freer to place the events within the long sweep of time, the ups and downs of unfolding years, and he did so. Thanks to him, we know that in retrospect, certain indigenous envisioned the fates as setting up the pieces in the great game of life in which they were to suffer so dramatically in the mid-1560s.

In the entry for 1560 the author of the *Aubin* mentions that doctor Ceynos (the licenciado Francisco Ceynos), who had functioned as an Audiencia judge in the 1530s but then had returned to Spain, came back to Mexico again. At first, it seems an odd item to mention, surrounded as the notation is by important events. But the arrival of Ceynos is a forerunner, as it were. In 1563, multiple pieces fall into place. In January of that year, the marqués del Valle, son of Hernando Cortés, arrives in Mexico. In August, don Luis de Santa María Cipac of the royal line is installed as indigenous governor. In September, the visitador (or inspector) licenciado Jerónimo de Valderrama arrives to challenge the longtime rule of the viceroy, don Luis de Velasco. All the key players in the drama to come are now in place—except the church authorities. Perhaps unsurprisingly, the author asserts that in the same month of September, a bishop was installed in the indigenous chapel of San Josef. Here, it seems, is an error, a rare thing for this author, for Mexico City had no bishop of its own, and the reigning archbishop (fray Alonso de Montúfar) had been in place for many years. Presumably, however, some ceremony of investiture did occur for someone in that year, or perhaps the archbishop came once to attend Mass. It was apparently necessary that whatever occurred be interpreted as the seating of a powerful figure, for in that way the pattern was completed, and literally all the key players could be understood to have arrived in this critical year. The confluence of events boded ill. An epidemic of measles began.

The events that unfolded afterwards in the City of Mexico are nearly impossible to comprehend when we follow only one set of sources. Too often the tale has been told from the singular perspective of the viceroy or visitador, the marqués or the Audiencia, or even, more recently, the indigenous governor or else commoners.[41] Clearer vision involves multiple perspectives—as the makers of the traditional xiuhpohualli knew, when they had several performers go over the same temporal ground, or when a pictorial history placed events relevant to different altepetls above and below a timeline.[42] A multiplicity of voices does not have to confuse matters; if the threads are separated, each may help to clarify the other. In the style of the annals, then, we must turn to different speakers at different times, though in this case, all the while with a view to deepening our understanding of the perspectives of one particular set of speakers, the artisans of Moyotlan. They reveal their fear that their world was crumbling.

In a story with many possible beginnings, we may open with the arrival of the last key player to arrive on the scene, the visitador, or inspector. A significant facet of the Spanish Crown's policy regarding America was the practice of regularly sending inspectors to report directly to the Crown. In this regard the arrival of Jerónimo de Valderrama was nothing unusual. Yet his visit was particularly charged, for Philip II was strapped for cash (he would later declare bankruptcy) and Valderrama's implicit—and perhaps even explicit—instructions were to find a way to extract more resources from Mexico.[43] The tributes received from different sectors of the indigenous population varied, depending as they did on ad hoc arrangements made during the period of conquest. The indigenous people of the City of Mexico, for example, were not subject to paying tribute. This was in theory because they had not paid tribute in the years of the Mexica empire and it would thus have been difficult to demand it of them in the 1520s; it was also, however, because in the 1520s and 1530s they were in fact coerced into building the Spanish city and providing food, fodder, and service to the households of the Crown officials and the friars. As the conquerors themselves knew, there was only so much they could do. Now, however, a new generation of officials governed, and they did not see why the indigenous people of San Juan de México and Santiago de Tlatelolco should not pay a head tax, as most other indigenous people paid, either to an encomendero or to the Crown. The argument began in the 1550s and became energized in 1560.[44]

The indigenous citizens had their defenders, among them the Franciscans and the viceroy, don Luis de Velasco. These claimed that the people already labored as hard as they could, and that if the Spaniards persisted in attempting to extract more from them, the population of the city would fall as drastically as it had already fallen elsewhere in the empire. The urbanites, they reminded their hearers, did not have agricultural lands and could not simply raise more food or more goods to satisfy the tribute. Most Spaniards, however, fell over themselves in their haste to please the king and construct reasons why imposing the urban tax was the most just course of action. They argued that the indigenous craftsmen made good wages, and that the only reason they were not wealthy was that their own governing nobility fleeced them mercilessly, for they maintained their own ruling class just as they had in the past. It was the indigenous nobility—working hand in glove with the friars—who were the true enemy, and had to be curbed. The quantities taken, Valderrama argued in an early report in 1563, were enormous and were wasted. "All that has been taken from the Indians and has accrued to your Majesty used to be consumed by the [indigenous] governors and noblemen, and the friars. The governors and noblemen drink it up. The friars do, I am sure, use it for good in buying silver and ornaments for their churches and monasteries, but they do wrong to take the property against the will of its owners."[45] Indeed, Valderrama asserted repeatedly, the ordinary indigenous citizens would be only too glad to pay a head tax, if it meant they could be relieved of volunteering for public labor and paying taxes to their own nobility.

There were some in Spain who quarreled with the king's choice of inspector, for Valderrama's family was distinctly beneath that of Velasco, the viceroy. Valderrama, however, had extensive experience as an accountant, which would have been valued by the king in this period of financial need.[46] Valderrama must have felt he had the king's blanket approval, for literally as soon as he touched shore, he set himself up in opposition to the viceroy. Velasco had previously quarreled with the recently arrived marqués del Valle, the arrogant young son of Hernando Cortés; it was no accident that Valderrama chose to lodge at the Cortés mansion rather than in the Audiencia building, where the viceroy lived.[47] He was publicly distancing himself from the viceroy, even positioning himself as an alternate authority.

By January of 1564 the viceroy had lost the battle of the tribute. Though he predicted a crisis in the indigenous community, on the 18th of the month he signed into law an edict requiring from the indigenous people of the city over 14,000 pesos to be paid annually, as well as a substantial payment in corn (to be replaced by an additional cash payment if the people could not obtain the corn). Velasco could not stand alone, and all the oidores, or judges of the Audiencia, had written reports in compliance with the desires of the king. The law was effective immediately, with the first payments to be made in July.[48]

Three days later, the indigenous tecpan (or *casa de comunidad*) was visited by three judges of the Audiencia.[49] Don Luis Cipac and the reigning members of the cabildo were informed of the new law. They protested and appealed in the ensuing weeks, but to no avail. In February 1564, don Luis—threatened with prison—signed an acceptance of a *fait accompli*. In March, to convince the people that it was the governor's profligacy that was ultimately at fault, and thus weaken his leadership, some Spaniards—probably from Valderrama's office—arranged for a lawsuit to be filed against don Luis and his peers by some indigenous tradesmen from San Sebastián Atzacualco. They were led by Juan Daniel (a breadmaker) and Pedro Macías (a tailor). There was undoubtedly real anger in Atzacualco directed at the nobility of Moyotlan; perhaps whichever Spaniard was orchestrating the case would have done better to let the indigenous direct it. He clearly did not, however, for the charges these men brought were of a type that would have reverberated far more with Spaniards than with native peoples. They said that many of the reigning nobility, old chiefs who had been alive in the days of idolatry, still did not know how to read and write and were therefore laughable, that they conducted legal hearings in their homes in the mornings and accepted gifts from both sides, that they celebrated feast days with old-style dancing, even wearing the traditional clothing woven of feathers, that they did not care who was a polygamist or how many taverns there were in the city, that they forced commoners to work in pulque-making and feather-weaving establishments, and in general did not obey royal laws. Only at the very end were charges added that might have been of some interest to an indigenous audience: that they arranged cabildo elections among themselves and robbed the people of their money through their own tribute demands.[50]

As don Luis Cipac prepared for the public crisis coming in July and discussed the cabildo's legal defense with his attorneys, he also orchestrated a grand public ceremony: his marriage on June 4 to doña Magdalena Chichimecacihuatl, daughter of the late don Diego de San Francisco Tehuetzquititzin, grandson of Tizoc, one-time tlatoani and indigenous governor of the City of Mexico (from 1541 to 1554).[51] On the day of the festivities, the people sang traditional songs. Don Luis himself danced, holding a gold-painted drum. If there was a public gesture that could remind the people of who he was and what he stood for, that he saw his interests as indivisible with those of the altepetl, this marriage was it.

Like the chiefs of old, don Luis worked hard to muster support from key figures in the community. A week later, on June 13, he sent respected messengers to speak to the church painters and scribes in their workshop near the Franciscan convent.[52] The speakers were elderly cabildo officers,

Antonio Tlapaltecatl and Pedro Nicolás, and they employed the language that they had heard as youths. "Is it now that we throw it out, that it passes on, the breath, the words of the altepetl, its exhausting efforts, its sacrifices?" If such men as the church painters and scribes were going to be inharmonious, to rebel, all the community would be threatened, and the triumphs their altepetl had known would soon all be forgotten. "Because of your arrogance there will be nothing to be honored, to be renowned. Remember your commitment, your social contract." They also insisted that the high nobility were not uncaring people, as some were apparently saying. "They suffer anxiety in the night. They don't eat their bread with tranquility, for worrying about how they will care for the wings, the tail [the macehualtin]."

On Sunday, July 2, the guardián of the Franciscans said Mass, and then he spoke to the congregation about the upcoming tribute payment. He had been summoned to speak to the visitador the day before. In an attempt to reassure his indigenous listeners that he was on their side, he recounted an argument he had had with the visitador about whether or not the indigenous were hard-working people. But then he had in fact been reassured that the new cash tribute payments really would be less onerous for the populace than the old hodgepodge of duties and responsibilities. After Mass was over, Marcos Tlacuiloc and three other community leaders, including Pedro Nicolás, went to speak to him in private. Later they recorded the conversation for posterity: the ways in which they respectfully disagreed with him, the fraying of their erstwhile ally's temper, the rudeness he exhibited to them, the patience with which they forced themselves to respond. They tried to tell him that he was being naïve, that the administration was concealing some part of their plan, because the amount of money he claimed was to be the limit of what was imposed on them could not possibly cover all that had to be paid for, when one considered the cost of running the indigenous government—unless the amount was to be extracted not annually but every eighty days, or unmarried adolescents were going to have to pay. The friar continued to say that they were mistaken, to snarl that they should believe him. Finally Marcos said gently, "It's really a lot, isn't it, that will all come out of one peso?" Then the father said, "I really don't know. You are the ones who know about that. I'm just asking you to think about things."

Across Mexico such conversations had been unfolding for decades between Spaniards and local leaders, usually containing not direct threats but rather subtle inflection—repressed anger, embedded pleas to see another angle, condescension, or the stifled shame that comes with impotence to change a situation. As always, those with less power were undoubtedly generally more aware than those with more power of the various shades of meaning. Only rarely were the less powerful the ones holding the pen, and even more rarely did they write in such privacy that they could choose to record all that they had experienced.

The skeptical artisans were proven right. The next morning, Monday, seven regidores of the indigenous cabildo were arrested. They were to be held as hostages while the Crown's office demanded participation in public works in addition to payment of a cash tribute. On Friday it was announced that three hundred more people would be arrested and sold as indentured laborers if the community did not cooperate. An alcalde from the cabildo came to ask the friars to let the people know. He said, "I am not responsible for this. Can't you take responsibility to help the macehualtin in some way?" The next Monday morning, armed men went from house to house collecting "volunteers."

On Wednesday, the amount of the cash tribute was reaffirmed and the people were called to a great public meeting for the following day. The painters and scribes learned from their clergy that the friars had been given direct orders by the visitador not to interfere. At two o'clock on July 13, people poured upstairs to the second floor of the tecpan.[53] Don Luis de Santa María Cipac and the cabildo members (who had all apparently been released from prison for the occasion) were seated in the center, and the people surrounded them. Almost all community leaders and master craftsmen were present, but also many ordinary people, including women. Don Luis asked the clerk of the cabildo to read a statement he had prepared about the futile efforts he had made on the people's behalf, as well as a summary of the new tribute.

When the man finished, there was an instant uproar. Women and men cried out in rage. People shouted that the rulers had sold the interests of the altepetl in exchange for benefits for themselves. "Maybe the rulers . . . could have gambled something [on our behalf]? You come out after you have imposed on us what tribute we are to pay! The rulers should have spoken when the altepetl went to acknowledge defeat! Did Cuauhtemoc gamble anything in the last pass? Did he say anything he wasn't supposed to say?"[54] It was pandemonium. The governor and an official trying to protect him were attacked. Spaniards present drew their swords to escape, then brought armed guards back who wielded their weapons ferociously in an attempt to disperse the crowd. There was a crush; the courtyard wall gave way on one side. "Many really got hurt, and they hammered one old woman's face." At least thirty men were arrested. They were tied up and walked to the Audiencia prison, escorted not only by Spaniards but also by the now enraged cabildo members. "It was ringing Ave María," remembered the writer.

The Spaniards held a summary trial in the next few days, and one week later on July 20, thirty-one Tenochca and fifteen Tlatelolca (who had created their own separate disturbance) were made to go in procession.[55] Their heads were shaved and they were each given two hundred lashes. "The town crier went by shouting, saying, 'They are to be sold for terms of two years and five years.'" And this was what was seared into the memory of the writer of the *Codex Aubin* as well in his entry for July 1564: "When they had a court hearing, they sold the Mexica, some to labor for five years and some for two." "When they were made to go in procession," added the writer of the *Anales*, "the one leading was named Toribio Lucas, from Huitznahuatonco in San Pablo, he who was in prison before." Indeed he had been. He was a lesser noble who had quarreled with the governor over the tribute before and been jailed previously for his rebelliousness. Don Luis loathed him, calling him "a seditious, offensive outsider,"[56] but the writer of this section of the *Anales* implicitly offered him respect. The writer carefully listed the names of every arrested Mexica man following this Toribio Lucas Totococ whose names he knew—twenty-eight of them in all.

That Sunday, the writer mentioned, the "Chalca cihuacuicatl" was sung. It was an old song, associated for years with political protest on the part of the conquered. It did not offer direct resistance or a promise of rebellion. Rather, in the voice of a concubine taken prisoner in wartime (an image deeply familiar to everyone), it reminded the victorious ruler that his subordinate was in pain, and that he could use his power to create more pain or he could offer kindness and find some happiness. "It is infuriating. It is heart-rending, here on earth. Sometimes I worry and fret. I consume myself in rage. In my desperation, I suddenly say, 'Hey, child, I would as soon die.'" Yet the king himself will pay the price if he reduces his prisoner of war to helplessness and hopelessness. "What comes of it that it seems he makes me live as a concubine, dependent upon others? Because of me, you will have twice the kingdom to keep, my child. Maybe that's the way your heart wants it...."[57]

Spaniards and mestizos living as Spaniards carried their own memories of the great upheaval. Malinche's son by Hernando Cortés, who had been bound as a page to Philip II when he was still a little boy, had only recently returned to Mexico with his half-brother, the marqués.[58] There don Martín faced great isolation, for in this half-remembered homeland he lived by the patronage of the brother with whom he was sometimes at odds. In the early months of 1564, he was named interim *alguacil mayor* (chief constable) while the incumbent was being investigated by Valderrama.[59] It was therefore he who had to ride post-haste to the indigenous tecpan the day of the riot and address the multitude.[60] The people gave a great shout when they saw him. Was this because he represented the administration they were protesting? Or did our writers' interest in him indicate that they knew who his mother was?[61] Don Martín almost certainly had not spoken Nahuatl since he said farewell to his mother at the age of six. He faced the sea of indigenous faces, and, through the interpreter, told them that it was the will of the king that they return to their homes, that if they did not, they would be sold as slaves. "Everyone must go home. Go home, Mexica." Like his mother before him, he told them what was the bitter truth if they valued life above all else; he left no record of his thoughts.

Don Luis Velasco, the viceroy on whose behalf don Martín spoke, lay dying. His kidneys were apparently failing. From his sickbed, he was losing all ability to combat Valderrama and the oidores whom the visitador had enlisted as his allies. When the forty-six men were beaten in the streets and then sold into service, it was "sorely against his will."[62] He had spent his fourteen-year tenure as viceroy working to solidify relations between all sectors of the colony. Agonizing that the social disintegration he had feared was upon them, he withdrew yet more from life, and on July 28 he died.[63]

Valderrama, meantime, was not pained by the sudden violence of the angry mob, but rather stunned. He had convinced himself that what he had written to the king was true: that the haphazard, largely traditional system was onerous to the common people, and that they would be delighted to have it replaced by an orderly cash economy. He tried to minimize the event, concluding that the riots had been inspired by others, presumably rebellious Spaniards. "One can't believe that this riot by a few Indians could have happened if they hadn't been incited to it, because besides the fact that they are naturally so obedient, the [new] tax has been of great benefit to them. And an animal without reason understands and recognizes the good that is done for him, more than a man, even though he has a bit of reason. I have made a great effort to understand them, and the situation has not become clear."[64]

The Audiencia judges now governed in place of the deceased viceroy. The licenciado Francisco Ceynos, as the senior member, in effect acted as viceroy, supported by his close friend and associate, the visitador, who presently moved into the Audiencia building.[65] The exchange of Velasco for Ceynos was to come as something of a shock to the indigenous community. In Ceynos they were dealing with a man who felt no royal or patriarchal concern for the king's varied "children." He was content to pit them against one another, even to risk further public crises, as he was confident of the Spanish state's present ability to extract through coercion rather than negotiation and compromise. In August a church painter named Juan Ahuach, who worked for the Dominicans, was arrested for demanding an investigation of the governor's actions in accepting the new taxes. Ceynos sentenced him and one other companion to hang. Don Luis Cipac put his personal irritation with Ahuach aside—though he was still shouting that he would take the governor down with him if he died—and together with the entire cabildo and numerous friars pled for their lives; by the end of the day they were successful.[66] Ceynos had his own reasons for allowing the man to live, however: after Ahuach was released, the visitador took from him a painted record of the burdensome service he and his people had performed without pay in latter years, saying that this was more evidence for the king that the indigenous governors were draining the populace and thus shortchanging the king. They had undoubtedly received the men's payments and pocketed the money themselves. This was to be the strategy Ceynos and the visitador would employ in the next few crucial months, arguing always to the people that if it weren't for the expensive tastes of their governor and his ilk, none of these unfortunate events would have occurred.

While don Luis continued to work on practical matters—orchestrating the collection of the required tribute and breaking it down into specific quantities to be collected by specific people from specific neighborhoods—the friars continued to take an active political stand on behalf of their parishioners. They fulminated publicly against the visitador and the Audiencia and selected a group of delegates to go to Spain and address the king on the matter.[67] At the same time, however, as they urged the indigenous not to lose hope until the king was fully informed, they also urged them not to protest and risk prison, and most of all, not to turn on one another. "I beg you, you who are governors, alcaldes, and regidores, for the sake of Our Lord, meet together, meet with the macehualtin and the neighborhood officers. Calm your hearts. Do you not see what is happening? The altepetl is on the point of splitting apart. Don't let yourself disappear. Let love begin within yourself, so that your altepetl does not disappear." And the writer reporting these words commented, "He is a knowledgeable man."

But September only brought more bitter strife. First, the lawsuit against the cabildo that had begun in March was in effect reopened, albeit in the form of another case. The earlier case had foundered. The week before the disastrous public meeting, the attorney for don Luis and the cabildo members had filed an effective response to their detractors, arguing that their adversaries were discontented, intemperate, and litigious men who had personal cause to dislike them and were allowing their passions to sway their judgment. They themselves sounded highly rational and not overly defensive. They pointed out, for example, that although it was true that many cabildo members did not read and write, it was their understanding that this was not uncommon for community leaders even in Spain, and that although it was true that they danced on festival days in traditional featherwork outfits, these were costumes that they had had for more than twenty-five years, since their youth, and they certainly had never forced anyone to work in any feather-working establishments, which were in any case vastly diminished in number.[68]

Apparently the original plaintiffs were themselves not overly committed to their suit. In early September, their attorney appeared before the Audiencia and said that his clients had disappeared into the countryside during the tumultuous days of July and were ignoring his urgent messages to return to the city.[69]

Other craftsmen, among them a number of tailors, were found to head a suit against the altepetl, this time on grounds of greater interest to potential indigenous plaintiffs: that the ruling nobles had committed depredations against the people, demanding that they serve the Spaniards upon request and then pocketing for themselves monies intended to constitute their pay.[70] At some point, the previously arrested Toribio Lucas Totococ of San Pablo was released from his indenture, apparently in exchange for his participation. He joined the suit and produced various documents from the 1550s and early 1560s in which he had earlier demanded payment for services rendered by his people. Don Luis and the altepetl responded with records of their own concerning the services performed and with many witnesses insisting that they had done the best they could with very limited funds—that they had, in short, only been doing what the then-viceroy demanded of them.[71]

Meanwhile, numerous men continued to protest the new head tax and to be jailed for it, among them Marcos Tlacuiloc, who was in prison for weeks before someone paid the required tribute of four reales to secure his release. The Franciscan fathers felt deep sympathy. At the feast of San Miguel, the father asked, "Where is Marcos?" already knowing the answer. The Indians answered, "He is not here."[72] The oidor Ceynos, on the other hand, said scathingly to one group of petitioners that he found it ironic that they were so unwilling to give a few pesos to the king. "When it was still the time of Moctezuma, didn't the people use to give their children to have their breasts cut open for their devil-gods?"[73] On September 18, he decided to go himself to talk to the men who were imprisoned. Perhaps it was Marcos who told of the exchange Ceynos had with a craftsman named Pedro Acaçayol, a fellow prisoner. Through an interpreter, the would-be viceroy told the man he was wasting his time, that there was nothing more he could do to protest, that he might as well bow to the inevitable:

Ceynos said, "There's nothing more for you to wait for. You can't keep the pulque that you've already drunk. Look around! Things are becoming clear. You've been here for three Sundays. Doesn't it hurt you, all that has already happened to you? Are you here to make a point?" Then he said to Pedro Acaçayol, "Listen, you. Four pesos are what you have. In order to accomplish a little something, put down one peso and three tomines, and a basket of your corn. Three tomines can be instead of a basket of corn, because you don't have lands and fields. That is all you will give in one year." At that [Pedro] answered, he said, "It will not be possible, o king. Where will I get it from? I only have saved one medio and ten cacao grains. Please listen, o king. Even though they pay me four pesos [for my craftwork], it doesn't stretch [to cover everything]. It is needed for my children."

"And do you serve only your children?"

"Whom if not them, my children? Our Lord gave them to me....

And if I had the money? Yes, if I had it, I would put it down. But this [conversation] is to what end? Where am I to get it?"

Ceynos said, "Fine. You will be sold to a metalworks."

"Fine, you know what to do, for you are the king."[74]

The tone of Pedro Acaçayol was clearly laced with irony. In theory, a king by definition knew what was best for his people; this was the key criterion of a ruler. Yet this man who understood nothing about the community he ruled and was reckless with people's lives was nevertheless dubbed their king. The writer felt Acaçayol's rage along with him. (Indeed, Acaçayol had been deposited in the metalworks by the time of the writing.[75]) He did not comment explicitly, but in keeping with the tradition of the xiuhpohualli, put his critique in the mouths of key players, in this case, of other powerful Spaniards. The writer of the segment said to another man who had heard the Franciscan Provincial make an angry speech, "Write down exactly how it happened, exactly how it befell, in Xochimilco." And he carefully kept the response he got: "A man should not be chosen if his life is not righteous, even if he is a nobleman. He should not guide the community. He who scoffs at other people should not perform any post. Even if he is the viceroy or the visitador, if he doesn't do his job rightly, if he afflicts people, then he is from Hell. He belongs in Hell. He will go to Hell, and will be forever imprisoned there."[76]

Eventually, in his frustration with the constant stream of petitioners, Ceynos sent a group to see the visitador, as the one who had instigated the change. Valderrama, however, went into a rage. "Am I going to go to Hell because of you?!" He said it was their own governor who had unilaterally chosen to steal the money that had been collected from the community and thus now was not available to help allay the tax. "Whether you will help him with that is your affair."[77] Indeed, Valderrama had just arranged to have don Luis de Santa María Cipac carted off to jail on grounds that he had purportedly stolen 1,200 gold pesos of community money. Don Luis insisted that he had always spent community money on community needs—church, tecpan, salaries of neighborhood officials—but he spent three days in September in prison before being released to oversee the collection of the head tax that was shortly to begin.[78]

Don Luis seems to have begun to suffer emotional disturbances at this point. The day he was released, he saw a woman shouting outside, being pushed by a guard. He leaned out the window and shouted, "Bring her in! Tie her up!"[79] He had her beaten and at least one other woman as well. He was in an impossible position, hemmed in on two sides. There were some to whom he could not answer back; perhaps he punished the ones he could all the more brutally. The writer described the wooden stakes that they tied the women to and the blood that came from their torn flesh.

In the first week of October 1564, officials began to move through each barrio, collecting the tax. For the first time in their lives, the once-proud Mexica were being asked to give not their time to the community—that they always had done—but rather a significant portion of their income, even if it left their children hungry. It was the kind of tribute Moctezuma would have demanded of his most brutally defeated enemies. If the merinos, or community officers, returned with substantially less than the amount they were to have collected, they were to go to prison. A number of them did.

At every point that they could, the Spanish administrators attempted to reinforce the idea that it was the indigenous governor who was to blame for the new taxes. When the neighborhood of Tequixquipan collected 150 pesos relatively rapidly, don Luis was pleased and sent them to give the money to the Visitador. Valderrama, however, responded with anger. He had gone to great lengths to convince the people that their own *principales* were the source of their troubles, not he. "What tribute?! Is the tribute my job?! Did I come here for the tribute? Am I a mayordomo? Give it to your indigenous governor.... Maybe he will [use it to] pay back the money he took." The writer of the segment was not deceived, however. He commented laconically, "It *is* true that he came here [to New Spain] for that reason, came to demand the tribute." When the men of Tequixquipan returned with the 150 pesos, don Luis responded to them with resignation, as he had to. "Fine. Keep it a while longer. Later I will go myself and give it to him."[80]

If, however, Valderrama failed to deceive these indigenous reporters on the events, he was nevertheless effectively exacerbating a deep schism which existed in their community. The governor and his peers were regularly accused of having failed in their responsibilities to protect and care for the people, of having acted selfishly and in response to their personal interests alone. The nobility, on the other hand, argued vociferously that the commoners did not understand how difficult the situation was, how powerless they were, and that the people's obstreperousness was in fact rapidly becoming the worst problem of all, rendering any effective negotiation utterly impossible and escalating the violence. One ardent protester suggested that two men volunteer to sacrifice themselves, one pilli and one macehualli, so that people would perceive it as fair. These two could take a hard line against the government, utterly refusing to bend or buckle in any way. They would probably be executed, but the point would have been made that the Spaniards could not push them beyond a certain line. The governor and his men looked at each other, amazed at this innocence. They laughed harshly. "You propose that two will die? When they have died, then you will die."[81]

The Spaniards were to varying degrees aware of the depth of rage to which people were being pushed, partly owing to the symbolic significance of being rendered a conquered people, and partly owing to the prospect of hunger. There was another element, however, as yet invisible to outsiders—indeed, it is only visible now because of speeches recorded in the *Anales*. This was the extent to which the new burden would perforce be placed on the shoulders of women. The urban families had limited landholdings, as they had said. They could not simply grow more crops to pay the tribute. Nor could artisans drastically increase their earnings simply by working harder. A shoemaker who made more shoes than he could sell had gained nothing, only lost his investment. A church painter could not expect that if he painted faster, the friars would give him more frescoes to work on. Their women, however, had always been spinners, their daughters learning the art from the age of five. And if they worked into the night and produced more yarn and thread, they could always sell their handiwork to the Spaniards. In fact, this was largely what they did in order to come up with the funds. The people expressed their rage, and some took beatings. But then the city's women came up with several thousand pesos within a matter of weeks and handed it over to their men. They kept their husbands from prison and allowed the community's life to continue.

On Saturday, October 14, the cabildo members went to deposit 3,360 pesos in the Caja Real. They started out at the tecpan, where they made an official count. "When the tribute was collected in the tecpan, before those at the table, the ones who were counting it were the regidores Miguel Teicniuh, Andrés Cohuacuech, Pedro Chalchiuhtepehua, Antonio Tlapaltecatl, Tomás Quauhtliyolqui, and Miguel Itzac; also the mayordomos . . . and the notary, Miguel Xuárez. When they counted the tomines at the table before the regidores, a mayordomo wrote it down, putting it in color." The officials looked so exhausted and beleaguered themselves that it was difficult to blame them. Even people who had been arguing that they needed to replace their ruling families with others were chastened at that moment. "People said, 'Even if the lords and rulers from the time of the altepetl were still here, they gambled nothing in the last pass. How can you be confused? Are we not a conquered people?'"[82]

They were still short of the required one-third of 14,000 pesos, but they had gathered a significant enough installment to buy themselves some time. Later in the day, after the cabildo members walked to the heart of Spanish power and deposited the money—an event to which none of the writers was privy—they returned to the tecpan and met with anyone in the community who cared to come. A representative of each of the four quarters spoke. Two of the leaders wept—among Nahuas, a gesture indicating the political significance of the moment:

Tezcacouacatl was on the point of crying, and [the senior alcalde] don Martín [Ezmallin] really cried. He withdrew to a corner and spoke these words: "Here you are, you who are Mexica, you who are Tenochca. Your face, your heart [your honor] were satisfied. You went personally to deposit your tribute. You fulfilled it with the sale of the women's spinning, or with a loan they got somewhere. Are you happy? Are you content, you merino, you who got blamed in some places? Do we have fields? Do we have lands? We just work for a living. You elders, you men of experience, you have hurt the altepetl by confronting it and rising up. Did anyone here order this? It came from Spain."[83]

It had come from Spain. And they feared Spanish power had not exhausted itself yet. To some extent, everyone in the colony felt vulnerable to the winds of change, not just the indigenous. 1565 was a fraught year in the City of Mexico. Even Valderrama's position was no longer secure, for word of the grave troubles with the indigenous had made its way back to the king via the accounts of others (particularly those of the friars). The previously high-handed inspector fairly whined in the defensive reports he now submitted. "I have told the truth in everything that I have written, and your Majesty has been badly served here before I came. They had usurped [legal] jurisdiction and the treasury, and the land was badly governed."[84] Allying with the archbishop, who was a Dominican, Valderrama and Ceynos encouraged the announcement that many of the *doctrinas* administered by the Franciscans would henceforth be taken over by the secular priests. The author of the *Codex Aubin* found the style of the announcement memorable in the notion that the parishes would be "freed."[85] The authors of the *Anales* recounted the anger of the Franciscans, whom they knew well.[86] In the meantime, Valderrama also worked on the project of gradually arranging for the encomiendas that had been distributed in the period of conquest to revert to the Crown. This made the powerful class of encomenderos so angry that they actually began to speak of rebellion, of breaking away from Spain. How serious they were is not at all clear. At the very least, however, a group of young dissidents who moved in the circle of the influential and dashing marqués del Valle enjoyed some heady political talk.[87]

Later it would be said that the indigenous supported the belligerent friars and encomenderos in their secessionist thoughts. Certainly it is true that the writers of the *Anales* spoke with interest of the marqués and of his mestizo half-brother, don Martín. And they exhibited affection for the friars, sometimes tinged with the exasperation that only comes with close connection. In 1565, however, as they hung in limbo, seeking a way to survive as a community, it does not seem likely that they plotted rebellion. They were struggling to make improvements in their lives in practical ways. A careful house-to-house census was taken in the process of finalizing the amount of tribute the altepetl would henceforth owe; the indigenous writers all commented extensively on this. The pace of the lawsuit on the part of certain craftsmen against don Luis and the altepetl stepped up, and the cabildo was asked to produce detailed records of all service that had been done in the past ten years and any monies that had been received for such work.[88] The community set to work producing what would later be known as the *Codex Osuna*, a pictorial and alphabetic record of the extensive unpaid contributions they had made and even of the vicious treatment the workers had received at certain hands. It read as an indictment of don Luis de Velasco, now deceased, and his government. Such a tactic, their attorney would have informed them, was the indigenous cabildo's last best hope.

In May, don Luis Cipac suffered his breakdown and fall. Yet in August he was arrested again, on a claim that he had at one time stolen 170 pesos from the community. This time, he was in prison for weeks. He finally paid the 170 pesos—still insisting that he did not owe them—in order to secure his release, but his attorney had to beg the Audiencia once again before he was freed.[89] On this occasion, no one was outside protesting, and he did not vent his rage on anyone publicly; at least, no one commented on any such affair. He was a broken man. In December, the Audiencia dismissed the charges against him and his cabildo lodged by don Toribio Lucas and others. With the taxation crisis past and the people apparently quiescent, the authorities had no further reason to torment the indigenous rulers or continue to seek to pass the blame to them. Perhaps Valderrama personally would have liked to see the suit succeed, but if so, he no longer had the power he once had.

In that same month, don Luis died. His new young wife followed him to the grave a few months later, presumably as she attempted to give birth to their child.[90] It was unclear if the royal line could ever rise again, and people were shaken. A group of artisans presented to the tecpan a painting of "all those who had ruled Mexico during the time that the kingship has lasted," and it received much praise.⁹¹

In March of 1566, Valderrama departed for Spain. He had been legally bound to a stay of only two years, and it had been almost three, but the death of the viceroy had created unforeseen circumstances. The inspector took with him two Audiencia judges whom he had indicted for crimes and stripped of their office during his period of power. It might have been expected that the departure of these figures would leach some of the bitterness from the ongoing quarrels among the Spaniards, but it did not turn out so. Once Valderrama was gone, and along with him two of those who had opposed Ceynos on the judicial board, the aging Ceynos had more power than ever before. The young marqués was suddenly vulnerable, for Valderrama had been his friend and ally, even living in his home for a lengthy period. A few months later, on a day in July, young Cortés, his two half-brothers, and a number of their friends and associates were arrested for having plotted treason the year before.⁹² "And when they were arrested, muskets were brought to the tecpan, to the central patio of the building, and a Spanish military guard was prepared, everyone armed."⁹³ It seems Ceynos did indeed fear the indigenous. The indigenous were certainly watching the Spaniards.

Two brothers from an aristocratic family who had been at the heart of whatever intrigue there had been were summarily tried and executed in the public square, the grisly spectacle noted by the indigenous commentators.⁹⁴ The marqués was then tried in August before Ceynos himself. There was no hard evidence that he had ever been involved in a real plot, but there was evidence of his interest in such talk. He was found guilty. The harshness and rapidity with which Ceynos dared to act against members of the nobility, and even the marqués del Valle, who had been raised with king Philip as his childhood companion, would be puzzling if it were not for the context in which the events occurred. Mexico City's Spaniards clearly had grown fearful of the possibility of indigenous rebellion in the wake of the rage the populace had evinced two years earlier, in 1564. Throughout the trial, the accusers of the marqués assumed that he had had the support not only of much of the clergy, but also of the indigenous population. From their vantage point, it did not seem impossible to believe that they might have involved themselves. Fear must have fed the otherwise inexplicable strength of their rage.

In reality, the indigenous altepetl, rather than being a hotbed of political activism, was still reeling from recent events. In most households, the new taxes weighed heavily in daily life, and bitterness reigned, as the often overlapping social sectors no longer trusted one another. Different factions of the pipiltin struggled to gain control and salvage the situation as they saw fit. In January of 1566, not long after the death of the governor, Toribio Lucas Totococ and his associates (famed to the community for their participation in the lawsuit against the cabildo) had gone to the Dominicans and claimed that the cabildo elections had been rigged, as always. One of the fathers took them to see Ceynos, who, true to his irrascible style, exploded at them for trying to create more commotion. The next day, the fathers talked the San Pablo and San Sebastián residents out of pursuing their complaint, saying that ordinary people would only say they wanted to gain political power so they could be sure of winning the suit they still hoped to continue and thus enrich themselves.[95]

The mutual hatred continued. In May, the angry cabildo members received a complaint that the fiscal of the church of Santo Domingo, Miguel Chimalaca, had beaten a parishioner unmercifully. Before the Provisor (the judge of the ecclesiastical court), they accused him of wreaking havoc in the spiritual lives of the people, and he was imprisoned for a period. When one of the Dominican friars tried to defend him, the indigenous lords spoke more sharply than they were wont to do before Spaniards. One of the indigenous present who seemed to know the friar well sympathized with him. "He said nothing. He just suffered their angry words in silence."[96] One might wonder why a group of pipiltin who had themselves been known to order commoners whipped should be so enraged with the culprit; however, the lawsuit records tell us that the previous year, this same Miguel Chimalaca had acted as a primary witness on behalf of Toribio Lucas Totococ and his colleagues, claiming that the cabildo members had long had a habit of pocketing some of the money raised for communal projects.[97]

In October, the new viceroy, the marqués de Falces, finally arrived. He laughed away the fears of Ceynos and his cohort. Whether or not a few young hotheads had temporarily lost their good judgment, the people of the land were hardly in a position to rise against the king. He tabled the Audiencia's verdicts and sent the marqués de Valle back to Spain for King Philip to judge. (One of Cortés's half-brothers went with him, but Malinche's son, don Martín, was allowed to stay in Mexico.) The indigenous writers commented on the departure of the Cortés brothers, but mostly they were interested in the festive atmosphere that now prevailed; the end of the recent chaos seemed to render the usual ceremonies honoring the arrival of a new viceroy especially joyous.[98]

Amidst the festivities, under the benign influence of the new viceroy, plans were made to install a new indigenous governor, don Pedro Dionisio of San Pablo, himself a scion of the royal line and an experienced cabildo member. Suddenly, however, don Pedro was brought before the Spanish court, accused of having slept with his stepmother and a younger sister. He was declared unfit to rule.[99] It would be easy to assume that the rival faction of the nobility had at last destroyed the old peerage, but a close look reveals the matter to have been far from simple. One of the writers of the *Anales* records the names of the five men who went to lodge the complaint with the Spaniards. There was one representative from each quarter of the city (with two from Santa María). All but one were men who had served closely alongside don Luis Cipac during the recent crisis and who had themselves ushered don Pedro onto the cabildo. The only exception was the representative from don Pedro's home barrio of San Pablo; in that case it was a new, hitherto unknown man who went, not someone who had been a close associate for years.[100]

Don Pedro was, in short, suddenly betrayed by those whom he might have expected to support him, not by his political enemies. Of course, it is possible that the turn of events was due to his own behavior. Certainly the *Anales* contain numerous stories of men brought up on charges of polygamy. A stepmother left on don Pedro's hands at his father's death might have been a very young woman; another young woman in his household might have been his "younger sister" only in a figurative sense. But if don Pedro were promiscuous, such promiscuity is unlikely to have begun very suddenly at the end of 1566. No, there had to have been a political explanation for what transpired. We probably will never know what it was, but it may well be significant that the case against the cabildo was allowed to drop during the course of the next year and a half.

The rival factions may have made an arrangement: they would let the old peerage disband and give up its stranglehold on power in return for ceasing to be persecuted in court. The altepetl might yet find peace, despite what had happened.

The chaos was not quite ended, though. In the last part of 1567 and the beginning of 1568 it gave one last shudder. Back in Spain, Valderrama had prevailed upon the king to send two more inspectors to investigate Falces, who might, he said, be attempting to cover up the purported rebellion for reasons of his own. These two wielded their legal powers lethally. Several more Spaniards were hanged. Malinche's son was arrested once again. In January of 1568, he was tortured in the cellar of the Audiencia prison, his head submerged under water long enough to bring him to the very edge of drowning, over and over. In all that long affair of the purported conspiracy, he was the only one who said nothing under torture. He denied involvement with any kind of plot. "I have told the truth, and in the holy name of God who suffered for me I will say nothing more from this moment until I die."[101] They did not kill him, but they did condemn him to perpetual exile. They sent him back to Spain, with his sentence commuted to years of working in the galleys of North Africa. Word of these events spread in the indigenous community. They reported them with varying degrees of clarity. The author of the *Codex Aubin* said that the Spanish fleet "took the prisoners who were going to die—they will just take ships from the sea."[102] In the meantime, other notable events were occurring in the indigenous community in these same early months of 1568. New families—families who had opposed the old cabildo in the lawsuit—took over posts on the council. Men in the cohort of Toribio Lucas Totococ and Juan Ahuach took their places and began to govern.[103]

By the end of 1568, peace had been restored on most fronts. The indigenous reported that a new viceroy arrived to take the place of the toppled Falces, and fittingly, a month later, that the dreaded Ceynos had died.[104] On the indigenous council, an outsider came to serve as governor. It was arranged that some of the old families would likewise take their places alongside the new ones in 1569. And so it came to pass. The altepetl had survived the great crisis, it seemed. The painters and scribes went on with their work for the church, reporting on it in loving detail. Yet the aging Pedro Nicolás, now the fiscal of the indigenous chapel, warned the younger men not to forget their past, saying they no longer understood many things that they needed to understand. His words were memorable: "You no longer understand how to carry the altepetl, care for the spirit of the altepetl, the governance." [105] And one of the scribes began to paste together, to copy out, the many testimonies about the speeches of 1564 that had been collected. He would try to see that posterity did not forget, or at least did not forget why his generation had had to let go of so much, including so much of the past.

***

Several of the men whose words or deeds are recounted in the pages of the *Anales* were in their mid-fifties in 1564.[106] This is logical: they were of an age to have the respect of the community and to take their own role very seriously, and at the same time not too old to participate energetically. As a cohort born circa 1510, they bridged two worlds in their very being. They remembered a time when the Spaniards had never been heard of, and yet also had been educated by Spaniards during their adolescence. Most of their parents spoke only Nahuatl; as church artisans, they themselves spent many of their days with Spanish friars. Such figures are in a position to tell us a great deal—if we are willing to strain to hear.

When these men were young, they would have been present at old-style historical performances. Very possibly, such performances continued even during their young adult lives. They knew, then, that such presentations involved representatives of several sub-entities of a given polity stepping forward to speak. They would cover the same temporal ground more than once to offer multiple perspectives and create a more widely acceptable whole. Ideally, there would be two or four treatments of crucial periods, for the tendency toward reciprocity and symmetry ran deep in their world.[107]

Hernando Cortés, the first European to write of what has since been termed the cellular nature of Nahua culture, made something of a joke of it all. In November of 1519, he was met on the causeway leading to Tenochtitlan by a collection of chiefs. "Each one performed a ceremony which they practice among themselves; each placed his hand on the ground and kissed it." He meant that the leader of each segment of the polity needed to complete the act separately and in the proper order. "And so I stood there waiting for nearly an hour until everyone had performed his ceremony."[108] The impatience of Cortés notwithstanding, however, this was no joke. Later he would learn to his cost what it meant if only some leaders participated, but not all. It indicated that a community was breaking apart to follow opposing strategies, and he was naïve if he continued to treat with the people as a single kingdom.

The *Anales* written in the 1560s have sometimes seemed disorderly even to the most astute observers. But they are not: close investigation reveals that they, too, place the contributions of varying subunits of the polity side by side. The version that survives today was copied out in a single hand in about 1580, probably by a man named Martín de la Cruz of the barrio of Necaltitlan, in San Juan Moyotlan, in a sheaf of bound paper that a prior owner had intended to put to another use.[109] It was based, however, on words written by other men in the 1560s. At first, one might assume that Martín (or some such figure in the later period) had access to a collection of separate papers containing the disparate testimonies collected years before, and himself became the first person to copy them into a single document, a kind of notebook consisting of bound folios. That might explain the fact that the entries seem to jump about in time. In fact, however, there had to be someone acting in the 1560s who ordered them to a large extent—very possibly the Cristóbal Cuauhtli mentioned before—because when examined closely, the entries actually follow a highly orchestrated order that no one decades later would have been able to reconstruct from loose pieces of paper. Nor is it at all likely that someone working decades later would have begun with the political crisis of 1566, and only when the situation became calmer in 1569, moved backward to cover 1564 in detail, unless he was copying a single document that already proceeded thus. But someone working during the 1560s might well have done exactly that; indeed, he would even have been likely to do so.[110]

The writing begins in 1566. In fact, in a style that appears odd at first, the copyist begins in 1566 twice. That is, he puts down one set of testimony beginning with the crises occurring in 1566 and the rampant arrests, even the threatened arrest of indigenous people, and mentioning the arrival of Falces, the viceroy who calms the situation. Then he moves back in time to the beginning of 1566 and recounts the story of the year once again in a careful month-by-month manner. At this point, one might well assume the writer is merely disorganized. But he is not, for he repeats the pattern for every year he covers. He backs up and restarts the story of 1567—during which the Hydra-like, unending struggles between the Spaniards and the indigenous factions as to who would rule the cabildo raise a head once again—not one time but three times, for a total of four testimonies. By 1568, the city is calmer again, and that year's story restarts twice, as does that of 1569. The writer ends this part with the dire words of Pedro Nicolás concerning the people's loss of ancient knowledge, and then launches what is undoubtedly the heart of the production: the detailed testimonies concerning the year 1564 and continuing into 1565.

The story proceeds month by month in great detail without starting over at all, until the horrendous period of the collection itself, in late September and early October. Then, suddenly, the writer proceeds to do as he has done before. He repeatedly backs up in time to cover that highly charged ground again. This time, the tellings are so detailed that we can glean something of the vantage points of the different speakers. They do not come from the four quarters of Mexico City but rather from at least four different barrios of San Juan Moyotlan—Tequixquipan, Atizapan, Tecpancaltitlan, and Huehuecalco are named—moving from the heart of the old Mexica center of power, near what is now the Zócalo, and passing gradually westward.[111] Differences of opinion show in the different sectional contributions; sometimes even probable authorship shows. The compiler may well have written the longest and richest segment himself, or he may have taken all four from others. Whether he simply took down the verbal statements of others, or was handed written testimony by other authors, is unknown. Judging from the varied tone, it seems likely that both procedures occurred.

The author of the *Codex Aubin* seems to have behaved similarly in his history when he approached the important—and in his time still much debated—period of conquest between 1519 and 1521. As 1519 opens, he tells the reader that in this year Moctezuma died and Hernando Cortés arrived. An account of the *ahuiani*, or pleasure women, being of interest to the Spaniards is begun, with Moctezuma making a speech that then breaks off and is never finished. Then the text says again, as if for the first time, that the Castilians arrived in that year, on a certain day in November. The narrative passes through various events, focusing on the Toxcatl massacre (the famous incident in which a jumpy Pedro de Alvarado ordered warrior dancers in the temple to be killed). Then suddenly, it veers into a story completely different in tone, recounting a vicious rivalry between Cuauhtemoc (Moctezuma's eventual successor) and a fellow lord. These details in themselves would indicate that the compiler was layering multiple accounts on top of one another, but there is yet more. By the end of this choppy entry for 1519, the author has summarized the entire story of the conquest through to the final submission in 1521 (though he does not explicitly say that he has moved forward into other years). Then in his actual entries for 1520 and 1521, he backtracks in time, describing the brief 1520 reign of Cuitlahuac (Moctezuma's immediate successor), then moving on to events that occurred in 1521. Thus we can be certain that for this important period, the author definitely included at least two sources, and that he probably had recourse to four, given the three distinct trajectories found under the heading "1519."

Those who remembered the old ways understood that in recounting the history of troubled and contentious times, it was particularly important to have speakers representing different subgroups be given the floor, one after another. Don Alonso Castañeda's courtroom drama indicates that they had not forgotten this at midcentury; so also do the community meetings to which we are privy in the *Anales* themselves. When the church scribes and artisans wrote their history of the horrifying years in the mid-1560s, they seem to have abided by the old ways, introducing new perspectives on the same events one right after the other, without explicit comment. In doing this, they were allowing for divergence of opinion. Without such tolerance, there was no hope of the community holding together. They knew this from their own past. For them, truth was necessarily multivocal. From their own experience, they understood the political importance of multiplicity of perspective. In an oft-used metaphor of theirs, they swirled strands together into a cord that was much sturdier than any single strand otherwise could ever have been.

It was more than the format of the historical performances, however, that allowed for thought-provoking multiplicity of perspective. It was also the content that did this work. At moments of upheaval, annals centered on pithy dialogue that opened up worlds within worlds like the most memorable lines of great plays. This was as true in the *Anales* of the 1560s as it had been in the *Historia Tolteca Chichimeca*. In the latter, Icxicoatl demands, "Why are the Tolteca being destroyed? Was I the one who started it? Was I the one who sent for the women over whom we're fighting and making war?!" Listeners were asked to think about who was responsible for warfare and when it was right to launch such violence and how alliances should work. Over and over at moments of crisis, great men and women in the *Historia Tolteca Chichimeca* ask pointed questions, revealing that there had been grave differences of opinion in the period in question, and asking listeners to consider multiple possibilities. The *Annals of Juan Bautista* are no different. The action is propelled forward almost entirely through pointed speeches. "Are we not a conquered people?" ask the observers in the tecpan in the crisis of October 1564. Here was the heart of the matter: one's answer to that question determined one's political stance.

The expected performative response to such rhetorical questions was "No!" If the speaker had been trying to rile the people up to protest rather than trying to convince them to accept their destiny, he would have said, "Are we a conquered people?!" In either case, however, in positing a question, he allows for dissent. For indeed, many in the city at that moment felt that they were not truly a conquered people, not in a full sense—that they could not be made to pay the tax. They were becoming outnumbered, however, by those who saw the matter as did the alcalde don Martín Ezmallin. By the time he gave his grief-stricken, angry speech, almost everyone knew someone who had been put in irons, or beaten, or even sold into servitude. By asking his bitter questions ("Did anyone here order this?!"), he was perhaps more convincing than if he had shouted his own thoughts aloud—that he rued the day, that he had no choice.

In interacting with the text, the reader, like an audience member of old, perforce responds to the questioner, meeting him halfway, thinking of the alternatives, acknowledging complexity. If the indigenous people were ever truly thought of by outsiders as simple, then that is proof only of the outsiders' own simplicity, their own naiveté regarding the indigenous. That was as true for the inspector Valderrama as it is for people of more recent times. The ability to acknowledge complexity, to understand the decentered nature of truth, was perhaps the Nahuas' greatest gift. Marcos Cipac and his colleagues desperately desired that posterity remember both their intricate realities and their multifaceted responses. They had not lived through easy times; they had done their very best.

Fig 3.1 Fresco by indigenous artisan Juan Gerson in the church of Tecamachalco. Noah's Ark, with Middle Eastern doves and Mesoamerican herons soaring overhead.

3

Forging Friendship with Franciscans (1560s–1580s)

The *Annals of Tecamachalco*[1] span many years. Here follow some selections spaced over more than a century:

[middle of f. 2v.]

1442[2]

One House year. In this [year] Cuetzpaltzin died, when the altepetl found itself surrounded by war, when those who surrounded us defeated us. The people of Tepeyacac[3] hired everyone [to fight with them]—the Cholulteca, the Tlaxcalteca, the Huexotzinca, all who surrounded the altepetl. A great many things happened. Cuetzpaltzin had been king for twenty-two years.

Two Rabbit year.

Three Reed year.

Four Flint Knife year. In this [year] Quetzalecatzin returned to Tlacotepec from [the lands] where he had been struggling. He entered the [royal] household of Olin.[4]

[f. 3]

Five House year.

Six Rabbit year.

Seven Reed year.

Eight Flint Knife year.

Nine house year. ~~In this [year] Quetzalecatzin came to Wind Temple when he was coming back from Coaixtlahuacan~~

Ten Rabbit year.

Eleven Reed year. In this [year] the tlatoani Quetzalecatzin battled the Wind at Wind Temple.[5] In this same year he went up to the top of Tecamachalco and the royal household [and lands] were taken.

Twelve Flint Knife year.

Thirteen House year.

In the year One Rabbit the people were "one rabbited."[6] For three years the crops did not yield. The famine that occurred was terrifying. Here in this [year] Quetzalecatzin gave lands to our forefathers.

In the year Two Reed the people of Tepeyacac were blocked again, until the war abated in which the Mexica defeated them, so that it fell upon them that they had to serve people in Mexico, and give tribute in corn, beans, chili, pumpkin seeds, dyes, charcoal, etc. It was at this point that [the people of Tepeyacac] asked for the lands that they have today.[7]

Three Flint Knife year. In the third year, the crops yielded.

Four House year.

Five Rabbit year.

Six Reed year.

Seven Flint Knife year.

Eight House year.

Nine Rabbit year.

Ten Reed year.

Eleven Flint Knife year.

[f. 3v.]
Twelve House year.

Thirteen Rabbit year. In this [year] the people of Tepeyacac were defeated. Their tlatoani was Chiyauhcoatl. The one who came to defeat him was Axayacatzin, tlatoani of Tenochtitlan. He came to defeat him.[8]

In the year One Reed a common border was established that the people of Tepeyacac had asked for on the lands on which they served Tenochtitlan. It was done before four Mexica calpixque—Ecamecatl, Coacuech, Tlilayatl, and Cuauhtilma.

***

[middle of f. 4v.]
Eleven Flint Knife year.

Twelve House year.

Thirteen rabbit year.

One Reed year. In this [year] the Spaniards came here to New Spain, onto the lands of the Indians, in the aureu 19,[9] in the year 1519.

Two Flint Knife, 1520. Here [in this year] Tlehuexollotzin became tlatoani, but he did not last long. In this very year he died. At that point, don Felipe Juárez Motlatlalohuatzin became tlatoani, [sworn in] before the marqués [Hernando Cortés]. At this point began the time of no longer seeing the chieftainship clearly. Quetzalecatzin and other pipiltin were off in Mexico [for the war]. At that time what everyone called the teoçahuatl [the great pox, the divine scourge] was terrorizing people. Large pox formed, completely disfiguring people's faces. Because of it there was a great mortality. It would begin with blood, what is called the tlayelli (dysentery). It had never occurred in former times. Then began all the sicknesses that have been breaking out.

Three House, 1521. In this year Cuetzpaltzin was established as tlacochteuctli.[10] This year is the aureu number 2.

Four Rabbit, 1522. It is three, aureu number 3.

Five Reed, 1523. It is four, aureu number 4.

Six Flint Knife, 1524. It is aureu number 5. At this point, Tepalayo was established as tlacochteuctli [lord] in Tecamachalco.

[f. 5]
Seven House, 1525. Six, aureu number 6.

Eight Rabbit, 1526. Seven, aureu number 7.

Nine Reed, 1527. Eight, aureu number. In this [year] arrived don fray Julián, bishop of Tlaxcala.

Ten Flint Knife, 1528. Nine, aureu number. In this [year] arrived don fray Juan Zumárraga, archbishop of Mexico. He was a Franciscan father.

Eleven House, 1529. Ten, aureu number. At this point, Moquihuixtzin was established as tlacochteuctli.

Twelve Rabbit, 1530. Eleven, aureu number. In this year died Ytzcuinquani of Tetzcoco. The [Franciscan] fathers with fray Juan de Rivas set themselves up in Tepeyacac.

Thirteen Reed, 1531. Twelve, aureu number. In this year a comet appeared. At this time they hanged the rulers of Cuauhtinchan—the late Huilacapitzin, Tlacochcalcatl, and Tochayotl. They sang songs of the old gods. Then [they hanged] some women, because of the bathing of the enslaved [sacrifice victims]. They killed children, etc. They were hanged at the orders of fray Alonso Suárez, the guardián [of the Franciscans] of Tepeyacac.

***

It is 1557, and the region is in the midst of a major *congregación,* or reorganization of settlements:

[f. 11, towards the top]
When the viceroy established the laws and ordinances of the altepetl, he proposed various laws making Tecamachalco and Quecholac one single altepetl. And on the eleventh of the month of October, there met Baltasar Valiente, don Pedro León, and other noble councilmen in order to bring complaints against the governor, Juan de los Angeles. They then produced three written documents, one [to be] read by the provincial, Bustamente, one by the lord tlatoani the viceroy, and one by Francisco Jiménez, who was then in Xochimilco. And on the 14th of October, died the bishop, don fray Martín de Hojacastro. He had gone to Tlaxcala and came [home] to die in Cuetlaxcoapan [Puebla] and was buried on Friday in the early morning. A comet appeared. Afterwards there arrived a letter from the provincial. They came to give it to the guardián, fray Francisco de Toral. There it was written how they were bringing complaints against the governor, Juan de los Angeles. Then there also came a letter from the tlatoani viceroy, [asking] that he be given [the names] of those who were nobility so that he would know all about the matter and justice might be done. After that, father Toral brought together all the noblemen so that they might confess who [were those who] had complained. The names of Baltasar Valiente and don Pedro de León and various other nobles came out. There were also some others whose signatures had falsely been put down on the document. It was not truly done of their own volition. And

then it came out who was indeed the writer, Juan Bautista de Santa María. Father Toral got really angry about it. He took back from Juan Bautista the license that the viceroy had given him to carry a sword. Then he threw him out; no longer would he work in the church, he would just stay outside. In this judgment father Toral simply pardoned those who came out looking good. As for whoever in their names had complained of the governor, he said that the lord ruler the viceroy was going to exercise severe justice upon them. Before [all] this, the child Lucas was born to Mateo Sánchez. Catarina's first child was baptized in the arms of don Baltasar del Castillo[11] on the 18th of the month of October. And for the first time the fathers fray Francisco and fray Diego de Lemos etc appeared in Quecholac. Nineteen, aureu number, C. Dominica.

One Rabbit, 1558. In the year one thousand five hundred and fifty-eight, fray Alonso de Molina became guardián. The same Juan de los Angeles became governor. Mateo Sánchez, Baltasar del Castillo and Juan Josef became alcaldes. At this time the Ihuipanecatl[12] went to Cuauhtla to build a church. The canal in Toluca was also made.

[f. 12]
On the fifth of the month of January, the [Franciscan] chapter met in Huexotzinco. At that time fray Francisco de Toral became the provincial. At this point, on the 24th of the month of January, there arrived our [new] guardián, fray Alonso de Molina. At this point, when the said chapter met, they went to leave the comisario at Pinahuizapan, whence he left for Spain. When he left it was the 29th of the same month of January. The cabildo members went to meet the comisario in Altecallehcan, and then they accompanied them to Pinahuizapan on the Saturday. The comisario general, the provincial Toral, and our guardián, fray Alonso de Molina, dined there in Atlacozauhyan. Then [the comisario] sent the cabildo members back and they returned. When the provincial Toral got back from taking the people to the coast, he came by here to make his farewells. He brought together the different peoples [at his departure] because he would never see us again. We will not again see the like of how he educated and raised us. This was on the 19th of the month of February.

***

[It is 1575.]

[f. 26. towards the bottom]

¶Here [in this year] Martín Cortés[13] was taken to Tepeyacac when he was accused of idolatry by don Juan de Saavedra, the alcalde mayor, on the 18th of June. ¶Here don Martín[14] died. He fell from a height over in Quecholac. Father Francisco Goyti buried him, and he preached here on the 29th of June.

(The following was supposed to come in two paragraphs above, how—) There had come a man, a certain friar named fray Juan de Parada. He was just going to preach and hear confession until our guardián, who had gone to Yucatán, came back. And then fray Juan beat the governor, Mateo Sánchez. It was not good how he berated him. Thereupon the church authorities removed him. It happened on the 8th of June. He was here just forty-one days; he had come on the feast day of the Invention of the Holy Cross.[15] + At this time Diego Romano Mendoza sold his house. They gave him 300 pesos [for it]. Then he lent 100 pesos to Martín Cortés, his old companion, to help him [in his case] before the señor alcalde mayor, don Juan [de Saavedra]. On the 7th of July, fray Domingo de Arreyzaga left here. He was going to become the comisario in Guatemala. On the 27th of August, a Saturday, the repartidor came, bringing a decree. He informed the cabildo members that 160 men should be collected for rotary labor in San Pablo. (The one who came on the 27th of August was Hernando Quezada.)

On the first day of the month of September, a Friday, they went to meet the comisario, fray Rodrigo de Seguera. Likewise here in this year, there arrived thirty-three religious with the comisario general, fray Rodrigo de Seguera. He was the replacement for fray Miguel Navarro, the former comisario. He got here on the fourth day of September, Itzcuintonalli [day of the dog], the same as the third day of [the old month called] Ochpaniztli [with its festival of sweeping and renewal]. It happened in Two Reed, when it was the aureu number 18, and the Dominica B. And in the year count of our lord Jesus Christ, in the year one thousand five hundred and seventy-five. It was likewise in this year that the moon and the sun crossed paths. Just a half portion [of the sun] showed at seven o'clock on the second day of November. On the sixth day of September, our guardián, fray Clemente de la Cruz,[finally] came back. He had gone to Yucatán. It was already dark when he arrived.

***

[1576]

[f. 28, towards the bottom]

On the first day of August began the great sickness here in Techamachalco. It was really strong; there was no resisting. At the end of August began the processions because of the sickness. They finished on the ninth day. Because of it, many people died, young men and women, those who were old men and women, or children. It first began among the Xineteca macehualtin, subjects of don Baltasar del Castillo, the governor. When the month of October began, thirty people had been buried. In just two or three days they would die. Blood came from the nose, the ears, the eyes, the anus. Among the women, blood came from the crotch, among us men it came from our penis. Some died of diarrhea. They lost their senses.[16] They thought of just anything and would die. The 11th of the month of October, the Spaniard Juan Rodríguez died, the spouse of Isabel de Vega. The ninth of November, the fiscal Tomás died, losing his senses, nephew of Mateo Sánchez. The 13th of November, on a Tuesday, the spouse of the late Juan Osorio died. Her name was doña Lucía Osorio. The 15th of November, the altepetl bought an estancia which used to belong to Juan de Ocon, together with all the goats. It is in Huitziltepec. At this point Diego Ramírez died, on Wednesday, the 20th day of November, aureo number 19, A. G. Dominica.

Seven House, 1577. In this year of one thousand five hundred and seventy seven, fray Hernando de Oviedo became guardián. Don Tomás Gerson was going to become governor, but he couldn't. The Spaniards spoiled it. Then began a period when there was no governor anymore. Just the alcaldes were elected—don Francisco de Mendoza, Mateo López, and Juan Jiménez. It was done on the third day of the month of January. On this day of January 26, died doña Marta, spouse of Mateo Sánchez, daughter of the late don Martín of Tecalco. The first day of February, don Mateo Sánchez's sister-in-law died. The eleventh of February, Mateo Sánchez and Pedro Osorio were elected [special] alcaldes to take charge of the orphans so that their goods and properties would not be lost. At this same time died Juan Jiménez, pilli, who was an alcalde. Mateo Sánchez became his replacement. At first the alcalde mayor gave him only the position of official for the property of the dead; afterwards came the document making him a [regular] alcalde. He had been given the position by the alcalde mayor. [A total of] three people had now been made alcaldes, including don Francisco de Mendoza and Mateo López [who were still alive].

She died. Marta, doña Marta, had been little more than a girl when she entered don Mateo's home as his new bride thirteen years before. He had been a widower then, and he was besotted with her, recording the day he married her and brought her from Tecalco to his beloved Tecamachalco in nearly ecstatic tones.[17] Now, on the 26th of January, 1577, she stopped breathing, released from her torment of the preceding days.[18] Blood had come from every orifice and she had lost coherency. For her, the friars would have said, it was better this way, for she had gone to her maker who loved her. It was most likely Marta's sister who helped dispose of the body and tend to the other sick people in the house. She caught the contagion and one week later, she, too, was dead.

Don Mateo staggered forward, day by day. The epidemic had started the preceding August, with at least one person dying every other day, and then the numbers had grown. He had lost many who were dear to him, including his nephew, a credit to his family, the fiscal of the church. Now Marta was gone, and her sister as well. The town had held elections for the cabildo in early January, as they always did, but with special urgency this time. On February 11, the newly elected alcalde for Mateo's barrio himself died of the dread disease. Don Mateo, who had survived the onslaught of the sickness, was quickly chosen to replace him, and his community gave him the additional task of sorting out and protecting the property of all those who had been left orphans. He apparently wanted to be busy, for he took the task seriously. By early August, he was on his way to Mexico to plead with the viceroy that their tribute had to be lowered because their households had been decimated.

The deaths had abated, but a pall settled over the community. In September, the viceroy did send a representative to recount the populace, but unfortunately one of his first acts was to arrest a number of the nobility for noncompliance and hold them for a week while their records were investigated.[19] In November a comet with a long tail was visible in the night sky, a cosmic sign of the people's suffering. "A great comet started where the sun goes down [in the west]; we see it clearly on the road to Zoyapetlayocan. Its tail is long. As soon as it grows dark, it appears."[20] In his younger days, don Mateo would have been able to talk to the man he called Toraltzin, fray Francisco Toral. Even after Toral had left Tecamachalco, he had visited and sent letters.[21] He was a good friend, capable of listening and understanding, and he had the ear of powerful men. But if Mateo wanted to write to him now, he could not. For Toral, too, was dead. The aging don Mateo faced the future on his own. Steadily, he continued to record the events brought by time in the book he had kept for many years.

***

Don Mateo Sánchez did not remember the days before the Spaniards came. He had been born around 1530 to a pilli (noble) family seated near the village of Tecamachalco.[22] His father—or whoever headed his lineage—probably converted to Christianity around the same time, for the hangings of the Cuauhtinchan nobles in 1531 made a deep impression on him, judging from the stories he passed down, and someone in the family maintained a close connection with the friars who had a presence in Tepeaca.[23] Perhaps it was Mateo himself who spent some time with them there when he was a child, or perhaps it was some other relative. What Mateo actually wrote about in later years were his memories of the 1541 arrival of the friars in his own altepetl of Tecamachalco on the feast day of Santa Clara (the 12th of August, he added). "Our beloved father fray Diego de Estremera, who was the guardián in Tepeaca, came to leave them here."[24] They began to baptize all the people in large batches, and by the next year, 1542, they were even baptizing the resident Popoloca, a population usually marginalized by the more recently arrived and politically dominant Nahuas. In 1543, fray Andrés de Olmos arrived as their guardián, and with him came a young assistant, an enthusiastic, warm-hearted and intelligent friar just arrived from Spain.

This was fray Francisco de Toral, who had taken the habit in Jaen and had arrived in Mexico in 1542, in his late twenties.[25] Boys of the indigenous nobility who were of the right age and temperament immediately began to study with him and over time grew deeply attached. It is evident from the knowledge they later displayed that Toral's young scholars studied not only Christian precepts, but also reading, writing, arithmetic, and art. On his side, Toral learned to have unbounded confidence in their abilities, which he esteemed above those of many of his Spanish colleagues. (In later years, in his disparagement of his Franciscan colleagues' activities in Yucatán, he would actually write to the king that if any Mayans had learned the doctrine, "it was due to the other Indians who have taught them," and not due to any labors on the part of the missionaries themselves.[26])

Toral's arrival in the early 1540s coincided with a period of extraordinary enthusiasm for scholarly activity on the part of the friars. In 1544, fray Juan de Zumárraga, another Franciscan and first bishop of Mexico, arranged to have two works printed for use by the missionaries. One was *Doctrina cristiana: en que en suma se contiene todo lo principal y necessario que el cristiano debe saber y obrar* ("Christian Doctrine: which contains in summary all that is most important and necessary for a Christian to know and to practice"). He commented in the preface, "This will work better for beginners and the other [volume], the Tripartito de Juan Gersón, for the [more] proficient."[27] The latter volume, *El Tripartito del critianísimo y consolatorio doctor Juan Gersón* ("The Tripartite of the most Christian and consolatory doctor Juan Gerson"), likewise printed in Mexico City in 1544, soon became one of the most sought-after volumes in sixteenth-century Mexico. It consisted of a translation into Spanish of the influential writings of the French theologian Jean Gerson (1363–1429), whose enlightened views have often been compared to those of Erasmus. More than one copy was available at the school at Tlatelolco.[28] Toral, who confessed to being an avid buyer of books, clearly had a copy of the volume in his trunks and assigned it to his more proficient students, if not to all.[29] One of the most talented and creative soon took as his Christian name "Juan Gerson," and another relative—probably his father—became "Tomás Gerson."[30] This Juan Gerson was an extraordinary artist, and in later years Toral would encourage him to produce a rich set of paintings to be used in the church.[31]

In 1545, the bright days were dimmed for Mateo and his classmates. An epidemic, the first in his memory, swept through the land. "Blood came from the mouth, the nose, the teeth. It came upon us here in the month of May, in the time of the harvest. The dying was terrifying. When it was just beginning, in one day they would bury ten, twenty, thirty, forty. This was in one day."[32] Children younger than he was were the most vulnerable. Little ones whom he had once made laugh now died in extraordinary numbers. The head of his lineage, the old huey teuctli, also died. With him, implicitly, disappeared a symbol of the old days.

Mateo either remembered little of the time right after the epidemic or he could not bear to write of it, for he said little about it in his later writings, but he recalled quite specifically and accurately that in 1548, Toral became the guardián of the friary in Tecamachalco.[33] He himself became a full adult in this period, and in 1552, he was elected to the cabildo for the first time.[34] He worked eagerly at governing the altepetl, serving several terms in the 1550s. Toral continued as guardián except for a period of about a year and a half when he was in Spain, working to bring more Franciscans of a devoted stamp to the New World. If Toral looked forward to more years of satisfying work among people who welcomed him, don Mateo Sánchez also apparently saw the future in hopeful terms. Aside the diseases, conquest did not seem to have spelled disaster for his people.

The only crisis of this period occurred in 1557. In a wider project of *congregación* (also experienced by don Alonso in Cuauhtinchan), the Spaniards announced that Tecamachalco and Quecholac would need to combine to become one altepetl. Undoubtedly by design, given the tensions around the resettlements, the viceroy, don Luis de Velasco, chose to tour the area at this moment. Certain disgruntled noblemen seized an opportunity to submit a petition to him complaining of behavior they did not like on the part of their gobernador. They were to all appearances unprepared for the consequences. Toral clearly felt he knew "his" people, and he believed that there were no serious injustices occurring on his watch. He was also undoubtedly embarrassed by the imputation that all was not well in Tecamachalco being brought straight to the viceroy. He who was never angry grew enraged. He stripped the tokens of nobility from the ringleader, one Juan Bautista, and threatened worse punishments to any who dared to join him in insisting that there was a problem. The next year, the sitting governor was re-elected, with don Mateo Sánchez on his council. Tranquility had, at least on the surface, been restored.

The overt conflict, however, bore some fruitful results. The events seem to have caused to blossom in Mateo's generation a deep interest and pride in their past. When the viceroy came to visit, he was presented with a *tlachihualxochitl*, a sort of coat of arms in traditional style, this one showing on the community's highest hill the symbolic eagle and jaguar. Two of the friars in his entourage (a Dominican and an Augustinian) were escorted up the very hill portrayed in the painting and shown the impressive ruins of the palace of Cuetzpaltzin.[35] Finally, the visitors were shown a traditional pictorial history of their people, an *altepetlahcuillolli*, which their reigning tlatoani had signed with his own hand at the bottom.[36] All of this was well within normal practice for any indigenous town being honored with a visit from the viceroy. What was more noteworthy was that the desire to demonstrate civic pride did not wane with the departure of the visiting dignitary. Perhaps this was because so many of the town's young men were highly educated by world standards, and now envisioned themselves as existing in relation to other peoples of the globe. It would have been in this very period that Juan Gerson began to sketch out and work on his extensive set of paintings for the church then being planned, and it seems to have been at this time as well that don Mateo began work on his xiuhpohualli.

It seems so because in this period, his entries grow noticeably richer and more detailed, for the first time as if he were writing near to the time of the events, when he could still easily recall details. It is logical that he would begin to take the historical trajectory of his altepetl more seriously than ever before and to feel some responsibility for preserving it for future generations. There was a variety of reasons: he was a cabildo member now; the *congregación* demanded political changes that were of necessity rendered complicated by the past; and the viceroy himself, stand-in for one of the world's greatest monarchs, made his first visit to Tecamachalco. Furthermore, don Mateo had married and had a son (Lucas) in 1557 and daughter (Francisca) in 1560, so certain elements of the future were suddenly acutely visible to him. In short, it was probably no accident that he turned with special interest to the writing of history at this point.

He knew enough about the traditional genre of the xiuhpohualli to know that it was on one level to be an anonymous work. He wrote in the third person and never signed his name or stated explicitly that he wrote it. But the perspective he took was the perspective of his lineage, and indeed of his household and himself. Readers glean more information about the doings of Mateo Sánchez than they do about the activities of anyone else, including the highest-ranking nobles. It even details his personal life. There can be no doubt that it is his work. There were two sub-altepetls in Tecamachalco, as was typical of Nahua organization, each associated with the regular election of two different alcaldes (until the incorporation of Quecholac raised the number to three), and he knew enough about the old format to know that both sides should be included. At points of great crisis, especially at the deaths of important people, the same event is frequently mentioned twice, as if the author were incorporating another perspective at key moments. A musician speaks in the first person frequently, once even explicitly distinguishing himself from the cabildo (and hence implicitly from don Mateo): "The cabildo members let us know [of the arrival of the Marqués del Valle], so we went to await him in Puebla, with the permission of Puebla's alcalde mayor. We went to play wind instruments for him, on the sixth of the month."[37] An altepetl's musicians generally were of a particular lineage and usually were not the same people who served on the cabildo, so most likely don Mateo drew upon a record kept by a friend among the town's musicians.[38]

It is clear that don Mateo wanted to begin his year count in the deep past. His own parents would have been adults in their prime when the Spaniards arrived, so he had (or at least had once had) a direct source of information about the past. His mother still lived, and would for another decade, though we can know nothing of the state of her memory at this time or her interest in such projects.[39] In Mateo's early childhood, before he was old enough to go to the friars, he had probably been raised on the ancient stories. He knew some of them, at least in skeletal form, or else he found people who could narrate them to him. He had pictorials he could use to remind him, but here his own ignorance of the old ways frustrated him. In the busy year One House, when Cuetzpaltzin died and the altepetl was attacked by many enemies at once, the timeline was apparently surrounded by complex images he did not understand. He was reduced to throwing up his hands at one point and writing, "And a great many things happened." The account was not what it should have been—it was much more bare-bones—but it was the best he could do. The pictorials at least guided him securely through the old calendar. He followed the old-style dates right up until 1519, when the Spaniards arrived and with them the Christian years. Then he proceeded to give both the old-style year and the new-style throughout.

Don Mateo's acquaintance with European books had recently only added to his interest in variegated calendrical possibilities—multiple languages of time, as it were. The Old World almanacs of the sixteenth century devoted minute attention to celestial mapping of various kinds, and the fascinated Franciscans found rapt audiences in their indigenous students.[40] Beginning in 1519, at the arrival of the Christians, don Mateo noted that the year's "golden number" was nineteen. This was a reference to the Metonic cycle, the period of almost nineteen years that it takes for the solar cycle (the earth's revolution around the sun) and the lunar cycle (the moon's revolution around the earth) to realign perfectly. The cycle was—and still is—used to calculate the date of Easter, and so was important to Christians of the era who prided themselves on education and rationality. The years' assigned numbers were referred to as "golden" (*aurea*) because in many early manuscripts, they were painted in gold. However, educated readers no longer needed to consult these aging pages. Toral would have taught the young Mateo that even non-experts in the Metonic cycle could calculate the years, simply by dividing the Christian year number by 19, taking the remainder, and adding 1. So, for example, don Mateo learned: 1519 divided by 19 is 79, remainder 18. To 18 he would add 1, and end with the golden number of 19 (a rich coincidence, given that the Christian year was 1519). In the next year, the twentieth year, the cycle would begin again. It is easy to see how appealing the system would have been to one like don Mateo, whose father or uncle would have been deeply versed in the rotating, periodically interlocking calendars of the *ancien régime*, a system largely oriented around the number 20 (as well as 13).[41]

In 1558, don Mateo's beloved Toral left Tecamachalco. He had been named as provincial of his order, and he departed to take up his duties in Mexico City. Before he left, he made an emotional farewell speech. "He brought together the different peoples because he would never see us again." Don Mateo was himself feeling profoundly nostalgic for the passing of an era. "We will not again see the like of how he educated and raised us." The connection, in fact, between Toral and his friends in Tecamachalco turned out to be too deep to be severed easily by the friar's promotion and removal. He came back to visit twice in the following three years, in 1559 and again in 1561. On the latter occasion, he was called in to mediate a dispute between the indigenous government and the Spanish state regarding the new cash tribute they were in the process of instituting.[42]

Toral also left his protegés in positions of importance that they continued to occupy after his own departure. Juan Gerson, probably the most important of these, had several Bibles whose illustrations he was using as his inspiration for most of the paintings that were to adorn the ceiling of the church.[43] He selected only Old Testament scenes of dramatic struggle and the apocalyptic battle of Revelations, not images of Jesus Christ or loving saints. The pictures were drawn from his models, but they were nevertheless his. An eagle holding a book took pride of place. Waters churned in the style of the traditional aquatic glyph. A dove soaring overhead became a pelican, known to Nahuas as the tlatoani of all birds.[44] A hill sheltered a cavernous depth from which great mysteries emerged. When Gerson finished in 1562, don Mateo recorded the event proudly in his xiuhpohualli,[45] and the whole community commemorated the event for as long as stone should last by carving in the wall of the church the Nahuatl phrase, "1562 años ipan omochiuin" ("done in the year 1562").[46]

Don Mateo himself had been recommended—presumably by Toral—to act as a visiting *juez gobernador* in another town, apparently receiving in return a grant of an estancia for small livestock.[47] He went to Cozcatlan to serve, and hence was absent when the cabildo members were suddenly arrested for their failure to come up with the tithes that were to support the church. It was a difficult time for him. He wrote, speaking of himself in the third person, "Don Mateo arrived [back in town] as soon as his duties in Cozcatlan were finished, but it was for only a few days. Then he went to Mexico City to give an account to the viceroy. At the time he was there [in the city] he had a fever."[48] When these events had finally passed, at about the same time as the community's church was completed, a very welcome letter from Toral arrived.[49] He had been named bishop of Yucatán and had been to Spain to be consecrated. Now he was in Mérida and hard at work. Given the cheerful tone evinced by don Mateo, we can assume that what we might have expected was indeed true: in his letter, Toral had chosen to hide what he had actually found when he docked in Yucatán. Fray Diego de Landa had been leading a veritable rampage, arresting and torturing dozens in the indigenous community on grounds that they had purportedly been participating in continuing ceremonies of human sacrifice.[50] Perhaps it was as well that Mateo did not know of the brutal torments inflicted. Not long afterward, his wife, Catarina, died, perhaps in childbed, leaving him alone with two very young children.[51] He lost no time in remarrying. The next year, doña Marta, daughter of an indigenous nobleman of Tecalco, became his wife. They celebrated in Tecalco, and then he brought her to her new home.

In 1565, Toral visited Mexico City to attend the Second Council of the Mexican Roman Catholic Church. There, Marcos Cipac and his peers would have been aware of his presence, for he argued vociferously against the excessive taxes levied on the indigenous; he even sent a letter to Philip II.[52] He stopped for a visit in Tecamachalco both on the way there and upon his return.[53] Now indeed he must have told don Mateo and others something of what he had seen in Yucatán. He had written in a somewhat muted tone to the king what he had initially learned of Landa's activities, focusing on Landa's inflated sense of self-importance, and the danger he therefore presented to the conversion of the populace and the authority of the king: "[When I arrived] they were holding as prisoners a hundred and some nobles in the monastery of the city [of Mérida], and were going around seizing more in order to hold an *auto* and burn them all, showing great audaciousness and independence of action."[54] Another Spaniard writing at the same time had been blunter, but then, he had seen more with his own eyes, and in addition was less burdened by the imperative of appearing circumspect:

> They began the business with great rigor and atrocity, putting the Indians to terrible torture by water and rope, then hanging them up high by means of a pulley with two or three weights of 25 pounds attached to their feet, and, holding them suspended there, giving them many lashes, until blood ran from their backs and legs to the ground; then they scalded them like they used to do to black slaves, with lit wax candles, letting the wax from them melt over their flesh.[55]

Later Toral would be reprimanded for having spoken as harshly as he did of his Franciscan brethren to outsiders. Doubtless he was conscious of the need to be cautious when he was with his beloved Tecamachalcans, but having witnessed what he had, he could not have been fully master of his tongue, for he had long needed to talk to sympathetic souls on the subject. In his letters to Spain he condemned the Yucatán friars for failing to learn the language of those whom they were supposed to convert, and he himself had been feeling his own limitations in this regard in his new territory. "I am deaf and dumb because I don't know the language," he sighed.[56] There was a chasm between him and those who surrounded him in Yucatán. He had once learned languages easily, but he was older now, suffering health problems, and overwhelmed by the bureaucratic responsibilities regarding a large territory. So he remained isolated. During his visit to Tecamachalco, he could speak freely and easily, and the temptation to do so must have been extreme.

Don Mateo was delighted to see him. They had received a message that he was on his way and set out to find him on the road, as was traditional upon great occasions. "All of us cabildo members went to meet him at Atzonpan. He came from Yucatán on the 19th of the month of June. The very next day it was Corpus Christi and the feast of the blessed sacrament was celebrated."[57] Toral led them in prayer, as in former days. Then he went on to Mexico City, where he participated in the great meeting in Xochimilco attended by the angry Mexica.

For don Mateo, the late 1560s were a time of great activity. He was burdened by more difficult situations than in his youth, but his tone was undaunted, even unchanged. It is very clear that he was in constant touch with Spaniards—most likely the friars—for he knew the ins and outs of the contemporaneous Spanish political crisis in Mexico City even as it unfolded, beginning with the sudden death of don Luis de Velasco in 1564. Indeed, he had a very thorough handle on the events. When he wrote that the "tlatoani virrey" don Gastón de Peralta "caused himself to depart from Mexico" (*moquixti Mexihco*), or alternatively, "was ejected from Mexico," a modern scholar decided it was merely a way of saying he left Mexico in a reverential form—and indeed it was—but the particular word choice and the alternate meaning conveyed the flavor of what had happened: don Gastón was expelled by the residencia judges and forced to return to Spain.[58]

When the reasonable don Gastón de Peralta had first come to power, and it had seemed that the violent storm in Mexico City had exhausted itself, don Tomás Gerson (of Juan Gerson's family) had taken the opportunity to go to the capital and complain once again of the oft-serving governor, don Juan de los Angeles—the same one whom Toral had defended years before. In a bitter turn of events, the viceregal office had in fact agreed to remove don Juan, but then replaced him with one whom Gerson liked no better—Francisco Jiménez, apparently a favorite of the friars. Back to Mexico City went don Tomás Gerson and his colleagues. "Their hearts were not satisfied." Either the Crown turned a deaf ear this time, and/or don Tomás decided on his own that he had to make the best of the situation. A few years later, he and don Francisco Jiménez decided to have their two children become engaged and unite the lines. Yet the anger lingered, and don Tomás let the local friars know that he was still seething about it.[59]

Most people probably would have said that the most exciting news of the era came in 1568, when the English pirate and slaver John Hawkins was caught in the port of Veracruz by the convoy bearing the new viceroy. Hawkins's own ship managed to slip away, but two accompanying boats were trapped and the passengers taken prisoner. They were sentenced to hard labor in Mexico for years to come.[60] Don Mateo reported the event, but for him, the crescendo of the decade came in 1570, when for the first time he was elected gobernador of the cabildo. He set to work immediately surveying disputed lands and completing the construction of the tecpan, the community house.[61]

Then he received word that Toral was once again coming for a visit. It was a momentous occasion. It had been a full five years since they had seen each other. They had known each other for almost thirty years, and now, perhaps, were coming close to the end, though they still remembered the beginning so clearly. They were no longer a young teacher and his eager student. Toral was at this point the long-established bishop of Yucatán, and don Mateo was governor of his people. He held a great reception and recorded it in his book. "The governor Mateo Sánchez went to meet the bishop don fray Francisco Toral in Altecalehcan. On the 6th of June they came to San Salvador Quauhyaualolco to eat. On Thursday they arrived here in Tecamachalco."[62]

Toral was a shadow of his former self. He was ailing, but most importantly, he knew now beyond doubt that his relationship with the young men of Tecamachalco had been mutual, that he had learned as much from them as they from him, and that his heart could not be at peace without such exchange. He had never found it in Mérida. He lived there in isolation, for without the language, he was incapable of the give-and-take of conversation. His relationship with the people there stood in stark contrast to his connection with the people—or at least some of the people—of Tecamachalco. In April of 1567, a group of caciques of Maní wrote to the king to demand justice, which they felt they still had not truly received. Though they certainly did not blame Toral for initiating the crisis of 1562, they harbored bitter feelings against him nonetheless. "Even though he took us from prison and freed us from death and removed the San Benito hoods, he has not vindicated us from the lies and calumnies that were brought against us, saying that we are idolators and practicers of human sacrifice and have killed many Indians. Because, in the end, he wears the same habit as the friars of Saint Francis and takes their side."[63] Only a few days earlier, Toral had penned a letter of his own which showed that the feelings of distrust and distance were mutual. He wrote to Pedro Menéndez de Aviles, adelantado of Florida, who was in the midst of planning an expedition to the Chesapeake Bay area; Menéndez had as his middleman an Indian who had been kidnapped from the region years before and had been living with the Nahua artisans in the Dominican convent in Mexico City, privy to all the recent crises. Toral warned him, "The natives, fearing to lose their lands, will use a thousand betrayals and artful frauds, for which you will be responsable."[64]

When Toral arrived in the City of Mexico in 1570 after his visit to Tecamachalco, he wrote to the king in more depth about his feelings of being "deaf and dumb" among the Maya. "As I am already old, I have not been able to learn the language of the land, for which reason I have lived in great discontent, as I am unable to preach to my flock. . . . And if it please Your Majesty that I might serve in proper dignity and state, may it be in a cooler land, where I can fulfill my office, and the flock may hear my voice and I understand theirs." But then he added that he would prefer to set down his burdens altogether. "Although I would like even better to be in some corner free of the charge of human souls."[65] The king ignored the bishop's pleas, but Toral continued to wait in the city, hoping for a release from his duties. It came in another form. Early the next year, at the end of March, after a seven-day illness, he died.[66]

Word came to his friends in Tecamachalco. Here was one of several momentous occasions in his text on which don Mateo included the words of different parties, each recording the honors done to "Toraltzin", first in April, when they heard, and then again in May, when they had had time to prepare a special ceremony. The cleric who served as his Mayan interpreter, who had accompanied him to Mexico City, came in May, bringing with him Toral's personal effects, which were to be given to his friends in Tecamachalco, "the tlatoque here."[67]

Don Mateo's responsibilities as governor continued. Some involved local tensions. Don Francisco Jiménez died—he who was so disliked by don Tomás Gerson—leaving an orphan son whom don Mateo decided to take under his roof. Don Mateo became embroiled in lawsuits necessary to defend the child against his neighbors, who were doing their best to usurp his lands, which they claimed were his only by virtue of Spanish interference.[68] Most of don Mateo's time, however, was directed toward larger political issues relating to the Spanish authorities. The Crown was deeply embedded in the project of taking another census, so as to more efficiently collect the increased taxes that had been approved in the 1560s. In 1572, all the cabildo members had to go to Mexico City to have read to them in person the total quantities they would henceforth be responsible for collecting. "It was contested. The tlatoque said, 'It will not be possible. Let it be half.'"[69] They compromised. The cabildo members did their best to convince the people to pay, but tensions clearly percolated. In 1575, a good friend, Martín Cortés, who also often served on the cabildo, was arrested. The Spanish alcalde mayor, don Juan de Saavedra, accused him of idolatry and had him jailed in Tepeaca.[70] Another friend sold his house and gave 100 pesos of the proceeds to help Martín hire a lawyer. Around the same time, a fray Juan de Parada came to Tecamachalco to cover for the guardián, who had to travel to Yucatán. Fray Juan was completely unfamiliar with the social hierarchy and assumed that his prerogatives as a Spaniard would stand him in good stead. When don Mateo argued with him about something, fray Juan struck him and scolded him in public. "It was not good how he berated him," commented don Mateo laconically, speaking of himself in the third person as he always did. Then he arranged for word to be sent to higher-ranking churchmen, presumably to someone in Tepeaca. "Thereupon the church authorities removed [fray Juan]." Don Mateo was obviously pleased, but he could not rest easy until their very own guardián had returned. He was acutely aware of the moment of his reappearance. "It was already dark when he arrived," he remembered.

Only a few months later, the church hierarchy demanded a large collection for the cathedral—presumably the one in Puebla—and the regular tribute also was due. The cabildo members had great difficulty convincing the people to comply this time, so they themselves were jailed until their people came up with the cash.[71] It was the same cabildo members' responsibility to negotiate with some arrogant Spanish *estancieros* (ranchers) to pay them to take charge of some communally owned sheep, as apparently none of the tlatoque had unused lands extensive enough to put them to pasture. Worse, there was an ongoing legal battle over a local mill, and again many of the tlatoque, including don Mateo, found themselves imprisoned. The belligerent don Tomás Gerson went to Mexico City for a week and seemed to have made some progress in settling the affair.[72] Then in August of 1576, the worst epidemic in memory struck. Rumor had it that 2 million Indians disappeared.[73] Sahagún in Mexico City wrote that he feared they all would die. Among the dead was don Mateo's still-young wife, Marta, and several other family members.

In the wake of the scourge, the political problems only worsened. In January, don Tomás Gerson was elected governor, but the Spaniards—who were well acquainted with his strong political stances—refused to allow him to serve. Tecamachalco was left without a leader. In February, 500 people were demanded for public labor on behalf of the community, and the old tribute payments were also expected. In August, don Mateo left for Mexico City to plead for relief from these demands. While he was gone, the other cabildo members were jailed and held for a week, apparently to convince the people to cooperate with the taking of a new census.[74] In early 1578, the count was completed, but the Crown had no leader to charge with collecting the named tribute amount. The aging don Mateo was made governor at mid-year, in April. Apparently he was able to convince the people to pay, for there is no record of a disturbance.[75]

The sense of being buffeted, however, seemed to settle on don Mateo. Numerous entries recounted problems introduced by the Spaniards.[76] At the start of 1579, he accepted the charge of the governorship again, but his old friend, the godfather of his son, don Baltasar del Castillo, would not accept a post as alcalde.[77] Did don Mateo ever wonder about the actions taken by his father and father's colleagues, about the acceptance of Spanish rule? He may have. But he probably understood just how constrained their choices had been. He probably thought more about his need for Toraltzin in his dealings with the Spanish world: his exchanges with that Spaniard, at least, had been among the most meaningful interchanges of his life. But the days of such optimistic camaraderie between European and Indian seemed to have passed. The town's authorities at that point believed there were only two or three Indians living there who could read and write, when in fact there were at least that many in his family alone.[78] Certainly he no longer felt he had a political ally in the Spanish world. In April of 1580, don Mateo took to his bed. Six weeks later, he died. The heart of don Baltasar del Castillo softened, and he entered the cabildo after all and took up the post of governor and led the altepetl. Don Mateo's son, Lucas, now twenty-three years old, took charge of the xiuhpohualli. He recorded his father's death and moved forward into the future.[79]

***

Don Mateo noted in his work when his community received letters, twice from Toral, and on other occasions from friars who had left Tecamachalco to go on to Guatemala. If he himself wrote any letters, he did not say so. Intellectual exchange is implied to some extent in the conversations they had, but there is no actual record of it, unless we count Toral's longing for the interchange that once had been his. Other indigenous men of don Mateo's generation, however, did definitely correspond with the friars who had taught them. It is occasionally possible to glimpse the exchange of ideas. Around 1570, Pedro de San Buenaventura, one of the famous "trilinguals" trained by fray Bernardino de Sahagún to write in Spanish, Latin, and Nahuatl, sat down to answer an epistle from his erstwhile mentor.⁸⁰ He began in Spanish: "Muy reverendo padre." Sahagún had undoubtedly written to him in Spanish, the language in which he nearly always wrote. Pedro easily began with the familiar salutation, for which no analogous form existed in his natal language, not having been needed. Then, however, he switched to Nahuatl, the language in which he would be able to explain the matter at hand more accurately, knowing that fray Bernardino would be able to follow.⁸¹ He got right down to business. "I have received your honored letter asking where the ancients based and began [the year]." Literally, he began, "I have received and admired the breath of your words," but such flourishes were commonplace within his language and conveyed nothing more than polite respect. Sahagún would know this, and would understand that he meant to be quite direct. "I have considered the matter, and have before me a document concerning the [calendar] year," he went on.

San Buenaventura then launched into an explanation of the rotating calendar as it worked in his region, culminating in a discussion of *nemontli*, the frightening five-day period that fit nowhere in the calendar wheel of eighteen months of twenty days each.⁸² "*Nemontemi* means 'it belongs nowhere'," he explained, as he was using a verb likely unfamiliar to Sahagún. At the end of that period, the new year began as soon as the sun came up. "Everybody went to the water's edge while it was still dark." They waited there to see how the sun would rise and bring time back into being. Then they would bathe in the holy manner, puncturing themselves and shedding their own blood. "This is what the ancients say who are still alive," he added, for of course, he himself did not remember. But he trusted the knowledge of the old ones of his homeland, of Cuauhtitlan. "Pues, in Mexico City, where you are, it is not rightly known." "This is all with which I return your words," he said in closing, as his ancestors once had said when they made formal speech exchanges. Then he translated some stock Spanish phrases into his own language, at the same time managing to retain the mutuality of his forebears. "May our Lord God keep your soul. Pray to our Lord on our behalf. Your humble servant, Pedro de San Buenaventura."

In the late 1560s, Sahagún was living in the monastery of San Francisco in the City of Mexico, where he was working hard on the materials he had collected over the course of his career. "For three years, alone, I examined and reexamined all my writings. And I again amended them and divided them into Books, into twelve books...."[83] It was in this period that he decided he did not fully grasp the calendrical system after all; he could not, for example, say exactly when the Nahuas considered that a new year began, as his notes revealed discrepancies. He knew to whom he would write: Pedro de San Buenaventura, one of his favorite former students, then living at home in Cuauhtitlan, and a great expert in the old ways. When he received San Buenaventura's answer to his query, he explained carefully on the back in Spanish what it was, and then preserved it at the start of a draft of a chapter on the calendar.[84]

Sahagún had always rated San Buenaventura's abilities highly, from the time when he had been his Latin teacher at the Colegio Santa Cruz in Tlatelolco. In the mid-1550s, he had worked with him in interviewing aging men in the city about their experiences in the war against the Spaniards between 1519 and 1521. Then in 1558, fray Francisco de Toral, the newly appointed provincial of the Franciscan order, had given Sahagún instructions to undertake a great encyclopedic work on the history and culture of the ancient Nahuas, to be used to further their indoctrination. San Buenaventura had been one of four whom the delighted friar had chosen to accompany him to Tepepolco in the Aculhuacan region of Tetzcoco. There they began their researches. "With the [town's] principales and the grammarians [from the school at Tlatelolco], who were also principales, I conferred for many days over the course of two years, following the sequence of the outline that I had prepared. They gave me all the matters we discussed in pictures, for that was the writing they employed in ancient times. And the grammarians explained them in their language, writing the explanation at the bottom of the painting."[85] Remarkably, Sahagún did not condemn his four aides to anonymity. He gave credit to each. Alonso Valeriano from Azcapotzalco was "the principal one and the most knowledgeable." (He had already worked as a teacher at the Colegio, famous for his ability to speak Latin effortlessly, and later became gobernador of the indigenous cabildo of Mexico City.[86]) Martín Jacobito from Tlatelolco later became rector of the Colegio. And then there were two young men from Cuauhtitlan, Alonso Vegerano and Pedro de San Buenaventura.

In 1561, Sahagún was called back from Tepepolco to Santiago de Tlatelolco, the monastery next to the Colegio de Santa Cruz. The four grammarians continued to help him organize and expand the writings. Then another change occurred: Pedro de San Buenaventura apparently went home. In 1564, by the time the friar launched his next major project, organizing the notes taken on the 1524 exchanges between friars and native priests, and translating them into Nahuatl (the material now known as the "Coloquios y doctrina christiana"), Sahagún did not include him in the list of his aides. He again mentioned Antonio Valeriano, Alonso Vegerano, and Martín Jacobita, and then he added that Andrés Leonardo from Tlatelolco now worked with them.[87] By the late 1560s, San Buenaventura was definitely residing in his natal home of Cuauhtitlan.[88]

There, it seems safe to say, he was either writing a history or else conferring with someone who was. The anonymous *Annals of Cuauhtitlan* is a remarkable document, sixty-eight double-sided folios rich in language and stories of a style not generally brought before Spaniards. The fact that it was written in Cuauhtitlan in the late 1560s and early 1570s by someone highly skilled in alphabetic writing is not on its own enough to ascribe it to San Buenaventura or even to someone in his social circle.[89] Moreover, the handwriting is definitely that of a later copyist, not the original author.[90] But there is other evidence linking it to San Buenaventura, or at least demonstrating his influence. The work is in effect the braiding together of three histories: that of Cuauhtitlan, that of Tenochtitlan, and that of the Tetzcoco region, the three places where Buenaventura had lived and consulted with locals. The writer moves back and forth effortlessly between these, clearly having documentation from all three within his reach. He has an extraordinary grasp of the Nahua calendar, blending the three histories over many centuries and working entirely within the old-style calendar. Yet he is also aware of Spanish history. More, the writer demonstrates intimate knowledge of more than one segment of Sahagún's great work, including materials on the Spanish conquest and on the story of Quetzalcoatl, for example. Indeed, there are moments when the author seems to be talking to Sahagún and his students. It would seem impossible that with all these elements present, San Buenaventura had nothing to do with the project. We must assume that he did.

Perhaps the author was not San Buenaventura himself, but rather a friend, one who had shared materials with him but who had spent fewer years away from home living with Spaniards. That is certainly possible, for the stories sometimes seem startlingly removed from anything the student of a former friar would write. On the other hand, the writer often seems to have been strongly influenced by a Spanish-style education. He is critical of his sources, adding "so they say" or "this cannot be right," and insisting on a linear chronology rather than allowing different towns' perspectives to stand side by side, as if he could imagine what a Spaniard would say about the topic. We probably will never know if San Buenaventura wrote the words himself or merely read them as someone else worked, offering his thoughts and contributions along the way. In either case, the text gives us narratives the like of which we find nowhere else, including the life story of the famous culture hero Quetzalcoatl:

> [page 3][91]
>
> 1 House. In this year died the Toltecs' ruler, named Mixcoamazatzin, the one who had started the rulership. Then Huentzin was installed as ruler of Tollan.
>
> 2 Rabbit.
>
> 3 Reed.
>
> 4 Flint Knife.
>
> 5 House.
>
> 6 Rabbit.
>
> 7 Reed.
>
> 8 Flint Knife.
>
> 9 House.
>
> 10 Rabbit.
>
> 11 Reed.
>
> 12 Flint Knife.
>
> 13 House.

1 Rabbit.

2 Reed.

3 Flint Knife.

4 House.

5 Rabbit.

In the year 6 Reed died Quetzalcoatl's father, named Totepeuh. And then Yhuitimal became ruler, the ruler of Tollan.

7 Flint Knife.

8 House.

9 Rabbit.

10 Reed.

11 Flint Knife.

12 House.

13 Rabbit.

In this year of 1 Reed, according to what they tell, what they say, Quetzalcoatl was born, he who was called Our Lord Priest One Reed Quetzalcoatl. [page 4] It is said that his mother was named "Shield Mother," and according to what is said about him, Quetzalcoatl was placed in his mother's belly when she swallowed a piece of turquoise.

2 Flint Knife.

3 House.

4 Rabbit.

5 Reed.

6 Flint Knife.

7 House.

8 Rabbit.

9 Reed. It was in 9 Reed that Quetzalcoatl sought his father. At that point he was nine years old and had some perspective. He said, "What is my father like? May I see him? May I look at his face?" "He is dead. He is buried over there," was the answer. "Go see." Quetzalcoatl went right away.

He looked for the bones and dug them up. When he had removed the bones, he went to bury them in the temple of the [god] called Quilaztli.

10 Flint Knife.

11 House.

12 Rabbit.

13 Reed.

1 Flint Knife.

2 House.

3 Rabbit.

4 Reed.

5 Flint Knife.

6 House.

7 Rabbit.

8 Reed.

9 Flint Knife.

10 House. In this year Huactli died, he who had been ruler of Cuauhtitlan. He had been ruler for sixty-two years. He was a ruler who did not know how to plant corn for food. Nor did his subjects know how to make textiles. They still wore hides. Their food was just birds, snakes, rabbits, and deer. They did not yet have houses. They just kept going from place to place, kept moving on.

In 11 Rabbit, the noblewoman Xiuhtlacuilolxochitzin became ruler. She had her straw house in Tianquiztenco, where Tepexitenco is now. And it is said that the reason the altepetl was left to this woman is that she was Huactli's wife, and she had the power of calling on the devil [meaning the goddess] Itzpapalotl.

12 Reed.

13 Flint Knife.

1 House.

In 2 Rabbit Quetzalcoatl came to Tollan. He spent four years there and built his house of fasting, his house of turquoise beams. Then he went off toward Cuextlan. He laid down a stone bridge to cross [a river] at a certain place and they say it is there still.

3 Reed.

4 Flint Knife.

5 House. In this year the Toltecs went to get Quetzalcoatl to make him ruler of Tollan as well as their priest. The story of it has been written elsewhere.

6 Rabbit.

In 7 Reed died Xiuhtlacuilolxochitzin, noblewoman of Cuauhtitlan. She had ruled for twelve years.

In the year 8 Flint Knife Ayauhcoyotzin was installed as ruler of Cuauhtitlan, in the place called Tecpancuauhtla.

9 House.

10 Rabbit.

11 Reed.

12 Flint Knife.

13 House.

1 Rabbit.

2 Reed. According to what is told in Tetzcoco, Quetzalcoatl Topiltzin of Tollan Culhuacan died.

It was in 2 Reed that Topiltzin, or One Reed Quetzalcoatl, built his house of fasting, his place of penance, his place of prayer. He built four houses—his house of turquoise beams, his house of coral, his house of shell, and his house of quetzal feathers. There he prayed and did penance; there he fasted. In the very middle of the night he would go down to the water, to the place called the Water Palace by the Reeds. He punctured himself with thorns at the crest of Xicocotl and Huitzco and Tzincoc and Nonohualco Mountain. He made his thorns out of jade and his needles of quetzal feathers. For incense he burned turquoise and coral. He would kill snakes, birds, and butterflies as blood offerings. It is told, it is said that he worshipped and prayed to the heavens. He called out to Citlalinicue, Citlalatonac, Tonacacihuatl, Tonacateuctli, Tecolliquenqui, Eztlaquenqui, Tlallamanac, and Tlalichcatl. He was calling out, according to what he knew, to the place of the Two,[92] to the Nine layers in which the heavens are arranged. It was thus he believed about those who inhabited the heavens, those whom he called out and prayed to. He lived a humble life, a merciful life.

What's more, in his life and in his time he brought forth great prosperity, [working in] turquoise, jade, gold, silver, red shell, white shell, [and feathers of] the quetzals, cotingas, roseate spoonbills, troupials, trogons, and herons. And he introduced cacao and cotton in different colors. He was a great craftsman in all his works—his eating dishes, his drinking vessels,[page 5] his green, white, yellow, and red painted pottery, and many other things. And while he lived, Quetzalcoatl initiated and began his temple. He put up the serpent columns. But he did not finish it; he did not build it to the top.

While he lived, he did not show himself to people. He was guarded in a dangerous place.[93] His retainers kept him closed up in different places. Wherever he was closed up, a number of his retainers were there. That is where the jade mat was, the quetzal mat, the golden mat. It has been said, been related, that he had four houses for fasting.

And it is said, it is related that while he lived, demons [that is, sorcerers] wanted to deceive him into paying with human life, taking human lives [as sacrifices]. But he never wanted to, he did not consent, for he really loved his subjects, the Tolteca. The sacrifices that he killed were always snakes, birds, and butterflies. And it is told, it is related that with this he wore out the patience of the sorcerers. Then they began to mock and ridicule him. What the sorcerers said was that they wanted to torment Quetzalcoatl so that he would run away. Thus it became true; it is what happened.

3 Flint Knife.

4 House.

5 Rabbit.

6 Reed.

7 Flint Knife.

8 House.

9 Rabbit.

10 Reed.

11 Flint Knife.

12 House.

13 Rabbit.

1 Reed was the year in which Quetzalcoatl died. And it is said that he went to Tlillan Tlapallan in order to die there. Then one named Matlacxochitl became ruler of Tollan.

Then it is told how Quetzalcoatl left. It was when he did not obey the sorcerers about paying with human life, sacrificing humans. Then the sorcerers talked among themselves, the ones called Tezcatlipoca, and also Yhuimecatl Toltecatl. They said, "He must leave his altepetl behind and we will live there." They said, "Let's make pulque. We will have him drink it so that he gets confused and no longer does his duty." Then Tezcatlipoca said, "What I say is that we should give him a way to see his body." They agreed that that was what they would do. Then Tezcatlipoca went ahead. He took a two-sided mirror a hand-span wide and wrapped it up. When he got to where Quetzalcoatl was, he said to the retainers guarding him, "Say to the priest, 'A young man has come to give you, to show you, your body.'" The retainers went in and repeated it to Quetzalcoatl, who said, "What's that, grandfather servants?[94] What is my 'body'? Look at what he's brought, then he should come in." But [Tezcatlipoca] did not want to show it to them. He said, "I had thought I would show it to the priest [himself]. Tell him that." They went and told him, "He refuses. He really wants to show it to you himself." "Let him come, grandfathers," said Quetzalcoatl. They went to call Tezcatlipoca. He entered and greeted Quetzalcoatl, saying, "My child,[95] Priest One Reed Quetzalcoatl, I greet you, and I have come to show you your honored body." Said Quetzalcoatl, "Welcome, grandfather. Where do you come from? What is my body? Let me see it." Said he, "My child, o priest, I am your servant [subject] and I come from the foot of Nonohualco Mountain. Behold your body." Then he gave him the mirror, saying, "Know yourself, see yourself, my child, for you will appear in the mirror." Then Quetzalcoatl saw himself and was greatly frightened. He said, "If my subjects see me, they may run away." For his eyelids were bulging, his eye sockets were sunken, and his face hung in folds everywhere. Was he not a monster? When he had looked in the mirror, he said, "My subjects are never to see me. I will stay right here." Then Tezcatlipoca left him and came away. Then he consulted with Yhuimecatl about how they might not best belittle him. Said Yhuimecatl, "Let the feather worker Coyotlinahual go." They repeated [the story] to him, so that the feather worker Coyotlinahual would go. He said, "Very well. I'll go see Quetzalcoatl." And he went. He said to Quetzalcoatl, "My child, I say you must go out. Your subjects[page 6] must see you. Let me dress you up so they can see you." He answered, "Do it! I would like to see it [done], my grandfather." And so the feather worker Coyotlinahual did it. First he made Quetzalcoatl's head fan. Then he made his turquoise mask, taking dyes to make the mouth red, taking yellow to make the design of a cage on his face. Then he gave him serpent teeth and made his beard, covering the bottom with cotinga and roseate spoonbill feathers. When he had prepared [the costume]—in which Quetzalcoatl used to be dressed—then he gave him the mirror. When Quetzalcoatl saw himself, he thought it was really good. Instantly he went out from where they were guarding him. Then the feather worker Coyotlinahual went to tell Yhuimecatl, "I have brought Quetzalcoatl out, now you go!" "Very well," said he. Then he sidled up to one named Toltecatl and they went together. When they were ready, they set off for Xonacapacoyan. They lodged with the keeper of the fields there, Maxtlaton, keeper of Toltec Mountain. Then they made greens, tomatoes, chili peppers, green corn, and beans. In just a few days it was done. There were also maguey plants there, which they requested from Maxtla. In just four days they made pulque of it, then they decanted it. They were the ones who discovered little [hives of] honey in trees and with it they decanted pulque. Then they went to Quetzalcoatl's home in Tollan, bringing all their greens, chilis, etc., as well as the pulque. They got there and tried to enter, but the ones guarding Quetzalcoatl would not allow it. Twice, three times they turned them back. There was no admission. In the end, they were asked where their home was. "At Priest Mountain, at Toltec Mountain," they answered. Quetzalcoatl, hearing such, said, "Let them come in." They went in. They greeted him, and at last gave him the greens, etc. When he had eaten, they urged him again, and gave him the pulque. He answered, "No, I won't drink it. I'm abstaining. Is it intoxicating? Or poisonous?" They said, "Just taste a bit with your finger.[96] It stirs people's blood, it's sharp."[97] Quetzalcoatl tasted it with his finger. When he found he liked it, he said, "Let me drink, grandfather." When he had had one drink, the sorcerers said to him, "Four is what you'll drink." Thus they gave him [a total of] five.[98] "Your portion," they said. When he had drunk, then they gave it to all his retainers. They all had five drinks. When the sorcerers had gotten them completely drunk, then they said to Quetzalcoatl, "My child, please sing. Here is a song for you to sing." Then Yhuimecatl recited it. "I must leave my house of quetzal, quetzal, my house of troupial, my house of coral...."[99] When he had gotten into a happy mood, Quetzalcoatl said, "Go get my elder sister,[100] Quetzalpetlatl. Let the two of us get drunk together." The retainers sent to Nonohualco Mountain where she was doing penance and said, "My child, lady Quetzalpetlatl, fasting one, we have come to get you. The priest Quetzalcoatl is waiting for you. You are to go be with him." She said, "Very well, let's go, grandfather servant." When she had placed herself beside Quetzalcoatl, they gave her the pulque. Four draughts plus another were hers, thus five. When Yhuimecatl and Toltecatl had made everyone drunk, then they sang for Quetzalcoatl's elder sister. They sang: "My elder sister, where are you, Quetzalpetlatl? Let's get drunk, ay yay ay!" Having gotten drunk, they no longer said, "Let us do penance." They no longer went down to the water. They no longer punctured themselves with thorns. They no longer did anything at daybreak. But after dawn came, they were very sad; their hearts were miserable. Then Quetzalcoatl said, "Woe is me!" Then he sang a lament, composing a song saying that he would have to go away. He sang:

[page 7]

Aya ... itlapohual çe tonal nocallan

Ma nican ayaque ya

Ma nican no nican an ma ye on

Ma niyequehua tlallaque

Çan ya cococ tlacoyotl

Ayca ninozcaltica[101]

He sang the second part of his song, "Ay yay, she used to carry me, my mother Coacueye, noble goddess, ay yay, I am weeping...." When Quetzalcoatl had sung, all his retainers were saddened. They wept. Then they too sang, saying: "Our lords made us rich, and Quetzalcoatl, who braids his hair with turquoise has [only] wood. Would that we might see him! Let us weep!"

And when Quetzalcoatl's retainers had sung, he said, "Grandfather servants, let that be enough. I must leave the altepetl. I must go. Give the command that they make a stone chest." Right away a stone chest was carved. When they had carved it, had finished it, they laid Quetzalcoatl in it. But he lay only four days in the stone chest. When he felt discomfort, he said to his retainers, "Enough, grandfather servants. We must go. Everywhere put away, hide what we discovered, the joy, the riches, all our property, our possessions." And his retainers did so. They hid it at Quetzalcoatl's bathing place, the place called Water Palace by the Reeds. With that Quetzalcoatl left. He got up, called together his retainers, and wept for them. Then they left, heading for Tlillan, Tlapallan, Tlatlayan. He went looking everywhere, exploring. Nowhere was he happy. When he reached the place he had been heading for, again he wept and was sad. It is said, it is related that this year of One Reed was when he arrived at the ocean, the coast. Then he stopped and wept and gathered up his attire, putting on his head fan, his turquoise mask, etc. When he was ready, by his own hand he set himself on fire, cremated himself. That is why they called the place Tlatlayan [Land of Burning], it is where Quetzalcoatl went to set himself afire. And they say as he burned, right away his ashes rose, and what appeared, what they saw, were all the precious birds rising into the sky. They saw roseate spoonbills, cotingas, trogons, herons, green parrots, scarlet macaws, white-fronted parrots, and all the other precious birds. As soon as his ashes had been consumed, they saw the heart [that is, the soul] of a quetzal bird rising up. Thus they knew he had gone to the heavens, had entered the heavens. Old people used to say he was changed into the star that appears at dawn. Thus they say it appeared when Quetzalcoatl died, and they called him Lord of the Dawn. What they said is that when he died, he disappeared for four days. They said he went to Mictlan [the land of the dead] and spent [another] four days making arrows for himself. Thus in eight days, the great star appeared, which they called Quetzalcoatl. They said at that point he became a lord. Thus they used to think when he goes forth on certain day signs, certain groups are the ones he breathes on, shoots arrows at, vents his anger on. If he goes on 1 Alligator, he shoots old men and old women, all equally. If on 1 Jaguar or 1 Deer or 1 Flower, he shoots little children. And if on 1 Reed, he shoots rulers. The same for everybody, if on 1 Death. And if on 1 Rain, he shoots the rain, and no rain will fall. And if on 1 Movement, he shoots young men and young women. If on 1 Water, there is a drought. So each of these [day signs] was venerated by the old men and the old women from former times. [page 8] As for the one called Quetzalcoatl, the span of his lifetime was such that the years he lived are counted as fifty-two, being born in One Reed and also dying in One Reed. So he finished in the year One Reed. It was said that Matlacxochitl succeeded him and ruled in Tollan....

The writer of this tale had undoubtedly heard many versions of it told on evenings of song and story, and he had an ear for beauty and for drama. This Quetzalcoatl longed to know who he was, who his father was, but his mother held back in telling him. He remained a mystery even to himself. He was a great craftsman, maker of four gorgeous palaces of the finest materials possible—turquoise, coral, mother-of-pearl, and woven quetzal feathers. He was a wise and devout man who knew the names of all the gods and prayed to them and did penance. His hard work and spiritualism brought their own rewards: his people prospered. Yet life on this earth is never easy and certainly never static. Quetzalcoatl, too, was subject to torment—the mockery of those who were envious, and who used against him his innermost fears of himself. Unknown to his people, Quetzalcoatl, the creator of beauty, was himself, in secret, monstrously ugly. His undoing came at his own hands, in a sense. His enemies were able to bring him low owing to his own weakness and self-indulgence. He drank to the point of drunkenness, and he demanded sex from a proscribed woman. In forgetting himself thus far, he lost all track of his duties. And so he lost his kingdom. He was nevertheless a great man, and with extraordinary dignity and the shedding of tears, he traveled east seeking kin who had migrated that way long before. He fearlessly set fire to himself, dying in a great conflagration by the sea. Some said he became the morning star, and his arrows remained potent, dangerous to future generations.

A very similar story had been told years ago, in Tepepolco, written down by the trilinguals, among them Pedro de San Buenaventura.[102] That version was somewhat different, less lyrical, and the plot choppier, as if it had been recounted by multiple people—as it undoubtedly had been. The trilinguals also left their own imprint on top of what they recorded from the lips of others: at one point, for example, Tepepolco's Quetzalcoatl is wandering the land and decides to stop in Cuauhtitlan, which allows for certain key events to take place there. A few of the plot details of the two versions are significantly different. In the Tepepolco telling, for instance, when Quetzalcoatl reached the sea, he floated away forever on a raft made of snakes—or perhaps only twisted vines—rather than immolating himself and rising as the morning star. Ultimately, however, it is the same, recognizable story.

When Sahagún and his aides, including San Buenaventura, had returned from Tepepolco to the Mexico City, they spent significant time discussing the material they had gathered, gathering more from local people, organizing, adding, and copying. Enough of their process survives for us to see the stages of work experienced by San Buenaventura years earlier, before he produced his own rendition of the story.[103] The original Tepepolco narration actually concerns the god Quetzalcoatl; it follows on the heels of the stories of Tezcatlipoca and other divinities. Sahagún, however, like other Spaniards of his generation, was determined to see him as a man, a great leader who had traveled east. He wrote in Spanish in the margins, "Here is the story of the one who was Quetzalcoatl, another Hercules, a great wizard, and of what happened when he left."[104] Then he went through and periodically added summaries casting the immortal figure as a mortal hero. In the next stage of writing, these marginal comments in Spanish (minus the reference to Hercules) were translated into Nahuatl and incorporated into the body of the story, thus effectively changing Quetzalcoatl from a god into a great religious leader.[105]

However, the Quetzalcoatl of the text still has not exactly become a human king: he is a priest and sorceror, and a separate character, named Huemac, winds through the Tepepolco version of the story, serving as a political leader. On a different occasion, the trilinguals wrote another version of the life story of Quetzalcoatl, and by that time, two significant alterations had occurred.[106] First, in the new text, there is no mention of Huemac. Quetzalcoatl is simply both priest and king. The second major shift occurs in the very nature of Quetzalcoatl: he is no longer a figure of foibles, with weaknesses for others to exploit. Instead, he is a profoundly good man, in a veritably Christian sense, and the god to whom he is devoted is equally good. For the first time, one of the characters says, "There is only one god. His name is Quetzalcoatl. He requires nothing of you. You will offer him, you will sacrifice before him, only snakes and butterflies."[107] The writer added, "And everyone obeyed the command of Quetzalcoatl's priest." For the first time, there was a reference to his being immolated at the seashore.

In 1570, the writer of the *Annals of Cuauhtitlan* accepted both major changes as they had unfolded, although he did so with evident hesitation. He employed much of the plot and even the language of the Tepepolco version, but he turned Quetzalcoatl into a king as well as a priest (Huemac becomes a later king), and described him as abhorring human sacrifice (he desires only butterflies and snakes). Yet oddly, despite the author's decision to do this, he apparently was not entirely comfortable with it, perhaps because he could not find any evidence for either amendment among his local sources. He wrote, "5 House. In this year, the Toltecs went to get Quetzalcoatl to make him ruler of Tollan as well as their priest." He did not quote any dialogue or offer any details as he usually did in cases of such moment, adding only, "The story of it has been written elsewhere." Apparently, he knew that the pages rendering Quetzalcoatl a king were safely stored in Tlatelolco.

The author faced a comparable conundrum not many pages later, when he needed to assert that human sacrifice did not begin until after the time of Quetzalcoatl: "Every kind of human sacrifice that there used to be got started then [in his successor's reign]. It is told and related that during his time and under his authority, the first Quetzalcoatl, whose name was One Reed, absolutely refused to perform human sacrifice. It was precisely when Huemac [later] was ruler that all those things that used to be done got started. It was the devils who started them."[108] Yet the narrator now had a problem, for even in his own account, humans had been sacrificed on prior pages. He needed, once again, to refer his readers elsewhere, almost disowning personal responsibility for the assertions he was making. "This has been put on paper and written down elsewhere," he added. Nowhere else in his long narrative, beyond the story of Quetzalcoatl, did he make comparable comments.

There was one element that was written on certain pages stored on the shelves in Tlatelolco that the writer in Cuauhtitlan did not mention. That was the prophecy of a return of an apotheosized Quetzalcoatl, which later became so prominent. He may have rejected it, but it is possible the writer did not even have to wrestle with the question of whether to include it, for he may not have known of it. It did not appear either in the version of the story originally taken down in Tepepolco, or in the later rewritten one. It did appear elsewhere in Sahagún's great work, but in the briefest of accounts and the oddest of formats. The first time it appeared, in a series of descriptions of the evil natures of the old gods, the friar's writing team spent more time denying the validity of any such belief than they did in describing it: "The ancients held that Quetzalcoatl went to Tlapallan, but that he will return. He is still expected. This is not true. It is falsehood. For his body died. Here on earth it became dust, it became filth. And our Lord God damned his soul."[109] Only in a text from the mid-1580s, the period in which Sahagún finalized Book 12, the story of the conquest, do we find a mention of the prophecy with no qualifiers or disavowals, simply as an important element of the story as it unfolds.[110] It had not yet appeared in any other indigenous writings whatsoever, but only in the work of such Spaniards as Motolinia, Andrés de Tapia, Francisco López de Gómara, and Bartolomé de las Casas.[111] They were widely read, but not yet by many indigenous,[112] so San Buenaventura may have left Mexico City before the notion of a significant prophecy became an issue in general conversation.

If the author of the *Annals of Cuauhtitlan* could not help but be engaged in discussion with the men he had known so well in earlier years, it is nevertheless clear that such debate was certainly *not* his primary goal. What he was trying to do—at least in a conscious sense—was to record for posterity all that he could of the history of the ancients. Such knowledge was well within his compass. There is no text that reveals more clearly the political realities of the preconquest world, for example.[113] The world the author represents is one that teems with life, with shifting political alliances and identities. Its people struggle to control resources and hence to bend one another to their will. Indeed, in some ways it can be characterized as a drama of mutual captivities and of fecund unions. Sometimes, it is a story of both at once. "Quetzalcoatl was placed in his mother's belly when she swallowed a piece of turquoise." In Mesoamerican lore, Chimalman was not the only woman to be impregnated almost against her will, through no knowing act of her own.[114] Nor was she the only woman to turn the tables on her captors or on those who duped her, and have her own son rise to prominence, whatever might have been expected at the time of his engendering.[115] The text shows itself at every turn to be a product of traditional Nahua storytelling. The author transcribed the words of those who grew up hearing the same kinds of tales as did don Alonso Chimalpopoca, the prime mover behind the *Historia Tolteca Chichimeca*. His purpose was not to argue with Spaniards, but rather to record a world of which they knew nothing.

In these annals, the historical characters are often mythic and are usually larger than life, yet that does not render them entirely unreal, for they are not flattened, but multidimensional. In different situations, they show different sides of themselves; they change. They render those who created them, who imagined them on firelit evenings, more visible in our own imagination. Certainly the speaker of the words, whoever he was, remembered clearly the elders who must have scared him when he was a child, telling him of the morning star's arrows of death reserved on certain days for certain people. Memories flooded him; he could still feel the chill, wondering, "Who is vulnerable to death today?" But the writer, the organizer of the text, was someone who could bring the voices to heel and order them coherently enough for others to hear them almost as well as he could. It was clearly a project he worked on for years.

One day, he sat with various notes in front of him, trying to recount the arrival of the Spaniards' first exploratory mission, the one that had come the year before the arrival of Hernando Cortés.[116] He apparently had with him some actual notes, or at least specific memories drawn from the work done years before in Tlatelolco.[117] These told him that the newcomers first arrived in Cuetlaxtlan, where the chief was named Pinotl. He went to speak to the Spaniards, accompanied by other leaders, two of whom were named Tentlil and Cuitlapitoc. The writer then made an equivocal comment, explaining that they first took the strangers for gods (*teotl*), because that is what they called their own devils, "such as Nauhecatl Tonatiuh and Quetzalcoatl," but it is not clear if he meant, as he had when he used the same word in his story of Quetzalcoatl, that such "devils" (*tlatlacatecollo*) were the priests and wizards of the old gods, rather than the gods themselves. In the same sentence he added that "later they called them Christians," as if he did indeed mean to imply that people were named for the gods they worshipped, embodied by their priests.

In any case, in the exchange that followed, the obviously human Spaniards learned that Moctezuma was the leader with whom they would have to treat, and they determined to visit him. They sent him gifts by way of the emissaries. Here the writer turned to a list that those who worked with Sahagún either had not had or had not thought important enough to use: the Christians presented one green cassock, two capes (one black, one red), another piece of cloth, a drinking cup, and some beads.

We do not know what the writer worked on next, or if he worked again at all, for there the text abruptly ends. Did he plan to go on to recount the years that followed? Did he in fact do so in documents now lost to us? Perhaps that was never his goal. He knew it had been done and was being done elsewhere. And it would have involved a much more direct reckoning with the Spanish presence than he had yet undertaken, a presence which had clearly been a significant factor in his own past life as well as that of his people. A few pages back, Moctezuma had received a most unwelcome prognostication: he must cease to demand tribute to honor the god Huitzilopochtli, or he would "invite the destruction of his people." A new lord and master, a new creator was coming. "He will arrive," he was warned.[118] Perhaps the continuation into the present was not a welcome project to the writer in Cuauhtitlan. Certainly he would not have been the first historian or the last to find the past most freeing to his mind.

In the end, it is difficult to tell exactly how disconcerted either this writer or don Mateo Sánchez was toward the close of life. What we can see in each case are signs of disturbance of what might be called their inner peace. Through their lives, they had spoken actively and had asserted themselves to some extent in their relations with their Franciscan teachers. Yet it would remain for future generations to learn to fit comfortably within this New World they had forged together.

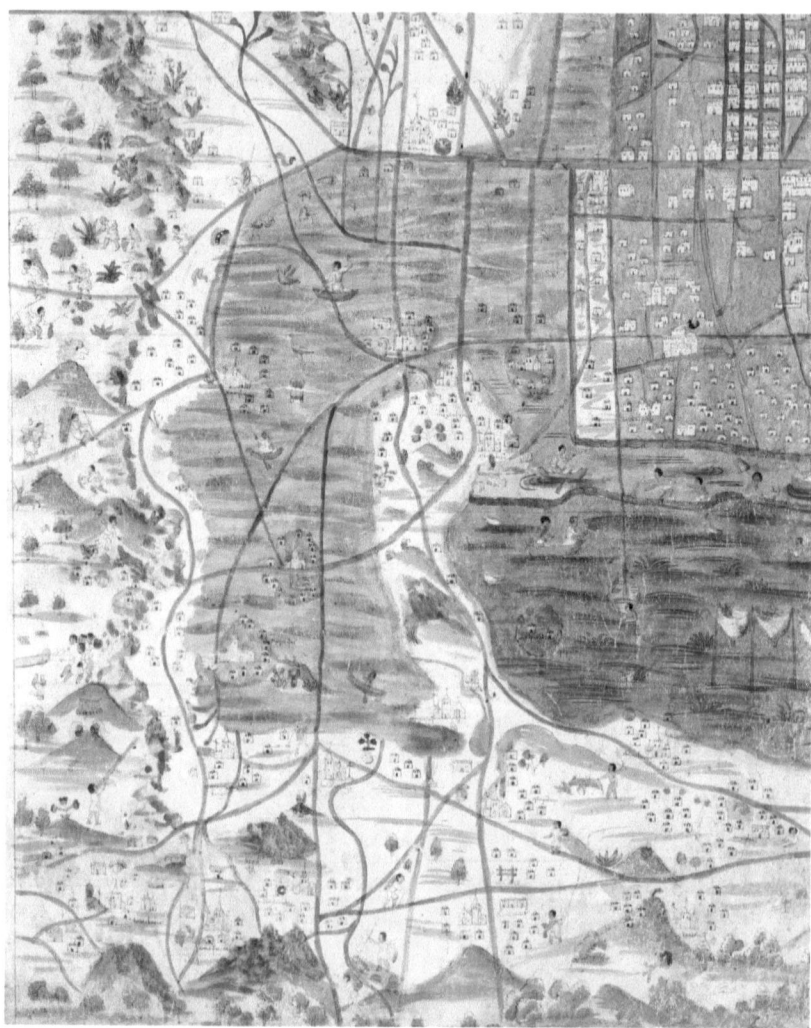

Fig 4.1 Segment of the *Mapa Santa Cruz*, painted by indigenous artists in Tlatelolco, mid-sixteenth century. This section shows Chimalpahin's world, ranging from Chalco (at the bottom) to the entrance to Mexico City (at the top) where he lived as an adult. He experienced the beginning of the attempt to drain this aquatic environment. Courtesy Uppsala University Library.

4

The Riches of Twilight (Circa 1600)

In the annals recorded by Chimalpahin,[1] many tales are told:

[f.174v]
13 Reed Year, 1479. In this year there was an earthquake. All the houses and palaces were damaged, and many of the hill[sides] crumbled. The people of Tochcalco were also defeated then. Then in the same year the Chalca people of Amaquemecan and Tlalmanalco went to sing in [the city of] Mexico for the first time. They went to perform the "Chalca Woman's Song,"[2] singing it for the tlatoani Axayacatzin. The singing and dancing began in the patio of the palace, while Axayacatzin was inside with his women. The song was moving slowly. A nobleman from Tlalmanalco was playing with bad rhythm. He fainted on one of the great drums. He just drooped over the drum, not knowing how to play. And there next to the drum was standing someone named Quecholcohuatzin. He was an Amaquemecan nobleman, a great singer and drummer. When he saw that the music, the song and the dance, were to be ruined, he quickly went over to stand by the drum and began to play it, reanimating the dancing so that it wasn't ruined. Thus Quecholcohuatzin guided the singing and dancing. The Tlalmanalcan nobleman, the one who was going to guide the singing, was just drooping. Inside, Axayacatl was listening, and when he heard how marvelously this Quecholcohuatzin played, and how he guided the singing, his heart was animated. At that he stood up, went out from where he was with his women, and went to dance. When he got to the dance floor, Axayacatzin lifted up one foot, completely happy in hearing the music, and began to dance and move in circles.

When the dancing finished [f.175], the tlatoani Axayacatzin said, "Greetings, my humble one! You will bring over to me the one who played and led the singing, without fail." The people answered him, "Very well, lord king. So it shall be." When Axayacatzin gave this order, all the Chalca nobles were really frightened, looking questions at each other. They were really frightened. They thought he meant the Tlalmanalcan nobleman who was first playing and leading the singing. (According to what the elders say, his name was Cuateotzin. Perhaps there was another nobleman with this name, for it had been thirty-four years since the death of the second of the two lords with this name who had ruled in Tlalmanalco; he was no longer with them.) The Chalca people thought that perhaps he was going to burn or stone the singer, the musician. The Chalca noblemen said, "Our singer hurt us, left us in a bad way. What are we going to do? Will we be burned [to death] here?"

The tlatoani Axayacatzin had gone into the palace to go sit with the noble ladies, his women. Then he sent to have Quecholcohuatzin, the one who danced and sang, called and brought to him. The messengers said, they asked the Chalca nobles, "Where is your singer, your drummer? The lord king summons him, and we have come to bring him inside." At that they answered, they said, "Yes, here he is, let the lord see him." With that the Chalca nobles called over the young Quecholcohuatzin. They thought that the tlatoani Axayacatzin would condemn him to death, would burn him. Thus he went in, pausing at the entrance, considering what judgment would come forth from the king. It was as though the Chalca were choking on a stone,[3] they were so scared. When Quecholcohuatzin arrived before Axayacatzin, he kissed the earth and went on one knee, saying to him, "O lord king, may you burn me, I who am your vassal, for we have done wrong in your presence." But the tlatoani Axayacatzin did not want to hear these words, saying to the ladies his women, "Women, stand up and meet him, seat him amongst you. Here has come your rival. Look at him and know him well, for I have deflowered him. May your hearts be happy, o women, for what has happened. This Quecholcohuatl made me dance and sing. Never before had anyone called me forth from inside, caused me to go out and dance as he has done. Henceforth he will be your rival. From now on I take him as my singer."

Then Axayacatl made much of him, giving him a cloak and breeches, even a cloak and breeches and sandals embroidered with turquoise that had been his. Quecholcohuatzin's gifts also included a headdress of quetzal feathers and a number of bundles of cloth and cacao beans.[4]

[The king] really loved him because he got him to dance. Axayacatl made him his own so that he would sing only for him and no longer go anywhere to sing for others.

Then the king commanded Quecholcohuatzin to go back outside. He was wearing his turquoise cloak and breeches and sandals, carrying his gifts of fabric and cacao. When the Chalca saw it they were really happy. They had been thinking that perhaps the [Mexica] had already enclosed him in a cage or burned him. They greeted [congratulated] whoever had been afraid!

The tlatoani Axayacatzin really loved and was made happy by the "Chalca Warrior Woman's Song." Again and again he summoned all the Chalca nobles, asking them for the song, especially those who were Amaquemecan, because "the Chalca Warrior Woman's Song" was really their property and their song. A nobleman there named Quiyauhtzin Cuauhquiyahuacatzintli had arranged [composed] it. He was a great creator of songs. There [in Chalco] the name of the tlatoani Huehue Ayoquantzin Chichimecateuhctli was mentioned in the song. He was the tlatoani of Itztlacozauhcan Totolimpan. But when Axayacatzin asked for the song, they made some exchanges in it. They took out and erased the name of the king, Huehue Ayoquantzin. They put into the song the king named Axayacatzin. There in the aforementioned year the said tlatoani Axayacatzin made the song his own, his property. He would have people sing it in his palace home when he wanted to feel happy, and he always wanted the said Quecholcohuatzin to sing it, the one who later [after the arrival of the Spaniards] was named don Jerónimo. He really loved him, and used to have him come to sing it in Mexico. This song became the property of Axayacatl's son, Tezozomoctli Acolnahuacatl, and of his son, Axayacatl's grandson, don Diego de Alvarado Huanitzin. He was tlatoani of Ehcatepec and afterward governor of Tenochtitlan. They, too, used to have people sing and dance in their palace in Mexico, because the song was really impressive. And because of it Amaquemecan was famous, an altepetl which now appears only small and unimportant.

***

Domingo was a well-loved child. As he grew up, his family told him about the night of his birth in rich detail. May 26, 1579, had been a Tuesday. He made his appearance near midnight, just before the turn of the next day, so it was on the eve of the ascension of the Christ, forty days out from the resurrection. The family thought about that as dawn came. When Domingo came into the world, he was the welcome ninth generation of a lordly family of Chalco, on the southeastern edge of the Valley of Mexico, near the pass between the mountains of Popocatepetl and Iztaccihuatl. Later, he would be known to his friends as Domingo de San Antón because he worked for so many years at the church of San Antonio Abad in the capital. He would become a prolific writer and style himself don Domingo Francisco de San Antón Chimalpahin Cuauhtlehuanitzin, the indigenous names coming down to him from his ancestors. Posterity would dub him simply "Chimalpahin." We know more about Chimalpahin than we do about any other colonial indigenous historian, but even in his case, the available facts are few and far between. We glean them not from legal documents, where he does not seem to appear, as he lived a quiet life, but from his own writings.[5]

Chimalpahin certainly understood himself to be a product of the history he loved to write. The Chalcan kingdoms he was proud to hail from had been settled by Nahuas coming down from the north between 1261 and 1303. They drove out the previous settlers alongside a great lake. The annals his ancestors preserved tell us this, as does the archaeological record.[6] The Chalca people were not a single ethnic group; rather, a series of migrant groups had arrived and gradually joined to form a polity by the banks of the emerald-green waters (Chalchiuhmatlalatl) that they identified with their green-skirted goddess, Chalchiuhtlicue, and they also borrowed the common root of these words to name themselves. "It is as if they called themselves 'people of the shore,'" explained Chimalpahin.[7] Chalco consisted of the Nahuas' usual four parts, in this case called Tlalmanalco, Amaquemecan, Tenanca-Pepopolla, and Chimalhuacan, always cited in that order, reflecting their size and importance. Each of the quadrants was itself knit together from varied political subunits, each with its own noble lineage. The subunits also often numbered four, but they did not always, reality sometimes not being so neat, as additional groups of migrants could show up and ask to join. Chimalpahin's family was from Amaquemecan, and within that, from the second of its five kingdoms, the one called Tzaqualtitlan Tenanco. (The others were Itztlacozauhcan, Tequanipan, Panohuayan, and Tlailotlacan.) Within his beloved Tzaqualtitlan Tenanco, there were six calpolli units or "great houses," one might say "lineages," or "clans," one of which traditionally ruled over the others. On his father's side, Chimalpahin descended from the line of kings (tlatoani) until four generations previously, when his branch of the family descended from a younger brother of the king. This was Huehue Chimalpahin, himself a great nobleman and progenitor of noblemen. On his mother's side, Chimalpahin was descended from the elder-brother king himself (Cuauhtlehuanitzin, his other namesake), but through a son who did not become king. Such figures were called *tlatocapilli*, or kingly noblemen, and they constituted the ruler's closest relatives, and indeed could be named king themselves should occasion arise, but their family did not normally in fact contain the tlatoani. So Chimalpahin was a scion of what one might call the lesser nobility, but proud of his ancestry nonetheless.[8]

The fertile lakeshore lands of Chalco rendered the state vulnerable, as did its proximity to the path leading to the lands of the east, with their varied tropical goods. The Chalca had come there as conquerors themselves, so it probably came as little surprise to them that they had to spend decades defending themselves from the rapacious Mexica once the latter's star began to rise. Eventually, they lost their war against the expanding Aztec state. The embittered Chalca became tributaries to Tenochtitlan in 1464. Twenty years went by before their protests at being treated as a conquered people bore fruit and they were allowed to reinstate their rulers and come to the table to counsel the Aztec overlord as supporters rather than as cringing victims. It delighted Chimalpahin that a clever nobleman from Amaquemecan, a talented poet-singer—who was apparently irresistibly attractive as well—played a key role in bringing this change about. In the epic multi-generational story narrated by Chimalpahin, it was the conquest by the Mexica more than the conquest by the Spanish that seemed to dominate his imagination. It was, after all, in the first instance and not the second that his people had lost their independence forever.

By the time Chimalpahin was growing up, even the conquest by the Spanish was two generations old. A revered grandfather for whom he was named, another Domingo, his mother's father, a tlatocapilli who could trace his ancestry back 369 years, had been born around the time of the conquest.[9] Those who had been born before then were not known to young Domingo and his peers. By then, Amaquemecan had long been a Dominican-run parish. Either the friars taught him his letters, or some indigenous person who had learned at their side did so, for he became fully fluent in Spanish and in the art of writing, as only someone who has been exposed as a child can be. The friars and their students talked. Fray Pedro del Castillo, who served in Amaquemecan, told Domingo (or perhaps someone else close to him) how awful he felt when, over twenty years before Chimalpahin was born, the Dominicans had married the tlatoani of neighboring Tequanipan to a young woman named Juana from Cuitlahuac, and within a year and a half, he had murdered her.[10]

When Chimalpahin was no more than twelve, he was sent to Mexico City. Most likely his scholarly abilities had recommended him to the friars and they sent him to an acquaintance to work and continue his education, but we cannot be sure. It is also possible that his family sent him to stay with relatives, as the Chalcan nobility maintained connections with kin living in the metropolis.[11] The annals Chimalpahin later wrote about his own times center on Mexico City, and he begins to say "here" in the metropolis with some regularity in 1590, when he was eleven. The entries become much more detailed, with a true first-person perspective, in the early months of 1591. "The grasshoppers came at four o'clock, raised up like a wind-axe...." "Sunday the 26th was when they sent two jaguars off to Spain. They took the two that had been housed in the community palace [in San Juan Moyotlan]."[12] He also later commented in Spanish that he had lived in the city "from the time he was a very young child,"[13] which he would not have said if he had been older than twelve when he came. We do not know where he lived, but he seems to have worshipped at the church of San Francisco and the associated indigenous chapel of San Josef de los Naturales, the doings of which he knew a great deal about.

Meanwhile, certain local events were unfolding which would have a direct impact on his life. Immediately after the conquest, in 1530, one Alonso Sánchez had purchased a piece of land for an *hermita*, a little chapel, in Xoloco, at the edge of the causeway leading from Iztapalapa into Tenochtitlan. It was exactly where Hernando Cortés had first come face to face with Moctezuma. In 1570, a younger relative, perhaps a son, named Diego Sánchez de Muñón began to build a real church there. It was completed in 1591, when the sacrament was taken out in procession from the church for the first time. A family member named don Sancho Sánchez de Muñón was the church's patron. He was a prominent priest, a leading member of the cathedral council who in the 1580s had even briefly served as acting archbishop. What he undoubtedly learned rather quickly was that managing a specific church, even a small one, required a great deal of work. He needed reliable help; he would ask his fellow church men whom they recommended.[14]

Chimalpahin simply tells us that on Tuesday, October 5, 1593, when he was fourteen years old, he "entered the church of San Antonio Abad."[15] Not long after, apparently sometime in 1594, the highly competent adolescent was made the mayoral, the general manager of all matters relating to the indigenous parishioners, and probably of the physical plant as well. He would remain in that position for three decades, until the church closed. But he could not know then that it would turn out so. At the time, he was a very young man trying to make sense of his place in the world. In the record he was keeping, he wrote from the perspective of the church—except sometimes, when he became very explicitly an Indian in a Spanish world. In 1595, "a proclamation was made at the San Hipólito market about how we are to pay tribute in chickens in the [city of] Mexico; we were assigned a tribute of 7,400-odd chickens."[16] The city's indigenous peoples suddenly had to come up with the money to contribute toward a massive annual purchase of chickens for use in various Spanish institutions. The Spaniards were not perturbed by how difficult it would be for them to find the money, or the poultry. It was a sharp reminder of what it meant to be an Indian, no matter how privileged, and Chimalpahin suddenly used the form "we."

Then a few months later, a terrible epidemic of measles began. It would abate but then return. For two years this went on. "The epidemic raged terribly, there was a great deal of death. Infants who could already raise themselves up quite well and crawl, youths and maidens, grown men, mature men and women, and old men and women, all died."[17] The language he used was reminiscent of ancient prayers to Tlaloc in times of drought, though he surely did not realize this. "With pallid eyes live the babies, the children, those who totter, those who crawl, those who spend their time [as farmers] turning dirt and potsherds in their hands," the priests used to intone. "All the people face torment, affliction."[18] The prayer, in a sense, had come down to him as a manner of speaking, and it remained part of his thought in the Spanish city as people fell sick around him.

If in some ways the young Chimalpahin felt isolated and even terrified, in other ways he felt himself to be part of a great project, a far-flung network of Christian men leaving their homes and traveling great distances to work on behalf of the souls of all earth's people. In 1591 he had reported on the departure of hundreds of Tlaxcalans for the northern wildlands of New Mexico. They would become the pillar of the Franciscans' settlement effort there. In 1598, a long letter came from friars in Santa Fe, reporting on all that had happened since their departure. Two indigenous musicians known to Chimalpahin had gone, as well as an indigenous lay brother from Amaquemecan. He proudly referred to each of them by name. "There was great rejoicing here in Mexico [after the letter was read], and a procession was held at the cathedral."[19] Only a few months later, sadder news came from Asia: "Sunday, the 6th of the month of December of the year 1598, in the afternoon, was when the bones of the Discalced fathers who died in Japan in the land of China arrived. It was afternoon when the friars arrived; they came carrying them enclosed in chests. All the religious who are here in Mexico went to meet them; when they reached [the church of] San Diego, the guns were discharged. How they died and what happened there was painted on four cloths which were hung at the church of San Josef; everyone saw and admired them, the Spaniards and we indigenous."[20] Chimalpahin went on to record with fascination all the Mexican dealings with Japan and the Philippines. He cared not only about the conversion story, but also about those faraway people's secular realities. And he understood them to some extent. At one point, he even referred to the "indigenous" people of the Philippines.[21]

In December of 1600, when Chimalpahin was twenty-one, his patron don Sancho Muñón died.[22] The young Domingo had been interested in his people's history before, but now he began to think of the passage of time in a new way. In April, when they took down a decades-old monument, he thought about the rise and fall of earthly leaders:

Wednesday, the 11th day of the month of April of the year 1601, was when they took down the big cross, very high, that stood in the churchyard of San Francisco, that was raised by our precious father fray Pedro de Gante, the lay friar and teacher, along with the twelve friars who first arrived here in Mexico. It was raised in the year of 1531, 13 Reed in the old year count; it was thirteen years after the Spaniards arrived when it was put up. And the cross had stood for 69 years and three months on the 11th day of April, and when it fell and was taken down, it had been a time of eighty-two years, three months, and eleven days since the Spaniards arrived. Many lords died in its time—viceroys and Audiencia judges who came to rule in Mexico, and Mexica rulers and nobles, and bishops and friars....[23]

In 1604, great flooding began that lasted for several years and swept away old buildings and causeways that stood a long time. In 1606 typhus came. In July it took Chimalpahin's father, and in October his seventy-two-year-old maternal grandmother.[24]

In the rainy season of 1607, even more terrible flooding began. Mexico City, in the center of a geological basin, was largely submerged in waters that rose about a foot over street level. People built temporary footbridges so they could get about. Those Spaniards who could left town. It was a desperate time, especially for the commoners living in adobe houses, which often fell in when their foundations got soaked.[25] In this crisis, the Spanish government concluded that they must take drastic steps to preserve their grand metropolis. They would begin a great drainage project. Thousands of indigenous people would undertake the labor. The people of the four parts of Chalco were told they must all contribute to digging a great channel that would direct some of the melting snow from the mountaintops away from the city; after months of work the project failed and was abandoned.[26] But the city fathers had not abandoned their principle. They had concluded that the water was best drained through the mountains to the north. They launched the project known as the Desagüe de Huehuetoca. Domingo of San Antón went somewhat mournfully about his business, working to preserve the church for which he was responsible and trying to help the waterlogged parishioners. On Christmas day, he heard a great commotion on the road coming from the south that went right past the church. Hundreds of huge logs had been brought as far as they could be by canoe and were now being carried on carts to further the reconstruction effort.[27] He looked, and saw that he knew the men who were bringing them. They were old comrades from Amaquemecan. They had been charged with bringing 11,000 logs down from their mountain woodlands to the city to aid in the public works project. "They were greatly afflicted by it; the married men of each household were assigned thirteen each. Everyone went together, no one stayed behind [at home]."[28]

It turned out that a modicum of good stemmed from the onerous assignment. Because of it, the Chalca were not called up in January along with all the other valley people to work on the great drainage project being undertaken at Huehuetoca. "There was an excavation so that the mountain was opened up, cut into, and a hole made in it. And they removed the bones of the dead from there; some of their bones were like those who lived formerly here on earth, whom the ancients, our grandmothers and grandfathers, named and called giants. . . . Very many indigenous people died there [at the drainage works], and some of the people from the various altepetl fell sick [or were hurt]."[29] In that very year, Chimalpahin began to write the history of his people's deep past. He would not see it swept away in the general devastation he saw everywhere.

His great work eventually took the form of eight sets of annals—usually called his *"ocho relaciones"*—set forth in one massive document of 272 folios, all written in his own hand. Four times in the course of his work he mentioned the year in which he was writing: in 1612, 1620, 1629, and 1631.[30] He had begun the project in 1608, however. In that year, in the annals of his own time that he consistently maintained, he suddenly made a major digression, traveling back many centuries to the ancient Nahuas' departure from Aztlan, and then continuing through time in a thumbnail sketch, as it were, of his people's historical annals. In effect, he wrote an outline that he would later fill out richly. And there is further evidence that he began his project in about 1608. In 1606 two published works appeared that clearly fell into his hands in the ensuing months and influenced him. One was Enrico Martínez's *Reportorio de los tiempos e historia natural de esta Nueva España*, large passages of which Chimalpahin borrowed and used in his 1608 digression as well as in the early sections of his new manuscript. Another was fray Juan Bautista Viseo's *Sermonario en lengua Mexicana*, published in Mexico City. We know that Chimalpahin read it, for a segment is incorporated in the annals he kept of his own times. In short, not long after his father and grandmother died, and as his people entered the crisis of the flooding, he read two works that made a deep impression on him—one a compendium of history, the other a beautiful new book printed in Nahuatl. Small wonder that he began to copy out his first set of historical Nahuatl annals in the midst of his write-up of the events of 1608 and had made significant progress on a full manuscript by 1612.[31]

Chimalpahin may have begun to collect materials—or at least note their whereabouts—years before. In his eighth and last "relation" he explained in detail what his sources had been, noting quite accurately that someday his readers would want to know.[32] One important book recording ancient doings in alphabetic text had been left to him by his father, who had himself obtained it from his father-in-law, don Domingo Hernández Ayochpotzin, the man's own sons (Chimalpahin's uncles on his mother's side) being but children at the time of his death. Certain pictorials had in fact been left to those uncles, who let Chimalpahin copy from them what he wanted. An additional short but valuable alphabetic account he obtained from his maternal great-grandfather's brother's family, who let him borrow and copy it.

Another extraordinary set of annals came from don Vicente de la Anunciación, a cousin of the same revered grandfather, don Domingo. Don Vicente said he had copied it from a book that had been in the possession of his own father-in-law, don Rodrigo de Rosas Xoecatzin, a nobleman from Itztlacozauhcan who had served as Amaquemecan's scribe in the 1540s. He would have been among the first generation of children to learn the roman alphabet, and he had put his skills to good use. In 1547, because the five sectors of Amaquemecan were squabbling about which of them should have a tlatoani, and which should be politically subordinated and pay tribute to the others, the viceroy don Antonio de Mendoza sent a judge, a high-ranking nobleman from Xochimilco, to settle the dispute. Don Rodrigo de Rosas acted as his scribe, transcribing all statements made. There was a great public meeting:

> So that the judge could investigate all the ancient pronouncements of all five segments of the altepetl, those who were the noble elders from here deliberated over it in a great gathering and put forth certain ancient tellings (*huehuetlatolli*). And they put down in written form, in a book, how the five segments had been organized, so that they could present it to the said judge. What the elders sought to present was really a true account, just like it had been, because it was impossible to lie before the others.[33]

Thus it was that Chimalpahin had access to the rich, swirling language and detailed stories of his great-grandfather's generation, almost as if he had been in the room with people who spoke differently and thought differently than he himself did. He had in fact stumbled on a 1540s transcription of ancient speeches very much like that which don Alonso de Castañeda, the orchestrator of the *Historia Tolteca Chichimeca*, had participated in producing elsewhere in the 1540s. Don Vicente and Chimalpahin both bemoaned the fact that the former had copied only part of the book that had been in his father-in-law's attic. Don Vicente had recently gone back to try to get the rest of the account, but the book was gone, presumably crumbled and then discarded, he said.[34]

These were Chimalpahin's sources for the ancient stories, but he had not yet finished explaining all his sources. Whence, his readers might want to know, had come the more recent materials, from the time around the conquest itself and all the years of the sixteenth century? For these accounts he turned not only to his relatives, but also to community elders (including at least one woman) whom he knew personally, who either loaned him accounts they had kept or spoke to him directly of what they remembered.[35] He was always aware of possible sources, noting, for example, when the people of Chalco sued the Jesuits over some land that all the related documents were now stored in the community palace archive.[36]

From the materials he gathered, Chimalpahin absorbed far more about traditional annals than that they proceeded year by year and focused on the polity as a whole. Perhaps from the document recording the great 1547 forum, or perhaps from fragments of recitations he had heard from elders as a child, he had gleaned, consciously or not, that his people's histories were in a sense pastiches, collections of accounts giving multiple points of view to audiences who heard a performance through. Like his ancestors, he believed that these varied accounts should appear in an orderly way, for taken together, they should prove a point. He used the words "arrange" and "order" to describe his role. Twice, he actually announced to his readers that he was about to paste two accounts together.[37] Then he did so, noting where each one began and ended. At other times he simply patched texts together as he saw fit, telling readers at other points that he had drawn from multiple sources, but not letting them see the seams.

As Chimalpahin worked, he frequently found himself interweaving the history of Tenochtitlan; it was, in fact, an essential element of the history of Chalco. But Tenochtitlan also had a claim on him in its own right. By now he had lived for most of his life in Mexico City. He had dear friends there; his relations with them constituted his daily life. He began to collect documents from among them. Eventually, he included among his eight relations one set of annals entirely devoted to the history of the Aztec state ("Memorial de Culhuacan"), and he also wrote a separate "Mexican chronicle," one version in Spanish and one in Nahuatl.[38] In his work on Tenochtitlan and its environs, however, Chimalpahin spoke less directly to posterity about the nature of his sources. In this case, he does not seem to have felt any urgency to prove that what he was writing was the truth or that it was important. There in the capital, surrounded by the remnants of the Aztec state, it would not have seemed necessary to defend accounts of the history of the Triple Alliance; nor would it have been his place to do so, as an outsider. But he recorded the various sets of annals that came his way nonetheless and then wove them into his own versions of history. Perhaps the most important document he copied was a history written by Tezozomoc.[39] He was of the royal line, the son of the same Huanitzin who inherited the rights to the beloved Chalca Woman's Song. Chimalpahin also copied numerous other texts that sometimes came with names, but often did not.[40] It was, apparently, quite easy to find people in the city who had accounts to share in this period, for a number of the texts written then survive to this day.[41] Tezozomoc certainly had a sense of his own importance—on one ceremonial occasion he was carried in a litter dressed in traditional garb in order to represent Moctezuma—but he was far from the only one to sense that the days were waning when there would be elders left alive who could give accounts to posterity. Even the early Nahua scholars who had been trained by the Franciscans and made their people proud were dying off by the early 1600s.[42]

Living in Mexico City at the same time was don Fernando de Alva Ixtlilxochitl, a mestizo historian from the Tetzcoco region who wrote in Spanish for an audience of Spaniards. He was a remarkable man who identified entirely as indigenous though he would not have had to, since his family was well-to-do and his father was a Spaniard who wanted him to go to university and become a priest. Of course, don Fernando's indigenous identification was partly so that his family could retain the chiefly lands they had inherited on their mother's side as descendants of the tlatoani of Teotihuacan (a vassal state of Tetzcoco), but it was also because he felt a deep pride in his maternal ancestors and a conviction that they and their history should be recognized as worthy of attention. His mother's family had raised him, and he spoke Nahuatl—indeed, numbers always came easier to him in Nahuatl than in Spanish, though he learned to write much better in Spanish[43]—so it was no fiction that he felt himself to be Indian. He spent decades collecting traditional pictorials and accounts in Nahuatl, then writing epic histories of the Nahuas in the European style. In his work, he insisted on the ancientness of Nahua history, on its intrinsic interest, and on its importance to the eventual historical outcome in the New World.[44]

Did don Fernando and Chimalpahin inspire each other, or share any sense of mission? There is no direct evidence that they knew each other, as neither ever mentioned the other's name in any extant writings, but there is significant indirect evidence that they were well aware of each other. Chimalpahin knew Ixtlilxochitl's Spanish grandfather, Juan Grande, personally, as he was the well-liked interpreter for the Audiencia for decades and often participated in projects himself, at least once alongside Chimalpahin, when they helped to measure out a drainage area in nearby Xochimilco.[45] Chimalpahin commented with deep sadness when Juan Grande died and probably attended his funeral. He also knew the Franciscan scholar fray Juan de Torquemada, constantly recording his comings and goings, and Torquemada was the special patron of Ixtlilxochitl: indeed, he was the one who had gotten the young Tetzcocan started in collecting Nahuatl documents from beyond his hometown.[46] In 1617, Ixtlilxochitl, who had sought a position as an indigenous judge-governor, was installed in Chimalpahin's home country of Chalco, first in Tlalmanalco, then in 1619 in Chalco Atenco.[47] Given these connections, not to mention their mutual interest in history, it would seem almost impossible that the two men never interacted. It should not surprise us that when he died, Chimalpahin's papers came into the hands of Ixtlilxochitl, who eventually left them in the keeping of his son. His son's longtime companion, the famous Carlos Sigüenza y Góngora, who was too young to have known Chimalpahin himself, referred to him as "el buen don Domingo" when he was sorting out the inherited papers.[48] Such a term of endearment for a man he had never known could only have come to him through the Ixtlilxochitl family.

It is difficult to picture the exact nature of Chimalpahin's relations with such local dignitaries as Tezozomoc or Ixtlilxochitl. Certainly he would have been deferential when he borrowed Tezozomoc's historical account to copy it, or perhaps offered Ixtlilxochitl condolences or congratulations. They were not his social equals, the one a grandson of Moctezuma who lived in wealth, the other in later years an interpreter for the Audiencia. Tezozomoc or Ixtlilxochitl, for example, could certainly have entered the library at the church of San Francisco as patrons; the latter undoubtedly did so, given the nature of some of the texts he mentions in his work. It is extremely doubtful, however, that an apparently ordinary indigenous man working as the mayoral of a small church could have entered as a library guest. On the other hand, the library would have been staffed by indigenous copyists who were friends and acquaintances of Chimalpahin's. He may even have worked part-time as just such a copyist. He probably could have borrowed any text he liked. References in his work certainly indicate that he read widely not only as a young student, but also as an adult (Enrico Martínez's 1606 *Reportorio*, for instance). We know that he copied out Bernardo de Sahagún's *Ejercicio quotidiano* as well as a copy of López de Gómara's proscribed biography of Hernando Cortés.[49] Whether or not he obtained them at San Francisco's library, sitting side by side with the likes of Ixtlilxochitl, he certainly had access to the Spanish world and Spanish print culture and, like the others, felt himself to be part of wider historical endeavors.

Domingo of San Antón's social stature increased over the years, as more people came to know of him and his work. He moved about the world speaking Spanish with only the faintest accent. (When he wrote out Spanish names he had never seen in writing, such as that of Juan Cano, the chosen husband of Moctezuma's daughter, he sometimes wrote them as Nahuas would have pronounced them, in this case, as "Juan Gano."[50]) He almost never misunderstood Spanish references or asides, except when his own frame of reference misled him. (For example, the causeways he had seen all had arches, but Aztec causeways had no arches, so he misunderstood Gómara when he mentioned "*ojos de la calzada.*"[51]). His classical education was always evident in the comments he made. He was known to the indigenous elite in the city and welcomed when he went home to Chalco for visits. Clearly, he met with respect when he looked into the eyes of others. Eventually, in his writings he even began to refer to himself by the long, grand name he chose ("Domingo Francisco de San Antón Muñón Chimalpahin Cuauhtlehuanitzin") and to include the title "don."

Chimalpahin's writings in the record he kept of his own times tell us that he remained a quiet man, with an understated sense of humor and a dry tone. In 1602, he attended a meeting of indigenous people who gathered to lodge a complaint about the rotary draft labor. Everyone had something to say. "Discussion was rather long," he commented, and in the end, of course, "it could not be abolished."[52] He could have told them that and saved the community some time. Years later, two factions at the university were arguing over who should be given the faculty position for the study of Latin. The winners (whose candidate Chimalpahin did not personally approve) put their man up on a horse and "went about like crazy people" shouting and celebrating.[53] This was a muted way of saying that the students and Augustinian friars involved should have been ashamed of themselves. Perhaps Chimalpahin's most memorable commentary appeared after a supposed plot on the part of the enslaved African population was uncovered. One can almost see the faint smile as he writes, "We Mexica indigenous were not at all frightened by it but were just looking and listening, just marveling at how the Spaniards were being destroyed by their fear, and didn't appear as such great warriors [after all]." [54]

Yet beneath the quiet exterior, without any grandiosity, Chimalpahin nevertheless apparently came to feel strongly that his life had a significant purpose. In 1613, a new viceroy arrived and was ceremoniously installed. "May our lord God deign to guard him for me for many years, may he give him good health and a long life, as we people everywhere wish—and especially to me separately it is an even greater obligation and duty that I, don Domingo de San Antón Muñón Cuauhtlehuanitzin Chimalpahin, wish it."[55] This was a polite manner of speaking in the Spanish world, and it was certainly in the Spanish world that Chimalpahin had first heard something like it. Yet he was not in the habit of employing flowery Spanish phrases in his histories. It was unusual for him. In 1613, he had been at work on his project for several years. The pages he had written thus far were filled with the deaths of great men and ordinary men. There had been an epidemic around the time of his birth and others since. Yet he himself still lived, and was still able to do his important work. Perhaps he truly felt that he was a particularly fortunate man and had a special duty to pray for good fortune for others. He often turned to Saint Augustine's *Confessions*, an old favorite of his, one of the first books he quoted as he began his great work, mentioning the first part of the work in particular.[56] At the close of Book I, he read:

> And yet, Lord, even if you had willed that I should not survive my childhood, I should have owed you gratitude, because you are our God, the supreme Good, the Creator and Ruler of the universe. For even as a child I existed, I was alive, I had the power of feeling: I had an instinct to keep myself safe and sound, to preserve my own being, which was a trace of the single unseen Being from whom it was derived; ... and even in the small things which occupied my thoughts I found pleasure in the truth. I disliked finding myself in the wrong; my memory was good; I was acquiring the command of words; I enjoyed the company of friends; and I shrank from pain, ignorance, and sorrow. Should I not be grateful that so small a creature possessed such wonderful qualities? But they were all gifts from God, for I did not give them to myself. His gifts are good and the sum of them all is my own self. Therefore, the God who made me must be good and all the good in me is his. I thank him and praise him for all the good in my life....[57]

***

Looking at it matter-of-factly, we do not have to wonder why Chimalpahin wrote. He told his readers that it was to ensure that the past would not be forgotten. He felt this even in the relatively little things in life. "The reason that I have recorded here that there are still only three houses facing the church of my precious father San Antonio is that the Mexica and citizens who live and are born later will see and know that it was still just like this when I set down and recorded the account of the lake that is there now, in case it is later seen at some future time that it is filled with churches, monasteries and houses that are there where now nothing appears yet, and it is full of water all around."[58] If such changes mattered to him, so much more urgent did the preservation of his people's past seem. He made passionate promises, using the old-style metaphors of his people: "It will never be lost or forgotten. It will always be preserved. We will preserve it, we who are the younger brothers, the children, grandchildren, great-grandchildren and great-great-grandchildren, we who are the beards, eyebrows, nails, color and blood, we who are the descendants of the Tlailotlacas, we who have been born and lived in the tlaxilacalli segment of Tlailotlacan Tecpan, where lived and governed all the precious ancient Chichimeca kings."[59]

Because Chimalpahin so frequently asserts the ancientness and importance of his own altepetl in his writings, he has often been thought of as addressing Chalcan posterity, preserving their records for future generations, so that they would have them when they needed them, whether in a literal or figurative sense. And indeed, inserts within his papers do show that in the 1660s, after his death, they were loaned to the community of Itztlacozauhcan to help them in a legal battle.[60] But Chimalpahin was participating in a wide and deep Nahua tradition that went far beyond Chalco when he asserted the need to keep chaos at bay by remembering and passing on to a changing future the way things had been, and the reason they had been that way. The artisans of San Juan Moyotlan quoted their ancestors on the supreme importance of remembering the old ways of one's people, one's community, and the danger of forgetting: "Is it here [at this point in time] that we throw it out, that it passes on, the breath, the words of the altepetl, its exhausting efforts, its sacrifices? Thus they used to speak, the old-timers."

As one scholar has noted, the Nahuas' very religion was based on the carefully kept record of a succession of imploding and renewing worlds, none of which was ever forgotten.[61] And ever since the beginning of this the fifth world, mortals had dealt with the overwhelming passage of time ordained by the quixotic gods by remembering. They even remembered how they had remembered. Writing an alphabetic text in black ink so that the stories would last forever, Chimalpahin nevertheless paid homage to the older form of writing, so that at least all reference to it, to the red and the black, would not disappear:

> Here will be said and told, the relations about the ancient way of life, the painted words about the ancient kingships. This accounting is no simple fable, story or invention, but rather is the truth about all that happened. Thus they left us, spoken and painted, their ancient words, the elder men and the elder women, the kings and nobles of Tzacualtitlantenanca, our grandfathers and grandmothers, great-grandfathers and great-grandmothers, our ancestors who came to live here. Such is the relation that they made, that they left for us. This relation of the altepetl and of the altepetl's kingly lines, painted and written on paper in red and black, will never be lost, never be forgotten. It will be preserved forever.[62]

Several historians have noted that Chimalpahin was in fact imagining an audience beyond the Chalca people.[63] Of course he wrote for his own ethnic group's posterity, but he wrote for others as well. It was not that he addressed himself to Spaniards. He never petitioned them for anything. He never seems to have feared their censorship, though it was theoretically forbidden to write of the old pagan ways in the period when he worked, assuredly because he knew they would not bother to read what he wrote.[64] He betrays no defensiveness toward them in his tone; he does not seem to have thought of them as an audience at all. No, the readers he seems to have imagined, like the closest friends he mentions in his work, were indigenous, but not all Chalca. He wrote for educated Nahuas of future generations, whatever altepetl they might hail from. He collected material and recounted stories not only from Chalco, but also from Tenochtitlan, Tlatelolco, Tetzcoco, Azcapotzalco, and Coatlichan, among others. And he commented reverently, assuming that his readers would be interested, when descendants of the nobility of other altepetls whom he knew passed away. But there is more subtle evidence than this that in his mind's eye he was speaking to a more generalized Nahua audience. One historian points out, for example, that in commenting on Gómara's *Conquista de México* as he copied it, he explains that the old god Ome Tochtli was very like Bacchus, or that the wild Otomí warrior should be thought of as a sort of Arab.[65] This is the type of aside one might make if one wanted to communicate with a fellow Nahua who had had a good European education but knew little about the ways of his own ancestors. At times, Chimalpahin even seems to have expected some skepticism among such readers. He assures them that he will tell them where he obtained the information in these old histories, "so that you the reader, you who are a Christian, may not doubt or waver."[66] When he refers to "Christians" in this case, he does not mean Spaniards, as he might have meant if he were writing nearer the conquest; he means simply Indians of the Christian faith, who have a modern, Hispanized outlook and will need to be convinced that he has done more than look at some of the old paintings that no one can read anymore and then make up a good yarn to go with them. We can be certain of this, because he then launches into his detailed explanation as to which families in Chalco gave him which documents, and how the rich source of 1547 was produced in the midst of the major intra-altepetl dispute, facts that most Spanish readers could not have followed and would not have been interested in even if they could have.

Only once did Chimalpahin write a whole text in Spanish. It was a history of the Mexica, and judging from its content and its placement among his papers, it seems to have been intended as a sort of introduction to—or explanation of—Tezozomoc's "Crónica mexicayotl," which followed. Tezozomoc's words were clearly addressed to Mexica posterity: "What [the ancestors] came to do, what they came to establish, their writings, their renown, their history, their memory, will never perish, will never be forgotten in times to come.... We shall always keep them, we sons, grandsons, younger brothers, great-great-grandchildren, great-grandchildren, we, their descendants, their offspring; and those children of the Mexica, those children of the Tenochca yet to live, yet to be born, will go on telling of them, will go on celebrating them." As Chimalpahin's general reason for writing (or recopying) lengthy histories was very much in accord, it is safe to say he found no fault with

Tezozomoc's thinking. He would not have included a Spanish synthesis and interpretation for the benefit of a Spanish audience, for he did not imagine one. Why go to the trouble, then? Perhaps he included it for the same reason we today are glad to have it: on their own, Tezozomoc's statements, taken down as he says from his father and uncle, are hard for later peoples to understand: "And the Mexica thereupon performed penances there at the place named Quinehuayan Tzotzompan. They laid down their fir branches. Four times they returned. . . . [The leader] spoke. 'Our friends,' he said to the Mexica, 'for this we have come; for this have we emerged from our home in Aztlan.' "[67] It would have been almost as much a relief to Chimalpahin's neighbors as to us to read elsewhere in clear Spanish, "They were a most robust, wise and warlike people . . . the people of Quinehuayan. Having emerged and come from their land in the north, called the great province and island of the city of Aztlan, they then came out at the site of Chicomoztoc or the Seven Caves, site of sacrifices."[68] If Chimalpahin really wanted Tezozomoc's words to be preserved and valued for all time, then he would have wanted to be certain posterity would understand enough of their content to render them useful.

Tellingly, Tezozomoc was not the only illustrious personage whose work Chimalpahin felt free to take and use as he saw fit in his work on behalf of educated Nahuas. Europeans were likewise fair game. He paraphrased or translated into Nahuatl passages from Plato, Saint Augustine, and many other European authors with perfect aplomb. When he copied out Gómara's work, he periodically made corrections and side comments, and in so doing, as one historian has put it, he truly "turned the tables"[69] on the Spanish, given their practice of borrowing and using indigenous sources however they liked. (Indeed, if Chimalpahin did work on that project in the library of the San Francisco church, he would not have been many yards distant from Torquemada, sitting in another room at the same time, busily extracting from his protegé Ixtlilxochitl's work whatever he liked, and then distorting it in preparation for use in his *Monarquía Indiana*.) Yet Chimalpahin did this without any ostentation or even any apparent self-consciousness.

It was not that Chimalpahin was entirely unaware that certain tensions existed in his world between Spaniards and indigenous. When there was a threat of a slave rebellion, he gently mocked the Spaniards who showed fear despite all their power, and he once showed real discomfort when it turned out that a prison breakout that left several dead had been orchestrated by Indians. "Nothing like this, like what these fellows did, had ever happened before; because of it the Spaniards thought very badly of us."[70] He showed pride when a feisty indigenous woman named María López, a chocolate seller, brought justice down upon a particularly cruel friar, the chaplain at San Josef, by going to the higher authorities when he whipped her husband. The chaplain had long behaved atrociously, according to Chimalpahin. "He thought nothing of the Mexica." Yet a lowly woman broke the silence. No one would have dared to, "if it hadn't been for the said María López, who was so bold as to accuse him before the lord judges of the Audiencia."[71] But Chimalpahin did not generalize about Spaniards from his experiences with this chaplain. According to Chimalpahin, this friar was a particularly evil man who would receive his due in the next life; he was not at all the norm. Chimalpahin also definitely gave the Spaniards credit where he believed they deserved it: he explained the nature of eclipses as he had learned of it from European scientific works, commenting to his potential Nahua audience that "our forefathers" had not been able to understand the phenomenon because they lived in confusion until God arranged for the discovery of the New World.[72] In the end, he respected the social order, commenting with a trace of disapproval that the relatives of doña Isabel, daughter of Moctezuma, "have become Spaniards."[73] He especially did not approve when those who crossed lines turned and looked back at those left on the other side with anything short of respect. "The admirable mestizo and mestiza people honor us, as they descend from our lines, but some mestizos and mestizas without reason do not recognize that some of them carry our blood and nobility. They just try to be Spaniards, belittling us and mocking us, as some Spaniards do."[74] That, however, was as far as his anger took him. He closed by commenting simply that Adam was father and Eve mother to all living people.

His contemporary Ixtlilxochitl—one of the mestizos who fully acknowledged his descent from indigenous lines—felt more belligerence, perhaps because he interacted on a regular basis with a wide array of Spaniards. In the 1580s, when rising censorship was causing a decline of the indigenous scholarly community at Tlatelolco, students there put on a play of their own writing. One character commented, "According to the opinion of many, we the Indians of New Spain are shams, like magpies and parrots, birds that with great effort learn to talk, and soon forget what they have been taught."[75] Ixtlilxochitl may never have seen the play. But he was living in the mixed world that produced both those hostile ideas, and the resulting bitterness on the part of educated indigenous people who were exposed to them. As the years passed, Ixtlilxochitl grew increasingly strident in the language he used when he wrote about his work. "Having considered the varied and contrary presentations of the [European] authors who have treated the history of New Spain, I did not want to follow any of them."[76]

Chimalpahin seems to have lived his life well away from any such political or epistemological struggles. He was aware of the power differentials in his world, but he was not burdened by them. He saw them as ordained by God and seemed to feel that all would be well if everyone—including wicked Spanish chaplains—followed the rules. He had not been made to feel unintelligent, he was cosmopolitan in his education and perspective, and he had perfect confidence in his ability to interrogate texts. He had no desire to reject Spanish ones that came his way. He also had confidence in his fellow Nahuas' ability to fathom the workings of history if they were offered any worthwhile account of it. It became his life's work to leave them materials they could use.

***

Don Domingo apparently worked on his project in bits and pieces, presumably as time allowed him, recopying segments at various moments. Eventually, however, he ordered the "eight relations" as he wanted them. The dates they contain (that is, 1612, 1620, 1629, and 1631) do not appear in order, so he did not maintain them in the order in which he had originally written them, but placed them in a sequence that by then made sense to him. It seems highly unlikely that some future person simply gathered them together in no particular order, for the document is a seamless whole in the kind of paper and the style of handwriting, and the order of the sections is profoundly logical.

Once Chimalpahin commented that the segment he wrote first (his first *amoxtli*) was about Chalcan history,[77] but the section he ultimately placed first and actually labeled "first chapter" (employing the Spanish word *capítulo* to express this) was about Adam and Eve. In his first lines he defended his decision: "Even if it doesn't seem relevant to treat it here, it is necessary that all of us people here, we indigenous people from New Spain, that we know that what is called the first human generation was created from the earth, from the mud, was created only one time, and from it we all come and are born; from it all of us people on earth descend, even though there have been gentiles and idolaters—they who engendered us, we people here in Mexico Tenochtitlan and all the altepetls of New Spain."[78] All humans, he asserted with vehemence, have one origin. This idea was important to him because it was what he had been taught as a Christian; it was also politically important to him as an indigenous person that all souls be recognized as equal. Then he told the story of Adam and Eve in colorful style, taking his material not just from Genesis, but also from Saint Augustine and Saint Thomas Aquinas and from his own imagination. Man was not to be pitied, for example, just because he did not have brilliant plumage like the birds, or sharp teeth like the animals, for he had the greatest gift of all, his soul.[79] He left out the story of Eve's transgression entirely, perhaps because he himself did not tend to blame women for much, or perhaps because he instinctively recognized that the notion that women were the original wrongdoers would be alien to his Nahua readership. Or perhaps it was because he was interested here only in the first creation of humanity, not in any later divisions.

Chimalpahin wrote explicitly that he must begin with God. In this, he was conscious of following authors of the Old World. "The ancient writers always used to begin in the name of God."[80] He quoted Diogenes, who wrote in the name of his divinity, then Saint Augustine, whom he remembered as speaking directly to the Lord from the first line of his first book. Then he passed on to more recent writers, who all acknowledged, as he did himself, that all that they were and could ever be came to them as a gift from God. This was the purport of his first section. Now he was ready to launch into the tales of history he longed to write.

In the second relation, Chimalpahin began immediately with his own people's calendrical system. "Here begins the ancient Mexican year count, instituted by the ancient Chichimecs, our ancestors and grandparents, those who came to live here long ago."[81] He explained the fifty-two-year cycle, started the wheel of time turning, and then had Jesus be born into it and die thirty-three years later. Sixteen years after that, the ancestors of the New World's people set off from an unspecified place in canoes, landing on the island of Aztlan.[82] Later, he would suggest that they had probably come from the Baltic, perhaps being akin to the fierce Latvians and Livonians as per a suggestion made by Enrico Martínez in his *Reportorio de los tiempos*. The twelfth- and thirteenth-century Frankish Christians had found the Baltic peoples to be savages almost impossible to defeat; certainly they formed the last bastion of paganism within the confines of Europe.[83] At the time of writing, Chimalpahin probably did not feel his potential Nahua readers could understand that reference. Instead, he offered an outline of the four continents—Europe, Asia, Africa, and the New World. Without ever having traveled beyond Chalco and Mexico City, he provided a clear summary of the places found in each continent and their general disposition, relying for his information again on Enrico Martínez. The fourth and last continent on the list is the New World, which receives short shrift here, as the remainder of Chimalpahin's work is to delineate its lands and histories. Here, the author repeats and even embellishes what must have been to him the most memorable sentence he found in Martínez's section: he says, as a closing thought, "This land of the world completely surpasses and exceeds the value of any of the other three."[84]

Third in order comes the story of the Culhua people, the most ancient Nahuas to arrive in the Valley of Mexico, whose history eventually envelops that of the more recently arrived Mexica of Tenochtitlan, who conquer Culhuacan. The Culhua story began earlier than—and was the necessary backdrop for—the history of the people of Chalco. It was they, these first arrivals, explains Chimalpahin, who began the practice of the "tying of the years" every fifty-two years, initiating a cycle that all Nahuas had abided by ever since.[85] Chimalpahin had gathered enough texts, or listened to enough elders, to have imbibed the ancient language we have heard before. "As for those Chichimec Totolimpanecas, this is what their shooting was like: their arrows never missed. When they shot toward the heavens they got an eagle or perhaps some other bird, and if they got nothing in the sky, then as it was coming back, as it was shooting towards the earth, the arrow of those Teochichimecs got a wolf, or a puma or a deer or a snake or a rabbit."[86] In the classic historical drama, when the daughter of the Mexica chief Huitzilihuitl has been taken in war by the angry Culhua king and deprived of her clothing (as in the histories of chapter 1), she belligerently demands that they hurry up and get on with the sacrifice, as she does in every version. But the storyteller to whom Chimalpahin had listened, or whose words he had read, had even more ethnic pride than some of the other narrators. In this version, the disdainful Culhua people refuse to sacrifice the princess and her followers just yet. So the valiant Mexica do the job themselves, turning and cutting open each other's hearts in the ultimate demonstration of fearlessness. [87]

As always, Chimalpahin clearly had more than one source either open before him or in his head. He also regularly incorporated material he had gleaned from the Spanish world—references to the number of years yet to come before the arrival of Hernando Cortés, or to the fact that when Cortés came, the Nahuas would mistake him for the leader Quetzalcoatl, who had traveled to the east to Tlapallan and was thought not to have died.[88] Interestingly, the three comments he made in this regard do not at all resemble those of Torquemada, who had written the fullest account of the subject to date, and whose book had been published and brought back to Mexico in 1615. Instead, they seem to be clearly extracted from the early work of Ixtlilxochitl. It would seem that either don Fernando had showed him his unpublished work, or that the two men had talked at length, or both. Ixtlilxochiltl in his earlier work had likewise said that a culture hero (he called him Topiltzin, Our Lord in those years) had traveled east to a land called Tlapallan, where he died, but then was mistakenly thought to have gone on living.[89]

Chimalpahin's "third relation" is a full set of annals devoted to the people who came to settle in Chalco, at the side of the green lake. The author includes material about all the Nahuas, as in the previous section, but this time the focus is on the ancestors of the Chalca. They wander, struggle for land, fight, sometimes win and sometimes lose. They face the elements; they suffer.

> 11 Reed, 1451. This was the second year in which there was famine. Then the coyotes began to eat people in Chalco and in other places, and the vultures also ate people. For the young men and women [who left home] were dying all around in the woods, the hills, the grasslands. The flesh of the young men and women shriveled up as though it were the flesh of old people. The famine strengthened.[90]

By the 1480s, Chimalpahin was interpolating material from his Spanish books, but still with the purpose of elucidating the history of Chalco. Columbus makes an appearance: he begins to sketch out his plans for traveling west, and he visits the crowned heads of Europe. Then, back in the New World, the Chalca fall to the Mexica; in fact, many kingdoms fall to these ambitious imperialists. Back in Europe, it is 1492, and Columbus secures permission to sail. He discovers the New World. Meanwhile, the wars in Mexico continue, with the Chalca now fighting on the side of the Mexica. In 1519, Cortés arrives in Mexico. Within a few months, he and his allies from Tlaxcala and Huexotzinco are driven from the city in the darkness of night; the annals end. The Chalcans have suffered, but they are far from extinguished.

Then follow four more sets of annals focusing on the Chalca in the fourth, fifth, sixth, and seventh relations. They have different purposes: one, for example, clarifies Chimalpahin's belief that the ancestors of the Chalca came from the Old World, probably from the Baltic, before their boats came ashore on Aztlan, whence they eventually traveled southward to the Valley of Mexico, where some discovered the wide green lake.[91] (The author comments vehemently that they should by no means be mistaken for a lost tribe of Israel; he says the timing precludes the possibility, as they had gotten all the way to Aztlan before the Romans destroyed Jerusalem. He insists that there be no mistake about this, that his people were not Jews.[92]) Another has only brief, factual entries covering the years 1258–1612 in relatively short order; this may well have been one of the materials Chimalpahin simply copied from one of the informants he mentioned. (Indeed, the piece gives its date of composition as 1612, though the two pieces placed immediately after date themselves to the 1620s.) The two other texts are richly interwoven accounts of Chalcan history, moving from the deep past through to the end of the sixteenth century; the second ("the seventh relation") is an extraordinary work of over eighty folios. It brings the preconquest world to life in a way that no other existing text does.

The seventh relation's story of the famous musician Quecholcohuatzin, for instance, opens a window into the world of Chimalpahin's grandparents' generation. Indeed, being from Amaquemecan, his grandparents almost certainly knew Quecholcohuatzin and probably were related in some way. He was apparently a very young man in 1480, a much older one when the Spaniards became a significant presence in Chalco in the 1530s. He was high-ranking enough at that time to be baptized and take the "don" along with a Christian name, becoming "don Jerónimo." The cohort who accompanied him to the city of Mexico when he was a young man clearly loved to tell the story of his meeting with the tlatoani Axayacatl, conveying in the telling all the tension they had felt and displaying no shyness in recounting that Quecholcohuatzin soon became the king's lover. It was a politically charged moment: the Chalca people had been defeated in the 1460s, and by the 1470s they were growing restive under the strictures of Mexica control. In their choice of what to perform, Quecholcohuatzin and his companions were lodging a political protest of sorts. The popular "Chalca Woman's Song" was written down in the latter half of the sixteenth century, so we know the words. As a political metaphor, it ventriloquizes a concubine captured in war, who laments her fate—her loss of home and independence—and asks her new lord not to treat her with disrespect, but to make a loyal friend of her instead.[93] Chimalpahin tells us, even if it is a partly apocryphal tale, all that we would want to know about the dynamics of the initial presentation of the song to the Mexica overlords, as well as how songs were authored and performed and changed over time, and how they could be gifted to certain "owners" in a widely recognized cultural gesture. The story is a fine example of all that the "seventh relation" can offer.

The last section of Chimalpahin's great work (his "eighth relation") is in some senses the denouement. It, too, contains a set of annals of the history of Chalco, but it offers much more than this. It is here that the longtime scholar chose to explain to his readers why he had written what he had, and where he had found the information. It is here that he chose to include an explanatory essay on Chalco's history, jettisoning the year-count format in favor of an analytical one that he felt posterity would need. It is here that he chose to comment explicitly on where injustice had been done, where the early colonial government had made mistakes regarding Chalco's welfare. Modern scholars have regularly turned hungrily to the eighth relation, using it to make sense of Chimalpahin's more traditional annals, which might otherwise remain somewhat inscrutable to modern eyes.

Interestingly, the central argument about the Spaniards' mistaken judgment concerns their conviction that where the male line had failed, a chieftainship could not pass. Chimalpahin went to great length—using up more than ten folios on the task—to show historical examples of moments when royal lines had been carried by sitting queens, who then passed the rulership on to male children.[94] First he gave two Nahua examples. Then he veered into a long disquisition on Spanish history and gave two illustrations from there, including the very recent and important example of the line of Ferdinand and Isabella passing through their daughter Juana to her son Charles. Chimalpahin's view has sometimes been considered self-serving, in that it was only through his mother's line that Chimalpahin could claim a direct-line connection to a royal past. But we should take seriously the time and energy Chimalpahin expended on this project. He was clearly genuinely interested in his subject for itself, not merely pursuing it because it indirectly lent grandeur to his own past. He would not have needed to research the fates of each of Queen Juana's sisters to gain that end.

Throughout his texts, Chimalpahin remains interested in the complex question of Nahua marriage politics. For him, as for don Alonso Castañeda Chimalpopoca years before, the sexual liaisons of Nahua chiefs were not merely matters of salacious gossip from the preconquest world; rather, they were integral to the nature of inter-altepetl relations. When a girl from one altepetl was given to a chief of another, did she go as a slave, a respected secondary wife, or a first wife whose children would inherit? In short, what was the nature of the political relationship of which she was the embodiment? Or if a girl was taken from her home by the chief of a foreign altepetl, was she a hostage who would be treated with some respect in order to elicit good behavior from her people, or were her people so thoroughly conquered that she could expect to be abused as proof of that fact? Details of this nature come through in the Chalcan annals yet are difficult for us to understand fully today. Sometimes we can understand the matter clearly, as when Chimalpahin points out that the Mexica king Itzcoatl was not the son of a royal wife, but rather the son of a vegetable seller; he used his own wits and charisma to rise to seize the kingship.[95] Frequently, however, it is far more difficult for outsiders to bring the matter into focus.

When Chimalpahin made his copy of Gómara, he several times felt the need to correct the European writer's myopic vision of the politics of gender. When the defeated Tlaxcalans give women to Cortés as a peace offering, he inserts the word "hostages" in describing them, as the intention was that they were given as a guarantee of their people's loyalty.[96] When the disdainful and recalcitrant Nahuas entertain the Spaniards in the city, he wants readers to understand that the women they offered were not truly tokens of good faith, but "servants" in whom the Mexica would have had no real interest.[97] In Amaquemecan, Hernando Cortés had reported receiving a gift of "as many as forty slave women."[98] Gómara repeated it in his version. Chimalpahin copied this without comment,[99] but he did not forget; the term "slave" apparently troubled him. In his own previous annals, he had addressed the question of Amaquemecan's decision to side with the conqueror early on. In his text, as in numerous other altepetls, the chiefs face the question of whether fighting the Spaniards would be a worthy or a foolish act. In Amaquemecan, in Chimalpahin's prior annals, they decide fighting would only yield needless death. Then, in the eighth relation, clearly the last history written, and in the wake of having read Gómara, Chimalpahin introduces the subject of the forty women for the first time. He wants to make sense of the situation. Given the decision Amaquemecan's leaders had made, they would in reality have offered local girls, not slaves, dressed as honored secondary wives, not servants, for in doing so they were symbolically offering fealty. Chimalpahin writes very explicitly:

> The two kings gathered together forty good and beautiful women, daughters of commoners from here. The two kings and the other noblemen had requested them, asking that they choose young women. They

dressed them up, giving them whatever it was then customary for the wives of rulers to wear, beautiful skirts and huipillis. And it is said that they bathed them in temazcal, decorated their feet, and combed and shaved them.[100]

The politics of gender was not a minor interest of Chimalpahin's, for the central focus of the Chalcan annals is the question of lineage and the complex interactions between lineages. The land also matters, but the people matter more. And if descent and human relationships are the crux of the matter, then gender politics must be central. Before the conquest, it was not just a literary feature but a socio-economic reality that the rules governing male and female lines of descent, and thus the significance of varying types of marriage, were extremely complex. In Chalco, some roles passed only through the male line: for example, in the 1540s, all those who spoke on behalf of their people, giving voice to the huehuetlahtolli, had to have inherited their status as a tlatocapilli through the male line, or be the sons of a tlatocapilli's daughter.[101] Beyond such sons, even to their own children, the role could not extend. Even more stringently, the role of tlatoani passed from father to son. Sons who did not inherit became tlatocapilli (able to inherit the rulership at some future point if needed, but not kings themselves). Their sons likewise were tlatocapilli, and on through the male line, but the status was lost in the girls. However, when there really was no son left alive, a woman could and did hold the royal line within her. Chimalpahin was not saying this because it was in his own self-interest. It was not. His uncles, his mother's brothers, were categorized as tlatocapilli and one did indeed serve as gobernador of Amaquemecan;[102] he himself never would be able to inherit according to what he was saying, for his mother had had living brothers. Chimalpahin was apparently speaking here as he so often was, as a scholar, as one who wanted to get the facts right and communicate them to others, not as a propagandist.

He was well aware that the inverse situation, in which power passed through the female line, was often the dominant reality. He used the ancient Nahuatl term *inhueltiuh,* "their elder sister," to describe not only a literal older sibling, but also a young woman who was the bearer of the royal line in a matrilineal context. In such a world, the chieftainship did not pass from a man to his son, but from a man to his sister's son. The *inhueltiuh* did not usually wield power herself, but it was understood that her children would rule. Usually Chimalpahin employed the term in telling the story of the foundation of an altepetl; the need for an ennobling matrilineal inheritance seems to have been almost universal in Nahua stories of origins. Most of the Nahua altepetls were no longer matrilineal, or at least not purely so: men passed their power sometimes to their younger brothers and nephews, but at least as often to their sons. But the authors of other annals still used the term in discussing the politics of their modern, generally patrilineal world: if an altepetl offered a woman who was *inhueltiuh* to the Mexica king as a wife, for example, they were promising that his children would rule over their altepetl. She was not necessarily the chief's sister anymore. She might be his daughter, for example. But the important point was that in titling her *inhueltiuh* her people were promising to acknowledge her son as their lord.[103]

Chimalpahin's interest in gender may have stemmed from more than just his awareness of its political importance to his people. He seems to have felt significant sympathy for disempowered people generally, and women specifically. In his present-day life, he admired María López for her gutsy defiance of the wicked chaplain. He commented quietly when Isabel Machado, the daughter of a Jewish tailor, was burned at the stake by the Inquisition: "She was a young girl."[104] He mourned the deaths of old women who had been kind to him. He always noticed nuns. He brought Malintzin out from the shadows in his annals, referring to her by name, explaining that she was the one who was translating. When he recopied Gómara, he even gave her an indigenous name, "Tenepal."[105] Indeed, Quecholcohuatzin, the ancestral singer of whom he was so proud, gave voice to Chalco's woes in "The Chalcan Woman's Song" by comparing the fate of the conquered altepetl to that of a miserable war-prize concubine. And then Quecholcohuatzin was placed among those very concubines and found himself in a feminine position, both literally and figuratively.

Chimalpahin carefully copied out an illuminating story given to him by Tezozomoc. He would have had human fellow-feeling for the appealing young girl the story concerned, but also have seen her political importance in Mexica history. Indeed, the gendered dynamics of political marriages sometimes required some wit to follow. This story went as follows: before the rulers of Tenochtitlan were as powerful as they later became, they craved access to the cotton of the Cuernavaca region. So the tlatoani asked for the hand of the Cuernavaca princess in marriage. But the Cuernavaca king turned him down, saying scornfully, "What will he give my daughter there in the midst of the water? Will he clothe her in marsh plant thread?" The Mexica tlatoani sought divine advice and was told that he should shoot a precious greenstone dart over the wall into the home of the beautiful Miyahuaxihuitl:

> And when the reed fell in the middle of the courtyard, when the maiden Miyahuaxihuitl saw that the reed came from the heavens, that it fell into the courtyard, that it fell as if it was truly given from the heavens, then she took it up in her hand. When she had thus taken it up she marveled at it, now that she saw how the reed was varicolored. Never had she seen the like. So then she broke it in half; within it she saw the precious green stone, which was most valuable, which shimmered brightly. Then the maiden took it up; she said to herself: perhaps it is powerful. Then she put it in her mouth; she would crunch it with her teeth. It went directly within her; she swallowed it; she could not take it out. Thus at that moment she became pregnant. Moctezuma Ilhuicaminatzin was conceived.[106]

Perhaps Miyahuaxihuitl was taken by treachery and Cuernavaca immediately after defeated in war, but her people had the last laugh. The Mexica people's need for their cotton guaranteed that she served not as a miserable concubine, but as the mother of the heir. The duped princess lived to see her sons rule over many tens of thousands.

Chimalpahin, like historians everywhere, was interested in power and shifts in power; he was sympathetic to the underdog, whether the status was temporary or permanent. That, however, did not mean that he felt like an underdog himself. Quite the contrary. He felt himself to be a privileged, thoughtful observer, one who had been allowed to survive, and gain knowledge, and preserve it for others. Where he went after San Antonio Abad was closed down in 1624 we do not know; he was, however, still scribbling away in 1631,[107] and quite possibly for years after that. Chimalpahin's death is unrecorded. In our mind's eye, we can leave him still alive, adding another entry to a xiuhpohualli, rightly convinced that by dint of years of effort he was emblazoning his people's past permanently in the world's recoverable memory.

Fig 5.1 Cover created for don Juan Zapata's "Historia Cronológica" of Tlaxcala by his friend, don Manuel de los Santos Salazar. Méxicain 212, Courtesy Bibliothèque Nationale de France.

5

Renaissance in the East (The Seventeenth Century)

In the seventeenth century, there still lived individuals who continued the tradition of the xiuhpohualli, especially in the region of Tlaxala:[1]

[f. 92]

Now in the new year, on the first of January in the year 1675, don Diego Martín Faustino of Ocotelolco became judge-governor for the first time. The Ocotelolca will hold [the governorship] for a second year; with this the term is complete. The new alcalde [from Ocotelolco] is don Manuel de los Santos, the regidores don Juan Francisco—who lives in Tepeitic—and don Diego Felipe Nahualtzintli. The new alcalde for Tizatla is don Luis Diego, the regidores don Juan Nicolás and don Juan Nicolás [sic]. The new alcalde for Quiyahuiztlan is don Diego Pérez Cuixcocatzin, citizen of San Francisco Temetzontlan, the regidores don Juan Nicolás Tezpantzin and don Sebastián Gabriel Zárate. For Tepeticpac, [the new alcalde is] don Diego Martín Pérez, the regidores don Nicolás Salvador and don Juan Pérez. Don Josef de San Francisco is alguacil mayor for the first time. The cabildo notary is Juan Pablo. The Spanish governor is the same don León de Arsa, whose spouse is doña Tomasina. In this year [the construction of] the [bridge's] pillars started up on the 11th of January,[2] and now half have come to be finished at the end of the month of March, everything on San Miguel's side.[3] Then began [work on] the part on our side.[4] The one who paid for everything was Josef de Alva, cobrador of the cabildo.[5]

Today on the 16th of the month of February, in the same year of 1675, was begun the earthen canal to provide a channel for the Zahuatl river. Only three altepetl dug it—Ocotelolco, Quiyahuiztlan and Tepeticpac. The people of Tizatla did not want to do it. They paid 300 pesos that the three altepetl divided among themselves. At the beginning of March they began to close off [the river] [f. 92v] to divert it. But they could not control it. Until the end of March they couldn't close it up with stones.[6] It just stayed open. Everyone in the three altepetl was really upset. And the people of Tizatla who did not want it and demurred spent a month and half in the big jail. They were going to lash them about in the streets[7] and banish them, but the whole cabildo spoke on their behalf, and our father the preacher Diego Martín de Valdés pled with don León de Arsa that they be pardoned. They vowed that they would obey.

Today on Sunday, on the 24th of March in the year 1675, on the eve of our precious Mother of Incarnation, they brought an accusation against a sorcerer from Santa María Acuitlapilco. It had already rung nine o'clock when they brought him out from the jail. They took him to the home of the vicar, Antonio González Laso. There they put a rope around his neck and placed a green candle in his hands. Once they brought him into the church of San Josef the Mass began. He heard it on his knees. They admonished him with what was in the sermon. Everyone who belonged to our chapel went to San Josef. They brought him back to the jail tied up.

Today on the feast day, at dawn on the feast day of San Juan Papa Mártir, on Tuesday, May 27, in the same year of 1675, six thieves entered our home. Two of them came in the window. First one came in. The one who was leading the way grabbed me first of all. When I was overpowering him, he called to his friend, so that they doubled up on me. When I grabbed his knife, he really cut up my hands. The other four kept guard outside my house. They had swords[8] and a musket. As for money, [f. 93] 200 pesos [were taken]. As for our raiment,[9] they did not take it. Not a rag did they remove. And they didn't leave us hurt.

Today, Monday, June 20, was when it was begun, when I began [building] an oven. On the feast day of San Silverio Papa Mártir,[10] the foundation was begun. The one who began it was also the one who finished it. Juan Gabriel is his name, an old man like me. It was fired for the first time on Thursday, July 11. Our father the preacher, Diego Martínez de Valdés, who lives here next to my house, came to bless it on the feast day of San Pío Papa Mártir. The oven was fired for two days. Bread[11] came out for the first time right on the eve of San Buenaventura, my [name] saint, Saturday, at dawn on Sunday, the precious day of don Juan Buenaventura Zapata y Mendoza.

[margin, almost a parallel column] And at this time the pipiltin went to see the border, where the border of the Tlaxcalans ends at [or edges] Tepeyacac. A road will go there. Don León de Arsa went personally, along with the [indigenous] governor, don Martín Faustino, and the alcaldes, the regidores, the whole cabildo. The party went on exactly this day month and year; at that time I, Juan Buenaventura Zapata y Mendoza, was teniente.

Today on the feast day of San Apolinar Obispo Mártir, Tuesday, July 23, two days before[12] the day of Señor Santiago, the Zahuatl river overflowed and knocked down the new bridge that had been made by the tlatoani don León de Arsa together with Josef de Alva. Right away half was carried away, [bringing it] toward San Miguel's side. Next the Zahuatl took the part made first, just flipped it on its side, [taking it] toward the solares going to San Juan Totollan.

Today Monday [sic], July 25 the Zahuatl overflowed and knocked things down again, so that everything was carried away, so that a new bridge, a wooden bridge, was started again. [f. 93v] Our father named Juan Merino really put himself into it. Soon after, our father the guardián whose name is fray Juan Moreno went to see it, so that they could cut cypress trees [for the project] in Quaquauhxiuhtla. Four were cut, then they were dragged and brought to the river's edge, where they are now. Afterward offerings were solicited by all three curates, Antonio González, Juan Merino, and the preacher, Diego Martín de Valdés. Everyone brought their offering—Spaniards, mestizos, Indians, mulattoes—whatever they could. It was just done voluntarily. Juan Merino was right there when it was done; he spent all day every day there; he [even] ate there.

Today on the 15th of August, on the precious feast day of our precious revered mother, Santa María de la Asunción, the feast day of the altepetl was observed in grand style. Never had the like been done, ever since the times of our forefathers and foremothers, as the honoring of the precious lady Santa María was carried out [this time].. There were bonfires when she was brought out and taken on procession. And when she was taken back to [the church of] San Josef, there were big fireworks when thirteen big árboles[13] were burned. The people from the towns all around really marveled. All the people were really appreciative[14]—the priests, the Spaniards, all the different kinds of people. At every flowerhouse altar[15] fireworks were set off from an árbol.

[f. 94]

Today on Tuesday, August 20, a Tuesday [sic] the bridge was blessed, when our precious mother Santa María who presides here in Ocotlan, was in [the church of] San Josef. She was brought out from there. There were many litters and litanies chanted as she was taken to the bridge. All the priests went in procession, and the three curates got dressed up. When she got to the bridge it was really nicely decorated. On the San Miguel side an altar was placed. There they rested our precious mother of Ocotlan, and there the singing of litanies ended. The vicar Antonio González Laso blessed the bridge. He went about spreading incense and sprinkling. When she was brought back again to San Josef there was a high Mass. By ten o'clock it had already ended and concluded.

[f. 94v]

Now in the year of 1676 new officeholders were installed.

Today on the first day of January, a Wednesday, in the new year of 1676, don Diego de Santiago of Tizatla became governor for the first time. The new alcalde [of Tizatla] is don Juan de la Corona, his new regidores don Diego de Santiago and don Luis. From Ocotelolco the new alcalde is don Juan Francisco from Tepeitic, the new regidores don Diego Osorio and don Juan Pascual. From Quiyahuiztlan the new alcalde is don Salvador Ramírez, his regidores don Simón de la Cruz and don Juan Francisco. From Tepeticpac the alcalde is don Francisco Ruiz, an old man, and his regidores are don Nicolás Salvador and don Diego Ruiz, a new regidor who is don Francisco's son. The new cabildo notary is don Manuel de los Santos. The alguacil mayor of the prison is Miguel de Celis. He was not elected; another was elected. They just gave it to him the next day. The tlatoani is the same don León de Arsa, and the notary Miguel de Ortega. [Alcaldes de] provincia: for San Francisco Topoyanco, don Francisco Ximenes held it for the second year. For San Luis Huamantla in Tizatla it came out to be the one named don Juan Antonio, son-in-law of don Francisco Cecetzin. For San Felipe the new alcalde is don Pascual Ramírez, and for San Juan Atlancatepec, don Josef Pérez, a citizen there. Those mentioned above are all the officeholders who were installed.

[f. 95]

Today, Sunday, on the 16th of February in the year 1676 the church of Jesús Nazareno was consecrated in San Pablo Apetatitlan. Many things were done [to celebrate], including flying and spinning from a pole.[16] All three curates from here went. On Monday and Tuesday there was bullfighting. And on Wednesday a new market was established. At first only a few people went and set up stalls. My children Juan Gabriel and Juan Cristóbal brought their bread; they were the only ones yet. The next week there were already a lot of people selling things. It was the day of ashes [Ash Wednesday]. The curate of Santa Ana Chiauhtempan, whose name is Mateo Rivera, was the one who invited the people, and by his hand the church of Jesús Nazareno was blessed.

Today on the first day of May in the year of 1676, on Friday afternoon at four o'clock came a document from the [new] tlatoani don Melchor Melo Ponce de León.[17] In it he gave authorization [for the cabildo] to receive the one who will be teniente on the evening before the day of Saints Felipe and Santiago, [which would come] at dawn on Saturday. And don Gerónimo de la Fuente received the office during the night, at maybe nine or ten o'clock. At that time don Francisco Ruiz [the elderly alcalde from Tepeticpac] had a stone fall on his foot. He was opening the postern gate of the cabildo when it came to fall on his foot. They just carried him, to take him to his home. At dawn on Saturday he was already ailing. There was a great deal of anxiety because don León de Arsa and the notary, Miguel de Ortega, wished each other ill. Of the alcaldes, only three appeared, those from Tizatla, Quiyahuiztlan, and Tepeticpac. They were the only ones who took their places.[18]

[f. 95v]
Today the tlatoani don Melchor Melo Ponce de León entered [Tlaxcala], on Tuesday, June 3, in the year 1676. We went to meet him. At five o'clock he came by San Felipe and we went to meet him at San Nicolás. They gave him his staff of office[19] a bit closer to here. They didn't read him his commission yet, but just went to pray in the cabildo. He came straight to the church, passed outside our chapel, went inside San Josef, and from there entered the cabildo. Then he went up to the palace to stay. That was when we went to get the teniente, who was at the little market. We brought him on our horses as we went by the palace. Everyone went— alcaldes, regidores, and the pipiltin currently not in office.

Today, on Friday, October 2, in the year 1676, on the feast day of Santo Tomás Obispo, there arrived a document announcing that the bishop of Guadalajara will come. He will come here as he is coming to take charge of [the bishopric] of Cuetlaxcohuapan [Puebla]. [Another hand[20] adds: his name is doctor don Manuel Fernández de Santa Cruz.]

Today, on Wednesday, October 28, and in the year 1676, right on the feast day of San Simón Judas, at eleven o'clock, they read the document that came from Mexico announcing that our tlatoani king over in Spain has taken up his crown and office. The whole day they were ringing the bells. And at four o'clock a proclamation was made. The pipiltin went in procession playing wind instruments for him, and the Spanish notary went about ordering that there be bonfires all over town. The next day, Thursday and also Friday, there was bullfighting. A week later also on Thursday and Friday there was bullfighting again. There was a procession of the governor, alcaldes, regidores, and all the pipiltin currently not in office. They put themselves in formation. First was the clarín, then the chirimías. Then on top of the church boys bearing the royal arms[21] played a great drum. Everyone went on horseback, no one on foot. They left the Palacio going past the doorway of the church, then turned at the inn on the way to Quaquauhxiuhtla. They went straight toward the market. They followed the same route as when there are processions at Lent. The town crier went calling out the whole way.

***

As Chimalpahin bent his head over the wooden table and scribbled furiously, lest what he knew be forgotten by generations to come, a new baby was crying lustily. When the child was old enough, he would happily receive the historian's torch from his forebears—but he did not live in Mexico City, or indeed anywhere in the Central Valley. There, just as Chimalpahin had feared, people were already beginning to forget how the ancient ones inscribed their histories, as well as what exactly those histories contained; the young people knew almost nothing about it. The child who was to be different lived to the east. There was a colonial road leading out of Mexico City following the old Aztec track that traversed the pass between Popocatepetl and Iztaccihuatl, and then gradually descended through the pine forests toward the sea. Eventually, after about seventy of today's miles, the road came to a wide, flat valley, dominated by the sight of Matlalcueye, the green-skirted volcano. At the north end of this valley lay Tlaxcala, the quadripartite kingdom that had jealously guarded its independence for centuries. There, even the chatter in the public streets was nearly all in Nahuatl, and the old ways of doing things lived on. There, many people still knew what a xiuhpohualli should be. Elsewhere, people remembered the form in a vaguer sense: they might try to record the history of their altepetl in a year-by-year format, but they had little sense of what to say, and before they knew it, they might find themselves using the record to keep the altepetl's financial accounts.[22]

The Tlaxcalans' decision to ally with the Spaniards almost exactly one hundred years before had borne fruit for the present generations. At the time, however, consensus had not been easily come by. The chiefly families had hotly debated the matter. Certainly they welcomed the opportunity to attack their old enemies, the Mexica, with a greater degree of confidence than they otherwise would have had, but there was great risk involved. What if the Spaniards were not as strong as they seemed to be, and they ultimately lost? Or what if they were all that they boasted, and the Tlaxcalans found themselves the permanent junior partners of an insufferably arrogant set of erstwhile accomplices? In the end, the Tlaxcalans had concluded that their best option was to ally with the newcomers from across the sea and do their best to help bring down Moctezuma. Victory had been theirs, and they pressed Hernando Cortés hard to keep promises that he had made to them. Thus it was that they were never given out in encomienda to individual Spaniards, but rather paid their only tribute directly to the Crown. No major Spanish settlement was planted in their midst. Instead, Puebla was founded in the southern part of the valley, and after some dickering, even the region's cathedral was built there. The two to three hundred noble families who had ruled Tlaxcala in the past continued to exercise substantial control, now through the Spanish-style governing body known as the cabildo.[23]

The baby boy who would later become a serious historian, christened Juan Buenaventura Zapata y Mendoza, was born into a lordly family from Quiyahuiztlan. Tlaxcala consisted of four subaltepetls—Ocotelolco, Tizatlan, Quiyahuiztlan, and Tepeticpac, always named in that order—and each of these contained a given number of *teccalli*, or lordly houses. In Quiyahuiztlan, there were twenty-nine of these noble lines at the time of conquest,[24] and young Juan Buenaventura was the scion of at least one of them, possibly of two. In the surviving mid-sixteenth-century records of the cabildo, there is no mention of any leading family with the surname Zapata, but this was a time when the indigenous nobility was still in the process of adopting Spanish names as markers of their status, and not all had done so by the period for which we have records.[25] It is also possible that Zapata was only noble through his grandmother. The ostentatious insistence on the part of his grandfather, Buenaventura Zapata, on the surname Zapata *y Mendoza* may indicate that he was a particularly successful commoner who managed to gain control of a teccalli through marriage to a daughter of the house.[26] But it might also simply indicate that everyone recognized the Mendoza family to be of higher status than other noble families in the sub-altepetl. Zapata's grandmother, doña Magdalena de Mendoza, came to the marriage with some significant landholdings, and she was likely closely related either to don Juan de Mendoza, the last man to act as hereditary tlatoani of Quiyahuiztlan before the line died out for lack of a male heir, or to Francisco de Mendoza, tlatoani of Tepeticpac.[27] (Mendoza was an apt choice of surname for a newly baptized high chief in the era of the mid-sixteenth-century Spanish viceroy don Antonio de Mendoza.)

However it had happened, there is no question of the high status of the Zapata family by the early years of the seventeenth century. They lived in the central, urban section of Tlaxcala, a town nestled between the four hills that had once been the fortified hearts of the four sub-altepetls.[28] They referred to themselves as *caciques y principales* in Spanish documents and were major landholders in the Quiyahuiztlan area. Like other heads of noble households, young Juan's grandfather, don Buenaventura Zapata, not only held lands that belonged to his family, but also governed lands that belonged to the community. As the dynasty's overlord, it was one of his traditional duties to distribute usufruct rights to members of the teccalli and the associated commoner families. There is an extant drawing of some holdings near the church of Santa María Nativitas Atzatzacuala, in the direction of Cholula. It reads at the top *Yn itlalpa don Buenaventura Zapata y Mendoza* ("What [or who] is on the land of don Buenaventura Zapata y Mendoza") and includes such comments as "Juan Guerrero and his son Felipe have held their land for some time."[29]

As he grew older, young Juan Buenaventura learned what to expect in his own future by watching the men in his family. His grandfather was elected to the cabildo in 1619 as an alcalde, a position second only to that of the gobernador, or head of the indigenous council.[30] Indeed, an alcalde generally was later elected as gobernador. But don Buenaventura served only two months before dying suddenly of an unnamed disease. The tragic timing became part of family lore. In 1626, little Juan's father, also named don Juan Zapata, became a regidor, or councilman, on the cabildo. He acted for several years in that capacity, and then, in the 1630s, gave up serving on the cabildo and worked as the fiscal of the Franciscans' indigenous church.[31] This was a time-honored and highly responsible position in an era when much of daily life revolved around church activities: when a gobernador stepped down from office, he often worked as the fiscal.[32] During the period of his father's service, the younger Juan Zapata would have been constantly exposed to the idea that he could himself potentially have a close future association with the Spanish world.

It was, however, an idea he rejected utterly. In his writings in later years, he would demonstrate no close ties to any church figures. This was so even though he almost certainly was educated by the Franciscans, unless perhaps his father hired an indigenous tutor who had been educated by the Franciscans. He definitely learned to read and write Spanish quite well, but he never acknowledged as much directly or left any writings in Spanish. We know of his ability in this regard only because he was later elected as clerk of the indigenous cabildo, a position he could never have held without a good knowledge of Spanish, and because late in life he took it upon himself to attack the competency of the man who was serving as interpreter, a stance he would never have taken if he had no ability to judge.[33] As his own career unfolded, don Juan stuck tenaciously to a life in Nahuatl, at the side of Nahuas. He became almost defiant in this regard.

In 1641, when don Juan Zapata—as his contemporaries called him[34]—was no more than a very young man, an epidemic swept through the region. It started in a nearby village and spread rapidly. Thousands died. First it took two friends who sang beautifully, silencing their voices forever. Then it came to his home and took both his parents. He survived, rattling about in the emptiness. "All over, where the saints are [that is, in the villages] there were no more people; those who remained were very few."[35] Yet he learned to laugh again. A beloved aunt Pascuala from the Mendoza family remained on earth with him and cared for him, and he had a younger brother and a sister who also survived and with whom he remained very close. A companion a few years younger than he, don

Bernabé de Salazar, from another Quiyahuiztlan teccalli, also lived through the horror and remained a lifelong friend.

Not many years after the devastating epidemic, Zapata entered into a romantic liaison with a commoner woman from the barrio of Tochitzin, undoubtedly with the full intention of marrying someone else later. In the not so distant past, his forebears had thought nothing of one man having more than one woman, and even within Spanish tradition it was not considered terribly reprehensible for there to be a long-term relationship prior to a marriage. He spoke with affection of the two sons born of the union, Juan Gabriel and Juan Cristóbal, but he never called them "don" or mentioned their mother's name; later, they took no part in the legal wrangling among his legitimate children over the estate.[36] While the two boys were still children, don Juan took a suitable bride, doña Petronilla de Paredes, from a noble line of Tizatlan. When his first son by Petronilla was born, he wrote as eloquently as Chimalpahin's father once had done for him. "During the night on Monday, July 3, 1662, a child was born, at 7:30. At dawn on Tuesday he was already born, on Saint Martin's day, but he did not take the saint's name. He is called Juan Buenaventura; he bears my name."[37]

By the time this child was born, Zapata had become the politically important personage he was raised to be. In 1645, he became a regidor for the first time, and in 1646, an alcalde. By 1651 he was gobernador. Later he served numerous times as alcalde again, often with his trusted younger brother or his sister's husband as part of "his" slate of regidores from Quiyahuiztlan.[38] Toward the end of his career he accepted the important positions of treasurer and then notary. As an officeholder he was constantly active in cabildo affairs—collecting taxes, organizing labor contributions for the building of bridges, fountains, or bell towers, orchestrating public ceremonies and participating in them, arbitrating disputes, drawing up petitions, sending legal representatives to Mexico City or Puebla, or acting as such an emissary himself. Occasionally he, like others, even helped voluntarily with these tasks in years when he was, as he put it, "resting," meaning not serving in any official capacity.

While he was gobernador, Zapata also acted as a sort of patron of indigenous artisans. Throughout his life, he noticed their contributions to city life ("The cross was made here in Tlaxcala. The one who made it was Juan Bautista, an Indian"),[39] but while he was in office, he could do more than comment. He made it his business, for example, to get back for the altepetl a beautifully crafted cloak that had been made years before for an icon of Santa María Asunción and then had been pawned in Mexico City by a profligate former governor.[40] He also saw to it that the musicians in two different indigenous chapels learned to play the chirimía, a wind instrument invented in France and brought over by the conquerors, but adjusted in Mexico to be played with the great drum, the huehuetl. Zapata loved music—bells peal throughout his pages and singers are mentioned wherever they can be—and he clearly wanted his people to partake in all it had to offer.[41]

Zapata also loved pageantry, but for him it constituted far more than a display of icons and finery.[42] It was a statement of the political importance of his people. Every procession organized by church or Crown represented the various peoples who together comprised the polity or the religious community. Every procession was thus a public reminder to everyone, old and young, high and low, indigenous and Spanish, of the importance of each and every group that was part of the greater whole, for without the many groups, there would be no greater entity. This was an ancient Nahua principle, and for Zapata the Spaniards' pageants provided an ideal opportunity to reaffirm it. "Our tlatoani king over in Spain has taken up his crown and office. The whole day they were ringing the bells. And at four o'clock a proclamation was made. The pipiltin went in procession playing wind instruments for him, and the Spanish notary went about ordering that there be bonfires all over town."

What is most remarkable about Zapata's ethnic patriotism, perhaps, is that he commented explicitly on the importance of using the Nahuatl language to keep the tongue alive. Zapata returns to the subject repeatedly; there can be no doubt that the issue was as important to him as it is to any modern day activist. In the entry for 1668, an order comes from the Holy Father to celebrate a jubilee. The entire indigenous cabildo takes a prominent role in the processions that follow: "On Thursday it was done the same way, there was a procession . . . Again there was preaching by the entrance of the cabildo. Again the doctrine went along being said in our Nahuatl language."[43] A year later, another entry smacks of satisfaction: "Thus the sermon was begun in Spanish, but finished in our Nahuatl language." That same month, Zapata was delighted to be named as one of six representatives of the altepetl to be sent to Mexico City to be questioned by an Audiencia judge. That high-level personage asked the Tlaxcalan delegation about their priests, not only if they treated the people well and were devout, but first of all—according to Zapata—if they knew enough of the language (of "our words") to preach effectively to people and to hear confession.[44]

In more subtle regards as well, Zapata made it clear that he considered it important to preserve indigenous language usage. Even when a loan word was in common use, he would choose an older form if he could.[45] For example, when he reports in his writings that an entire bridge had dramatically fallen in, or that a bridge had been ceremoniously blessed by the fathers, he uses the ancient Nahuatl word, *quappantli*. It is clear that he is doing this on purpose, for when another subject is the real item of interest, and a particular bridge is mentioned only in passing, he tends to forget himself and use the word that really was common in his daily life, the Spanish *puente*. When the river Zahuatl floods and everyone for miles around is caught up in the drama of the event, linguistic traditionalism is the least of his concerns, and he refers unselfconsciously to a *puente* that has been washed away along with so much else. In the same way, although Zapata himself often uses the Spanish word *reina* to refer to the Spanish queen or the viceroy's wife, in a self-conscious, almost stylized passage where he is describing a memorable ceremony (a cabildo meeting where a letter from the widowed Spanish queen to the city of Tlaxcala was read aloud) he speaks with emotion of their *cihuateuctli*—despite the fact that the letter was from a European monarch and was obviously read in Spanish.[46]

About the time of his marriage and then the birth of his legitimate son, Zapata made another decision: he began to keep his own annals, to write his own entries in a xiuhpohualli. His political career—and his interest in Nahua culture—pre-dated his detailed writings by at least a decade. In the mid-1650s he took a trip to Mexico City and may well have acquired then the history of the central valley that he later incorporated into his own work. Reading the old documents circulating in the great metropolis might have inspired him, but such works could not have been his only models. He certainly had had access to his father's papers and those of other older men in his community for many years, and he did not begin to write his own entries until the early 1660s.[47] That was the point at which his own progeny became part of the greater drama and he himself a link in a chain.

Zapata's annals in some ways closely resemble numerous others that were written elsewhere in the greater altepetl of Tlaxcala in the same period. In fact, it is evident that he and others copied extensively from one another, happily borrowing and then passing on others' work.[48] In certain regards, however, Zapata's text is much richer and more detailed than that of any of his contemporaries. It is thus worth examining with some care. If we come to understand what such a man—who was certainly conscious of being a guardian of his people and their ancient ways—thought a truly valuable xiuhpohualli should contain, then we can see how history and history writing were envisioned by the community in which he lived, over one hundred years after the conquest.

***

To begin with, Zapata knew that no story has a single beginning, and no history should be told in only one way. Chimalpahin knew this, too, but the knowledge is more surprising in Zapata's case. For in his generation, it is inconceivable that he had ever seen an old-style performance, or ever known anyone who had. No friend of his could tell him that his father-in-law had transcribed a great public performance of old histories in the 1540s. In Zapata's case, it had to have been the old, decaying written texts that had communicated to him the essence of the old ways. One might assume that the multiple sources on a single era were simply crystallized forms in older documents he copied, except that he maintained the practice of overlapping multiple voices even in the later periods.

There is strong evidence that Zapata had at least three documents before him as he worked on the earliest portion of his history; he then glued them together, figuratively speaking, into a seamless whole. The first part of his text was later labeled in another hand "The Origins of the Nation of Tlaxcala," and it reads differently from classic annals, more like a narrative than a year-by-year account. He possessed a document containing text written by someone whose father's generation had been children at the time of the conquest. "To the late Benito Itzcacmacuextli and Lucas García, father of don Juan Ponce de León, the Spaniards gave a big book for them to study. They were disciples of fray Martín de la Coruña...."[49] Apparently the Tlaxcalans, like many other altepetl, had turned two commoners over to the friars, rather than two princes, as they both lacked the title "don." They were clearly talented. When Lucas García grew to manhood, he served on the cabildo as alcalde of Tepeticpac and as governor, eventually earning the title "don" in cabildo records, and after him, his son, called don Juan Ponce de León, likewise served on the council.[50] Nothing more is known of the other student, Benito, as there is no Spanish surname to trace. Purportedly, the statement Zapata had, though at least partly recorded by the next generation, contained some text actually written by this Benito Itzcacmacuextli, using the alphabetic literacy he had gleaned from the friars to record Tlaxcala's history prior to the conquest; at least, this is what Zapata told don Bernabé's son, don Manuel, about the material. "It is told, it is said, in the papers of the Tlaxcalans, that a nobleman named Benito Itzcacmacuextli, one of the first who was taught by the Franciscan fathers who baptized him, wrote this in his own hand . . . " don Manuel would later write.[51] Thanks largely to this text, apparently written by a man who remembered the *ancien régime*, Zapata was able to recount the tale of his migrant ancestors with energy and zest, including bits and pieces from the old performances. The figures occasionally even speak. "It is said that the Mexica declared, 'Never will [these other] Chichimeca settle near us. They are really bothersome. Let them leave. Let's drive them east!'"[52]

Zapata also had a copy of the document now known as the "Annals of Tula" at his elbow. The latter is an interesting work consisting of a mixture of pre- and post-conquest-style drawings along with brief statements written out in Nahuatl. For a fifteen-year stretch in the fifteenth century, Zapata's entries come nearly verbatim from this piece.[53] Elsewhere in the preconquest period, however, where the "Annals of Tula" cover matters of interest only to the people of Tula, his entries take different paths, not found either here or in the Itzcacmacuextli document, but apparently originating somewhere else—perhaps in a single additional document, more likely in several. At least one of these others must have come from the Mexico City area, for before the late fifteenth century a great deal of Zapata's material concerns the Mexica.

In his annals, after the Spaniards arrive, Zapata turns to accounts clearly written in direct response to Christian teachings. He goes over the story of the critical years from 1519 to 1527 twice in succession, presumably inspired by two different texts covering the same period. The first item he had before him was apparently a version of a famous story of the immediate and voluntary baptism of the four kings of Tlaxcala. Historians know now that the story was a mid-sixteenth-century creation, designed to help everyone conveniently forget that the Tlaxcalans initially waged violent war against the Spaniards; the speaker may or may not have been aware of that.[54] The second source was an indignant recitation of the violence practiced by the Spaniards during those years. In both sections, Zapata has an edge to his voice, though whether it is his own tone or that of the author whose words he was probably copying—someone much closer to the period of conquest, perhaps Benito Itzcacmacuextli or Juan Ponce de León—it is impossible to say with certainty.

In the first telling, the events themselves sound quite familiar, but the Spaniards appear a bit more like buffoons than they generally do. Upon the arrival of Cortés, the padre Juan Díaz immediately baptizes the four kings, but in this telling, the act seems hollow, not spiritually uplifting. "People could not yet know what it was about." Then there arrive three "of those people called friars." They were fray Juan, fray Pedro de Gante, "and another whose name we didn't know." Fray Juan, may he rest in peace, was very concerned. "He really wanted to teach people, but he could not yet speak Nahuatl." He did what he could. "He used to just stand there, pointing his finger at the sky and mentioning Dios and Santa María, then pointing downward toward Mictlan [the land of the dead], saying, 'snakes, toads.'" The Spanish friars proceeded with the desired baptisms, but not of adults, only those pupils whom they were teaching. An indigenous man named don Juan Tzohuacpopocatzin taught the boys something worth remembering: not only the Pater Noster and the Ave María, but also accounting and the reading primer. Eventually the friars began gathering the people together every Sunday to preach to them. "Sometimes the prior [Francisco de] Soto would preach, with his eyes just stuck on the book. He got the words out with difficulty because he was already an old man."[55]

As Zapata starts over to tell the story of those years from some other point of view, the tone darkens considerably. The second version does not seem to have come from an affectionate if somewhat mocking former student. According to this other teller, the four kings, rather than consenting to baptism, simply asked, "What do the Christians worship in Castile?" One man began to argue vehemently against baptism and was whipped in the public market. Soon an investigation of idolatry began everywhere in Tlaxcala. "They did it, the students of the priests." Then the hangings began. The speaker remembers specifics and names. "They hanged the ruling nobles Temiloteuctli, Tlaltochtzin from Quiyahuiztlan, Quauhtotohuan from Atenpan, and don Francisco Tecpanecatl and Tenamascuicuiltzin from Topoyanco. Adulterers [that is, pagans married to more than one woman], they killed them, still the way they were. People were killed without reason." After the hangings of the kings, "a great fear spread." In fact, "it was at this time, when the kings died, that everyone began to go for baptism." The friars apparently had not really cared to save the souls of the indigenous. If they had, if they had been true and responsible caretakers, they would not have condemned pagans to death without hesitation. People responded to them out of fear, not out of understanding, and this apparently did not distress them.[56]

Zapata then moves back in time once again to begin his main project: a classic annals-style political history of the altepetl from the year 1310 to his present day. This time, when he gets to the arrival of the Spaniards, he treats more worldly matters: the formation of an alliance with them, the terrifying epidemic of smallpox, the learning of carpentry and shipbuilding from the foreigners' artisans, and the defeat of the Tlaxcalans' age-old enemy, the Mexica. The tale of the Spanish victory in this case is told without rancor or bitterness: the Tlaxcalans are the Spaniards' allies and move forward with their political structure essentially intact. In fact, it is if anything strengthened, thanks to the removal of the Mexica menace. After the founding of the Spanish-style council, the annals continue to move forward year by year, telling of the rotation into cabildo offices of the various noblemen, generation after generation, who work on behalf of the altepetl in every way they can. In tending to its business, great and small, they preserve the recognition of its past and guard against its dissolution in the future.

Zapata's work includes materials from other Tlaxcalan annals, and other Tlaxcalan annals copy materials from him. Indeed, they are literally all genetically related, each sharing a peculiar phrase or error with at least one other.[57] However, it is far from sufficient to say that Zapata was simply one of many authors borrowing from others. His annals are far more detailed than any others in his region or era. His contain materials found in no other Tlaxcalan annals. What did he consider a worthy source? Chimalpahin, working years before, had considered anything and everything that came his way as food for thought. He did not agree with everything he read, as he sometimes bluntly said, and he could certainly be selective, given what he chose to omit and include. But in his opinion it was all worth considering, and we find ancient Nahuatl sources side by side with gossip, adjacent to materials from the Bible or an astrological almanac or a Spanish chronicle. Zapata was far different. To his mind, materials in a xiuhpohualli had to come from a text in Nahuatl, and one in a traditional format at that.

As a member of the indigenous cabildo, he would have had access to its records, but these Spanish-style narrative records apparently were not what he was looking for, for he did not use them. It is clear that he did not, because although he always correctly recorded the terms of the indigenous office holders, he regularly introduced a significant error he would never have made if he had consulted the cabildo's Actas: he always got the dates of the Spanish corregidores wrong. Interestingly, he always began a corregidor's term with a year during which the man actually did serve. This suggests a probable explanation. Indigenous annals referred to Spanish officeholders only when their lives directly touched that of the altepetl—when a corregidor made a certain taxation demand, for example. Thus it is likely that Zapata was looking at notes written in Nahuatl, but not the official cabildo record, in which corregidores made periodic appearances to collect taxes, issue decrees, or die. He then assumed it safe to record that they served from the year of their first appearance in his record, until the year before some other corregidor was mentioned. This would also explain how Zapata was able to include details from the mid-sixteenth century about cabildo business that do not appear in the surviving Actas. In 1550, for example, the cabildo decided to build a European-style town clock and recorded their determination in their annals, but it is Zapata who tells us that they actually constructed it in 1560 and who the builder was.[58]

The same phenomenon exists in Zapata's treatment of church matters. As the son of a fiscal and a respected cabildo member who knew some of the friars personally, he could have consulted church records, but he did not. Instead, he consulted an alternate, highly detailed statement, apparently in Nahuatl. In the entry for 1622, for instance, he says, "On the 16th of November the bishop named fray Alonso de la Mota came here to the city of Tlaxcala to confirm people. He did not come from Spain. He came from Guadalajara to establish himself in Puebla."[59] In his own diary, bishop Mota—who, it is true, did not come from Spain, having been born in the New World, and having served as bishop of Guadalajara first—had this to say: "The 13th of November I set out on the tenth tour, toward the province of Tlaxcala, and stopped [first] at Topoyanco, where the Franciscan friars are.... And in the three days that I was there, I confirmed 518 people, Spaniards as well as natives. On the 22nd I left for the city of Tlaxcala, which is the head town of this province."[60] As it is clear that Zapata had a detailed record in front of him, the reader must ask why he would say that the bishop arrived on the 16th of November, when he was only drawing near to the village of Topoyanco on that day. The family of Zapata's close friend, don Bernabé de Salazar, lived near Topoyanco and definitely supplied other commentary to Zapata, as his name was included elsewhere. Someone in the family must have recorded the bishop's arrival at their home on the 16th—touring Spaniards often stopped at wealthy indigenous households for room and board—and Zapata presumably had that commentary before him.

Even Zapata's treatment of lands far away, such as Spain and Peru, seems to have come from local Nahuatl sources. Those with intimate knowledge of Spanish history were close at hand, but these, too, he seems to have eschewed. In the late sixteenth century, a Tlaxcalan mestizo named Diego Muñoz Camargo, the son of a conquistador and a local noblewoman, returned from his education in Spain and wrote a narrative history of his people, incorporating his knowledge of European affairs as well as all that he had gleaned from his mother's people. He lived in the native community and married a cihuapilli, the last remaining heir of the kings of Ocotelolco. As a wealthy man with ties to the Spanish world, Muñoz Camargo did favors for many of his neighbors, and they thanked him with gifts of land.[61] Zapata's grandfather or great-grandfather apparently gave him one such plot.[62] And the historian's son served on the cabildo at the same time as Zapata's grandfather, so it is certain that members of the two families knew each other personally. Yet Zapata, despite his avid interest in his people's history, never consulted Muñoz Camargo's great work. The narrative arc and the great events mentioned are quite different. It seems that even in the case of distant events, Zapata was looking at someone's notes in Nahuatl. In the entry for 1539, for example, he added a brief statement that in this year Carlos V died, as well as Francisco Pizarro. He was only a few years off in the case of Pizarro, and 1539 was the year of the great crisis with Almagro, intermittent rumors of which would have filtered back to Mexico. But Carlos V died in 1558. Clearly, no Spanish source could possibly have been so wrong or said anything to create confusion on this point. It is probably significant that Zapata was exactly nineteen years off, because one of the writers in the Tlaxcalan chain of annals writers had in fact gotten most events in the first half of the sixteenth century nineteen years off, as he thought that Cortés's arrival in 1519 must have occurred in 1500, a sort of year-zero, and he was widely copied.[63] Once again, it is seems sensible to conclude that Zapata was looking at notes in Nahuatl.

Who wrote these notes or made these statements? In the early twenty-first century, an era of language revitalization, readers can easily value Zapata's desire to preserve the Nahuatl language and consult only Nahuatl sources. Yet the full answer he would have given to the question will unsettle some. He didn't want just any Nahuatl speaker to tell him whatever he remembered. He wanted to hear only from tlatoque—literally, rulers, the plural of tlatoani, though by his era it had come to mean cabildo members, or more broadly, the pool of men from whom cabildo members were drawn. It will come as no surprise that Zapata frequently covered a particular year from more than one perspective, including more than one voice, especially in the period before he began to generate long and detailed entries stemming from his own experiences. Sometimes these speakers rise out of anonymity and declare their names; at other moments, it can be deduced who they are. There are six recognizable figures whom he quotes, and all six fit squarely within the category of "tlatoque."

In 1609, someone who called himself a fiscal of an unnamed church spoke "here in Tizatlan," explaining, "We were asked to pay [the tithe] every week."[64] Zapata's wife's family was from Tizatlan, so such a segment could have come from her father or grandfather, or any of various other good friends among the indigenous nobility in the vicinity who might have served as church officer and been responsible for the collection of the tithe. In 1616–1617, a man styling himself "I, Sebastián de Rosas" contributed text.[65] He lived in the city of Tlaxcala and served as clerk of the jail and later as the teniente in charge of work parties, an assistant to the gobernador. In the 1620s and 1630s, someone contributed who clearly had a close relationship with the Spanish church hierarchy in downtown Tlaxcala: in a most unusual stance, he reported on who filled various church positions with almost as much interest as he showed in the indigenous cabildo. Zapata's father (or perhaps uncle or other relative) served as fiscal in this generation.[66] This could have been his work, or that of some close acquaintance of his. In 1643—in the wake of the death of Zapata's parents and thousands of others in an epidemic—one Antonio Diego spoke in the first person, explaining that he had often acted on behalf of the governor and his teniente as well as the cabildo's notary because he could write well.[67] From the early seventeenth century, comments are often made from the reference points of Topoyanco (as in the case of the bishop's visit in 1622) or else Acxotlan, both pueblos in Ocotelolco and both homes to branches of the Salazar family, with whom Zapata was on intimate terms. Don Bernabé Salazar seems to have been Zapata's closest friend, and his son, don Manuel Santos Salazar, the age of Zapata's own children, actually managed to attend university and become a priest. They each contributed first-person signed statements.[68] Others in their extended family or circle of friends probably added segments as well, but these are two whose participation is certain.

All six distinguishable contributors were of sufficiently noble status to fill important posts. Antonio Diego might not have been of the nobility—given his undistinguished last name and his comment that the gobernador's teniente "permitted me to be the clerk"—but he was both educated and close to powerful men, so most likely he, too, was born a pilli and meant only that he had not actually been elected; if he was not a pilli he had proven his worth in a time of great need, like the quauhpilli in generations before.[69] These were not just any noblemen; they were all scholars to some extent, qualified by their education to serve as cabildo scribe or fiscal or even to enter university in one case. In short, Zapata's manuscript was the work of the elect, of those anointed by virtue of their line of descent to speak for a teccalli and by virtue of their skills to keep its history.

Yet there is no evidence that Zapata's assumptions stemmed ultimately from deep-seated snobbery or a bent toward exclusivity. Rather, they seem to have been a mark of his belief in the responsibility of the pilli class to represent their people effectively and preserve the community. Indeed, his greatest fear was that they would relinquish this responsibility and lose the trust of the commoners. And if they faded from the scene, there would be no one else who could maintain the intellectual life of the community. It was not that the elderly male pipiltin were the only people of value. In Zapata's text, women are important for their lineage and for the children they bear, and laboring men are honored for their work. Certain Spaniards can be loved, and certain Africans respected. But none of them can be the indigenous people's history keepers. It was simply not the role assigned to them—and, as Zapata well knew, it was never likely to be.

In the years in which he is narrating events himself, Zapata's tone is neutral or generous, with certain significant exceptions. Specific clues to his perspective on his relationships with others can be found in his use of the term "we." In his writings, he ties himself to those who surround him in his parish when he speaks of "our father" (meaning the priest) and "our precious mother" (meaning the beautifully dressed icon of Mary that they carry in procession). Never was he more delighted to belong to a group of neighbors than when they worked together to purchase a bell, for he had long been a lover of chimes. "The bell came to our chapel, and we could no longer hear what we said to each other," he reported gleefully.[70]

Sometimes Zapata's "we" refers to the indigenous people of Tlaxcala as a whole, not just those of his own chapel or neighborhood. For instance, some cabildo officials once traveled to Puebla to try to bring back some Tlaxcalans who had left secretly to settle in that town, hoping to avoid paying tribute in either place, and he called the absconders "our Tlaxcalan children."⁷¹ Once he even reported on a highly self-conscious use of the notion "we Tlaxcalans," claiming that he and his peers continued to follow in the loyal tradition of their ancestors. (Indeed, he was so intent on making this point that he forgot to change the word *puente* to *quappantli*.):

> On Saturday, February 15, at eleven o'clock the tlatoani [meaning the viceroy] entered San Juan Atlancatepec. And this is what happened when we—the gobernador and the other pipiltin—went to meet the entourage. The gobernador was don Francisco Ruiz from Tepeticpac, governor for the first time; the alcalde of his sub-altepetl was don Martín Pérez, the regidores don Nicolás Salvador and don Francisco Hernández. For Quiyahuiztlan, there was the alcalde don Juan Buenaventura Zapata y Mendoza, don Francisco Pascual, and other nobles from Quiyahuiztlan, together with the residents of San Juan Atlancatepec. Everybody got undressed down to the *sotanilla* or *ropilla* [meaning short doublets—they had removed their outer garments] and everybody carried a walking stick to meet him at the bridge [*puente*]. And our king said, "Why do you do this?" and they [the tlatoque] answered him, "We will accompany you wherever you go. We are already aware of your concerns [meaning your needs]. Thus did our ancestors, so that the marqués [that is, Cortés] conquered all the altepetls." The king was very grateful for these words. He said, "Truly you are impressive, you Tlaxcalans. You make clear both the respect you deserve and the respect you give to others. May our Lord God keep you. I thank you deeply."⁷²

Remarkably, when Zapata said "we" he often meant not only members of his own immediate community, or of his beloved Tlaxcala writ large, but all Nahuatl speakers or even all Indians. He used a word frequently which is not generally found in other indigenous texts. He adopted the Spanish word *indio*, rendered it in Nahuatl pronunciation as *itio*, and added a suffix of honor and respect, thus *itiotzin*. The first time he used it he said *titiotzin*, meaning "we who are Indians."⁷³ Usually when Nahuas wished to distinguish between Spaniards and themselves, they used the term *macehualli*, or "commoner" in the old tongue. Chimalpahin did this consistently. But this would not do for Zapata, as his thinking and his social experience were steeped in the distinctions between macehualli and pilli. And unlike most other indigenous writers, he frequently wanted to draw a circle around people of native descent, distinguishing them from all others. He never did this pejoratively. Either he was conveying a simple fact about ethnicity, or, if there was any subtext at all, he was implying a positive statement about the worth of the indigenous: that they had participated in creating art or music, or had heard and responded to the word of the king alongside all the other peoples of the realm. Neither the traditional word for "commoners" nor the concept of a "person from a certain altepetl" would do for Zapata. He needed a more inclusive rubric.

Perhaps the crux of the matter, in considering Zapata's understanding of his relations with others, lies in his concept of "tlatoque." Clearly, he felt at one with the people of his immediate community and with the indigenous people of Tlaxcala as a whole and with Nahuatl-speaking Indians everywhere. But within this generous-spirited connectedness, what do we make of his unshakable conviction that only certain people could rule, and only certain ones give voice to history? How important was it to him to define himself in opposition to, and as superior to, the macehualli majority that surrounded him? What to make of his certainty that he had a right to represent the latter both intellectually and politically, but they could not do the same for him?

Who, in short, were his tlatoque? The tlatoque of his text are by no means all-powerful. Indeed, in the second half of the sixteenth century and the first part of the seventeenth, their primary role was to be periodically taken prisoner and occasionally executed by the Spanish government when they could not manage to deliver whatever the Spanish overlords demanded from their people. In the 1670s, when a tax crisis erupts during Zapata's political career, the tlatoque are once again subject to such dangers. It is true that the tlatoque speak on behalf of their people, organize their people, and give orders to them, but they are likewise the ones held responsible when all does not go well.

Nor are the tlatoque of Zapata's world consistently honorable and good. In the preconquest period, many are dreadful schemers, and in his own lifetime, he does not hesitate to criticize indigenous governors who he feels have been irresponsible or profligate. He tolerates a mestizo who enters the cabildo and even ends up serving as governor for many years until he is caught in a corruption scandal; then he turns on him bitterly, calling him "that mestizo from Hell." "At his hands were destroyed the inheritances of the pipiltin.... That one, he destroyed everything."⁷⁴ Communal funds were lost and the people's trust irreparably damaged. His views echo those of another traditional Nahuatl annalist writing a century before, who in the *Annals of Juan Bautista* railed against a drunken and abusive Spanish official: "He should not be chosen [to lead] if his life is not righteous, even if he is a nobleman. He should not guide the community. He who scoffs at other people should not perform any post. Even if he is the viceroy or the visitador, if he doesn't do his job rightly, if he afflicts people, then he is from Hell. He belongs in Hell. He will go to Hell, and will be forever imprisoned there." Like many of his ancestors, what Zapata saw clearly when he thought of the tlatoque was apparently not their power and wealth, but rather their vulnerability to crisis and their responsibility to others. Such men owed much to posterity, not least rectitude and the use of their intellects.

Most tellingly of all, perhaps, for Zapata the word "tlatoque" referred to a social role exclusively, not to the actual humans who temporarily filled that role. The tlatoque represented all the people; in effect, they were the sum and substance of the people. Thus specific individuals could not identify themselves as tlatoque. For semantic reasons, it was grammatically impossible to do so. In the Nahuatl language, all nouns are in effect also predicates and must have an accompanying subject pronoun. "We [who were] musicians played our instruments," Zapata might say, or "He [who is] the governor gave the orders." On numerous occasions, Zapata would list all those who had been elected to office in a given year, including himself. Then he would describe, for example, a procession in which all cabildo members participated. He would say, "They [who are] the tlatoque" gathered or went in procession, and in the very next sentence something like, "we [meaning the individuals walking] went around the building" or "we went in a line." In context, the fact that the preceding sentence always read simply *in tlatoque* ("they the tlatoque") rather than *titlatoque* ("we the tlatoque") is notable indeed. Once, Zapata avoided a grammatically awkward situation—when the word "tlatoque" was needed but using the third person was going to render his sentence horribly unclear—by saying *timochitin cauildo* ("all of us of the cabildo").⁷⁵

Yet this construct was shattered in 1671. Zapata could not say (or even think) *titlatoque* ("we the tlatoque") as long as the tlatoque were understood to be not a subset of the people, but rather the equivalent of all the people, the stand-in for the whole, not simply a set of individuals. He could do so, however, once a great social crisis occurred, and the macehualtin began to place themselves in direct opposition to the governing pipiltin, to the tlatoque. In February of 1671, popular anger over increasing taxes on maguey plants—increases that the tlatoque had in fact vainly attempted to stave off—boiled over. "Everyone got angry and confronted us," Zapata wrote. "They really shouted."[76] He did not say that everyone confronted the government or even the cabildo. They simply confronted "us"—in context, clearly the tlatoque. This is a first in his lengthy text. He is now aware that the people are blaming their own leaders, that they no longer trust them to speak on behalf of the community.

One might assume that the people were angry because their noblemen had proven to be ineffective advocates, but the situation was worse than that. They were convinced that it was their own tlatoque who desired to see them pay higher taxes (so as to further enrich themselves), and the Spanish were only too happy to encourage this popular distrust. In May, viceregal officials issued a statement declaring that they themselves were attempting to lower the per capita tax by taking a new head count: the city's total quota would remain the same but be divided by the greater number of people uncovered in the count. Following tactics reminiscent of the 1560s, they said that the people's own governors were attempting to prevent such a change. Rumors ran rife: "The people of all four altepetl and from all of the villages went inventing things about us, that we were taking money from them and that the [Spaniards] were going to lower the tribute by half."[77] It is clear that Zapata feared social chaos would result from the kind of talk being instigated by the Spanish authorities against his newly defined "us," but the Spaniards remained blithely unaware of any danger. Responding with alacrity to the people's suspicions concerning their governing nobles, Mexico City sent auditors to the cabildo. "They came to investigate us about everything," wrote Zapata.[78]

What the tlatoque had been saying soon proved to be correct: the Spanish had no real intention of lowering individual tax payments, and in 1672, as soon as the new census was complete, they raised the total amount of tribute considerably. The city exploded in riots. It was what Zapata had been expecting. This time, however, the people laid the blame on the Spaniards and surged toward the royal offices. "It was a real war that was made," commented Zapata laconically.[79] The violence was soon put down. As treasurer, it fell to Zapata to deliver the newly collected taxes not long after. He could barely contain his loathing for the royal officials who had caused this crisis in his community. He and his peers deposited the money and "left without further ado."[80] He expressed the latter in a sentence of perfect alliteration and rhythm, *çan iuhqui yaque* or "San Yuki Yaki," just as he would have told the story to a roomful of listeners who still valued the aural component.

The next year it came out that the longtime mestizo governor had in fact been involved in some kind of racketeering, and Zapata's pain and anger knew no bounds. The angry populace dragged "the mestizo from Hell" to Mexico City, where he was imprisoned. Then Zapata and his community worked to put their lives back together. A few years later, when he was robbed by fellow Tlaxcalans, he was relieved that they wanted only cash. They did not destroy his manuscript. They did not destroy his historical costumes and accoutrements. "Not a rag did they remove," he said. He continued his labors on behalf of the altepetl. He went on writing the xiuhpohualli. In some ways, no real changes were discernible in his day-to-day life. Yet certain subtle shifts were occurring for Zapata. He largely replaced his use of the cumbersome "tlatoque" with "pipiltin," a term that did allow for "us" vs. "them." He complained with a touch of bitterness when other mestizos and people of the macehualli class rose to political prominence, usurping the positions of the pipiltin. Implicitly, if the pipiltin were losing their status as defenders of the altepetl, and anyone wealthy enough could claim the title, then the pipiltin must also eventually lose their position as the altepetl's legitimate historians, preservers of its memory. Once that role was gone, the pipiltin would indeed be envisioned only as parasites, as collectors of tribute produced by the sweat of other people's brows. The notion of entrusted representatives of the indigenous community who were inherently wise, who knew how to speak on behalf of others, both in the present and across the generations, would disappear. It was not only the nobility who would be the losers. All the indigenous would lose their history, for the men and women laboring in the fields, though they might preserve a tattered lienzo or even a set of folios comprising a xiuhpohualli, would be unlikely to have the time and energy to preserve knowledge of such an object's inner workings. As it turned out, he was far from wrong.

***

Such fears must explain the plaintiveness of some of the later entries. In 1685, an aging Zapata went with another council member, a much younger man, to see the Spanish governor. They complained that the indigenous alcalde from Quiyahuiztlan, don Pascual Ramírez, had held a post for eleven years, which was against their custom of rotation and led to corruption. In his book, Zapata wrote, "He is not a pilli. He was just raised among the priests and dresses like a Spaniard."[81] Zapata was beginning to feel very tired, saying that he was "already an old man." A few years later, it had become entirely clear that they were not going to be able to dislodge the Spaniards' protégé, even though he broke all traditions, to the point of selling corporate land without discussing the matter with his peers while he was governor. "How many years he has held the charge," murmured Zapata in 1688, which would be his own last year.[82]

Even within his own circle, Zapata was forced to face the idea that change was coming, that success might have to be defined differently than he had always done. The young people in his life made this clear to him. One of his daughters, doña María Jacoba, had a baby out of wedlock.[83] Despite the shame, however, the child, whom they called doña Antonia Sebastiana, grew up to be a delightful girl. Zapata's younger son, Salvador Mateo, married her, protecting the family honor and burying her illegitimacy. (It was perhaps fortunate that Zapata himself did not live to see this granddaughter Antonia Sebastiana widowed, for her next husband was a commoner, a successful goldsmith. He called himself "don Juan Diego," but his in-laws said he was really "*el indio* Huehueton."[84]) The son who bore Zapata's name inherited the cacicazgo and married a young woman of an established family.[85] Zapata's other daughter, Felipa, also married well. In 1686, Zapata had the satisfaction of seeing Felipa's husband and his own younger son, don Salvador, elected to the cabildo; he carefully recorded it in his annals.[86] He mourned the fact that the power of the governorship no longer rotated among the four subaltepetls as tradition dictated; he undoubtedly warned his children to be on their guard and to attempt to protect Tlaxcalan tradition, but he knew there was little they could do. [87]

Don Bernabé's son, Manuel de los Santos, had crossed the line and was dressing like a Spaniard. He was to be forgiven, however, or even celebrated, for he had become a priest and a scholar, succeeding according to his own culture and that of the Spaniards. He was a contemporary of Zapata's own legitimate children, but when he was an adolescent, his life took a different turn. Undoubtedly with the encouragement of the Franciscans in Topoyanco who had educated him, his father sent him to Puebla to enter the monastery there as a novitiate.[88] Entering was a long process. In April of 1675, the family made application and the friars agreed to begin the process of investigating his "legitimacy, quality and other conditions." They did not refer to his "purity of blood" as they did in the case of all other applicants; they simply avoided mention of the subject altogether. Theoretically, indigenous novices were prohibited, but just recently there had been increased discussion of the need for more religious with knowledge of indigenous languages. Fray Agustín de Vetancurt, already a longtime resident of the friary, had published his *Arte de la lengua Mexicana* two years previously, and he was at work on a Nahuatl version of the Vía Crucis. On May 27, don Manuel's friends and family arranged for three natives of Topoyanco then resident in Puebla to appear before the committee of the friars who handled these matters. One of the witnesses was relatively highborn and could read and write Spanish with ease; one could barely sign, and the other left his mark. When questioned, the educated one swore that had known the applicant all his life and then demonstrated his knowledge of local history. He was able to list the young man's progenitors on both sides by name, going back three generations, thus proving that don Manuel was legitimately descended on both sides from ancient nobility, indeed on his father's side from Citlalpopocatzin, the ruling king when Hernando Cortés arrived. He had always been a well-behaved youngster, and his family had means and did not need his support. Implicitly, it was clear that on the contrary they would be able to make donations to the order. The two other witnesses made briefer statements to the same effect. That very day, don Manuel was approved.

Sometime in the ensuing weeks or months, the Salazar family received word of the results and arranged to send the young man to Puebla. Probably one of the friars took the boy when he had to go to the city on business. His father definitely did not travel with him, for fray Luis de Garro, the master of novices, had to write to don Bernabé in October to say that he would be needing money to purchase clothing to wear during the novitiate.[89]

The boy's teachers reported that he conducted himself well in the community of friars, but not long after he donned the habit of a novice, he became "indisposed," suffering from acute stomach pains that went on for about two months. Some thought it was the work of the devil, but eventually they decided that he was genuinely ill. Don Manuel decided that he could not take up the vocation after all. He left. Whether someone had been tormenting him within the abbey walls, or he simply had realized he did not have the temperament to become a monk, or he was in fact suffering from disease, we shall never know. It is enough to know that he was convinced he should not be there. In April 1676, fray Luis de Garro wrote a reassuring letter to his father to tell him that his son had left voluntarily because of his ailment; he had not been expelled.[90]

Somehow in the following year don Manuel made the acquaintance of Puebla's brand-new bishop, Manuel Fernández de Santa Cruz (the same who would a decade later take the pen name of Sor Filotea and write a public letter to Sor Juana Inés de la Cruz, chiding her for her secular pursuits). Most likely an ally within the monastery made the introduction: Vetancurt could have done it. Certainly don Manuel later spoke of him with affection and admiration, mentioning his "accustomed humility and great modesty."[91] However the connection was made, the intellectually active bishop liked the young indigenous man and became his mentor. He insisted that he enroll at the university in Mexico City. There, don Manuel studied Otomí—the most common language after Nahuatl in his home region of Tlaxcala—with Professor Francisco de Aédo y Peña, who held one of the university chairs in indigenous languages. Don Manuel de los Santos Salazar graduated as *bachillerato* in five years, in May of 1684, and then the bishop of Puebla summoned him home, made him a deacon, and licensed him to say Mass.[92]

Don Manuel de los Santos Salazar said his first Mass on October 28, 1685 at the church of Santa María Acuitlapilco, the town his mother hailed from.[93] The indigenous governor attended, as did the alcaldes of Tizatlan, Tepeticpac, and Quiyahuiztlan (none other than don Pascual Ramírez, the indigenous man raised by the friars). Of course don Juan Zapata was there to hear. He was angry that no representative of Ocotelolco came to complete the representation of Tlaxcala but quietly pleased that "many Spaniards" attended.[94]

Over the next six years, as was customary for the newly ordained, don Manuel worked as a vicar who assisted older priests with established parishes. He was sent to various villages on the eastern slopes of Matlalcueye, the green-skirted volcano, which the Spaniards were calling La Malinche. On December 2, 1685, he was already signing baptism certificates.[95] In 1691, bishop Fernández awarded him a parish of his own, and then in 1693, after an extensive redistricting, he installed don Manuel as the first *cura beneficiado* of a new parish, San Lorenzo Quauhpiastla. It was a difficult assignment, for it was a large district with parishioners of various linguistic backgrounds, but the bishop already had reason to believe don Manuel could manage it. There were tensions—not everyone, whether Spanish or indigenous of other backgrounds, welcomed a Nahua cleric—but don Manuel worked hard, even investing his own personal funds in the parish. Soon his younger brother, don Nicolás Simeon, who had gained admission at the university in his older sibling's wake, joined him as his vicar, and they lived and worked together. They found that the locals did not want to deal with the responsibilities the redistricting entailed. They had been ordered to build a church, for instance, but had responded by constructing only four walls with a relatively useless thatch roof. "I and my brother the vicar personally hauled the [needed] materials—sand, stone, water and wood—because it had neither altar nor door nor roof."[96]

However, despite his efforts, after fourteen years at the post don Manuel still felt himself to be *persona non grata* in the area. He and his brother had accused locals of practicing the old religion in a nearby cave, and at one point he even felt his life was threatened. He may not have been exaggerating about that, for the tone of some of his writings occasionally bordered on the vitriolic.⁹⁷ He had lost the sight of one eye and was feeling some strain in the other. By 1707, a middle-aged don Manuel was pleading for a more congenial assignment. The authorities responded positively, and in February of 1710 he became *cura beneficiado* of Santa Cruz Cozcaquauhatlauhco, very close to his hometown. His brother took over Quauhpiastla, and don Manuel lived happily in his declining years among people who celebrated his accomplishments rather than resenting them.⁹⁸

For his new parishioners, he orchestrated a lively morality play, *Colloquio yn quenin oquimaxili yn tlazomahuizquauhnepanolli Santa Cruz intla cemic nopilhuiani Sancta Elena* ("Colloquy of How the Fortunate Saint Helen Found the Precious Revered Wooden Cross"), and dozens of community members presented it in May of 1714 to celebrate Corpus Christi. They even performed indigenous dances in the midst of it.⁹⁹ The villagers of Santa Cruz, as their town was generally known, would have been delighted to perform a play about the most famous Holy Cross of all; indeed, some version of what don Manuel redacted was probably traditional holiday fare in their town, given that don Manuel did not claim authorship but only editorship.¹⁰⁰ Though all the ideas may not have been his, he certainly immersed the work in the style of conversation and local culture he knew so well, even allowing for humorous distancing from the past. Says a peasant from the Holy Land before a battle: "I will cut the throats of some [of our enemies] and drink their blood; I will flay some and dress myself in their skins!"¹⁰¹ Nahua realism and a cultural penchant for teasing are evident in his companion's answer: "What are they, then? Little sheep, or piglets, or little chickens?" And the author also shows himself well versed in the power dynamics intrinsic to conquest: when some captured Jews are threatened with torture if they do not reveal the whereabouts of the Holy Cross upon which Christ died, one poor prisoner answers, "I don't know! It's been two hundred years!"¹⁰²

Don Manuel, however, had another, perhaps deeper interest close to his heart, beyond his work as a parish priest. For years he eagerly collected and encouraged the production of xiuhpohualli texts.¹⁰³ He took an abiding interest in the work of don Juan Zapata. He and his father lent materials to Zapata, which were then incorporated into their friend's great work. In 1688, the venerable Zapata died; his book remained carefully stored away in his family's keeping. Probably his sons meant to write more, but several years went by and no one did. Then in 1691, a sequence of events touched them deeply, and one of them at last put pen to paper. On Thursday, August 23, there was an eclipse of the sun, and the next day their mother, doña Petronilla, departed the earth.[104] Now the son holding the pen was truly of the senior generation, the next in line for death, and it was his duty to keep the annals that his father and the ancient ones had put such faith in. Yet somehow, he did not want to take up the task.

The Zapatas' friend since childhood, don Manuel, had at that time just been given his first parish, San Hipólito Zoltepec, in Tepeaca. He took the book there, promising to take good care of it. He guarded it well over the years. And he turned it into a work that others would recognize as deserving of reverence. In his finest handwriting (and he had been trained well), he added an ornate title page in Spanish, complete with a medieval-style insignia of a fortified town, calling the work the *Cronológia de la muy insigne, noble y leal ciudad de Tlaxcala* ("Chronicle of the Very Remarkable, Noble and Loyal City of Tlaxcala"). In his opinion, there were important facts missing. Where space had been left, he sometimes added more material, generally in Nahuatl but often in Spanish. When he had an important addition to make in a particular year and no space had been left, he used the margins. He inserted mentions of the year according to the traditional calendar, and even year signs, including, in the beginning, some charming rabbits for the *tochtli* years. He added red and green lines, bringing the work closer to *in tlilli in tlapalli*. Henceforth, he thought, no one could doubt the work's credentials as an indigenous history in the ancient tradition. [105]

At some point, don Manuel sat down to write his own history. Long before, his beloved teacher fray Agustín de Vetancurt had introduced him to the published works of fray Juan de Torquemada and Carlos Sigüenza y Góngora, among others. The same question that had once plagued Chimalpahin had also animated don Manuel's conversations with his tutor: Whence had the indigenous peoples of New Spain come?

Vetancurt had gone over twelve widely varying theories elaborated by a number of scholars, and then he had said that the truth probably lay in more than one idea. The peoples of the New World were so varied that it seemed to him more than probable that they had come in waves from different places. Don Manuel agreed to some extent. He personally believed, however, that the majority must certainly have come from Asia (one of the twelve theories), given their physical appearance. Boatloads of people might have left in the midst of the turmoil caused by various invasions, such as that of Alexander the Great. He could not document his people's ultimate origins, but he could show that according to their own ancient texts ("histories painted with hieroglyphics," he would later call them, using Spanish words) the people had arrived in waves from different places.[106]

He wrote the ancient history of central Mexico in Nahuatl in a series of twelve "chapters," using the Spanish word to express that idea. He began, "It is said, it is told, that those who were the Toltecs were very great in size. Their clothes were long and white, reaching to their feet. These men were the ones who first arrived."[107] Relying partly on Torquemada and partly on other manuscripts he had collected over the years, he outlined the arrival first of the Toltecs and then of the Chichimecs, including the peoples who became the citizens not only of Tenochtitlan, but also of Azcapotzalco and other places. Finally, in the fifth chapter, he recounted the adventures of the arrivals in the region who eventually became known as the Tlaxcalans. To tell this story he turned to the work of Zapata, though he cited not him but his sixteenth-century source, Benito Itzcacmacuextli. Clause by clause, he took what he had to say from Zapata, even unintentionally copying an error, referring to Cuauhtitlan when Cuauhtinchan was intended.[108] He adjusted the language. He modernized the spelling somewhat, replacing many a "y" with an "i," for example, and leaving out Zapata's old-fashioned periods between clauses. He simplified the story, expunging incomprehensible sixteenth-century jokes as well as references to obscure peoples or gods. And the dialogue all but disappeared. The chiefs had shouted insults at each other and orders at their underlings for the last time in Zapata's rendition. Their voices were silenced now, but their deeds lived on as don Manuel filled page after page.

Having united and made sense of the cacophony of sources he had long been familiar with regarding ancient Mexico, don Manuel wanted to do more. He wanted to make the work more widely available. Thus he began the project of creating a concise Spanish version of his work, later called the *Cómputo cronológico de los indios mexicanos* ("Chronological Computation of the Mexican Indians").[109] There, he explicitly placed the work in the context of the work of Spanish scholars and specifically the comments of his former teacher Vetancurt concerning the origins of the peoples of Mexico. He followed this discussion with the first three chapters of his earlier work, taken largely verbatim, though with some strategic cuts made for brevity's sake. Then he presented a version of some work once done by Sigüenza y Góngora, who had undoubtedly himself used the annals of Chimalpahin: don Manuel wrote out a lengthy chart giving the equivalent years of the indigenous calendar for every European year from 1186 to the year in which he wrote, 1711. Extracts of the material on the Tlaxcalans (which don Manuel had in his prior work included as a fifth chapter) were placed at the margins of the timeline itself, along with key facts about the Mexica. The Tlaxcalan material thus was rendered relatively prominent, although it was not presented in the introduction along with the material on the Toltecs and the earliest arriving Chichimecs. Perhaps don Manuel proceeded in this way because in the case of the Tlaxcalan material, he would have had to cite Tlaxcalan authorities, rather than Europeans such as Torquemada; or perhaps he had given himself a word limit and wanted to use his space to treat the Nahuas best known to Europeans. Whatever his reasons for arranging it as he did, he succeeded in incorporating what he believed should be there.

Don Manuel may have wanted to have his *Cómputo cronológico* printed. He had once paid for the printing of some copies of a brief treatise he wrote on "the good death."[110] The copy he left behind when he died seems to have been intended as a draft: his handwriting, which had sometimes been so very elegant, was here poor and difficult to read.[111] Though he did not actually print it, an early manuscript copy was widely circulated, and one hundred years later an eager and patriotic Mexican creole had it printed.[112] In any case, it is clear that don Manuel de los Santos Salazar, descendant of Citlalpopoca, saw his people as the equals of all other peoples and wanted their origins in the Old World clarified before the reading public; he wanted his people's calendar and the European calendar synchronized for the telling of coherent history. He desired that the two traditions be brought together in a mutually intelligible way. Zapata, now dead for a number of years, had wanted to communicate with his own posterity, not with the wider European world, but he undoubtedly would have approved the younger man's project in its scholarly essence: after all, it insisted that Nahua truths were the equal of all others. He would have had reservations about aspects of don Manuel's proceedings—not least his use of Spanish—but even these he would have understood.

As don Manuel grew old, he could look about and find himself a sort of a patriarch despite his legally celibate state. The nearby countryside was populated by nephews and great-nephews who had followed in their uncle's footsteps, attending university and entering the church; others had moved to Mexico City as relatively privileged citizens.[113] He and his younger brother don Nicolás each had a young family member as vicar. Indeed, the bishop of Puebla seems to have realized early on that cultivating such a family network was a significant element of the potential success of his plan to encourage indigenous priests. These were large parishes and in each case the cura beneficiado needed a vicar, but it might have been difficult to find a Spanish vecino willing to serve under an indigenous priest. There were at least two other younger men in the Topoyanco area who shared don Manuel's interest in history and who kept historical annals resembling ones in his collection, but who had considerably less education. These were more than likely the illegitimate sons of one or another of the Salazars; there would have been nothing unusual in that. One local annalist who styled himself "I, Marcelo Salazar," whose mother's name was María Concepción (not "doña), is not found anywhere in the carefully recorded Salazar family tree.[114] Marcelo's field of vision included only local concerns; he was very chatty, and not at all wealthy, complaining bitterly about the price of paper.[115] Another wrote the year 1710 as 17010, 1711 as 17011, etc., having grown used to writing his years as "170—" plus another number. He recorded don Manuel's death with care when it occurred, giving the exact date, August 19, 1715.[116]

When don Manuel died, his books and papers—among them Zapata's annals and his own historical writings—almost certainly went to his younger brother, don Nicolás, who still served in his old parish. But when don Nicolás died in 1733, the younger relative who received them, whoever he was, apparently decided to sell. The famous collector Lorenzo Boturini was serving as lieutenant to the Spanish governor of Tlaxcala in the late 1730s. Don Manuel's leading treasures ended up in his "museum," appearing in the list he prepared in the 1740s. At least the Salazar who sold to him managed to convey the priceless quality of the documents he was passing on. Boturini gave credit to don Manuel de los Santos and wrote enthusiastically that Tlaxcala's history deserved to be written "in letters of gold."[117] Zapata would perhaps have ached to see the indigenous histories pass out of pilli hands, and even out of the hands of *itiotzin*, but he was of a philosophic turn of mind and almost certainly would have been satisfied that they were not destroyed. Future generations would read them, not only in foreign lands but also in Mexico and in Tlaxcala itself, just as he had always wanted.

Fig E.1 Folio 10 of the *Annals of Puebla*, version located in the Archivo del Venerable Cabildo de la Catedral de Puebla. Year 1665. Courtesy of the Arzobispado de Puebla.

Epilogue

Postscript from a Golden Age

House 1683. Here in this year, the judge don Fernando Delgado took a census. He was still really just a youth. He counted people in the month of April, in Lent. (–) At this same time, on Sunday, the 5th of April, in the afternoon, during prayers, there arose a great wind. It grew very dark. Then everywhere in the churches the bells were tolled. The next day, on Tuesday, the 6th day of the month of April, the heavens crackled very loudly at half past eight in the morning. Absolutely everyone, everywhere, was frightened. (–) Once again on that day, Tuesday, as night was coming on, there was a great sparkling to the east. Once again the bells tolled in all the churches everywhere. What happened was terrifying. At that time a bad cough broke out, of which many people died.

Englishmen

In this same year, on Thursday, the 13th of the month of May, there arrived a dispatch saying that English enemies were in Vera Cruz; they had already laid waste to the land. Some of the people there they killed, some they carried off with them, priests and ordinary Spaniards alike. And they amused themselves with the women; they dishonored them. They killed many people. They just wheeled them off in carts in order [f.18v] to bury them. They took from them all the goods that they had. On that Thursday, at the palace, they quickly unfurled the standard of blood, which had never come out before, which never before had been unfurled. Quickly proclamations were issued that all the Spaniards there were should outfit themselves for war. Then all the city people grew agitated. All the banners there were were raised.

The next day, Friday, the 14th day of the month of May, the mulattoes for the first time raised a banner, and their captain turned out to be a mulatto named Felipe Monzón y Mujica, a chili vendor.

Then on Saturday, May 15, the blacks raised a banner, and a black named Lorenzo de Tapia turned out to be their captain. Thus both of them raised [banners] for the first time.

On this day the Lord Bishop disrobed

Right after that on that same day, Saturday, the lord bishop went in the chamber where his robes and ornaments are, and when he came back out, he just came barefoot and had already disrobed as a soldier. He came carrying a very large cutlass. Then mourning cloth was displayed inside the chamber of the ornaments. And when they saw him like that, coming disrobed, [f.19] everyone wept about how he was now going to battle in Vera Cruz. Then quickly a proclamation was made at the cathedral door that all the secular priests there were should outfit themselves for war, that all were to accompany him. Then all the priests armed themselves for war; they put on swords, daggers, and carbines. All the secular priests thus armed themselves for war in order to accompany him into battle. And the lord vicar general turned out as their captain, and they were going to leave on Monday, but then at that moment there suddenly arrived a dispatch that no longer should they go, because the enemies had pulled back and were already at sea at what they called Isla Sacrificios, so that they didn't go after all. Then on Monday, the 17th day of the month, began the departure of the soldiers. They all went to Veracruz. And all that month of May there was nothing but tolling of bells and the weeping of the Spaniards' wives because all the men they were connected with were going to fight. And no one went about on horseback any longer, because all [the horses] were taken away from people, whether they belonged to a Spaniard or anyone else. They even took the poor little donkeys from them. There was only fear. What happened was really terrifying; never had it been seen ever since the arrival of the Faith.

The Covered One

At this same time, on Wednesday, the 19th day of the month of May, there arrived one who came saying he was supposedly an inspector who had come to inspect [f.19v] the equipment that the Spaniards call arms, all that were here in the city of [Puebla de] los Angeles. And then quickly he saw to it that a proclamation was made that those who had war equipment—maces and bullets—should manifest it. And the alcalde mayor, don Estacio, gave him money. And he was here Thursday, Friday, and Saturday. Sunday, early in the morning, he was going back to Vera Cruz. When the viceroy who is in Mexico City learned of it, he quickly sent don Frutos[1] to come arrest him, wherefore he was accused [of wrongful behavior] here in Cuitlaxcohuapan. The viceroy said, "If he is an authentic inspector, why did he not come here to Mexico to see me? Perhaps he is just a friend of the English who entered Vera Cruz. Go arrest him." And don Frutos came here to Cuitlaxcohuapan very quickly. He just came to appear here briefly to satisfy himself if [the inspector] was authentic. He returned and told him he was authentic, then he went away. Altepetl to altepetl [don Frutos] went looking for him. And he caught him in the town of Córdoba, at the conde de Orizaba's [sugar] mill, and he arrested him there and restrained his hands with fetters. He brought him to Cuitlaxcohuapan on Tuesday, the first day of the month of June, at 8:00 in the morning. He brought him straight to the home of señor don Juan de Avila on the street of the [f.20] Carnicería where one goes up to the convent of Santa Catalina. And when he brought him to the door, when don Frutos got out of the coach, he went dragging him with a golden chain to take him indoors. Then he quickly stationed guards at the entrance, and they were standing watch at the walkways and windows. And the next day when he was going to take him out he put irons on his feet to take him to Mexico City until word should be sent to Spain so that it could be known what was to be done. And they named the inspector "the covered one."

In the 1680s, don Miguel de los Santos loved to stand on the rooftop of his church, San Juan del Río, named many decades earlier at the time of the founding of the city for Saint John the Baptist. Don Miguel was an indigenous builder—indeed, he had helped to build the stairway up to the platform where he stood—and he was very active in his community's cabildo, even serving once as gobernador. From his vantage point, whenever the sun shone, he could see almost all of his beloved Cuitlaxcohuapan, or the Ciudad de Puebla de los Angeles, as the Spaniards persisted in calling it. Standing there, don Miguel was perched in the midst of his own hillside neighborhood of Tlaxcaltecapan (meaning "where the Tlaxcalans are"). Saint John's metaphorical river was here in actuality a stream that gushed from the foot of the church on which he stood down through a multileveled washhouse toward the Río San Francisco at the base of the hill. Just to his left, on the same side of the river, towered the church and convent of San Francisco, home of the friars who had brought his Tlaxcalan ancestors here in the 1530s—when the place was just an empty plain—to build a great Spanish-style city. Before his eyes, on the other side of the river, he could see the fruits of his people's labors over the course of the generations since. The multicolored tiles of the lovely town glinted in the light. What might otherwise have been an undistinguishable sea of streets was punctuated by the heights of the churches rearing up amidst the bright colors, marking the locations of different neighborhoods. The cathedral signaled the location of the great plaza in the heart of the Spaniards' traza, or downtown area. Beyond the traza were two additional indigenous altepetls, as don Miguel called them: to the west, that of Santiago Apóstol at the start of the road towards Cholula, and to the north, that of San Pablo de los Naturales, on the way to Tlaxcala. It was the three indigenous altepetls of San Francisco Tlaxcaltecapan, Santiago, and San Pablo that had come together to form a greater indigenous altepetl of Cuitlaxcohuapan, with a well-organized cabildo, in the time of his grandfather, in 1610. Helping to govern and defend this community had brought don Miguel much joy over the course of his life; with complaisance he surveyed his world from the church where he worshipped.[2]

But if don Miguel ever turned away from the view looking west and turned instead to face the east, gazing at the road that ran eventually to Veracruz and the sea, he might have felt his heart sink. From that direction came enemies who were potentially as dangerous to his people's welfare as the Mexica had once been to his forefathers'. In 1682, eight buccaneer captains met in the Gulf of Honduras and planned a massive joint attack on the wealthy city of Veracruz. Only two of them were actually English (the others being French and Dutch), but since it was the English who had aided and abetted Caribbean pirates over the years, they all became *Ingleses* in the minds of their victims. They landed without warning and rampaged through the area, then withdrew to an island in the bay called Isla Sacrificios while they waited for ransom for the hostages they had taken. In the meantime, some of them spent their days kidnapping anyone of even partial African descent from the streets, as these people could be sold as slaves in the English Caribbean.[3]

When the pirates finally left—with the hundreds of people whose lives they had destroyed—one of their accomplices from Santo Domingo stayed behind. He could not go home because of illegal contraband activities he had engaged in there. Instead, he donned some of the fine clothes he had stolen and added a title to his name, transforming himself into a Spanish nobleman called don Antonio de Benavides. He went to Puebla and announced that he was a visitador, an inspector sent by the Crown. He demanded to see what kind of weaponry the town had available. Then he began to collect the bribes that were customary. Fortunately, the viceroy was not convinced that the new arrival was a bona fide inspector, and he sent an Audiencia judge to confront him. When Benavides slipped away after an initial meeting, the government soldiers went on a wild search through the villages of the countryside. They found him, but not before he had done more damage to unarmed people in his way. For don Miguel, these months were the most unnerving he had ever lived through: it had seemed that outsiders still had the power to upend the polity, just as in the days of old.[4]

Working on a xiuhpohualli he had begun years earlier in the 1670s helped don Miguel reconstitute his sense of certainty concerning his altepetl's continuity.[5] He wrote with verve and energy, producing a text of greater intrinsic interest to almost any audience than any annals writer had done for generations, perhaps since before the Spaniards came. He was able to do this because he was so deeply versed in multiple traditions, yet without being constrained by any of them. On the one hand, he knew all about the genre of the xiuhpohualli. At some point during the sixteenth century, one of the migrants from Tlaxcala who moved to Puebla had brought along a set of annals among his most treasured possessions.[6] That document had been widely copied by the families who ended up settling permanently in Puebla. There, they added to it the history of their own conglomerate altepetl, newly founded as a single political entity in 1610. Always they maintained a timeline, a bar running down the left-hand margin, where they placed the old-style year glyphs, and then they would begin their paragraphs with the unusual phrase *Nican ipan xihuitl* ("here in this year"), almost as if they were pointing to the place on the timeline that they were discussing. Don Miguel's family had clearly inherited one of these documents—the surname "de los Santos" was prominent in Tlaxcala—and he had been taught what to do with it, how to maintain it. He carefully and without fail recorded the rotating governorship, for example.

At the same time, don Miguel was also an active citizen of a proud and lively Hispanic city. By the second half of the seventeenth century, Puebla de los Angeles was living in what might be called its golden age. Mexico's second largest city, it was a crossroads of merchant trade, and its wheat and sugar plantations and its textile mills rendered it productive in its own right. The city was thus renowned throughout the kingdoms of Spain for its many churches (more than any other city in Mexico), as well as the craftsmanship and music which the churches sponsored.[7] Don Miguel, a builder, would have been involved in many exciting projects in his time, eliciting both pride and a sense of connectedness to a wider world. His language use demonstrates that he was completely bilingual, his spelling that he was a reader.[8] He tells us himself that he heard and loved the most impassioned Spanish sermons and moving public readings of his day. In the midst of one revival movement, he says, "No one wanted to go to sleep at night!"[9] Yet despite his full immersion in Spanish language and art, no one had offered him a classical education or even an extensive Christian one. In short, no one trained him young as to which lines of thought to follow, which questions to ask or answer. His immersion in rich Spanish literary prose had only freed him to pursue many different kinds of stories and similes.

So when don Miguel turned to his writing project, the pen in his hand did not constrain him in the least. It did not feel awkward compared to the act of speech, as it sometimes apparently did even for Zapata. Nor did it call to mind hours of conversations with friars and teachers, as it did for Chimalpahin or don Manuel Salazar. With the pen he expressed a range of his thoughts and even occasionally his feelings as he moved down the timeline given to him by his forebears.

And the events of his life offered him a great deal to comment on, in both years of peace and moments of crisis. In 1685, don Miguel was elected gobernador of the indigenous cabildo. Then he learned to his cost what so many indigenous leaders had learned in the past century and a half: how unbearably difficult it often was to act as an emissary to the powerful Spaniards. Despite years of living side by side with Indians, with apparent respect for them, the Spaniards were nevertheless liable to exert their power in cruel ways without notice if it suited them. In August, the Spanish alcalde decided that too many Indians were diluting the purity of the traza. Those living in the demarcated downtown area were given a week to vacate their homes and find a place to live in one of the three indigenous barrios, upon pain of public whipping. The governor was told that lands would be made available for them to settle at the outskirts of town, but no deeds were forthcoming. Don Miguel went to the alcalde and convinced him to rescind the order on grounds that under the present circumstances, he simply would not be able to collect the full amount of the annual tribute. The people were allowed to return to their homes. Don Miguel would continue to argue with intrusive and overbearing Spaniards throughout his life whenever he felt it necessary, but this was the most trying moment for him because of his great responsibility as head of the cabildo.[10]

Don Miguel de los Santos seems to have died in the terrible epidemic that swept through Mexico in 1691–1692; certainly he wrote no more after that. Almost immediately, family members and other connections began to borrow and copy his text.[11] It is little wonder that they felt a need to preserve the past: there was a sense that the world might truly be ending, and certainly that the survivors would have to accustom themselves to a new earth. In June of 1691 torrential rains began that caused flooding in many areas and rotted the crops. A frightening eclipse followed in August; even the birds made doleful cries.[12] The event was considered the harbinger of the plague that followed, killing thousands. Terrible rioting occurred in Mexico City in June of 1692; it seemed the government might truly topple. Puebla escaped violence, but none living there were unscathed by the recent months. In copying out don Miguel's xiuhpohualli, the people of his world tethered themselves to a past—and implicitly, a future.

***

By the latter part of the colonial era, it was not uncommon in moments of crisis, when political or economic change was occurring and lands needed to be defended, for indigenous people to use what they knew of their history to create documents that might shore up their claims regarding their past even in a Spanish-style courtroom. For there, they had learned, knowledge passed down "time out of mind" would no longer be enough to secure a deed; they would need written documentation.

Furthermore, many of them wished to record histories that answered to the cultural needs of their own times, whether or not they ever went to court. So it was that they worked creatively and thoughtfully to produce historic texts we now call *títulos primordiales*, because the authors embed their claims as native peoples in the primordial or ancient past, even if their actual knowledge of that past was by then limited.[13] But the set of annals originally penned by don Miguel de los Santos was quite different from any of these other proliferating and creative histories. It was intrinsically tied to the past not only in its substance but in its very form.

Of course, in a text produced in the 1690s, one has to look hard to find these elements. At first glance, it seems that there is in fact very little that is precolonial left in don Miguel's annals, apart from the fact that he wrote in Nahuatl. After all, the text opens with the arrival of the Spanish and the Christian faith, and quickly moves through various military expeditions orchestrated by the Spanish in which the writer's people help them conquer other indigenous. It is, however, worth reading through the material again, looking at it from a different perspective (in true Nahua style). After the Spaniards arrive, there is a mention of the first viceroy and the first bishop arriving to rule in Mexico City—called by the same name as the Tlaxcalans had once used to refer to the much-hated Aztec capital. The very next event is the founding of "Cuitlaxcohuopan," which the writer adds is "known as the City of the Angels." There is no mention at all of the word "Puebla," nor is there in later years, when don Miguel was residing in a city that had by then been called "Puebla" by the Spaniards for a century and a half.

The writer proceeds to cover the very same themes that his forefathers would have treated in any xiuhpohualli that they had produced: the installation and death of reigning figures, wars and conquests during each reign, major building projects, and overwhelming acts of the forces of nature. Of course, these ancient elements have shifted shape and have realigned themselves in terms of relative importance. In don Miguel's text, besides the consistent treatment of the governance of the tripartite altepetl, we find a litany of high appointments—Spanish kings and queens, viceroys, alcaldes, archbishops and bishops—punctuated by mentions of the deaths of certain important people. The old pictoglyphs would have reminded performers to speak of the sacrifices made or the songs chanted at the various kings' coronations and funerals; here we learn of the impressive processions or the prayers offered, and once even the number of candles needed for an important feast day.[14] In ancient times, a king was responsible for mammoth building projects requiring communal labor, such as palaces, pyramids, or water works. Naturally, as a builder himself, one of don Miguel's favorite subjects is building projects: now they mostly relate to churches or convents, but water projects have not lost their fascination.

Wars once dominated political life. That was no longer true in don Miguel's time, but he finds enemies to dwell on nevertheless. First there are the expeditions against "savage" Indians undertaken by the Tlaxcalans. In later years, there are rebelling slaves and dangerous criminals, and eventually, of course, the English pirates. (Indeed, they return to Campeche when don Miguel himself is governor.) Generally there are no prisoners of war to be brought home, as there once were, but when English women prisoners are brought back from the piracy-related battles in the Caribbean, it is a matter of special interest, though don Miguel himself probably never saw any of them.[15]

The natural world looms as large as it ever did, with epidemics, floods, eclipses, and comets serving as defining experiences. A reader can almost feel that a pantheon of gods still watches over these dramatic events encircling mortals, for don Miguel seems to feel the presence of each and every saint who marches through his pages, giving the ceremonial icons almost lifelike qualities. They seem to go up and down hills almost of their own accord: rarely does he mention that they are actually being carried. "There she slept," he says of Mary, when a beautifully dressed figure is left in a particular church overnight.[16]

Don Miguel marked his text with evocative illustrations that also are reminiscent of the way glyphs were used, though these too have undergone a transformation. He used a skull to indicate passages about epidemics or deaths in war, a sun or a comet in discussing meteorological phenomena, a crown to note the accession of a king, and a picture of the structure itself to record the building of a church, cathedral, fountain, or other structure. In past times, a Nahua painter would have used a bundled corpse to denote death and a reed mat to signal the installation of a new king, but the categories, and the places where such reminder glyphs would appear, remain largely the same. In the old days, a comet was often a heavenly serpent, and in these seventeenth-century pages we find recognizable comets, but it is also noticeable that these modern ones have remarkably long and undulating tails.

Perhaps most importantly, in times past the public performances of the historical annals would have involved speakers from the multiple sub-communities that together made up the altepetl. Sometimes these would have worked together to create a deeper picture; sometimes their accounts would have conflicted. Sometimes a performance would have been used to bring people together; sometimes it would have marked a crisis in which alliances were in danger of unraveling. Certainly don Miguel continuously reiterates the presence and importance of the two other indigenous altepetls that combine with his own to form the greater whole, and sometimes he distances himself from them. (Indigenous lawbreakers, for example, are always from the barrio of Santiago, where people of Cholulan descent lived, not Tlaxcalans.)[17]

Living in his cosmopolitan world, however, don Miguel makes room for other sub-communities as well, for it is people of Spanish and African descent who are his actual neighbors, with the Spaniards living right across the river in their traza, and the free blacks and mulattoes in a populous neighborhood just to the northwest.[18] Generally all is well, and if we readers were to change a few names, we might imagine we had gone back in time, with the altepetl working quietly to resolve its own problems and the Aztecs only occasionally interfering from on high, and with people from neighboring villages tranquilly living their own lives, sometimes even being accepted as marriage partners. Then of course, as in the old times, just as the Aztecs might suddenly make inordinate demands or reorganize the local chieftainships in inappropriate ways, the Spaniards suddenly order all the indigenous out of the traza, or tell them that they are no longer allowed to make tortillas to sell to the public. And as in the old times, when the friendly people from neighboring communities might suddenly become enemies, so does don Miguel's opinion of free blacks periodically deteriorate. In 1682, the year of the pirates, don Miguel seems to have felt nothing but admiration for his black and mulatto neighbors who organized themselves to go and fight; they went at great risk to themselves, since they could so easily be enslaved, as events had already proven. In that very year, the son of a mixed marriage between and Indian and an African, one Mateo Jaén, was actually serving as gobernador of the indigenous council. But then two years later Jaén was accused of treating indigenous elders disrespectfully, and don Miguel and others sent messages to Mexico City to induce their Spanish overlords to forbid Jaén and all other non-Indians the right to serve on the indigenous cabildo.[19]

Last but not least, the language itself, the very voice of don Miguel, harkens back to decades past, not in a stilted sense but in a very natural way. The vocabulary don Miguel uses to describe an eclipse or an election, as well as the syntax that structures his sentences, could easily be that of Zapata or Chimalpahin or Mateo Sánchez, or even Alonso Castañeda. Minor shifts have occurred, indicating a more advanced stage of acculturation, but the essentials of don Miguel's self-expression would have been utterly recognizable to people of decades before.[20] Perhaps most remarkably, his annals even harbor vestiges of the old colorful dialogues that once were used to underscore the heart of any political conflict. When the pirates come, the bishop goes to the door of the cathedral and issues direct orders to the priests to arm themselves and follow him to battle. Later, listeners are even privy to the exact words of the angry viceroy far off in Mexico City: ""If [this man] is an authentic inspector, why did he not come here to Mexico City to see me? Perhaps he is just a friend of the English who entered Vera Cruz. Go arrest him!" He sounds like the angry high chief of ancient Huexotzinco, as recorded by Zapata, when the ruler first perceived the arrival of the Tlaxcalans: "Xiuhtlehuin . . . observed that smoke was rising from the top of the hill of Tlaxcala. He sent for someone and said, 'Who are they? Go and see who is making smoke on the hill of Tlaxcala. Go and see if it is due to those Chichimeca!'"[21]

Remarkably, the genre of the xiuhpohualli had proven strong enough and flexible enough to incorporate the new without obliterating the old. This was true on multiple levels: the year count, the format and agenda, the subjects, the language usage. Unfortunately, however, this was not the end of the story. After the burst of copying of don Miguel's text during the crises of the 1690s, no one else in his world ever wrote another xiuhpohualli, at least not as far as we know. If the genre was strong in its flexibility, it was also vulnerable to erasure, once the very premises were forgotten in busy interactions with the wider world. Don Miguel's marvelous text was only made possible by the fact that the Tlaxcalan community had kept older forms alive longer than had been feasible elsewhere, owing to its greater degree of cultural isolation, and then had transported those traditions to the earliest generations of their settlement in Puebla. Don Miguel's text is the exception that underscores the rule: elsewhere, by this time, histories that purported to come down from the past were mostly savvy contemporary creations.

We live in an era that admonishes us not to speak of cultural loss, but only of cultural change. Culture is not a frozen form that cracks and breaks, but a template that humans use to order and reorder their shifting realities in meaningful ways. If indigenous culture was transformed during the colonial period, it nevertheless remained authentically indigenous. If what Indians of later generations wrote could no longer be called a "xiuhpohualli," it was nevertheless the work of Indians. Nothing could be more clearly true. Yet perhaps we should not simply let the matter rest there, as we have sometimes done in recent years. Don Alonso Chimalpopoca, Marcos Tlacuiloc, don Mateo Sánchez, Chimalpahin, don Juan Zapata, and the bachiller don Manuel de los Santos would not have wanted us to. Don Miguel Santos would not have wanted us to. They would all have wanted us to ask certain politically charged questions out loud, as they were in the habit of doing. Is it wrong to acknowledge that don Miguel would have been saddened to think that no grandson of his, and no grandson of any of his contemporaries, would take up a pen to continue his work and write a xiuhpohualli? I think not. For if we deny him that grief, then do we not also implicitly deny the complexity, the sophistication, and the intermittent humor and beauty of the cultural forms he wished to protect?

If we face the painful truth that much of the knowledge that the native historians in the generations after conquest wished to preserve was in fact later lost for many generations, are we saying that their descendants were somehow less indigenous? Let the Nahua chorus answer, "No!" The people who came later had their own worlds to live in, and they experienced those worlds as indigenous people. Could the knowledge of the ancestors have lasted forever in the new worlds in which the descendants lived? No, indeed. The loss was no one's fault. And if the knowledge was lost, are the aging papers that the indigenous historians carefully wrote and preserved now valueless? No, four hundred times no, as the Nahua chorus would say. If we study the papers closely, we can still piece together and puzzle over and come to understand much of what the indigenous historians wanted posterity to know about the worlds they inhabited. They *did* succeed in doing what they wanted to do, in the long run if not the short, for they preserved an intricate, multifaceted contribution to the human experience. Perhaps their grandsons and granddaughters lost touch with it for a while, but they were the very ones who carefully guarded many of the documents until they eventually landed in libraries, thus keeping the voices of the ancient ones present here on earth. Listen, for as if from a distant hill, they still call to us across the centuries.

Appendices

THE TEXTS IN NAHUATL

Historia Tolteca Chichimeca

[F. 1v]

¶ yzcate yn ialtepepouan ȳ tolteca yn imaçicayo in cattca yn ueycan tollan centecpantli yn altepetli. yn ima yn icxi Mochiuhticac yn toltecatli. yn iyapo yn itepepo cattca çan oncā xixinque. yn ueycā tollan ynic quitlatlamaçehuito yn imaltepeuh

¶ Pantecatli		¶ Nonoualca	
¶ ytzcuitzoncatli		¶ Cuitlapiltzinca	
¶ tlematepeua		¶ Aztateca	
¶ tlequaztepeua		¶ tzanatepeua	
¶ tezcatepeua	5	¶ tetetzincatli	5
¶ Tecollotepeua		¶ teuhxilcatli	
¶ Tochpaneca		¶ zacanca	
¶ cenpoualteca		¶ Cuixcoca	
¶ Cuetlaxteca		¶ quauhchichinolca	
¶ cozcateca	5	¶ chiuhnauhteca	5

[F. 2]

[**glyph**: ce tecpatl]

¶ Ica . i . tecpatl . xihuitl . Ynic acico ȳ tollan yn ompa ualleuaque ȳ colhuacatepec yn tolteca chichimeca . ȳ icxicouatl . ȳ quetzalteueyac . ȳ tezcauitzill .

ȳ tololouitzin . yuan y nonoualca chichimeca . ȳ xelhuā . yn ueuetzin . ȳ quauhtzin ȳ citlalmacuetzin . cexiuhtica yn oc pacticatca . yn imaçica ȳ tolteca chichimeca .

[**glyph:** ome calli]

⸿ . 2 . Calli . xiuitl . y n ipā y ya monetecheua ȳ ya imochallania y ya quineyxnamictia yn itoca memac [sic] . ça quimoteliq̄ ȳ tolteca y piltzintli . auh nimā conmaniliq̄ yeuantin quizcalltique quiuapauhq̄ ȳ tolteca . auh tlacaço yueyo ȳ tezcatlipoca ça ye ytlachichiual ynic xinizque ynic moyauaz yn tolteca chichimeca yuan nonoualca chichimeca ynic mixnamiquizq̄ ȳ tolteca yn imaçica y nonoualca . Auh yn iquac ya telpochtli ȳ memac . nimā ya quinahuatia ynic ychan tlapiazq̄ y nonoualca yn memac . auh nimā quilhuiq̄ y nonoualca . ma yui . nopiltzin ma ticchiuacan ȳ tlein tocōmonequiltia . nimā ya yc ychan uallapia y nonoualca y uemac [sic] . auh nimā y quimitlanillia çiua quimilhuia y nonoualca ānechmomaquilizq̄ çiua . namechnonauatillia yeuatl y nahuiztetl ynic tzī-tamalpatlauac . oquilhuiq̄ yn nonoualca ma yui ma oc tictemocā campa ticanatiui y nauiztetl ynic tzintamalpatlauac . auh nimā quimonanaco yn çiua nauime yn aoc auilli ynic ueueȳ . amo yxquich yn itlatamachiual oquimilhui yn nonoualca amo yxquich y nicnequi amo açi y nauiztetl yn intzintamall cenca uey y nicnequi . nimā cenca oquallanteuaq̄ ȳ nonoualca

[F. 2v]

Auh nimā ya yc quimonana ȳ nonoualca nimā ya quimihilpia ytzteuepaltetech auh nimā qualanteuaq̄ yn nonoualca quitoua aquinon yn ya toca mocacayaua macha çā quitlatlalhuia yn tolteca . macuelle ma titoyaochiuacā can ticanatihui ȳ techitlanillia . auh nimā yc tlacueteuetzq̄ ȳ chimalli yn itzquauitl yn mitli yn nonoualca nimā ya ymaçica moyaochiua ȳ toltecaya momictia ouelquallanq̄ yn nonoualca yeuan ya quincocoua ȳ tolteca ynmaçica ȳ uemac quitoua ȳ icxicouatl . yn quetzalteueyac . tle y cauia tle ypampa yn ya yxpoliui ȳ tolteca cuix neuatl notlapeualltitl cuix neuatl niquitlani yn çiuatl yn ipampa ya timixnamique ya timoyaochiua ma onmique ȳ memac otechneyxnamicti . nimā ya quimilhuia ȳ nonoualca . ȳ xelhuā . ȳ ueuetzin ȳ quauhtzin yn citlalmacuetzin . macamo ximoquallanaltican nopiltzin cuix neuatl nicchiua ma onmiqui yn uemac . auh yn iquac oquicac yn uemac yn ya motlaçeçeuilia ȳ tolteca yuan ȳ nonoualca . auh nimā ya yc choloua ȳ memac . auh niman ya quiualltoca ȳ nonouallca quimintiuitze quitzatzillituitze coyouitiuitze yn ya quiualtoca quicallaquitiuetzico ȳ cencallco oztoc niman ya ypan callaqui yhicpac conanato quiualquixtia nimā ya oncā quicacalli yn oztotepā comictiq̄ auh yn iquac omiqui yn uemac nimā ya yc yaui ȳ tollā ȳ nonouallca ȳ xelhuā ȳ ueuetzin . yn icxicouatl ȳ quetzalteueyac auh yn iquac ouaçique ȳ tollan nimā omocētlaliq̄ omononotzq̄ ȳ nonoualca .

oquitoque tla xihualhuia tla xicmocaquiticā quen titlaca aço otitlatlacoque ma ytla ypan mochiuhti yn topilhuā ȳ toxiuiuā maçatiuian ma titlalcauacā quen oc tinemizq̄ ca ya otechneteche ca ya otechneyxnamicti yn uemac ma tiquincauacan ȳ tolteca nimā ya youallquixiua mochi quitqui quitqui [sic] yn itlatquin quetzalcouatl yn ixquich quipiaya . &c.

***

[F. 11v]

¶ Nimā ya tetlapaloua yn icxicouatl ȳ quetzalteueyac ȳ tezcauitzil ȳ tolo-louitzil ȳ couenan tlamacazqui quimilhuia ȳ tolteca tla xicmocquiticā nopil-huane toltecaye cuix quita cuix quicaqui ȳ totepicauh ȳ toteyocoxcauh yn amochoquiz yn amixayo yn otocōtlalito yn imixpā yn innauac ȳ chaneq̄ ȳ calleque yn auaq̄ yn tepeuaq̄ yn tlatoq̄ ȳ xicallanca yn olmeca quiuel-caqui yn amotlatoltzin . ȳ tizacozq̄ yn amapane . ameuā antlaylhuitlaltizq̄ yn axcā nauhyopan . yn ipan yn imaltepeylhuiuh amechualcentlatlacoltiya tle anquimati nopilhuane ma çotlauati yn amomatzin yn amocxitzin ximochicauacā yn at teyxco teycpac otamechnemitito campa tiyazq̄ ca ya nicā otechpo otechnito ȳ totepicauh ȳ toteyocoxcauh at ya nicā tictlatizq̄ ȳ tix yn toten quē quitoua quē techyeyecoua ȳ totepicauh yn toteyyocoxcauh yn ipalnemouani oc ycuatl quimati cuix aya nicā techpopoloz quē tlacauaz yn iyollotzin ma titotemachicā toltecahe acouic xomapanacā xomotetzillocā yc pachiui yn amoyolotzin yn otiqueuato yn otiquitoto yn imixpā yn tlatoq̄ yn teteuhctin ynic tiquinmaceuilizq̄ quiuelcaqui quitoua uel xicyeyecocā yn amouic mahantlapihuahtitin oncā anquicēquixtizq̄ ȳ tlatoq̄ yn olmeca ȳ xicallanca. ameuan anquimi[lhui]tlaltizque tla xiccaquicā. yuin. ȳ quitoua. yn tle anquimati ma ytla ancontecuilitin yn qualli tlauiz-tli tla ximouicacan tla xicmotlaneuiti ȳ tlauiztli amo anceyazq̄ yx tla cana amacozq̄ ȳ yancuic tlauiztli ça ye anquimotlaneuizq̄ ȳ chimalçoltzintli yn itzquauhçoltzintli ȳ cana uetztoc. yn oquimayauhq̄ auh tlaxiccaquicā ȳ tla cana amechmacazq̄ yn yectli chimally yn yectli ytzquauitl amo anquicelizq̄ çan inpeuaya quichiuazq̄ ȳ tla ouantlapozteque ȳ tla ouantlatlacoq̄ auh yn axcan tla xiccaquicā atle tiquincuilia atle tiquimeleuillia yn axcan yn iuh tichiuallo yn iuh tipololo ynic techixatequiya yn innextamalayouh yn içiuauā. ȳ tometzpā yn ya tocuitlapā ya momamaxotla. auh ynin ac teuan yn iuh technemitiya cuix titzcuintin ma ytla anquicelitin yn imaxca yn intlatquin yn chaneq̄ auh yn tla oamechmomaquilliq̄ ȳ chimalçotzintli yn itzquauhçoltzintli ynin nimā ya uel anquichichiua ȳ chimalçoltzintli yn itzquauhçoltzintli yn at cana oytlacauhqui ca toncuizq̄ ca ypan tiyaotizq̄ cuix techquaz cuix noço yeuantin quinquaz yn olmeca ȳ xicalāca yn olmeca

yn inchimal yn imitzquauh nimā ya mochoquilia yn icxicouatl ȳ quetzalteueyac quitoua o nopilhuane tle āquimati toltecahe.

[F. 12]

☞ Niman quimonanquililiq̄ yn imicniuā ȳ tolteca quimilhuia ouatechmoc-
neliliq̄ otoncacq̄ yn amotlatoltzin yn antonauā yn antotauā quē tlacauaz
yn iyollo ȳ totepicauh ȳ toteyocoxcauh at ya yxquich at ya ocā techmiya-
niliz techmotlatiliz at ya nicā topoliuia ouanmotlapalloq̄ ouantechapanq̄
ouantechtetzilloq̄ tla tonentlamaticā niman ya y xini. yn motlaneuitihui quimilhuia ȳ chaneq̄ mah amopaltzinco titotlaneuican yn amotlauiçoltzin cana
amochimalçoltzin yuan amitzquauhçoltzin amo yeuatl ȳ qualli amotlatquitzin
yn tla xitechmomaquillicā tontlapoztequizque/quimilhuia tle āquichiuazq̄
can anquinequizq̄/quimilhuia tla xicmocaquiticā tiquinmaceuilizq̄ ȳ tlatoq̄
ypan tomitotizq̄ yn ichan yn incallitec yn amauh yn amotepeuh/quimilhuia
aço ye anquinequi ȳ qualli totlauiz./quimilhuia amo conetle ça yeuatl yn ma
cana uetztoc nextamallayotitlā amotlauizoltzin: ma oc toconmochichiuilizq̄
ca ypan tiquimonelelquixtizq̄ ȳ tlatoq̄ ȳ totecuā./nimā ya quimilhuia ma yui
nepa ueuetztoc ȳ totlauiçol ȳ tochimazoll. ȳ titzquauhçol nepa xicpepenati
ca ya amo anquineq̄ ȳ qualli totlauiz/nimā ya nouian nenemi yn tlatlatete-
moua ȳ tecacalltenco yn tecacalltitlā yn cana tepan callaquitiui tlaquallo
atliua mach quinmonochillia çan inpan tlatlapiqui quinueuetzquillia auh
yn yeuā mocencaua ȳ motlapepeniya ȳ tlauizoltzitzintin yn chimalçolli yn
itzquauhçoli tla centoca y motlapepeniya auh yn iquac oconcuicuiq̄ nimā ya
mouica ynic tepal cacate yn ouaciq̄ yn techā niman ya uel quinmochichi-
uilia ȳ chimalçoltin yn itzquauhçoltin quintlauia quintexouia quimihitzoma
yn ichcauipilçoltzitzintin cenca uey ynic motolinique ynic tlayhiyouique yn
tolteca chichimeca

Annals of Tlatelolco

[F. 8]

Auh y mexica umpoualxiuhtique omome yn chapoltepec yc omey ynic nam-
oyeloque ce tochtli xiuitl ypa. Y uitziliuitl mexica ȳtlatocauh uicoc ȳ colhuaca
yoan ychpoch chimalaxotzi Xochimilco uicoque cimatecatl teuua tezcacouacatl. tozpaxoch . matlatzinco uicoque ciuatzitzintin quauhnauac uicoque
couatzontli yoa ciuatzitzinti Chalco uicoqq̄ Uitziltecatl yoā ciuatzitzinti
Acolhuaca ciuatzitzinti uicoqq̄ Xaltoca uicoque tepantzi teccatlamiaualtzi
ualcholoque amo mique uncan tepan acico colhuaca Azcapotzalco cihuatz-
itzinti uicoqq̄ maça [ualcholoqq̄ amo mique uncā tepā acico Colhuaca

Azcapotzalco ciuatzitzinti uicoqq̄ Maça]¹ uaca uicoc yaoçol ualcholo uncā tepā acico colhuaca yn oc quezqui mocauh acocolco motecato atlitic ye macuilihuitia yn teycnoittoto ỹ coluaca y uia tlatlatlauhtito eztloocelopan ỹ tlatlauhtiloto tlatoqq̄ Acxoquauhtli cuxcuxtli chalchiuhtlatonac achitometl. quimonilhuia y mexica ueuetqq̄ totecuiouane tlatoquehe techualiua ỹ tenoch auh yn iztachiauhtototl. auexotl . tenantzi . cunitoa . Ma xiquintlatlauhtiti ỹ tlatoqq̄ Coluaca motolinia y maceualli yn oc omocauh yn atlitic ỹ quihyouitoc ma noço titletlalica ma titlachpanaca, ma yntlan titocallaquiça yn tlatoqq̄ Quiualilhuia ỹ tlatoqq̄ Can oanmaquizque. quimonilhuia Ca atlitic uncā yn acocolco. nima ye yc conotza yn tecpoyotl conilhuia tla xiauh xiquinpoua quezqui ynic omaquizque. quimitato azoc untecpanti. auh y mexica yueltiuh ce utztli unca mixiuh yn atlitic quitocayotiqq̄ ỹ tlacat axolotl. Auh y uitziliuitl ayamo mique ynic untlatitlanqq̄ Conilhuia quē quitoa Cuix oc ypā aciquiui ymaceualhua ca ye uitze yn oc umocauhqq̄. nimā yc tzatzitiquiz y ciuatzintli quito. tleycā amo timiquizqq̄ tleycan topan aciquiui ma quimocaquitica yn tlatoque tleycā amo timiquizqq̄ ma tiçatzintli yuitzintli tocontitlanica cōcaqq̄ ỹ tlatoqq̄ quitoqq̄. Xoconilhuiti y uitziliuitl cuix no tiçatl yuitl quinequi. tecolli quimomaxaqualhuiqq̄ ynic tlequauitl quimonaniliqq̄. Auh ynic quintiçauiqq̄ ye ỹ tenextli ynic tlaauitectli tlequaztli elmomozco quimomictiqq̄ uncā tlatoca y ciuatzintli ye achto contlecauiqq̄ tzatzitiuh mochoquilitiuh quiualitoa. Colhuaqq̄ a ye niauh yn inemaniā ỹ can teutl y notzon yn nixti moch tlacaquiçaz. Çano yui tzatzitiuh uitziliuitl yn oumicque nimā ye yc quipopoua yn imezyo. Niman yc oyaqq̄ mexico yn coluaca uncā tlaliloqq̄ tiçaapa. quilhuia Oanquihyouiqq̄ mexicae ma ximotlalican uncā tiçaapa. Auh y ye matlaquilhuitia niman ye yc quinauatia coluaca tlatoqq̄. quimilhuia. Mexicae xicualhuillanaca ỹ chinamitl unca uallicatiaz yn aztatl unca uallonotiaz ỹ coatl. ciyotoc ỹ chinamitl unca anquitecaquiui ỹ tecpanquiauac yn oyuh quiualnauatique nima ye mochoquilia y mexica quitoa ototlauelliltic quē ticchiuazqq̄ yc quinotz y uitzilopochtli quimilhui

[F. 8v]
Macamo ximomauhtica ye nehuatl nicmati nech[ca]² temi chimamitl anquiuillanatiui namechititiz uel oquichiuhque ỹ quiuillanque ye ỹ cueptli tlatlatlalilli oypan ycatia yn aztatl auh yn coua yoli nemini³ tentiuh yn chinamitl yc cenca quimotetzauiqq̄ colhuaca tlatoque quitoqq̄. aquiqq̄ hi y mexica. yn oquiuillanqq̄ chinamitl. ye no quintequitia quimilhuia. Mexicae quimitalhuia ỹ colhuaca tlatoque ma ỹpaltzinco canati maçatl. yn acan tlamintli. ma cana cequi quitlaxiliti yn iyomio. yntla yuh quichiuazqq̄ ye tehuanti ticmati ỹ quenin tiquinchiuazqq̄. yn iquac onauatiloque cenca tlaocuxqq̄. nima yaque quitemoto y maçatl. nouiā nenqq̄ yn acuezcomac ỹ chapoltepec

ycauacatiui ȳ tlapeuia. ynic ȳpā quizato y xaltocā axiuiaca y mexico tepa yoā yueltiuatzi tezcatlamiaualtzi yn ȳpa quiçato yn acatitla yn unca motlatiaya nimā quimonanqq̄ aocmo quitoqq̄ ȳ timexica. yn oyuh tlamaqq̄. nima ye ynic untlayua y coluaca tlatoqq̄ quimilhuito. Ma quimocaquitica ȳ tlatoqq̄ Ca ayac y mazatl quimonequiltia Ca ye otitlamaqq̄ Ce oquichtli ce cihuatl yn oticaciqq̄. nima ye yc quiuica yn imalhua ycauacatiui yn tlapeuia yqu ipā quiçaco maçatl acatitla nenemi: nima ye yc quitoca unpa quitztiltiui ȳ colhuaca yc omoçoquiaquito çā quemach conāque cōquimiloqq̄ yc unca tlatocayotiqq̄ yn axca maçatla. nimā y couicaqq̄ yn imixpā tlatoqq̄ maçatl quihita yn acā quenami. Auh [ximonalhua] niman ye yc quintlatlania ȳ colhuaca tlatoqq̄ quimilhuia mexicae Catliqq̄ yn amomalhua quin ic ūcā tlacaque ȳ tepa ȳ tezcatlamiaual quin ūca y ye choca quitoua tlacaço timexica yn otechāqq̄ yc ye conitoua totecuiouane ca timexica ca tehuanti timexica y xaltoca taxiuaqq̄ otiualcholoque ynic çā yma quiualhuicaltique y mexica. Auh y ye yuh uncan onoque tiçaapa nima yc ui quitlatlauhtizque yn colhuaca tlatoqq̄. quimonilhuia nopiltzintzine tamechtoyollitlacalhuizqq̄ ca achitzi tocontlaliznequi tlalmomoztli yn unca oantechmotlaucolilique. Amo cizque ȳ tlatoqq̄ ynic nima ye quiuallitoua cuxcuxtli: Niccauhtzine ma ça quitlalica ynic nima ye quiualilhuia. Ca ye qualli ma xictlallica. Auh yn oyecauh tlalmomoztli. nima ye yc ui quintlatlauhtizque tlatoque. quimonilhuia. Nopiltzintzine Ca oyecauh ȳ tomomoz. ma noço nechca tiuallaciti aço cana ȳpā tiquiçatiui tochi anoço couatl ynic ouetztiz tlequauitl. quiualhuiqq̄ yn tlatoqq̄. Ca ye qualli tla xiuia

[F. 9]
Ça ueca xicallaquica xochimilcopa xitztiuia. Auh y ye iuhqui oyaque nima ye yc untlayua ȳ colhuaca tlatoque quimonilhia y xochmilca. Xochmilcae tle anquimati ca ye unpa ui y mexica ma oc ce anquicauhti. nima ye ic hui y mexico tlapeuitiui ycauacatiui ye unpā unca ualleuaque xochmilca oquintlatequilique nima ye yc micalli yc unca much tlamaque y mexica aca ome aca yey cacic. nima ye yc ualmotitlani y mexica quīonotzazque coluaca tlatoque quimilhuia. totecuiouane ca otlamaque y mexica ȳpan ocholoto y xochmilca yn oquicaque tlatoqq̄ cenca quimotetzauiqq̄ quitoqq̄ aquique y mexica. yn iquac momomoztique omaca xiuitl ypa ycuac no molpi yn ixiuh. nima ye mononotza ȳ colhuaca tlatoque ye quitoa. Cuix yncha mexica yn omomomoztiqq̄ ma quiualyollotiliti. yc ye quinotza amatlamatqq̄ yzquinauatia quin quiyollotilizque yn ymomoz mexica ynic tlayollotilique ica cuitlatl tlaçolli teuhtli malacatl ychcatl yn oyaqq̄ nima ye yc quiualquixtia y mexica yn tleȳ oquitocaco yn

intlaollouh mochiuh acatl nacazuitztli aueuetl auh ỹ cuitlatl ỹ tlaçolli ỹ teuhtli yn ichcatl yuitl. cate ytualnepātla quitocaque quitoque cuix tocha. Auh yn unca quitlaliqq̄ ymomoz tolxacalli quitlayauallochotiqq̄: much quincouanotzque ỹ tlatoque amo oyaque çan iyo oya yn cuxcuxtli quito. tla niquimita quenin quichiuazque mexica. Auh yn oya cuxcuxtli omanaloque y xochmilca uel tlenepātla ỹ quitlalique. nima ye yc ualtemo tetztzoualli nima ye yc ualtemo xiuhcouatl nima ye yc tetlecauillo nima ye yc mique y xochmilco qui ye y ya unca ylhuichiuhqq̄ ynic uallaque acā yuhqui quichiuhqui. yn iquac ye micoua nima ye quicacque y mexica yoā y cuxcuxtli ye nanatzca yn ilhuicatl uncā ypā temoc ỹ quauhtli ycpac moquetzaco xacalli yn īteucal yuhqui xacaltapazolli y quitlallico ycpac y moquetzaco quauhtli. Yn ountlanqq̄ miqui xochimilca nimā yc patla çano unpa ytztia y ualtemoc. Yn colhuaca onoca mexica cempoualxiuitl uncā mociuauatiqq̄ uncā mopiluatique. ye yc cēpoualxiuitl ye tlaquallania auh ynic ye tetlatilo yn ūpa ciuaua uncā tlatiloqq̄ yn ūpa moquichoati uncā tlatiloque chicuey tochtli xiuitl

Annals of Juan Bautista

[f. 20, bottom]
<u>v</u> Axcā martes. a xiii. de junio 64. a°s . yquac q̄nnonotzque. in tlacuilloque. sant juan tlaca. ytēncopa. gov.ᵒʳ quinnahuati. yn ātonio. tlapaltecatl . p.° nicolas ōpa teopā. tlacuillolcalli. quinonnotzato . oyuh mopehualti. in tabla. mochiua . yn iquac ōyaque quitoque. anell euatl. nicā tocōquixtilia. ōquiça yn ihiyo yn itlatol. yn altepetl. yneneçoliz .

[f. 20v]
ynetequiliz. yn iuh quitohuaya. in tlateotocanime at aca ytla. mitztequiuhtia. maticuicuili in mix in moyollo. ma amo tetetlacama. yn tlaca.° xitetlacmati. çān ōcan ticmacehuaz in huey ytetoliniliz. yn ipalnemohuani. Amo tlacacemeleque. in pipiltin. yxiptlahuā. in tt° nētlamatoque. in yohualli hitic. amo yhuiyan quiqua. yn achitzin tlamatzohualli. in quē quihuicazq̄. yn icuitlapil yn iatlapal.

<u>v</u> Toltecaye aoc ceme oāquicacque yn intlatol yn amotahuā tla oc xocōtepotztocacā. yn motlacatiliz yn oc huel ytech otiquiz. in motoltecayotl tla oc xōcallaqui in mictic yn itic in mopillo. yn tla çan ipāpa yn monechachamahualiz. amo momahuiçitaz. amo cēca yuh mahuiçolloz. tla oc xiquilnamiq̄. ỹ monelpil ỹ monenanahuatil. etc.

ynin tlatolli yehuātin q̄caque in joān yaotlaloc. matheo xamā. miguel tepotzitolloc. p.º chimalatl. fran.co canpolihuiz. ant.º huetō. mīn yaotlapā. miguel teyol. mīn cocho. miguel xochitl. migl matlalaca. fran.co xīmamal. joseph xochihua. xºval quauhtli. marcos çipac. mīn momauhti. mīn mixcouatl. alguacil p.º ahuatzal. ant.º tezcachimal. gov.or amechaltepehuiq̄ lia. amechaltepepialia . yuhq̄ yuhcayotl. ynic nicā otihualihualoq̄ etc.

<u>v</u> oy martes. a xvi. de mayo: 1564 aºs yquac teopā. mocouh tlapalli. ompa huiya. in tlatlapalnemacaque teopā. quimanaco. in tianq̄zco. auh in tlapalli. mocouh yc mochiuh in imagē. huey tabla. auh Regidore. in q̄couhque. tlapalli. fran.co quauhtli. ant.º tlapaltecatl. auh ypā māca. in p.º nicolas. tlaçihuitiaya . auh mayordomo catca m̄p̄r̄ josefino. yc yuh macuil xihuitl.

[f. 21]
topillecati. etc.

<u>v</u> Axcā Domingo ypā ylhuitzin visitaçion a. 2 . de Julio de mill E quiºs 64. aºs . yquac quimotenehuilli. in tlacalaquilli. totatzin gr.an frai melchior de venevēte quimitalhui. yalhua . ye tlaquallo. ohuallayhua . in visitorador. quihuallali yyamauh ynic nechualnotz. auh quin iquac in ce hora. otzillin . ompa tiaque oniquinhuicac. occequintin padreme. auh yn iquac otōyāque nimā onechilhui ca oāhualmohuicaque. ca yehuatl. ynic nimitzōnonochilia. ca nel hitic āmoyetzticate yn altepetl. ma xicmotecaquiltilli. ma xiquinmocaquiztilli. in macehualtin in tlacalaquilli. ynic tlacalaquizq̄ ca omotzōtec yn intequiuh ynic tlacalaquizque. ye miecpa. nōtlayhua. cōnotza gov.or amo nechtlacamati. amo hualauh. ymanel alide. ma noço Regior campa nemi. ayaque ualhui~~~~

<u>v</u> auh yn iq̄c onicac nimā oniquilhui ca in ticmotenehuilia. ca amo huelitiz yehica campa. q̄mocuilizque. cuix milleque. cuix ōca intlal. ye ticmottilia ynicate.

<u>v</u> auh nimā oquito tle ypāpa yn amo huilitiz ca ye omito. ca omotzōtec. auh miyecpa yn oniquilhui campa quimocuiliz yhuā cāpa quinextiz. ca cohuatlatequipanohua. çacacalaquia . yhuā techpalehuia. mochihua in tochan nohuiyā tlapalehuia. yhuan in Diezmos yc techpalehuia. in tlein monequi. quichihua . yc techpalehuiya~~~~

[f. 21v]
yc nimā oquito. ca polihui in tequitl. ca quicahua. ca ça quixcahuizque yn intequiuh. ca in ce xihuitl. chicopa quicalaquia. çacatl . auh in cohuatlatequipanohua. chiq̄cepa. auh in cētlamamalli. çacatl. melio q̄nmaca. auh

cēpoualtetl quimaca. ynic quimotlaquehuia. yn quimama. auh yn iquac cehuetzi ce tomin q̄nmaca. auh çan cēpohualtetl q̄nmaca yni quihualcahua nicā. auh in tla noço quichiuazque. tequitl. ca nahui tomines. tlaxtlahuilozque. ca quicenpolohua yn intequiuh~~~~

v auh nimā oniquilhui. Camo huelitiz tlatohuanie. ca ye nicmati: ca ye moch tlachichiuhque. ca yuhq̄ yn achi. quintlatzihuizcuitiz yhuā quinpolhuiz yn inyeliz~~~~

v auh nimā oq̄to ca cēca tlatzihui ȳ mexica. auh nimā oniquilhui ca quemaca. ca cēca tlatzihui. ynic techpalehuia. yn hualhui ye iz tonatiuh. auh in quiça no yz tonatiuh. in motlalohua. in tihualquiça aocaque. oyaque. yehica camo yntech momati yn tlateq̄panoliztli.

v çan yehuantin yn altepehuaq̄ huel techpalehuia in tlacopan. in tetzcoco. in xochimilco. oc yohuatzinco hualhui. auh ye yohua hiuh yehica ca nel oyntechmoma. yn elimiqui.

v auh nimā onechittiti in pintora. cēca miyec yn amoteq̄uh. 6. yn āquichiua. cohuatequitl. auh. 7. çacatl. auh nimā onechmacac yn sentencia. oniquittac onicpouh. opachiuh yn noyollo/auh yhuā oquito ca intla quichihuazque/in tlacalaquilli. Ca ōcā quiçaz in Diezmos. yhuā in tleī moneq̄z. ca mochi ōcā mocuiz.

[f. 22]
Ca oc actle. quimitlaniliz ca ça yuhqui espānolesme yc nemizque. auh in çatepan nimā cēca onipapac/oniquito. ca cēca qualli Ca actle/amotequiuh yez. ca quicēpolohua. yn ixquich amotequiuh. ma xicmacacā yn empdor. in ce p°s. iii t°s ca in ce p°s. huell amotlacalaquil. auh yn ey t°s. yxiptla. in tlaolli. cē quahuacalli yhuā ōcā quiçaz. ce tomines. ytech pohuiz yn amotlatocauh. auh in quenin amo huel iez amehuā anquimati. etc.

v auh in iquac otzōquiz. missa. nimā ye ic mocalaquia. in callitic.

v auh cōtocatiaque. in marcos tlacuilol. p.° chachalaca. fran.co xinmamal. yhuan p.° nicolas. auh in totatzin. nimā quilhui in marcos—yn yçiuhca tlami. in tabla. oquihualmotlalili yyamatzin in provincial. yn ōtzōquiçaz metztli: julio. yquac hualmohuicaz. yehuatzin quimomaniliquiuh in tabla. in iquac ynetlecahuiliztzin. asunption. qimoyomahuiliquiuh. auh nimā yc cōnāquilli in marcos.

v Conilhui. totatzine. quenin nel uel yçiuhca tlamiz. ca in tlacuilloque ca quichihua. in çacatle yhuā in couatequitl. yhuā yn ixquich tequitl ca mochi q̄chihua. ~~~~

v nimā quilhui in totatzin Cuix amo ticcaqui yn nicteneuh in iuh tlanahuatia in visitador. yn iuh ātequitizque. in cohuatequitl. anquicahuazque . yhuā in çacatl. yhuā in ixquich amotecpanchā in tlein ohamechtequiuhtiyaya. auh ypā polihuiz in ce pºs iii tºs. yhui onechilhui. in visitador. ça yuhqui. yn espāolesme y nicā nemizque. auh cēca yc ni

[f. 22v]

paqui yn nehuatl. yc cēpolihui in Diezmo. in tlein ohāquichihuaya.

v auh q̄ to. in marcos ca ye qualli totatzine. ma nimā polihuicā in tepixcatotōtin yn ixquich callā tlein quitetequiuhtia. ~~~~

v auh nimā conito in p.º de. s. nicolas . totatzine . Ca amo çā napohuallacallaquilli yez. in ce pºs. yhuan yey ts.

v auh yn iquac oq̄cac totatzin. nimā cēca quallā oncā quitopeuh in nicolas. nimā quilhui maçatl. amo tipinahua. tlein çā napohuallacallaquilli yez. cuix amo nicpouh. cuix amo huel nixtelolo yc oniq̄tac cuix aca çan onechnonotz~~~~

v auh niman yc conito. in p.º chachalaca. totatzine . ca ye yuhque yn ichtecque. yn iquac huitza tlaxcalteca jueztin in q̄tlallilique. yn tlacuilo ome tomin quimanaz in huel motlayecoltia. auh yn aya huel motlayecoltia. ce tomin. yhuan yn atle yc motlayecoltia çā no ce tomin q̄ manaz. auh yn icnoçihuatl. melio . auh yn yehuā tlatlacatecollo çā quicētlazque/yn ohome tomin. yhuā yn cecē tomin ca ye yuhque. Ca oyntechmoma. yn ichtecque in quihuelilia./Auh no ceppa. conito in nicolas. totatzine . ca tequitiz in telpochtli in ichpochtli. ~~~~

v Auh no ceppa quihualilhui in totatzin ximocahua. amo çā ye yyo in teq̄tiz. in icnoçihuatl yhuā in icnooquichtli. in telpochtli oc quipalehuiz yn itatzin. yhuā in ichpochtli quipalehuiz yn inātzin/quin iquac yn omonamicti. tequitiz . ~~~~

v Auh in marcos conilhui. in totatzī. Ca cēca miec. aço çā ixquich yez. in ce p.º/auh nimā quimitalhui. in totaztin. Camo nehuatl nicmati. amehuā anquimati/ca ça

[f. 23]

nicnamechtlalnamictia. aço çā ye anquitocazque in tlaxcalteca in tlatlalil ocox cāpa. qualcā ximoteylhuicā yc oc ayamo cēca hualneltia~~~~

v Auh ȳ nicolas nimā yc ya quinonotzato. in gov.ᵒʳ yn ōpa huehuetlā yquac ompa ylhuiquixtilloc./quilhuito. nopiltzitzine . yn axcan yc ōtemachti. in guardiā in tlacalaquilli oquitecaquiti. auh in marcos. cēca quipaccacaqui. in tlacalaquilli yn iuh titequitizque. auh niman ymoztlayoc. yc neixnamicoc. yn itlatol in nicolas./auh in yehuatin totatzin guardiā occeppa yc cahuac in nicolas~~~~

v Auh nimā ymoztlayoc. lunes . a . 3 . de julio. 64 . aºs . ycuac ylpilloq̄ Regidoresme. ypāpa cohuatequitl amo tlapihuixque. in macehualtin/yn ilpilloque. chicomētin. miguel teycniuh. fran.ᶜᵒ quauhtli. mīn cocolotl. mīn coçotecatl. andres cohuacuech. miguel acxotecatl. ypolito de sancta m.ᵃ~~~~

v viernes a vii de julio. de 1564 aºs. yquac mochicahuacatzōtec. in couatequitl. ynic mochi tlacatl. quichiuaz . in nepapā offiçialesme. yhuā inic teylpilloz. ynic castoltecpātli. monamacaz . s.ᵗˡⁱ yhuā in momōmoyahuazque. ye oncā. in tecpā/ynic chicahuac firma motlalli. ye teotlac/ȳ motzōtec. tequitl . viernes~~~~

v auh nimā hualla yn alcalde. teopan . conilhuico totatzin fray p.º totatzine. ca omotzōtec. in cohuateq̄tl omochintin mofirmatique. in tlatoque. auh nimā quilhui. in totatzī amo nehuatl nicmati. amehuā āquimati acaço tle yc āq̄npalehuizque. in macehualtzintli.~~~~

[f. 23v]

v oy lunes. a . x. de julio. de 1564 aºs ypan peuh in cohuatequitl. chicauac ōpa. peuh . in S.ᵗᵃ m.ᵃ tlaltecayohuacā quiyomahui yn alcalde. tequixti tecalpāhui yn aquin açitla quihuallitoz. nimā teylpilloyā quihuicazque.~~~~

v martes. a xi. de julio. 64 . aºs yquac ce espānol. Sant fran.ᶜᵒ quititzopinique. temicti . yn ōpan tecpā quiyahuac achi tlaçopilli quimicti. nimā oncan hualmotlallo. S fran.ᶜᵒ auh in iquac ocōmatque yhuā yolque yn omictilloc nimā moteylhuito. yn ixpā justiᵃ auh in justiᵃme. yuā oydoresme. nimā huallaque. teopā. canazq̄ çā tepā tlecoque. valeio ytlilticauh. in q̄ titzopine. etc.~~~~

v auh nimā ymoztlayoc. miercoles . tzatzihuac . in sanct ipolito. umpa huia yn alguazil mayor. auh ynic tzatzihuato. quito . in tecpoyotl. xiqualmocaquiticā. quihualmitalhuia yn amotlatocauh. in nepapā tlachichiuhcā in teyacana. yhuā in tlatlaxilacalpā merinosme. yxquich tlacatl. cēquiçaz yn q̄pa tecpā. amechmonahuatiliz yn amotlatocauh. in moztla.~~~~

v auh oyuh yehua motzōtec. yn tlacalaquilli. ynic tetequitzque ye tercia tzillini/in motzontec totequiuh yn iquac omotzōtec.

v niman huallaque. in Regidoresme. in teopā quilhuico. in guardiā totatzine. ca quimitalhuia. in visitador. Ca omotzōtec in tlacalaquilli. macaocmo tle quimilhui yn macehualtin. tleyca . quimacomana . in tlein yteopixcate

[f. 24]

quiuh. amo ye quichihua. auh in nehuatl. in tlein notequiuh ca nicchiuaz. auh yn oquimocaquilti totazin. quimitalhui . ca ye qualli.

<u>v</u> oy jueves. a xiii. de julio. 64 a°s. yquac mopouh. in sentencia. in ipāpa. tlacalaquilli . yn iquac ocēquixohuac yn inauhcāpaixti. yoā in nepapā tlachichiuhcā. ōpa tlecohuac. in tlacpa. tecpā tlamelauhcacalco. ye ome hora tzillini yn iq̄c onetecoc. huel temohuac messa. motecac . in tlanepātla yhuan silla momā hetetl. nimā yc hualmotlalli in gov.ᵒʳ yhuā a̶l̶l̶d̶e̶. dō mīn hezmallin yhuā chicueyntin Regidoresme yuan tequihuaque pipiltin melchior Diaz. thomas de aquino. dō lucas cortes. mīn cano. dō mīn momauhtin. p.ᵒ nicolas. auh omētin espānolesme. Joan cano. Juan bap.ᵗᵃ tlaopochcopa. hualmotlalique . nimā ye ic quihuallitohua/gover.ᵒʳ ca ohāualmohuicaque. ỹ nicā hitic altepetl. nicā catqui anquimocaquiltizque. nimā quihualilhui. yn escribano. miguel de los angeles. xicmopohuilli—nimā ye ic quipohua. in tlatolli yuh quito yn.~~~~

<u>v</u> ỹ nehuatl Don luis de sancta m.ᵃ gov.ᵒʳ por su mag.ᵈ yn nicā çiudad/mexᶜᵒ tenochtitlā. castolomey. Dias del mes. de henero. de 1564. años . yhuā tehuātin a̶l̶l̶desme. dō mīn de sant joan dō ant.ᵒ de sancta m.ᵃ yhuā in matlactin omome Regidoresme. yn quimohuiquilia. altepetl . yhuā pipiltin. in tiacahuā yn iquac oticacque/ynic tlacalaq̄zque in macehualtzintli. nimā yc o

[f. 24v]

titononotzque. timochintin otiaque. in ixpan.ᶜᵒ aud.ᵃ Real. yuan ymixpanᶜᵒ in tlatoque oydores. auh miecpa in apelacion. oticchiuhque . yn oc nen yc titlacuepa. aocmo uelliti. yhuā miecpa inic otitocētlalique in cabildo. hitic . ynic otitononotzque. çā nimā aoc hueliti yehica ohuelchicahuato. oneltic ./auh yalhua. ye quen ohueltzōtec/miercoles ypā. xiii. de julio. auh in xihuitl. çā ye no yehuatl in tlacpac omoteneuh. yn itlacaltilitzin. in tt° Ix° auh yn iquac otzonquiz yn intlacuepaliztlatol. nimā. yehuatl. in sentencia. auto. nimā ye ic quipohua. yn p.ᵒ de sanctiago yehuatl in nicā contenehua

~~~~~~~

<u>v</u> ỹ nican çiudad. mexico . tenochtitlā. a xviii. Dias del mes. de hebreᵒ. de mil 564 años. ỹ nehuatl. don luis de sancta m.ᵃ por su mag.ᵈ nicā catqui yn otitequiuhtilloque. ynic titlacalaquizque. yn tictomaq̄lizque in totlatocatzin. Empador . auh yn iuh otitlalililoque. ynic titequitizque. in ticcalaquizque. cē xiquipilli ypā castoltzōtli. ypan matlacpoualli pesos. ypan hepoual pesos. auh in cecē tlacatl. yn iuh tequitiz ce peso ypā nahui tomines. yhuā cēquauacalli. tlaolli . auh yn icnooquichtli ycnoçihuatl. nahui tomin yhuan

tlaco quahuacalli. auh yn telpochtli ychpochtli. çā no nahui tomin yhuā tlaco quahuacalli. auh yn tla ca tle tlaolli. cēquahuacalli. yey tomines. yc moxtlahuaz. anoce trico. motemaz . auh yn iquac pipixco. mochi tlacatl quitemaz. in tlaolli. tecētocaz. auh yn iquac omonechico. tlacalaquilli . yeuatl . quixexeloz in gov.^{or} yn tlatocatlatquitl. quimopielia . in thesorrero/yn icalpixcahuā Emperador. quin

[f. 25]

momaquilitihui. auh in altepetl quimohuiquilia. in gov.^{or} oncā quiçaz yn inemac yn itech pohui in tasaçion/castoltzōtli ypā castolpoualli ypā hepoualli pesos. ypā matlactli p.^{os} . yhuan . iiii t^{os} yuā m^o onca mopiaz. in Cōmunidad. yetetl yez in caxa. cētetl gov.^{or} q̄piaz. cētetl alde cētetl mayordomo. auh ōcan quiçaz. yn innemac in qui[m]ohuiqulia altepetl. in gov.^{or} in alcaldes. in Regidores. yhuā yn occequintin yn quimotititlania. yhuā in teopan quitemachtia doctrina. yhuan yn campa tlein teq̄tl. quimocuitlahuia . moch ōcan quiçaz ymnemac/yhuā in tlein moneq̄z oncā quiçaz. in aço teotlatq̄tl. yc mocohuaz. auh aocac tlein quiteytlaniliz. yhui in oquimotlalilique. yn tlatoque oydoresme. in presidente. yhuan in visitador = yhuā oyuh quimotlalili in su senoria visorrey. oyuh quimotzōtequilli yn ica yprovisionestzin. yhuā hica in autos. yn itlamachiyotiltzin. yhui ypā oquimotlalil auh ynic ticexiuhq̄çazque in cecē tlacatl. ce p.^{os} ypā nahui auh nauhtetl. metztli . in titlacalaquizque. yn iquac otzonquiz in sentencia. nimā ye ic quihualitoua. gov.^{or} Ca oācōmocaquitique yn iuh otitlalililoque. in totequiuh auh cuix aoc tel amopā^{co} oticchiuhque. ca oc hueliti ye ixquich cahuitl yn oticnemitique. aocmo q̄mohuelcaquitia. in tlatoque ~~~~

<u>v</u> Auh nimā ye ic quihualitohua yn miguel teicniuh ca otocōcac in timexicatl in titenochcatl. ynic tōmotequitiliz yn iuh oq̄motlalili yn totlatocatzin. in mag.^{d} cuix çā

[f. 25v]

nicā omoyocox. Cuix no ceceme tlatoque. nicā oquitlalique. ca ye ixquich cahuitl yn ticnemita ye axcā chiquacētetl. metzli . yn oc nē titlacuepa. aoc hueliti/aocmo titlahuelcaquililo. auh onehuatica. yn amotlatocauh cuix aoctle amopā quichiua. Cuix oamexiccauh cuix oquixicauh yn icuitlapil yn iatlapal. auh ye cuel iquac ō ye axcā chicuacētetl. metztli yn nicā anquimocaquiltico auh yn axcā ma ximotetlalhuilli yn timerimo. ma xiccaquilti yn motlahuilanal. ma ximotecalpāhuilli ȳ nicā ticmocahuilia. ȳ meliotzī. auh in iquac otzōquiz ytlatol nimā ye ic neacomanallo. auh in gov.^{or} oc nē q̄ hualito. ma tlapitzallo. nimā ye ic netēhuiteco. tlacahuaco . nimā yc hualtemohuac tlatzintla netēhuiteco. yhuā mochi tlacatl. quito . Can ticuizque.

auh ixquich çihuatl. yllamatzin . in chocaque. yhuā cēca quallāque. auh ce tlacatl quito. ytoca . huixtopolcatl amanalco chane. quito . aquinō tlatohua. Cuix tlillācalqui. cuix q̄uhnochtli. cuix hezhuahuacatl tle mochihua tlapaltōtli achac momati. ylhuiz tlacauaco. conitohua . cuix itla quitlanitotihui yn tetecuhtin yn tlatoque. yn oquipiaco altepetl. anquicā quin ye ye antechōtlalilizque. ynic titlacalaquizque. ma yehuā yuh quitotiani. yn tlatoque. yn iquac yah. altepetl ynic tipoliuhque. cuix itla quitlanito yn quauhtemoctzī cuix itla quicamacautia. cēca miec yn quitoque. in tlatolli. auh cequintin conitoque. nocne . yca xihualmayahuicā yn teicniuh yuā in cocolotl. yn ye ixquich cahuitl

[f. 26]
yc timoteilhuia āca çan otiqualnahualhuicac. ỹ motlatol. nocne çan ihuiyā xihualtemo. cocollotle . ylhuiz cēca quallanihua. tzatzihua . auh ynic conahua. gov.^{or} yehuatl ynic tepā cacalaquia. yn ayamo tlatocati. auh in p.^{o} maceuhqui. ye ōcalaquia. temaxelotiuh yhuā tetlacahualtiaya. quiquechpanotiuh . yn itopil/nimā quicuitihuetzque. ye quimictia huel cololhuique ynic quimictique. ahchi quitlaliliq̄ yn icamissa. ça petlauhticac. in quicauhque. auh q̄manahui in joan cano ./ quiquixti yn inespada. yni quitetlaçaltin yn tlac^o yehuatl huel temac miquizquia. auh yn iquac ye netenhuiteco. mochi tlacatl. tlapāco hualmoma. yn intlapāco. castilteca . yhuan cequintin. hualmotlatlalohua . ỹ ye huallacaqui tlein ye mochihua tecpā yhuā cequintin ompa. hualmotlaloque . in tiamiquia. sanct ipolito yn ixquichtin tlanamacaya. tianquizco . yxquichtin huallaque—yhuā in calli onoco. yxquich tlacatl hualquiz. yn illmatzin ỹ huēhuētzī yhuā in pipiltotōtin yhuā yn altepetl ypan tlaca. yhuā ontlatepacholloya. yn tlacpaccalco. quitēxixitinique. ỹ tlaquilyahualtotōti. xochitl ytēpayo. auh niman yc ce hualla espānol topille. nimā quicopin. yn iEspada. tetotoca . yhuā Espānoltin. cequi mestiçome. oncā teyhttaya. moch quicopinque. yn imespada. tececēmana. auh çihua. quicuitlacoyonique . yn tepantli ythualco. tlaopochcopa . yn ōcan hualnemamayoohuac. in çihua in toquichtin. çā monenepanotihuitzīnco. ynic hualhuetzque. yuhqui tlatzatzatzi. huel miyec yn ōcā mococo yhuā ce q̄nacazhuitecque. yllamantzi . cēca çan içiuh

[f. 26v]
ca hualcēquizque. Espānoltin topilleque. ye tetotoca. tececēmana. auh in topilleque. nimā ye ic teana yn onocecanque. quitlecahuia tlacpac ỹmac quimotlaztimani gov.^{or} q̄nmictia. yn oquimōmictique. nimā yc q̄mōmaylpitihui auh yn izqui otli. nohuiyā. quitzatzaquato. yn espānolesme. [*inserted between lines:* nohuiyā teanoc yn otlica etc.] lança chimalli. cequi armas. in commaquique. ..

Annals of Tecamachalco

[middle of folio 2v]

¶ 1. calli xiuitl. ypan ȳ micqui yn cuetzpaltzin yn ihq̄c yaoyaualolco motlalli yn altepetl yn ihquac quipohpoloq̄ yn ixquich techyaualohtoc mochi quitlaqueuh yn tepeyacac tlacatl. yn chololtecatl. yn tlaxcaltecatl. yn uexotzincatl. auh yn ixquich ynic quiyaualohtoc altepetl. auh çan miyec tlamantli yn mochiuh. auh yn tlahtocatic çempualxiuitl omome. xxii .

¶ 2. xochtli xiuitl.

¶ 3. acatl xiuitl.

¶ 4. tecpatl xiuitl. ypan yn ahcico tlacotepec yn quetzalehcatzin ynic canin motlaihiyouiltito. auh yn ichan calaquico. ytoca olin.

[f. 3]

¶ 5. calli xiuitl.

¶ 6. tochtli xiuitl.

¶ 7. acatl xiuitl.

¶ 8. tecpatl xiuitl.

¶ 9. calli xiuitl. ~~ypan inic onahcico yn quetzalehcatzin y noncan hecateopan ynic moquihquixtito couayxtlauacan.~~

¶ 10. tochtli xiuitl.

¶ 11. acatl xiuitl ypan yn quimicti yn ehcatl. yn tlahtouani q̄tzalehcatzin. yn ocan yn ehcateopan. çan no ypan xiuitl ynic ōpa tlehcoc yn tlacpac tecamachalco ynic ompa oman tecpācalli.

¶ 12. ~~tecptli~~ tecpatl xiuitl.

¶ 13. calli xiuitl.

¶ 1. tochtli xiuitl. ypan neçetochuiloc. ye xiuhtica yn atle mochiuh tonacayotl temamauhti ȳ mochiuh ȳ mayanaliztli. nican yn quimomaquilli yn tlalli yn totahuan yn q̄tzalehcatzin.

¶ 2. acatl xiuitl. y ye no ceppa ualmotzauc in tepecac [sic] tlaca. yn ixquichica [sic] ompa ceuito yn yaoyotl yn ihquac quinpoloco ȳ mexicatl ynic tetlan ouetz ynic tetlayecoltiaya mexico. yn quitequitia tlaolli. etl . chilli . ayouechtli . tlapalizuatl . tecollin . etc . yuan yhquac quimihtlanihque yn tlalli yn axcan ypan cate.

¶ 3. tecpatl xiuitl. yqu e xiuitl ȳ mochiuh in tonacayotl.~~~~~

¶ 4. calli xiuitl.

¶ 5. tochtl [sic] xiuitl.

⁋ 6. acatl xiuitl.
⁋ 7. tecpatl xiuitl.
⁋ 8. calli xiuitl.
⁋ 9. tochtli xiuitl.
⁋ 10. acatl xiuitl.
⁋ 11. tecpatl xiuitl.

[f. 3v.]
⁋ 12. calli xiuitl.
⁋ 13. tochtli xiuitl. ypan ȳ poliuhque yn tepeyacac tlaca. yn tlahtoani catca chiyauhcouatl. Auh yn quipoloco axayacatzin tenochtitlan tlahtouani. yn quipoloco.
  ⁋ 1 acatl xiuitl ȳ moquetz couatepantli. yn oquimihtlanihque tepeyacac tlacatl. yn ipan tetlayecolti tenochtitlan. etc . yn tlalli. Auh nauintin ȳ calpixque mexica. yn imixpan mochiuh yecamecatl. couacuech . tlillayatl . quauhtilma .

***

[middle of f. 4v]

⁋ 11. tecpatl xiuitl. Nican motlahtocatlalli yn quetzalehcatzin.
⁋ 12. calli xiuitl.
⁋ 13. tochtli xiuitl.
  ⁋ 1. acatl xiuitl. ypan ȳ uallahque yn españoles. nican noeva españa. yndiotlalpan . ypan 19. aureu . 1519 . años .
  2. tecpatl . 1520 . ⁋ Auh nican omotlahtocatlalli yn tleuixollotzin. amo uehcauac. çan ipan yn xiuitl omic. ye no yhquac ȳ contlahtocatlalin ȳ motlatlallouatzin. Dō felipe xuarez. yn ixpan marques. Auh ynin niman oncā ualpeuhtica yn aoccā oualixneztia yn tlahtocayotl. Auh ynin yhquac mexico nemito yn quetzalehcatzin. yuan occequintin pipiltin. etc . yhquac yn mochintin quitocayotiaya teoçauatl cēca temahmauhti ynic mochiuh uey çauatl mochi quihtlaco yn texayac. uel ic tlayxpoliouac quin ōcan peuhtica yn eztli yn tlayeli mihtoua. Auh y ye nepa ayc mochiua oncā ocempeuh yn ixquichica axcan ualquiztiuh cocoliztli.
  3. calli . 1521 . ⁋ Auh ipan in xiuitl yn motlalli tlacochteuctli yn cuetzpaltzin. auh ypā 2. aureu numero.
  4. tochtli . 1522 . ⁋ auh yei. aureu numero. 3 .
  5. acatl . 1523 . ⁋ auh naui. aureu numero. 4 .
  6. tecpatl . 1524 . ⁋ macuilli. aureu nuemro. [sic] Nicā motlalli yn tepalayo. ya ic tlacochteuctitia. tecamachalco .

[f. 5]
7. calli 1525. ¶ chiquacen aureu numero. 6.
8. tochtli. 1526. ¶ 7. aure [sic] numero. 7.
9. acatl. 1527. ¶ 8. aure numero. ypan ȳ ualla yn tlaxcallan Obispo don fray Julian.
10. tecpatl. 1528, ¶ 9. aureu numero. yPan yn ualla ȳ mexico arzobispo. Don fray Juan çomaraca. ynin s. fran.co patre.
11 calli. 1529. ¶ 10. aureu numero. Nican motlacochteuctlalli ȳ moquiuitzin.
12. tochtli. 1530. ¶ 11. aure numero. Nican micqui yn tetzcoco ytzcuinquani. Nican motlalihque yn tepeyacac padreme fray Juan terribas.
13. acatl. 1531. ¶ 12. aure n. ypan xiuitl yn çitlallin popocac. ynin yhquac pilloloque quauhtinchan tlahtoq̄ uilacapitzin catca. yuan tlacochcalcatl yuan tochcayotl. tlacateocolocuicatl queuhque. yuan nima ye cequintin ciuah. ynin ympampa tlaaltilli tlacanehtolli quinmictihque piltzintli. etc. auh yn tepeyacac gua.an alonso xuarez. ymac yn tepilloloc.

***

[It is 1557, and they are in the midst of a major *congregación*.]

[f. 11, towards the top]

Auh yn ihquaqu in conmotlalili yn altepetl ynetlauhtil yn ordenazas [sic] oncan cōmocemihtalhui yn ixquich nauatilli ynic çan çe altepetl tecamachalco. yuan quecholac. /¶ Auh ynic mahtlactli ozceyoc. metztli otobre. mocentlalihque. b̄az. valiente. Don p.o de leon. occequītin Regidores. pipiltin. ynic quiteyxpauizq̄ yn Juan de los angeles. gove.or yc niman conihcuilohque etetl. yn imamatlacuilol. centetl q̄ttac provincial bostamante. yhuan centetl yn tlacatl tlahtoani Visorrey. auh niman centetl. fran.co ximenez. yhquac catca xochimilco ./¶ Auh ynin ymahtlactli onnauiyoc. otubre. oncan momiquili yn tlahtouani Obispo. Don fray martin de ojacastro. tlaxcallan peuato. auh cuetlaxcouapan yn momiquilico. viernes motocac youatzinco./¶ No yhquac citlalin popocac. auh çatepan yn ualla yn ymatlahcuilol provincial quimacaco guardian fray fran.co De toral. oncan ualihcuiliuhtia. ynic quiteixpauia yn Juan. De los angeles. gove.or. auh niman no ualla yn iyamatlahcuilol. yn tlahtouani Visorrey ynic quimmacaz yn aquihque pipilton. ynic quimomachitiz. yuan ynic chiuililozque justicia. Auh çatepan niman quincentlalli yn totahtzin Doral. yn ixquichtin pipiltin ynic quim [f. 11v] cuitizque yn aquihque teteixpauia. Auh niman ōcan ualnezque yn intoca. b̄az. valiente. Don p.o de leon. yhuan occequintin pipiltin. auh no cequintin çan tlapictli oncan

quitlalihque ynfirma. yn ipan amatlahcuilolli. auh amo nelli ynitlah quimati yn iyollo. Auh nimā no oncan ualnez. yn mache tlacuilouiani. Juan bap.ta de santa maria. auh yc cenca ytechpa moqualanilti yn totahtzin toral. auh niman no concuilli yn licencia quimacac visorrey ynic quipiazquia Espada. yn Juan bap.ta . Auh niman yc conquixti yn aocmo teopan nemiz çan nemiz quiyauac. Auh ynin tlahtolli çan conmopohpolhuili yn totahtzin toral. yn tlauelneztiani yn aquihque yn tle yntoca yn quiteyxpauizquia. gove.or cenca uey Justicia. ympan quimochiuilizquia yn tlacatl tlahtouani bisorrey etc. Auh achtopa yn tlacat lucas ypiltzin matheo Sanchez. yyācuica coneuh catharina ymac moquatequi dō b̄az del castillo. ycastolli omeiyoc metztli octobre ./
℘ Auh no uachtopa yn quecholac quizque. padreme . fray fran.co yhuan fray Diego de lemos etc. 19 . aureo numero. c . dominica .

. 1 . tochtli . 1558 . ℘ yn ipan xiuitl. mill e quīs. en cinquenta y ocho. guar.an mochiuh fray alonso de molina. gove.or mochiuh çan yehuatl Juan de los angeles. ~~alldes~~ mochiuhque matheo Sanchez. b̄az del Castillo. Juan Joseph. ℘ No yhquac yahqui yn ihuipanecatl yn quauhtlan. yn ompa quiciuato teopantli.℘ No yhquac mochiuh yn apantli yn tolloh [f. 12] can.℘ ymacuililhuiyoc metztli enero. yn omihto capitulo. uexotzinco . yhquac provincial mochiuh fray fran.co de toral. nican yn ualla toguardian fray alonso. De Molina y cempualli onnauiyoc metztli henero.℘ Nican yn quicauato cōmissario fray fran.co De mena. Pinauizapan yc yah castillan yhquac mihto moteneuh yn capitulo mochiuh. auh yn ihquac yah y cempualli onchiucnauiyoc yn omoteneuh henero. Auh ompa quimonamiquilihtiahque yn tlahtoque yn altecallehcan. auh niman ompa quimouiquilihque yn Pinauizapan sabadotica. ompa motlaqualtihque atlcozauhyan yn comisario general. yuan provincial toral. yuan nican toguardian. fray al° De Molina. auh niman oncan quinualmiualli. yn tlahtoque yc niman ualmouicaqueh ./℘Nican tenauatihtiquiz yn provincial toral. yhquac yn ualmocuep. ynic tecauato atenco. Auh miyec tlamantli ynic otecentlali yn aoquic cenca techittaz. yn çatepan aocmo yuhqui tiquittazque yn quenami yc otechizcalti otechualpauh. auh ynin ycastolli ōnauiyoc metztli hebrero yn mochiuh.

***

[It is 1575.]

[f. 26, towards the bottom]

℘ Nican ouicoc. tepeyacac . Martin cortes. yhquac ytech tlanqui tlateotoquiliztli.ymac don Juan de sayabedra. allde mayor. y xviii. yoc . Junius . ℘ nicā mo [f. 26 v] miquili don mīn tepexiu ompa quecholac quimtotoquili fray fran.co goyti.

yuan nican temachti. y xxix. Junius . ¶ Ome capitulo. tlacpac . ypan calaquizquia. ynin . ynic uallaca ce tlacatl frayle ytoca fray Juan de parada. Çan nican temachtizquia. yuan teyolcuitizquia. yn oquixquichica uallazquia toguard.ᵃⁿ yn mouicac yocadan. auh yn fray Juan yquac quimicti ỹ gove.ᵒʳ Matheo Sanchez. yuan amo qualli yc cahuac nimā yc quiquixtihque yn teopixcatlahtoque. ỹ mochiuh yviii. Junius . yn nican catca. çan ompualilhuitl ozceyca. yn uallaca ypan yn vetio sancta cruz.

¶ No yhquac mocalnamacac Diego Romano mēdoza quimacaq̄ trecientos pesos. nimā contlacuilti macuilpualli pᵒs yn ihueuepo. mīn. cordes . yc mopaleui yn ixpantzinco. sʳ a~~llde~~ mayor Don Juan. +

¶ yvii. Julius . nican omoquixti fray Domingo. de arreyzaaga. Comisario mochiuhtiuh quauhtemallan.¶ yxxvii. augusto . ypan sabado oualla Repartidor. quiualcuic provision. quimoncaquiti yn tlahtoq̄ ynic motecaz. chicuitecpantli coualtequipano yn ompa. San pablo. yn ouitza hernādo queseda [sic]. yxxvii. augusto .

¶ ycemilhuiyoc metztli. setiembre . ypan viernes. oquinamiquito comisario fray Rodrigo de seguera.¶ Nican çan no ypan xiuitl. yhquac ahcico teopixque. xxxiii . yhquac ualla yn comisario general. fray Rodrigo de seguera.yn ixiptla mochiuh. fray miguel nabarro. comisario catca. yn nican ahcico. ynauilhuiyoc . setiembre . itzcuintonalli . ça yuh yeyopan ochpaniztli ome acatle ypan mochiuh. yn ihquac catca. aureo numeros. 18 . auh ydominica. b. Auh yn ixiuh tlapualtzin. yn tt.º j. xº yetzontli xiuitl. ypan castolpualli xi [f. 27] uitl ypan yepualli oncaxtolli xiuitl.¶ ynin çan no yhquac ypan xiuitl. monepanohque ỹ metztli yn tonatiuh çan centlacol. ỹ necia ypan chicome hora. yyomilhuiyoc noviembre.¶ ychicuacemilhuiyotl setiembre oualla toguar.ᵃⁿ fray clemente de la cruz. ouiyah yocadan ya youac yn ahcico.

***

[It is 1576.]

[f. 28, towards the bottom]

¶ ycemilhuiyoc augusto. ỹ nican tecamachalco Peuhqui cocoliztli çenca chicauac uey amo yxnamiquiztli./auh ytlamiyan yn Augusto yn peuhqui ya tlayaualolo. yn ipampa cocoliztli chiucnauilhuitl tlaqui. ynic miyec tlacatl momiquilihque. yn telpuchtli yn ichpuchtli. yn amiquehque yn ueuetque yllmatque yn pipiltzitzintin. yancuican yntech peuaco. yn xineteca. yn imaceualhuā Don b̄az del Castillo gove.ᵒʳ yn ihquac. ypan metztli otobre [f. 28 v.] tahcico. yn ye motoco. centecpantli omahtlactli çan eylhuitl çan omilhuitl. yn micoua. Estli teyacacpatenancazco. teyxco . tetzinco . quizaya ./Auh yn ciuah ȳmaxac quiztia yn eztli. toquichtin yntech quizaya. yn eztli yntotouh. cequi apitzalli. ynic micouaya. motlacuepilliaya yn çan tleyn conilnamiquia niman yc miquia. ¶ yxi. voc metzli otobre yn omomiquili Juan Rodriguez. español . ynamic ysabel De bega. ¶ Nican omic thomas fiscal çan motlacuepili. ymach Don matheo Sanchez. yix. yoc . nobiembre . ¶ yxiii. yoc noviembre. yn altepetl oquicouh en estancia. yyaxca . ocatca . Juan de ocon. yuan mochi cabras. ompa uitziltepec mani. ¶nican momiquili Diego Ramirez. ypan miercules. ycempualilhuiyoc noviembre. 19 . aureu nº a. g. Dominica~~~~~

7 calli. 1577 . ¶ yn ipan xiuitl. mille e quinientos e setenta y seite. guar.ᵃⁿ mochiuh fray hernando de oviedo gove.ᵒʳ mochiuazquia. don Thomas gerson. auel mochiuh españoles quihtlahcohque. oncan peuhtica yn aocac. gove.ᵒʳ ça yehuantin mopehpenque. a̶l̶l̶d̶es don fran.ᶜᵒ de mendoza. math.º lupez. Juan ximenez. yn mochiuh yyeilhuiyoc metzli. henero . ¶Axcan yxxvi. yoc . henero . yn omomiquili dona Martha. ynamic dō math.º Sanchez. ychpuch catca. Dō mīn. tecalco . ¶ ycemilhuiyoc. hebrero . momiquili yuehpol Don math.º Sanchez. ¶ yxi. yoc . herbrero . opehpenaloq̄ math.º Sanchez. ynic a̶l̶l̶d̶e yuan p.º Osorio. ynic quimocuitlauizque ycnopipiltzintzintin ynic amo poliuiz yn imaxca ytlatqui. ¶ ynin yhquac ypan xiuitl moquili ce pilli Juan ximenez a̶l̶l̶d̶e catca yxiptla onmochiuh yn don math.º Sanchez a̶l̶l̶d̶e çan oc miccatlatquitl yn ipan topilli quimomacaca. yn a̶l̶l̶d̶e mayor. çatepan ualla yn iyamayo yn a̶l̶l̶d̶e ōmochiuh. yniqu eyntin omochiuhque Don fran.ᶜᵒ de Mendoza. math.º lupez. a̶l̶l̶d̶es

Annals of Cuauhtitlan

side 3, towards the bottom

= 1. calli . ypan in xihuitl yn momiquilli yn intlàtocauh tolteca yn quitzinti yn tlàtocayotl yn itoca Mixcoamaçatzin niman onmotlalli huetzin yn tollan tlàtocat = 2 tochtli = 3 acatl = 4 tecpatl = 5 calli = 6 tochtli = 7 acatl = 8 tecpatl = 9 calli = 10 tochtli = 11 acatl = 12 tecpatl = 13 calli = 1 tochtli = 2 acatl = 3 tecpatl. 4 calli. 5 tochtli. = 6 acatl ypan mic in itatzin quetzalcohuatl ytoca totepeuh. auh niman yquac motlàtocatlalli yhuitimal yn tlàtocat tollan = 7 tecpatl = 8 calli = 9 tochtli = 10 acatl = 11 tecpatl = 12 calli = 13 tochtli = 1 acatl yuh motenehua mitoa ypan inyn quetzalcohuatl yn tocayotilo topiltzin

side 4

tlamacazqui çe acatl quetzalcohuatl. auh mitoa yn inantzin catca ytoca chimanan yhuan yuh ìtalhuillo ynic motlalli ȳ ytic ynantzin quetzalcoahuatl chalchihuitl quitollò = 2 tecpatl = 3 cali = 4 tochtli = 5 acatl = 6 tecpatl = 7 calli = 8 tochtli = 9 acatl. yn ypan in 9 acatl ypan quitemo yn itatzin quetzalcohuatl yquac ye achi yxtlamati ye chiucnauhxiuhtia: quito quenami yn notatzin ma nicytta? ma yxco nitlachia? auh niman ylhuiloc ca omomiquilli ca nachca yn motocac. ma xicmottilli niman yc ompa ya yn quetzalcohuatl. auh niman quitatacac quitemo yn iomiyo. auh ȳ oquiquixti ohmitl: ompa quitocato yn iteccal yytic yn motocoahotia quillaztli 10 tecpatl = 11 calli = 12 tochtli = 13 acatl = 1 tecpatl = 2 calli = 3 tochtli = 4 acatl = 5 tecpatl = 6 calli = 7 tochtli = 8 acatl = 9 tecpatl = 10 calli—ypan in xihuitl momiquili yn quauhtitlan tlàtoani catca uactli epohualli omome xihuitl yn tlatocattiticatca yehuatl ynyn tlàtohuani catca àmo quiximatia ynic motocoa çintli yn qualoni yhuan àmo quimatia yn imaçehualhuan ynic mochihua tilmatli. çan oc yehua tlaquemitl quiquemia. çan oc tototl cohuatl tochin maçatl yn intlaqual catca ayamo no calli quipiaya çan oc àhuic yatinemia quiztinemia = 11 tochtli ypan in motlàtocatlalli yn çihuapilli xiuhtlacuilolxochitzin oncan manca içacacal yn tianquiztenco axcan tepexitenco yn manca. auh ȳyn çihuapilli ynic ytech cauh altepetl mitoa yzihuauh catca yn uactli yhuan hel quinotzaya yn Diablo ytzpapalotl = 12 acatl = 13 tecpatl = 1 calli = 2 tochtli ypan in açico yn quetzalcoatl yn ompa tollantzinco oncan nauhxiuhti quichiuh yneçahualcal yxiuhhuapalcal. ompa quiçaco cuextlan yn çecni yc panoc tequappantli quitecac yuh mitoa onoc yn axcā 3 acatl = 4 tecpatl = 5 calli. ypan in xihuitl canato yn tolteca yn yehua quetzalcohuatl ynic quimotlàtocatique yn oncan tollan yhuan ynteopixcauh catca = çecni omicuillo yn iytolloca = 6 tochtli 7 acatl ypan mic xiuhtlacuilolxochitzin çihuapilli quauhtitlan XII xihuitl tlàtocat. 8 tecpatl. ypan in xihuitl motlatocatlalli yn ayauhcoyotzin quauhtitlan tlàtohuani ompa yn itocayocan tecpanquauhtla = 9 calli = 10 tochtli = 11 acatl = 12 tecpatl = 13 calli = 1 tochtli = 2 acatl. tetzcoco tlatolli ypan mic quetzalcoatl topiltzin tollan colhuacan = ynipan 2 acatl quichiuh yneçahualcal ytlamaçehuayan ytlatlatlauhtiayan yn topiltzin yn çe acatl quetzalcoatl nauhtetl yn quimamā ycal yxiuuapalcal ytapachcal ytecçizcal yquetzalcal yn oncan tlatlatlauhtiaya tlamaçehuaya auh moçauhtinemia. auh oc huel yohual nepāla yn apan temoya yn oncan motocayoti atecpan amochco. auh ōpa yn onmohuitztlaliliaya yn xicocotl yycpac yoā huitzco yhuā tzincoc yhuan nonohualcatepec. auh yn yhuitz quichihuaya chalchiuhtli yn iyacxoyauh quetzalli. auh yn quitlenamacaya teoxiuhtli chalchiuhtli tapachtli. auh yn inextlahual catca cohuatl tototl papalotl yn quinmictiaya = Auh motenehua mitoa ca ylhuicatl yytic yn tlatlatlauhtiaya yn moteotiaya. auh yn quinotzaya. çitlali ycue çitlallatonac tonacaçihuatl tonacateuctli tecolliquèqui yeztlaquenqui tlallamanac tlallichcatl = Auh ompa ontzatzia yuh quimatia ommeyocan chiucnauhnepaniuhcan ynic mani yn ilhuicatl auh yn yuh quimatia yehuantin ompa chaneque yn quinnotzaya yn quintlatlatlauhtiaya huel m[oc]nomattinenca tlaocoxtinenca = auh yxpan ymatian yequene yèhuatl quinexti yn huey necuiltonoliztli yn chalchiuhtli yn teoxiuhtli auh yn teocuitlatl yn coztic yn yztac yn tapachtli yn tecçiztli yn quetzalli yn xiuhtototl yn tlauhquechol yn çaquan yn tzinitzcan yn ayoquan. auh yhuan quinexti yn tlapapal cacahuatl yn tlapapal ychcatl. auh huel huey toltecatl catca yn ipan [ixquic]h ytlachihual yn itlaquaya yn iatliya yn tapalcatl xox[oc]⁴

side 5

tic quiltic yztac coztic tlapaltic tlacuilolli yhuan oc çequi miyec. Auh yn iquac nemia quetzalcoatl quitzintica quipehualtica yteocal quimaman coatlaquetzalli yhuan amo quitzonquixti àmo quipātlaz = Auh yn icuac nemia amo monextiyaya teyxpan huel ohuican calitec yn catca yn pialloya auh yn quipiaya yn tecpoyohuan mieccan yn quitzaquaya. auh yn izquican tzacuia yzquican çe çentlamantin oncan catca yn itecpoyohuā. auh yn ipan catca chalchiuhpetlatl quetzalpetlatl teocuitlapetlatl. auh omito omoteneuh nauhtetl yn quimaman yneçahualcal = auh mitoa motenehua yn iquac nenca quetzalcoatl miecpa yca mocayahuaz nequia yn tlatlacatecollo ynic tlacatica moxtlahuaz yn tlacamictiz = auh ayc quinec àmo çiz çenca quintlaçotlaya yn imacehualhuan yn tolteca catca çan mochipa yehuatl ynextlahual catca yn quinmictiaya yn coatl tototl papalotl. Auh motenehua mitoa yeehuatl yc quinxiuhtlati yn tlatlacatecolo yc oncan quipehualtique ynic yca mocacayauhque ȳic quiquèqueloque yn oquitoque yn oquinnecque yn tlatlacatecollo ynic quitollinizque yn quetzalcoatl. auh ynic quichololtizque yuh neltic mochiuh yn. = 3 tecpatl = 4 calli = 5 tochtli = 6 acatl = 7 tecpatl 8 calli 9 tochtli = 10 catl [sic] 11 tecpatl = 12 calli = 13 tochtli. 1 acatl yn ipan in xihuitl yn mic quetzalcoatl. auh mitoa çan ya yn tlillan tlapallan ynic ompa miquito niman onmotlàtocatlalli yn tollan tlàtocat ytoca Matlacxochitl = niman motenehua yn quenin çan ya quetzalcoatl catca yn iquac àmo quintlacamati tlatlacatecolo ynic tlacatica moxtlahuaz tlacamictiz niman mononotzque yn tlatlacatecolo = yn motocayotiaya tezcatlipoca yhuan yhuimecatl toltecatl. quitoque ca monequi çan quitlalcahuiz yn ialtepeuh oncan tinemizque. quitoque ma ticchihuacan octli ticytizque ynic tictlapololtizque ynic aocmo tlamaçehuaz. auh nimā quito yn tezcatlipoca ca niquitoa yn nehuatl. ma ticmacati ynacayo quē quitoz quimonepanylhuique ynic yuh quichihuazque. niman achtopa ya yn tezcatlipoca. concuic tezcatl necoc çemiztitl conquimilo. auh yn oaçic ompa ca quetzalcoatl quimilhui yn quipiaya ytecpoyohuan xicmilhuilitin yn tlamacazqui ca ohualla telpochtli mitzmomaquilico auh mitzmottitilico yn monacayo callacque yn tetecpoyo quicaquiltito yn quetzalcoatl quimilhui tleynon cocol tecpoyotl tleyn nonacayo yn oquihualcuic xicyttacan quin iquac hualcalaquiz. amo quimititiznec quimilhui ca nonomatca nicnottitiliz yn tlamacazqui xiquilhuitin quilhuito àmo cia cenca mitzmottilizneque. quito yn quetzalcoatl ma hualauh cocol. connotzato yn tezcatlipoca. callac quitlapallo quilhui nopiltzin tlamacazqui ~~ca nimomaçehual umpa nihuitz~~ çe acatl quetzalcohuatl nimitznotlapalhuia yhuan nimitznottitilico yn monacayotzin quito yn quetzalcoatl. otiquihiyohui cocol campa tihualla tleyn nonacayo ma nicytta. quilhui nopiltzin tlamacazqui ca nimomaçehual ompa nihuitz yn nonohualcatepetl ytzintlan ma xicmotili yn monacayotzin niman conmacac yn tetzcatl quilhui ma ximiximati ma ximotta nopiltzin ca ompa tonneciz yn tetzcatl. auh niman mottac yn quetzalcoatl cenca momauhti quito yntla nechyttacan nomaçehualhuan aço motlalozque ypampa çenca yxquatol mimiltic yxtecocoyoctic huel nohuian xixiquipiltic yn ixayac amo tlacaçemelle. yn oquittac tezcatl quito ayc nechyttaz yn nomaçehual ça nican niyez. niman hualquiz quitlalcahui yn tezcatlipoca auh mononotzque yn yhuimecatl ynic amo huel yca mocayahua quito yn yhuimecatl ma oc yehuatl yauh yn coyotlynahual yn amantecatl quicaquiltique ynic yehuatl yaz coyotlynahual in amantecatl. quito ca ye qualli ma niyauh ma niquitta yn quetzalcoatl niman ya = quilhui yn quetzalcoatl nopiltzin ca niquitoa ma ximoquixti ma mitzmottilican yn maçehualtin. ma nimitznochi

side 6

chihuili ynic mitzmottilizque. quilhui xicchihua niquittaz nococol auh niman quichiuh yn amantecatl yn coyotlynahual achto quichiuh yn iapanecayouh quetzalcoatl niman quichihuilli yxiuhxayac concuic tlapalli yc contenchichilo concui coztic ynic quixquauhcallichiuh niman quicòcoatlanti niman quichihuilli yn itentzon xiuhtòtotl tlauhquechol ynic quitzinpachilhui. yn oquiçencauh yn iuhqui ynechichihual catca quetzalcoatl niman conmacac tezcatl yn omottac çenca moqualittac niman huel yquac quiz yn quetzalcoatl yn oncan pialoya. auh niman ya yn coyotlynahual yn amantecatl quilhuito yn yhuimecatl. ca onicquixtito yn quetzalcoatl oc te xiauh. quito ca ye qualli. niman quimocniuhti ytoca toltecatl yn inehaun yaque yn ye yazque niman huallaque xonocapacoyan. ytlan motlalico ycuenchihcauh yn maxtlaton toltecatepec tlapiaya niman no quichiuhque yn quillit yn tomatl yn chilli yn xillotl yn exotl. auh çan quezquilihuitl yn mochiuh auh no yhuā oncan catca metl quitlanilique yn maxtla çan nahuilihuitl yn conoctlalique niman concontenque yehuantin quinextique yn quauhneccontotontin yehuatl yni cōcontenque octli niman yaque yn ichan quetzalcoatl yn ompa tollan mochi quitquique yn inquil yn inchil et.ª yhuan octli. açito onmoyeyecoque amo ciaya yn quipiaya quetzalcohuatl ynic calaquizq̄ oppa expa quincuepque amo celiloya çatepan tlatlaniloque ỹ canin ynchan. tlananquilique quitoque ca oncan yn tlamacazcatepec yn toltecatepec yuh quicac yn quetzalcoatl yc quito ma hualcalaquican callacque auh quitlapaloque yequene quimacaque yn quilitl. etª Auh yn oquiqua oc çeppa quitlatlauhtique quimacaque yn octli. auh quilihui ca amo niquiz ca ninoçahua aço teyhuinti. anoço temicti. quilhuique ma momapiltzin yn xicpallo. ca tetlahueli ca huiztli. yn quetzalcoatl ymapilltica quipallo yn oquihuelmat quito ma niqui nococol yn oçe conyc quilhuique yn tlatlacatecollo nahui yn ticmitiz yuh quimacaque yc macuilli quilhuique motlatoyahualtzin. auh yn oqu ic niman mochintin quinmacaque yn itecpoyohuan mochintin mamacuilli yn quique yn oquincentlahuantique. oc ceppa yn tlatlacatecollo quilhuique yn quetzalcoatl nopiltzin ma ximocuicati yzcatqui yn mocuicatzin yn ticmehuiliz. niman quehuili yn yhuimecatl . = quetzal quetzal nocall i çaquan nocall in tapach nocall in nicyacahuaz anya . = auh yn ye pactica. quetzalcoatl quito xicanatin yn nohueltiuh quetzalpetlatl ma tonehuan titlahuanacan. yaque yn itecpoyohuan yn ompa tlamaçehuaya nonohualcatepec quilhuito nopiltzi çihuapilli quetzalpetlatl moçauhqui ca timitztanilico: mitzmochilia yn tlamacazqui yn quetzalcoatl ytlan timoyetztiyetiuh quito ca ye qualli. ma tihuian cocol tecpoyotl. auh yn ohualla ytlan motlalli yn quetzalcoac niman oquimacaque yn octli nahui co çe ytlatoyahual yc macuilli. auh yn teltahuantique yn yhuimecatl yhuan toltecatl niman ye no yc quicuicatia yn ihueltiuh quetzalcoatl quehuilique = nohueltiuh cā tiyanemeyan tiquetzalpetlatl in mā titlahuanacan ayya yya ynyean = yn oyhuintique aocmo quitoque yntla ça titlamaçeuhque. auh niman aocmo apan temoque. aocmo mohuitztlalito aoctle quichiuhque yn tlahuizcalpan. auh yn otlathuic cenca tlaocoxque ycnoyohuac yn inyollo. niman oncan quito yn quetzalcoatl onotlahue[litic niman ye] ic tlaocolcuica ynic quicuicayoti ynic yaz ocan queuh.

side 7

aychtli [on]⁵ pohual çe tonal nocallan: ma nican aya queya ma nicā no nican an ma ye on ma niyequehua tlallaque çan ye cococ tlacoyotl ayca ninozcaltica = yc oncamatl queuh ycuic aya nechytquiticatca yehua nonan an ya coacueye an teotl ay pillo yyaa nichoca yya ye an . = yn iquac ocuicac quetzalcoatl niman mochintin tlaocoxque yn itecpoyohuan chocaque niman yc no oncan cuicaque yn queuhque. aya techonyacuiltonoca yehuā noteuchuan yehuan quetzalcoatlan mochalchiuhpapahua quahuitl yeço cana tlapa⁶ ma ticyaytzcā yehuan man tichocacan ean. auh yn ocuicacque ytecpoyohuan quetzalcoatl niman oncan quimilhui cocol tecpoyotl ma yxquich ma nictlalcahui yn altepetl ma niyauh xitlanahuatican ma quichihuacan tepetlacalli niman yziuhca quixinque çentetl tepetlacalli. auh yn iquac oquixinque yn oyecauh niman oncan quitecaque yn quetzalcoatl. auh çan nahuilihuitl yn tepetlacalco onoca yn icuac àmo mohuelmati niman quimilhui yn itecpoyohuan ma yxquich cocol tecpoyotl ma tihuiyan nohuian xictzatzaquacan xictlatican yn oticnextica yn paquiliztli yn necuiltonolli yn yxquich taxca totlatqui. auh yn itecpoyohuan yuh quichiuhque oncan tlatlatique yn inealtiayan catca quetzalcoatl yn ytocayocan atecpan amochco = niman yc ya yn quetzalcoatl moquetz quinçennotz yn itecpoyohuan quinchoquilli niman yaque ompa tlamattiaque yn tlillan yn tlapallan yn tlatlayan auh nohuian quitztia moyeyecotia acan tlahuelittac auh yn oaçic yn ompa tlamatihuia niman oc ceppa oncan chocac tlaocox = ye ypan ynyn xihuitl çe acatl motenehua mitoa yniquac oaçito teoapan ylhuicaatenco nimā moquetz chocac concuic yn itlatqui mochichiuh yn yapanecayouh yn ixiuhxayac et . = auh yn iquac omoçencauh niman yc ynomatca. motlati motlecahui. yc motocayotia yn tlatlayan yn ompa motlatito yn quetzalcoatl. auh mitoa yn iquac yn ye tlatla niman ye yc aco quiça yn inexyo. auh yn neçiya yn quittaya mochi tlaçototome yn aco quiça yn ilhuicac quimonitta tlauhquechol xiuhtototl tzinitzcan ayoquan tozneneme allome cochome yxquich yn oc çequi tlaçototome auh ynontlan ynexyo niman ye ic aco quiça yn iyollo quetzaltototl yn quitta auh yn iuh quimatia ylhuicac ya ylhuicac callac quitohuaya yn huehuetque yehuatl mocuep yn çitlallin yn tlahuizcalpā hualneçi yn iuh quitoa yn iquac neçico yn mic quetzalcoatl ye quitocayotiaya yn iquac mic çan nahuilhuitl yn àmo nez tlahuizcalpanteuctli yn quitoaya yn iquac mic çan nahuilihuitl yn amo nez quitohuaya yquac mictlan nemito. auh no nahuilhuitl momiti yc chicueylhuitica yn neçico huey citlalli yn quitoaya quetzalcoatl yquac moteuctlalli = auh yn iuh quimatia yn iquac hualneztiuh yn tleyn ypan tonalli çeçentlamantin ȳpan mìyotia quinmina quintlahuelia = yntla çe çipactli ypan yauh quinmina huehuetque yllamatque mochi yuhque yntla çe oçelotl yntla çe maçatl yntla çe xochitl quinmina pipiltotontin. auh yntla çe acatl quinmina tlàtoque mochi yuhqui yntla çe miquiztli. auh yntla çe quiyahuitl quimina yn quiahuitl amo quiyahuiz. auh yntla çe olin quinmina telpopochtin ychpopochtin. auh yntla çe atl. yc t[l]ahuaqui[7] et. = çeçentlamantli yc quitenyotiayaya yn huehuetque yllamatq̄ catca.

side 8

yn omotenueh quetzalcoatl ynic nenca yn ixquich in otlacat ypan ce acatl auh yn mic çan no ypan çe acatl ynic moçenpoa ynic nenca Lij aᵒs yc ontlami yn ipan in çe acatl xihuitl omito conpatlac matlacxochitl yn tollan tlatocat =

Chimalpahin, Seventh Relation

Folio 174v

xiii. acatl xihuitl 1479 años. ypan in tlaollin mochi xixitin yn calli yn tepantli miec xixitin yn tepetl auh çano yhcuac yn pehualloque yn tochcalco tlaca auh çano yhcuac y achto yancuicā cuicato yn mexico yn amaquemeq̄ yhuan yn tlalmanalca chalca yehuatl quehuato yn chalcacihuacuicatl quicuicatito yn tlahtohuani axayacatzin yn peuh cuicatl yhuan macehualiztli tecpan ythualco yhcuac yntlan catca yn icihuahuan axayacatzin yn callihtic auh ye tlatlaconemin cuicatl ce pilli tlalmanalco yn tlatzotzonaya tlatlacoco yn ~~tepxxxx~~ tlatzontzonaliztica çotlahuac ypan ȳ cen nequetzalhuehuetl, ça hualtollo ypan yn huehuetl aocmo quimati auh oncan huehuetitlan ycaya yn itoca quecholcohuatzin (*inserted:* amaq̄mecan pilli) huey cuicani yhuan tlatzotoznqui yn oquittac ye tlatlacahui tlatzotzonaliztica cuicatica yhuan macehualiztica yc niman yehuatl onmoquetztihuetz yn huehuetitlan quicuitihuetz yn huehuetl quipahti yn nehtotiliztli ynic amo necahualoc yc ye tecuicatia ye temacehuitia yn quecholcohuatzin auh yn tlalmanalco pilli ça hualtollo yn otecuicatiaya auh yn axayacatzin callihtic huallacacticatca auh yn ihcuac ye quihualcaqui yn cenca mahuiztic yc ye tlatzotzona yhuan ynic ye tecuicatia omoteneuh quecholcohuatzin yyollo tlahto moyoleuh yc niman moquetz niman callihticpa ȳtlan yn icihuahuan hualehuac y ye mitotitihuitz yn oahcico yn oncan macehualloyan centlapal cacoctihuitz yn icxi axayacatzin cenca paqui yn quicaqui cuicatl ynic ye no mihtotia ye tlatlayalhuallohua. Auh yn ihcuac ontla yn macehualiztli [f.175] quihto yn tlahtohuani axayacatzin nocne ynon tlapalpol nican annechhualhuiquizq̄ on otlatzontzon yn otecuicati (*inserted:* amo anquicahuazque) conilhuique ca ye cualli tlacatle tlahtohuanie ma yuhqui mochihuaz. Auh yn oyuh tlanahuati (*inserted:* ȳ axayacatzin) yc cenca momauhtique mochintin yn chalca tlaçopipiltin mootta tlatollihui cenca huel momauhtique yn iuh momatque yn achtopa otlaztzotzonaya yhuan otecuicatiaya tlalmanalco pilli yn iuh quihtohua huehuetq̄ ytoca cuateotzin catca no ahço ~~c~~ ce pilli yuhqui ytoca ȳ ypāpa yn ihcuac yn ye oyuh cenpohuallonmatlactli ypan nauhxihuitl momiquilli yn ic ome tlatoque yntoca catca cuateotzitzin yn otlahtocatico tlalmanalco yn ihcuac ȳ aocmo mixpan auh yn iuh onomatca chalca ahço quitlatlatiz ahço quitetzotzonazque yn tecuicatiani yn tlatzotzonqui quihtoque yn pipiltin chalca otechoncahuilli otlatlaco yn tocuicacauh tleȳ ticchihuazq̄ amo nel ye titlatlatillo nican auh y ye oiuh callac calihtic tecpan tlahtohuani axayacatzin yntlan motlallito cihuapipiltin yn icihuahuan yc niman ye huallatitlani yn canazq̄ yn quinotzazq̄ yn quecholcohuatzin yn oquihtoti yn oquicuicati axayacatzin ye quihtohua yn titlanti ye quimilhuia yn chalca pipiltin catlia yn amocuicacauh yn amotlatzotzoncauh quimonochilia yn tlacatl yn tlahtohuani ticanaco oncallaquiz callihtic yc niman quinnanquilliq̄ quimilhuiq̄ ca nican catqui ma quimottilli yn tlacatl yc niman connotzque ỹ telpochtli quecholcohuatzin yn chalca pipiltin huel iuh momatque ca ompa quimiquiztlatzontequiliz yn tlahtohuani axayacatzin quitlahtlatiz ynic ye callaqui quitlatenmachilia quiyahuac quichia yn quenma ye quiçaquiuh ytlahtol tlahtohuani yuhqui tetl oquitoloque chal ynic momauhtia auh yn ihcuac onacic quecholcohuatzin yn ixpan axayacatzin niman ontlalcua motlancuaquetz conilhui tlacatle tlahtohuanie ma xinechmotla [175v] tilli nican yn nimomacehualtzin ca otitlatla[coque]⁸ yn mixpantzinco auh ynin tlahtolli amo qui[ne]qui quicaquiz yn tlahtohuani axayacatzin ye nim[an] quimilhui yn cihuapipiltin ycihuahuan cihuaye ximoquetzacan xicnamiquican amotlan xictlalican nican huitz yn amochauh huel xiquittacan xiquiximaticanca onicxapotlac ma amoyollo yc pachihui (inserted: cihuaye) ca oquichiuh ca onechitoti onechcuicati ynin quecholcohuatl ayc ceppa aquin yuh nechihua callitic nechquixtia nechitotia yn iuhqui omochiuh ca amochauh yez mochipa axcan noconana nocuicacauh yez yc niman ye quitlauhtia yn qimacac tilmahtli yhuan maxtlatl huel ye yn itonal axayacatzin yn xiuhtilmahtli yhuan xiuhmaxtlatl xiuhcactli auh yn quetzaltlalpilloni yhuā quezqui quimilli cuachtli yhuan cacahuatl ynn [sic] inetlauhtil mochiuh quecholcohuatzin cenca quitlaçotlac yn ipampa yc oquitoti auh huel quimotonalti yn axayacatzin ynic ça ycel ycuicacauh yez aocmo çan ilihuiz canin tecuicatiz yc niman quinahuati yn tlahtohuani yc ye hualquiça quecholcohuatzin xxxxcencauhtihuitz yn ixiuhtilmah yn ixiuhmaxtla yn ixiuhcac yhuan quihuiquilitze yn inetlauhtil cuachtli yn cacahuatl tlamamallo yn oquittaq̄ chalca cenca yc mopahpaquilitique yn momatia ahço cuauhcalco oncontzacque ahnoce ocontlatlatique quitlapalohua yehuapan nemauhtillo. auh yn tlahtoahuani axayacatzin cenca quelehui quipaccacac yn chalcayaocihuacuicatl occeppa no yehuantin quinhualtenotzalla yn mochitin chalca pipiltin quintlatlauhti quimitlanilli yn cuicatl oc cenca yehuantin yn [f.176] amaquemeque ypampa huel yehuantin yntlayllotlaque yncuic amaxca yn chalcayaocihuacuicatl ompa ytlatlalil yn ce pilli ytoca quiauhtzin cuauhquiyahucatzintli huey cuicapiquini yn oncan ypan tenehualloya cuicatl yehuatl yn itoca tlahtohuani huehue aoquantzin chichimecateuhctli tlahtohuani catca ytztlacoçaucan totollimpa auh ynic quitlan axayacatzin yhuan yc quicuepque cuicatl quiquixtique quipoloque yn ipan yn itoca tlahtohuani catca huehue ayoquantzin auh oc yehuatl ye yn itoca axayacatzin yn ipan concallaquique cuicatl oncan in ypan in yn omoteneuh xihuitl qimaxcati quimotonalti yn cuicatl yn omotenuh tlahtohuani axayacatzin ye tecuicatiaya yn itecpanchan yn ihcuac connequia pahpaquiz yhuan mochipa yehuatl yc quicuicatiaya yn tlacpac omotocateneuh quecholcohuatzin yn çatepan ytoca don Jeronimo cenca quitlaçotlaya quihualcuicatiaya mexico auh ynin cuicatl ca no yehuantin quimaxcatique yn ipiltzin axayacatzin yn itoca teçoçomoctli acolnahuacatl yhuan yn ipiltzin yxhuiuh yn axayacatzin yn itoca don Diego de alvarado huanitzin tlahtohuani mochiuh ehcatepec auh çatepan governadortico mexico tenuchtitlan ca no yehuantin in yc tecuicatiaya yc temacehuitiaya yn intecpanchan mexico ypampa ca cenca mahuiztic yn cuicatl yhuan ynin ytenyo yn altepetl amaquemecan yn axcan yc neztica ca ça altepetepitzin.

Don Juan Buenaventura Zapata y Mendoza

[f. 92]

Axcan Yn ipa yacuic xihuitl de henero yc. 1 . de 1675 años. Yacuican mochiuh Jues go.[or] ocotelulco D. Diego martin Faostino Ynic ome xihuitl. quihuicazque yn ucotelulca yc maçi. Yacuican alld[e] D. mañuhuel de los Santos Regidortin D. Ju.° franc[co] tepeytec motlalia D. Diego felipe nahualtzintl. tiçatla yacuican alld[e] D. luis Diego Regidortin D. Ju.° nicolas. D. Ju.° nicolas [sic]. quiyahuiztlan yacuican alld[e] D. Diego perez cuixcocatzin chane S[t] fran[co] temetzontlan Regidortin D. Ju.° Nicolas tezpantzin D. sepas.[n] grabiel çarate tepeticpac D. Diego martin perez Regidortin D. nicolas saluador. D. Ju.° perez. alhuiçil.[or] yacuican D. Josep . de S[t] fran[co] s.criuanu de cauildo. Ju.° Bablo. go.[or] espanul ça Ye yehuatl D. leon de arsa Ynamic D.[a] thomaçina. yn ipan peuhqui yn Pilartin = yn ipan de enero yc 11. auh yn uyecahuico yn tlaco axcan ypan meztl ytlamia março ynic mochi yn itechhuic S.[t] migueltzin yhuan opeuhqui y nican totechhuic yehuatl mochi quixtlahua yn Josep de alva coBerador de cauildo~~~~~

Axcan yn ipan meztl de feprero yc 16. ça yanu ypan xihuitl de 1675 años yn upeuhqui tlalapatl yni cohuitia çahuatl. auh y quichquaque çan ey altepetl. ocotelulco quiahuiztla tepeticpa = auh yn tiçatla tlaca amo quineque quichihuazqui = quitlaxtlahuique. caxtolpuhuali pesos. quimoxexelhuique yn ey altepetl = auh yn ipehuayan março quipehualtique yni quiçaqua [f. 92 v] Ynic cohuitizque ahuel quixicoque. azta ytlamia março ahuel quitetzaque ça ye motlapuhua huel omoxixicoque yn tlatlacatzintzintin yn ey altepetl = auh yni tiçatla tlaca ynic amo quineque ynic otlanananquilique çe mestica yhuan tlaco yn catca hueycan telpiluya quimecatlayahualoltizquia yhuan quitotocazquia ça ypā tlato mochi cauildo yhuan totatzin temachtiani Diego martinez de Baldes. quimotlatlauhtili D. leon de arsa ynic quitlapopulhuique monetoltique ynic tlatlacamatizque~~~~~

AxcanYpan Domigo yc 24 de março yhuan ypan xihuitl de 1675 ās [sic] ypan yBisperatzin totlaçonatzin yncarnaçio yn uquiteyxpahuique tetlachihui chane S.ᵗᵃ maria acuitlapilco quihualquixtique telpiloya ypan. 9 . oras . ya oçili quihuicaque ycha Antonio gosales laso Bicario ychan opa quiquechmecayotique yhuan ymac quitlalilique cadela. quiltic ynic quicalaquico teopan S.ᵗ Josep. ypan peuhqui misa tlaquaoli quicac ypan mochiuh sermo ocan quinonozque yn quexquich omopuh tocabillia mochi opa yaqui S.ᵗ Josep. ocçepa quihualhuicaque telpilyan hualilpita~~~~~

Axcan YPan ylhuitzin hualathui ylhuitzin S.ᵗ Juan Papa martil. martes . a 27 de mayo. ça ya nu ypan xihuitl de 1675. años . yn utopan calaque yn ichteque = 6: tlacatl. yn umetin ocalaque betana achtopa çe ocalac yn utlyecan huel achtopa onechquizque yn iquac ye nicxicohua ynic oquinutz yn icniuh ynic ye nechocahuiya = auh ynic oniquiquitzquili yn icochilio. huel onechmamatec y nahuin nechcaltepia yespada çe argapus. quihualhuica . yn tomintzin [f. 93] matlacpuhuali pesos = auh yn totilmatzintzinhuan Amo quihuicaque maçanel çe tzotzomatl amo quixtique yhuan amo techcocotehuaque~~~~~

Axcan lunes. a: 20: de junio Yn upeuhqui yn unicpehualtin yn urnu ypan ilhuitzin Sᵗ siluerio papa. martil . yn peuh çemento. yn quipehualtin ca nu yehuatl quitlami yn itoca Ju.º grabiel nuhuehueputzin = auh yn Yacuican tlatlac Juebes. a 11 de Julio quiteochihuaco totatzin temachtiani Diego martines. de Ualdes. nican motlalia yn nucalnahuac. ypan ylhuitzin S.ᵗ Bio paba martil. homilhuitl yn tlatlac. yacuican ytec quizqui in tlaxcaltzintl huel ypan yn iBisperatzin Sᵗ Bueʳᵃtzin nusantotzin. sabado . hualathui domigo yn itlaçoylhuitzin. D. Ju.º Bueʳᵃ çapata y mendoza~~~~~

[On the right margin appears a passage almost as large as the main text, almost as if two columns were intended, or two entries for the same date on an old-fashioned xiuhpohualli line] yhuan yquac yaque pipiltin quitato tepatl yn capa tlatica in itepan tlaxcaltecatl tepeyacac yetoz caminu ynuma yaqui D. leon de arsa yhuan g.ᵒʳ don martin faostinu alcaldesme Regidorestin mochi cauildo huel ypan i meztl tonali xihuitl yaluhuac yn iquac niteniente nimochiuhticatca Ju.º Buenaventura çapata y mendoza

Axcan YPan ylhuitzin S.ᵗ apulinar oBispo martil. martes a: 23. de julio yhuiptlayoc. ylhuitzin S.ʳ S.ᵗtiago . yn uquixitinitiquiçaco yn çahuatl yacuic puete yn oquichiuhca tlatohuani D. leon de arsa yhuan Josep de alva. ça nima çe tlacoltica. yn uatococ. yn itechhuic S.ᵗ migueltzin = auh yn achto tlachihuali çatepan yn uquihuicatiquiz çan uquinacaçictecatiquiz yn çahuatl yn itechhuic xolal yahui S.ᵗ Ju.º totollan.

Axcan lunes: a 25 de julio. yn uçepan. hoquixitiniquiçaco çahuatl ynic çemi ohuatococo. ynic ye ocan hoc çepa pehua yancuic puete quahuitl puete huel ypā [f. 93v] mochicauh yn totazin cora un itoca J.º merino. nima quitato. totazin guardia yn itoca fray Ju.º morenu ynic quitequizque a.huehueme quaquauhxiuhtl. nahui y moteque nima mohuihuilaque hopa huicoque Ateco yn axca mamani nima çatepa tlayeuhque yn imeyxtin corastin antonio gosales Ju.º merinu temachtiani Diego martin de ualdes mochi tlacatl quitlali yn ihuetzin caxtilteca meztiçotin ytiotzin molatotzintzin y tley ohuelique çan iyolucacopa mochiuh auh yn Ju.º merino huel yxpan mochiuh opa ceçemilhuitiaya hopa tlaquaya~~~~~

Axcan yc 15 de Agosto yn itlaçoylhuitzin totlaçomahuiznatzin S.ᵗᵃ ma.ª Assopsio Atepeyihuitl [sic]. y huel. omohueycachiuh yn ayc yuhqui mochihuani yn umochiuh yn ixquichica yn uc ocatca totahuan tonahuan yn imahuiztililocatzin yn tlaçoçihuapili S.ᵗᵃ ma.ª yn utlatlac ynic omoquixtin ynic omotlayahualoltin yhuan ynic omocalaquito S.ᵗ Josep huel otlatotopucac yn utlatla. arbul: 13 huehuey. huel çeca otlamahuiçoloc yn altepehuaque ynic çenuya nepapa tlaca huel mochi tlacatl omotlaçocamat ma teopixque caxtilteca ynic mochitin nepapa tlaca y çeçe xochicali çeçe otlatlac arbol~~~~

[f. 94]
Axcan martes. a . 20 . de Agosto martes. yn umoteochiuh quapatl yn iquac. nican mehuiltitica totlaçonatzin S.ᵗᵃ mara [sic] Hocotla mehuiltiticatca S.ᵗ Josep. ocan moquixtin huel miec andas yhuan letanias ynic mohuicac yn upa y quapaco mochitin teopixque tlayahualoque yhuā yeyme coras mochichiuhque yn iquac maxitito quapaco huel oyectlachichiualoc yn itechhuic S.ᵗ migueltzin altal motlali. opan quimoçehuilique yn totlaçonatzin ocotla letanias. opa tlanqui quiteochiuh Bicario Antonio gosales. laso . huel nuyan tlapupuchhuitine yhuan tlahuechitinne çan uçepa yn iquac hualmohuica huey misa mochiuhtaçico Sᵗ Josep ya matlactl. oras yn tlaqui ynic tlatzoquiz~~~~~

[f. 94v]
Axcan Yn ipan xhuitl [sic] de 1676 años yacuican tequihuaque mochiuque~~~~~

Axcan yc çemilhuitl de henero miecoles yacuic xihuitl de 1676 años yacuican mochiuh Jues go.ᵒʳ tiçatla D. Diego de S.ᵗtiago . yacuica all~~de~~ D. Ju.º de la corona yn iRegidorhuan yacuican D. Diego de santiago D. luis hocotelulco

yacuican alt̶d̶e̶ D. Ju.º franco tepeytec regidortin yacuican D. Diego . Osorio
. D. Ju.º pasqual quiyahuiztlan yacuican alt̶d̶e̶ D. Saluador Ramirez. yn
iRegidorhuan D. simon de la cros D. Ju.º franco tepeticpac alt̶d̶e̶ D. franco
Ruiz. huehue tlacatl yn iRegidorhuan D. Nicolas saluador yacuica Regidor.
D. Diego Ruiz çan itelpuch yacuican secribanu de cacbildo. D. manuhuel
de los Santos alhuaçil mayor. telpiluyan miguel de çeli amo tlapepetl ocçe
yn tlapepenalli ça quimacaque ymoztlayoc auh yn tlatohuani ça yehuatl D. leon de arsa s.criº miguel de ortega. Brobiçia san franco topuyanco
yc ome xihuitl quihuicac D. franco ximenes. tiçatla çan upa nesqui S.t luis
quamantla ytoca D. Ju.º Antonio yn imo D. franco çeçetzin. St felipe alt̶d̶e̶
yacuican D. pasqual Ramires. St Ju.º atlacatepec çan ypa chane D. Josep .
perrez . yni mochitin tequihuaque yny mochiuhque yny moteneuhque
tlacpac~~~~~

[f. 95]
Axcan Domigo yc caxtoli oçe 16 de feBrero. yhuan ypa y xihuitl de 1676
anos yn umoteochiuh yn iteocaltzin Jesos nasarenotzin S.t Bablo Apetatitlan
huel miyec tlamatl yn mochiuh yhua quapatlanuhuac moquahhuilacatzoque
yhuan nica yaque coratin ymeyxtin lunes yhuan martes tlaminuhuac auh y
miercoles. yacuican motlali tiaquiztl çan uquezqui tlacatl y motlalique auh y
nupilhuan Ju.º grabiel yhua Ju.º x̄p̄ūal quihuicaque yntlaxcal çan uc yehuatin.
auh yn ichicomicayoc ya miec tlacatl. yn tlanamacaque ça yhu chicome nextl
y mochiuh S.ta Ana chiauhtepan cora ytoca matheo Ribera yehuatl tecohu-
anuz yhuan ymac moteochiuh yn teocaltzintl Jesos nasarenutzin~~~~~

Axcan Yc çemiltl [sic] 1 de mayo yhuā ypan xihuitl de 1676 años yn iquac
huala yn iyamauh tlatohuani D. mel.or melo Buçe de leon. Biernes ya teotlac
Ypannahui oras. quihualmacac yhuelitilis Ynic quiçelis ynic teniete yezqui
ypan Bisperas S.t felipe S.tiago hualathui sabado auh y quiçeli D. Geronimo
de la fuente ya yohuac yn itequi aço ypan 9 noço ya ypan. 10 . oras ya Yohuac
yquac yn uca omocxitepacho. D. franco Ruis quitlapuhuaya. postigo . cauildo
. ynic Ypan ohuetzinco yn icxi ça oquimemeque ynic quihuicaque Yn icha
hualathui sabado ya omococohua miec netequipacholi catca yca D. leon de
arsa mococoliaYa yhuan s.criº miguel de ortega. auh yn alcaldetin çan eyme y
monextique tiçatla quiyahuiztlan tepeticpac ça yehuātin monextique~~~~~

[f. 95v]
Axcan yn ucalac tlatohuani D. melchor merlo puçe de leo ypan martes a. 3: de
junio yhuan ypan xihuitl de 1676 años ya teotlac ynic uticnamiquito ypa
macuili oras. yc quiçaco S.t felipe ticnamiquito S.t Nicolas = auh y quimacaque yn itopil. matela [lu?] achi nican aocmo quipuhuilique yn icomixio ça

moteochihuato yn cauildo. hualamelauh teopan tocapillia calteco quizqui y calaquito S.ᵗ Josep yc calaquico cauildo yc nima tlecoc Balaçio mocahuato = auh yn iquac ticanato teniete ynic motlalia tiaquiztepitzinco ypā tocahualyohuan yc tiqualicaque palaçio ynic uca tiquizque ynic mochi tlacatl yaqui a~~lldes~~ Regidorestin moçehuiticate piPiltin~~~~~

Axcan Biernes Yc. 2 tonali de otoBre yhuan ypan xihuitl de 1676: años Ypan ylhuitzin S.ᵗᵒ Thomas oBispo yn uhuaçico amatl ynic hualmohuicaz S.ᵒʳ oBispo Guadalajara ynic nican hualmohuicaz cuitlaxcohuapan motlapiliquiuh. [*added into the same paragraph seamlessly, but in the handwriting of don Manuel de los Santos:* ytocatzin doctor don Manuel Fernandez de Santa Cruz.]

[f. 96]
Axcan miercoles a 28. de octoBre Yhuan yn ipan xihuitl de 1676 años huel ipan Ylhuitzin S.ᵗ simon Judas ypan matlactloce oras yn uquipuhque yn amatl yn uhuaçico mexico ynic ocaqui yn icoronatzin ytequitzin totlatocauh Rey. yn upa caxtilan huel çemilhuitl. yn utlamatzilinticaya = auh yn ipan nahui oras. mochiuh Brigo tzatzahuac tlayahualuque y piPiltin quitlapichilitaque yhuan s.crio caxtiltecatl tlanahuatita ynic nuya tlatlatlaz. yn xolalpan yn imoztlayoc Juebes yhuā Biernes tlamiminaloc. hoc çepa yc 8 yn otlayoc ça nu Juebes yhuan Biernes ça ya nu tlaminuhuac y tlayahualoque

Jues go.ᵒʳ al~~lde~~ Regidorestin yhuan mochitin moçehuiticaque piPiltin mohuihuipaque tlaya [*sic*][for tlayacan] clarin nima chirimias nima teocalticpac motzotzona huelhuetl [*sic*] yhuan tetepitzintzin marselos. cahuaoytipan yeYetaque mochitin ayac tlacxihui palaçio quizque yc teopan caltenco yc mocoloto mexo yc quaquauhxiuhtla yc tlamelauhque tiaquizco y capa yc tlayahualolo quaresma ça yc quitocaque çemotlica tzatzinta tecpuyotl

NOTES

Introduction

1. The best summary of what is known of Nahuatl historical annals remains James Lockhart's treatment in *The Nahuas After the Conquest* (Stanford: Stanford University Press, 1992), chapter 9. For recent work on reconstructing what occurred at the traditional performances, see my "Glimpsing Native American Historiography: the Cellular Principle in Sixteenth-Century Nahuatl Annals," *Ethnohistory* 56 (2009): 625–650.
2. The literature is vast. To begin, see Elizabeth Hill Boone, *Stories in Red and Black: Pictorial Histories of the Aztecs and Mixtecs* (Austin: University of Texas Press, 2000) and more recently her "Ruptures and Unions: Graphic Complexity and Hybridity in Sixteenth-Century Mexico," in *Their Way of Writing: Scripts, Signs and Pictographies in Pre-Columbian America*, edited by E. H. Boone and Gary Urton (Washington, DC: Dumbarton Oaks, 2011). For an excellent study of a specific text, see Lori Boornazian Diel, *The Tira of Tepechpan: Negotiating Place under Aztec and Spanish Rule* (Austin: University of Texas Press, 2008). For an introduction specifically to the glyphs, see Gordon Whittaker, "The Principles of Nahuatl Writing," *Göttinger Beiträge zur Sprachwissenschaft* 16 (2009): 47–81. On the issue of glyphs encompassing varied registers, see Katarzyna Mikulska Dabrowska, "'Secret Language' in Oral and Graphic Form: Religious-Magic Discourse in Aztec Speeches and Manuscripts," *Oral Tradition* 25 (2010): 325–363.
3. Editions of various texts have been published, primarily in Mexico, and these will be cited throughout the book. Luis Reyes García was instrumental in forwarding the translation of the annals before his untimely death, and Rafael Tena has done particularly valuable work on Chimalpahin and the *Annals of Cuauhtitlan*. Nevertheless, analytical monographs remain rare. The major exception is the work of Susan Schroeder. To begin, see her *Chimalpahin and the Kingdoms of Chalco* (Tucson: University of Arizona Press, 1991).
4. On possession of fragments of religious or spiritual texts, see David Tavárez, *The Invisible War: Indigenous Devotions, Discipline, and Dissent in Colonial Mexico* (Stanford: Stanford University Press, 2011).

5. Some extraordinary work has been done with such sources, despite the heavy-handedness of their production. For the very best, see Inga Clendinnen, *Aztecs: An Interpretation* (New York: Cambridge University Press, 1991).
6. Here I give only what a reader most needs to know. To pursue the subject in more depth and to place the Nahua calendar in the full context of Mesoamerican calendars generally, I refer the reader to Munro Edmonson, *The Book of the Year: Middle American Calendrical Systems* (Salt Lake City: University of Utah Press, 1988). Calendrical counts varied between altepetls, naturally, because prior to Aztec rule there was no authority insisting on perfect correlation. For the ways in which indigenous leaders manipulated the calendar to suit their own political needs, see Ross Hassig, *Time, History and Belief in Aztec and Colonial Mexico* (Austin: University of Texas Press, 2001).
7. See, for example, Timothy Reuter, ed., *The Annals of Fulda* (Manchester: Manchester University Press, 1992). The translation and commentary make this work accessible even to those from outside the field.
8. Jorge Cañizares Esguerra, *How To Write the History of the New World: Histories, Epistemologies and Identities in the Eighteenth-Century Atlantic World* (Stanford: Stanford University Press, 2010).
9. William H. Prescott, *History of the Conquest of Mexico*, vol. 1 (New York: American Publishers, 1843), 87–88. See especially his note 10 on his opinion of Humboldt.
10. Enrique Florescano, *Memory, Myth, and Time in Mexico: From the Aztecs to Independence*, translated by Albert B. Bork (Austin: University of Texas Press, 1994); Serge Gruzinski, *The Conquest of Mexico: The Incorporation of Indian Societies into the Western World*, translated by Eileen Corrigan (London: Polity Press, 1993 [1988]).
11. Miguel Leon Portilla, "Have We Really Translated the Mesoamerican 'Ancient Word'?" in *On the Translation of Native American Literatures*, edited by Brian Swann (Washington, DC: Smithsonian Institution Press, 1992), 315–316.
12. The students of James Lockhart have led the way, though many have participated. Dozens of works will be cited throughout this book. Other scholars, following trails blazed by Louise Burkhart, have been engaged in studying Nahuatl sources that very definitely were produced under the auspices of the European religious, but within these they have been seeking Nahua perspectives. Readers should begin with Burkhart's *The Slippery Earth: Nahua-Christian Moral Dialogue in Sixteenth-Century Mexico* (Tucson: University of Arizona Press, 1989).
13. Lockhart, *The Nahuas*, 378; Luis Reyes García, ed., *¿Como te confundes? ¿Acaso no somos conquistados? Anales de Juan Bautista* (Mexico City: CIESAS, 2001), 21. Reyes, like Lockhart, had the greatest respect for Nahuatl language and culture. His comment is a testament to the difficulty of following the annals as an uninitiated outsider.
14. Günter Zimmermann, ed., *Die Relationen Chimalpahin's zur Geschichte Mexico's* (Hamburg: Cram, de Gruyter, 1965). Zimmerman wrote each year once, and placed all events that occurred in that year there, no matter where they appeared in Chimalpahin's corpus.
15. Townsend, "Glimpsing Native American Historiography."
16. For example, Federico Navarrete Linares, *Los orígenes de los pueblos indígenas del valle de México: Los altepetl y sus historias* (Mexico City: UNAM, 2011). See also Schroeder, *Chimalpahin and the Kingdoms of Chalco*.

17. In the North American context, the ever-expanding list includes such works as Lisa Brooks, *The Common Pot: The Recovery of Native Space in the Northeast* (Minneapolis: University of Minnesota Press, 2008); Philip Round, *Removable Type: Histories of the Book in Indian Country, 1663–1880* (Chapel Hill: University of North Carolina Press, 2010); and Hilary Wyss, *Writing Indians: Literacy, Christianity and Native Community in Early America* (Amherst: University of Massachusetts Press, 2000). In the Latin American context, readers might begin with Kelly McDonough, *The Learned Ones: Nahua Intellectuals in Postconquest Mexico* (Tucson: University of Arizona Press, 2014); Gabriela Ramos and Yanna Yannakakis, eds., *Indigenous Intellectuals: Knowledge, Power, and Colonial Culture in Mexico and the Andes* (Durham, NC: Duke University Press, 2014); Joanne Rappaport and Thomas Cummins, *Beyond the Lettered City: Indigenous Literacies in the Andes* (Durham, NC: Duke University Press, 2012); Frank Salomon and Mercedes Niño Murcía, *The Lettered Mountain: A Peruvian Village's Way with Writing* (Durham, NC: Duke University Press, 2011); and Dennis Tedlock, *Two Thousand Years of Mayan Literature* (Berkeley: University of California Press, 2011).
18. Eric Auerbach, *Mimesis* (Princeton, NJ: Princeton University Press, 1953 [1946]). Auerbach discusses his methodology in his epilogue.
19. I ask experts among my readers to allow me to dispense just this once with the current state-of-the-art Nahuatl translation practice of giving the Nahuatl and a European language (generally Spanish or English) on facing pages. I gave careful thought as to how to connect best with most readers, and concluded that the inclusion of the Nahuatl at the start of each chapter might alienate non-Nahuatl speakers, when my dearest wish was to convince *any* reader who might possibly pick up the book that the indigenous annals are literature, and literature worth the reading. These texts are unfamiliar enough; let new readers at least face them the first time in a familiar language.

Chapter 1

1. The original *Historia Tolteca Chichimeca* is housed in the Bibliothèque Nationale de France, as Méxicains 46–50, 51–53, and 54–58. A facsimile edition is *Historia Tolteca Chichimeca*, edited by Paul Kirchoff, Lina Odena Güemes and Luis Reyes García (Mexico City: INAH: 1976). All references here will be to the latter edition, rather than to the original manuscript, but the translation is my own and differs slightly in meaning from the Spanish translation provided by the editors.
2. The word implies that they came to act as servants, custodians of his lands, and perhaps even as guards.
3. This unit of measurement covered the distance a typical person can encompass between the thumb and little finger, about six inches.
4. At times the reciters of old would move to the present tense, as though they were putting on a miniature play.
5. An "etc." ends the line, possibly replacing a list of ceremonial objects that once would have appeared here.
6. The phrase is an exhortation, meaning something like "Pay attention!" or "Focus!" or "Go to it with a will!" It is found in the spiritual incantations recorded by Ruiz de Alarcón.
7. The verb literally means to tighten or twist together, with the idea that they are gathering spirit to take action. I say "take heart" because of the English expression.

8. Literally, "ash water," meaning the lye in which corn was soaked for husking.
9. This is a way of expressing mockery found in other annals as well.
10. Such weeping on the part of leaders marks a significant public moment.
11. This is an example of polite social inversion.
12. The concept of *techan* (the homes of others) is very important, conveying the idea of people who lived at the mercy of others. Here it probably refers to their living on borrowed lands, but it might possibly indicate that they were living as servants in the actual homes of others.
13. *Libro de los guardianes y gobernadores de Cuauhtinchan*, edited by Constantino Medina Lima (Mexico City: CIESAS, 1995), 48. The figure at the heart of this chapter is for the first time called "don Alonso Castañeda Yxpopoyotzin" [meaning "blind one," spoken affectionately], in the entry for 1558 in the set of annals now known as the *Libro de Guardianes*.
14. He is listed as don Alonso de Castañeda Chimalpopoca in "Donación de Tierras de 1532" in Luis Reyes García, ed., *Documentos sobre tierras y señorío en Cuauhtinchan* (Mexico City: INAH, 1978), 101. This shred of documentation from this early era survived only because it was treasured by the people in question for a generation before being produced in a later court case, "Donación de tierras y macehualli a la cofradía de la Asunción, 1554" [AGN, Tierras, vol. 146, exp. 4].
15. Annals from the nearby town of Tlaxcala attest to the frigid temperatures of the season. See, for example, don Juan Buenaventura Zapata y Mendoza, *Historia cronológica de la Noble Ciudad de Tlaxcala*, edited by Luis Reyes García and Andrea Martínez Baracs (Tlaxcala: Universidad Autónoma de Tlaxcala, 1995).
16. *Libro de Guardianes*, 50. The friar was really Gerónimo de Mendieta. "niman ytencopatzinco in guardian fray Franisco de mendieta quinchichinalhuique in incal yn aquique amo ualaznequia auh in tlapantli xixitin" (In this chapter, more than in future ones, I include the Nahuatl in the notes, as the phrasing in these earliest sources may be particularly interesting to readers.)
17. We see don Alonso in this guise in a later court case now in the Archivo Municipal de Cuauhtinchan, published as "El Manuscrito de 1553," in Reyes García, ed., *Documentos sobre tierras* (Mexico City: INAH, 1978), 80–100. This aspect of don Alonso's history will be treated in depth below.
18. *Historia Tolteca Chichimeca*, 228. It has long been accepted by scholars that the *Historia* was written under the auspices of don Alonso's lineage. For a summary of the traditional argument, see Luis Reyes García, *Cuauhtinchan del Siglo XII al XVI* (Wiesbaden: Franz Steiner, 1977). On my reasons for believing that some parts of the *Historia* reflect the words of don Alonso himself, see below.
19. Ibid., 228–229. "Auh yn quinotzato ytoca mocnomatitzin pilli catca." "oquilhui nopiltzine tlatouane mitzmonochilia y machcauhtzin yn tecpanecatl yn tozcocolle." "ya onpa cate yn temictiyani" "amo canillique in iyollo niman oquicauhtiuetzque yn iquac oquelteque cenca omotlatlauitequi ynic omomiquilli."
20. Ibid., 229. "machiyaco yn atenco yn caxtillantlaca yn iquac uallaque."
21. *Libro de Guardianes*, 44. "aocac otli quitocaya."
22. Zapata, *Historia cronológica*, 270. "noyan santopan huel tlatlan tlacatl ça huel quezqui yn mocauh." Neither this nor the example above comes from the first epidemic in the land, but both record the writer's own earliest experience of one.
23. *Historia Tolteca Chichimeca*, 230. It is possible, though not probable, that Tecuanitzin died not of the disease but in skirmishes with the Spaniards which

occurred earlier that year, according to Spanish records. The *Historia* only records that he died in this year.

24. Stephanie Wood, "Nahuatl Terms Relating to Conquest," paper presented at the American Historical Association, New York, January 2015.
25. *Historia Tolteca Chichimeca*, 230. On the Atoyac having been at that time not a full-fledged creek or river but a wetland with discontinuous streams, see Bradley Skopyk, "Undercurrents of Conquest: The Shifting Terrain of Indigenous Agriculture in Colonial Tlaxcala, Mexico," PhD dissertation, Department of History, York University, 2010.
26. The *Libro de Guardianes* (30) says of Malinche: *yn oquiuh mitouaya in yauecauh in ualnahuatlatotia ciuatzintli cempoualtecatl* ("In olden times they used to say that the one who came along translating was a Cempoallan woman"). At another point on the same page, the writer describes her exactly as does the writer of the relevant segment of the Florentine Codex, as a *cihuateuctli* from Tepeticpac (in Tlaxcala). See Camilla Townsend, *Malintzin's Choices: An Indian Woman in the Conquest of Mexico* (Albuquerque: University of New Mexico Press, 2006).
27. *Historia Tolteca Chichimeca*, 230.
28. Ibid., 231.
29. Ibid., 231–232. Spanish records fully corroborate local memory. See Robert Himmerich y Valencia, *The Encomenderos of New Spain, 1521–1555* (Austin: University of Texas, 1991), 215. On the man's Tlaxcalan marriage and his relationship with Malintzin, see Townsend, *Malintzin's Choices*, 74, 141, 185–185.
30. *Historia Tolteca Chichimeca*, 231; *Libro de Guardianes*, 36. The sources contradict themselves as to exactly when this happened, and the memoirs of the Franciscans are no more exact. Probably some sort of mission was gradually established, beginning with a one-time visit followed by the foundation of a chapel, then a church. Later they built a monastery.
31. For more on both these figures see Ida Altman, *The War for Mexico's West: Indians and Spaniards in New Galicia, 1524–1550* (Albuquerque: University of New Mexico Press, 2010).
32. Edward Osowski offers a salutary reminder of the importance of this fact in his *Indigenous Miracles: Nahua Authority in Colonial Mexico* (Tucson: University of Arizona Press, 2010), 33, 43.
33. Don Diego Ceynos of Tepeyacac, appearing as an acquaintance and ally of don Alonso, swore to this in the "Manuscrito de 1553," in Reyes García, ed., *Documentos sobre tierras*, 80.
34. "Donación de Tierras," in Reyes García, ed., *Documentos sobre tierras*, 101.
35. *Libro de Guardianes*, 36. Previously, it has not been assumed that the words of the *Libro* were necessarily those of a descendant of don Alonso. It says explicitly only that it was written in the neighborhood of the church of San Juan Cuauhtinchan, and several lineages or *teccalli* resided there, not only don Alonso's; indeed, several first-person statements from two other lineages appear toward the turn of the seventeenth century. However, I believe that approximately the first half of the document originated with the Castañeda clan, as the perspective taken in that segment is consistently that of a family member. For instance, only don Alonso is given an affectionate nickname rather than a title, and only his grandson is referred to as "don Alonso, the younger" though other families also pass down names through the generations. In that period, a special interest is taken in Amozoc, and we know from mundane documents that the majority of the family's lands were in Amozoc.

(See Reyes García, *Cuauhtinchan*.) In the second half of the *Libro*, the perspective shifts noticeably. It is likely that the original document was taken and copied by a member of another lineage, and then added to in succeeding years. This was common practice. I would even say that it would have been expected, given that don Alonso had close family ties in other lineages, and the legitimate, male line of the Castañedas dried up in the generation of his grandchildren. If others are unconvinced, I will insist only that it is beyond doubt that the words in the document were those of someone in don Alonso's social circle if not immediate family, and the perspectives offered are thus still useful to us here.

36. *Libro de Guardianes*, 34 and 38.
37. "Donación de Tierras," 101–102. "mazeualzizintin motolinia y campa ueca tlali ualeuaque." The scribe called himself "Simón Buenaventura" and he appeared years later in the "Manuscrito de 1553" as well, still functioning as a scribe. He must have been a very early student of the friars.
38. *Libro de Guardianes*, 36. The *Libro* records that the execution happened in 1528, but it clearly happened in 1531 or 1532. First, in the *Libro* itself, someone has gone through and scratched out an original set of dates in this period, replacing them with earlier ones. The execution was thus first given as having happened later, in 1530. We must remember that the writer would have been working with the comments or notations of elders whose memories may have faltered and who still functioned in the old-style calendar, thus creating some confusion; plus, it was politically wise to push this event as far back as possible. In the *Historia* the event is inserted in 13 Reed, which I believe correlated with 1531–1532 in Cuauhtinchan, at least in the count don Alonso's teccalli kept. In the *Annals of Tecamachalco*, it is listed under a year termed "13 acatl 1531." According to the Spanish documentation, don Tomás was still alive in early Feburary 1532, when 13 Reed had not yet quite run its course. In the friars' memory of the event (see especially Mendieta), it was a young Tlaxcalan boy whom they had with them who discovered and reported the ceremonial sacrifice, but the Cuauhtinchan sources say nothing about this.
39. *Anales de Tecamachalco, 1398–1590*, edited by Eustaquio Celestino Solís and Luis Reyes García (Mexico City: CIESAS, 1992), 25–26.
40. Numerous recent works prove this beyond doubt. See, for example, Patricia Lopes Don, *Bonfires of Culture: Franciscans, Indigenous Leaders, and Inquisition in Early Mexico, 1524–1540* (Norman: University of Oklahoma Press, 2010); David Tavárez, *The Invisible War: Indigenous Devotions, Discipline, and Dissent in Colonial Mexico* (Stanford: Stanford University Press, 2011); and Eleanor Wake, *Framing the Sacred: The Indian Churches of Colonial Mexico* (Norman: University of Oklahoma Press, 2010).
41. *Historia Tolteca Chichimeca*, 231.
42. *Libro de Guardianes*, 36. "Amo xexeloloc çan pilcaya in inacayo Auh in iytzcuin yztac tlilmamanqui yn oncan yxquix cauh ytlan onoya ynic pilcac ytecuio." See also details in the *Annals of Tecamachalco*.
43. Lopes Don, *Bonfires*, 91–101.
44. *Historia Tolteca Chichimeca*, 232.
45. "Manuscrito de 1553," 90.
46. On fray Juan, one of the original "Twelve Apostles" who arrived in 1524, see fray Juan de Torquemada, *Monarquía Indiana*, vol. 3 (Mexico City: Porrúa, 1969), 443–444. In the indigenous sources, he seems to have been a trusted presence.

47. See the essay of Pablo Escalante Gonzalbo, "El Patrocinio del arte indocristiano en el siglo XVI: La iniciativa de las autoridades indígenas en Tlaxcala y Cuauhtinchan." In *Patrocinio, colección y circulación de las artes*, edited by Gustavo Curiel (Mexico City: UNAM, 1997). The surviving church he analyzes actually dates from the 1550s (see below), but there is no reason to think that the original edifice would have been more Christian in its decorative concepts than the later one. For a thoughtful segment on the significance of Nahua architectural monuments as revealed in the *cantares*, see Wake, *Framing the Sacred*, 235–256.
48. *Libro de Guardianes*, 40. "mochiuh moquetz in nemachtilcalli in colegio ynic oncan momachtia in ixquichtin nican tlaca Nueva España yn inpilhuan tlatoque yn nouian altepetlipan."
49. The original manuscript of the *Historia Tolteca Chichimeca* demonstrates this.
50. *Libro de Guardianes*, 40–42. One might assume that the young scholar had learned these things at the knee of a local friar in Tepeaca, except that in the same decade, he comments on current events in Mexico City as well.
51. *Libro de Guardianes*, entry for 1586, 62. The will of this man's daughter makes it clear that he was in direct line of descent from the tlatoani at the time of conquest. See "Testamento de doña María Ruiz de Castañeda, casica de Guatinchan, 1652," published in Reyes García, *Documentos sobre tierras*, 172–174.
52. Torquemada, *Monarquía Indiana*, vol. 3, 113.
53. *Libro de Guardianes*, 28.
54. "Manuscrito de 1553," in Reyes García, *Documentos sobre tierras*, 94.
55. See Altman, *War for Mexico's West*.
56. This number appears in a variety of indigenous annals, including the *Libro de Guardianes*, 44.
57. "Cuauhtinchan contra Tepeaca por los linderos establecidos en al año de 1467," [1546–1547], copy of a document from Mexico City found in the Archivo Municipal de Cuauhtinchan, paquete I, exp. 1, published in Reyes García, ed., *Documentos sobre tierras*.
58. Ibid., 28. The only witnesses they called who were not from the Cuauhtinchan region were "Pablo Suchicalcatl y Martín Tlapixque naturales de Tatelulco." They said they knew the names of the men who had followed Axayacatl's orders many years before in distributing the territory to the families of Cuauhtinchan.
59. Ibid., 13. They pled for speed, claiming "questan muy gastados."
60. Ibid., 11.
61. Ibid, 13–14. Juan Gallegos was a former conquistador, a companion of Hernando Cortés. It is not clear how he gained proficiency in Nahuatl. See Martin Nesvig, "Spanish Men, Indigenous Language, and Informal Interpreters in Postcontact Mexico," *Ethnohistory* 19 (2012): 748.
62. Literally all previous scholars who have studied the work date it to the late 1540s–early 1550s.
63. *Historia Tolteca Chichimeca*, 131.
64. Fifty-two was of course the number of years in a Nahua "century." The *Libro de Guardianes* also contained fifty-two folios, and in both sources, the writer explicitly noted the number of pages.
65. For an extraordinarily complete study of one such, see Davíd Carrasco and Scott Sessions, eds., *Cave, City, and Eagle's Nest: An Interpretive Journey through*

the *Mapa de Cuauhtinchan No. 2* (Albuquerque: University of New Mexico Press, 2007).

66. Keiko Yoneda, for example, has argued that the mixed iconography of the Mapa No. 2 should cause us to leave open the possibility that members of Nahuapan families may have participated in its production. See "Glyphs and Messages in the Mapa de Cuauhtinchan No. 2," in Carrasco and Sessions, eds., *Cave, City and Eagle's Nest*.

67. Testimony of don Diego Ceynos, "Manuscrito de 1553," in Reyes García, *Documentos sobre tierras*, 82.

68. Testimony of don Alonso *tezcacoacatl* et al., ibid., 88–89. Don Alonso's party consisted of don Juan Ixconauhqui, Diego Cuauhcitlatzin, Cristóbal Valiente, Baltasar López, Tomás Aztatl, and Andrés Morales.

69. For a discussion of the mixture of styles in the *Historia*, see James Lockhart, *The Nahuas after the Conquest* (Stanford: Stanford University Press, 1992), 348–351.

70. In several places in the "Manuscrito" don Alonso is listed as giving testimony as part of a group. It is impossible to know which man said what, except in rare cases where a single speaker is noted as speaking in the first person. But at one moment he definitely speaks on his own, recounting the significance of whom the daughters of Teuctlecozauqui took as their marriage partners ("Manuscrito de 1553," 97).

71. Ibid., 92. "neuatl amo nicmatqui amo nechnotzque za oniccaqui."

72. Fray Toribio de Benavente Motolinía, *Historia de los indios de la Nueva España* (Madrid: Alianza, 1988), 273.

73. Dana Leibsohn, *Scrypt and Glyph: Pre-Hispanic History, Colonial Bookmaking and the Historia Tolteca Chichimeca* (Washington, DC: Dumbarton Oaks, 2009), 9. Leibsohn's work is essential reading on the *Historia Tolteca Chichimeca*, providing extraordinarily perceptive analysis of the imagery.

74. Michael Swanton, "El Texto Popoloca de la Historia Tolteca-Chichimeca," *Relaciones* 22, no. 86 (2001): 117–140.

75. Fray Gerónimo de Mendieta, *Historia Eclesiástica Indiana*, vol. 2 (Mexico City: Salvador Chávez Hayhoe, 1945), 186–202. It makes sense that Mendieta tells the story in excruciating and highly believable detail, as he was himself part of the negotiations for a solution and then in 1558 went to Cuauhtinchan to head the new monastery.

76. See chapter 2.

77. France Scholes and Eleanor Adams, eds., *Sobre el modo de tributar los indios de Nueva España a Su Majestad 1561–1564* (Mexico City: Porrúa, 1958), 120–122.

78. "Testamento de doña María Ruiz de Castañeda, casica de Guatinchan, 1652," published in Reyes García, *Documentos sobre tierras*, 172–174.

79. Before turning to the experiences of the people of Cuauhtinchan, the *Libro de Guardianes* begins with material that is very similar to certain passages in Book 12 of the Florentine Codex, with its descriptions of the clanking, metal-clad Spaniards. Eleanor Wake likewise demonstrated an extraordinarily close linkage between certain images in the Mapa Cuauhtinchan No. 2 and some illustrations in the Florentine Codex. See Wake, "Serpent Road: Iconic Encoding and the Historical Narrative of the Mapa de Cuauhtinchan No. 2," in Carrasco and Sessions, eds., *Cave, City, and Eagle's Nest*.

80. Miguel León-Portilla, *Bernardino de Sahagún: First Anthropologist* (Norman: University of Oklahoma Press, 2002).
81. The *Annals of Tlatelolco* are housed in the Bibliothèque Nationale de France as Méxicain 22 (together with a later version, Méxicain 22 bis). A facsimile edition is Ernst Mengin, ed., *Unos annales [sic] históricos de la nación Mexicana* (Copenhagen: Einar Munksgaard, 1945). I worked with the latter and references here are to it.
82. Literally "elder sister." See chapter 4 for more on this concept.
83. Items needed for the ceremony of death.
84. Later this became the name of a tool for applying whitewash.
85. This may have referred to charcoal.
86. A common metaphor, meaning that the descendants and relatives she left behind would eventually grow strong and fight.
87. The phrase is illegible, but the visible "yol. . ." certainly suggests life and liveliness. Chimalpahin also records a symbolic story about a wriggling snake in the marshy grass at the moment of the founding of his people's town.
88. Literally "say," but this translation is closer to the sense of it.
89. Other annals include bloody details. The Mexica cut their prisoners' ears or noses off to prove to their overlords how many they had captured.
90. They meant, "Do these things represent our home?!" and the answer to such a rhetorical question was always implicitly "No!"
91. The word is literally "hidden" rather than "killed." This was a common metaphoric use of the verb. Recall that in the *Historia Tolteca Chichimeca*, the Toltec leaders ask, "Will we have to hide our faces?" meaning "Will we have to die?"
92. Zapata, *Historia cronológica*, 92.
93. *Historia Tolteca Chichimeca*, 226.
94. The foundational article on this subject is Pedro Carrasco, "Royal Marriages in Ancient Mexico," in *Explorations in Ethnohistory: The Indians of Central Mexico in the Sixteenth Century*, edited by H. R. Harvey and H. Premm (Albuquerque: University of New Mexico Press, 1984). For a full discussion see Camilla Townsend, "'What in the World Have You Done to Me, My Lover?': Sex, Servitude, and Politics among the Pre-Conquest Nahuas as seen in the Cantares Mexicanos," *The Americas* 63, no. 3 (2006): 349–389.
95. "El Manuscrito de 1553," in Reyes García, *Documentos sobre tierras*, 96.
96. Ibid., 97.
97. *Historia Tolteca Chichimeca*, 186.
98. Ibid., 218.
99. The ramifications of this are delineated in much greater detail in "El Manuscrito de 1553," 89.
100. This conversation appears in the Codex Aubin and in Chimalpahin.
101. Zapata, *Historia cronológica*, 84.
102. See also the Codex Aubin and Chimalpahin.
103. Zapata, *Historia cronológica*, 84.
104. Ibid., 90.
105. Ibid., 94.
106. "El Manuscrito de 1553," 96–97.
107. For a rich discussion of these issues, see Guilhem Olivier, *Mockeries and Metamorphoses of an Aztec God: Tezcatlipoca, "Lord of the Smoking Mirror"*

(Boulder: University Press of Colorado, 2003). Those who wish to explore the pantheon of Aztec gods must ultimately focus on the archaeological texts rather than the alphabetic. To begin, I suggest Rafael Tena, *La religión mexica* (Mexico City: INAH, 1993), followed by Leonardo López Luján, *The Offerings of the Templo Mayor of Tenochtitlan* (Boulder: University Press of Colorado, 1994).

Chapter 2

1. The original *Annals of Juan Bautista* text is located in the archive of the Biblioteca Lorenzo Boturini of the Basilica de Guadalupe in Mexico City. A facsimile edition is Luis Reyes García, ed., *¿Cómo te confundes? ¿Acaso no somos conquistados?Anales de Juan Bautista* (Mexico City: CIESAS, 2001). All references will be to this edition, though my translations are independent.
2. It literally says "the idolaters," but to these speakers, this was simply a word used to refer to the people of the old regime.
3. The friar seems to mean that they will be less dedicated to their crafts and to participating in a barter economy as they desperately seek ways to earn the requisite cash. They would also find themselves unable to support their traditional nobility.
4. The friar was being sarcastic, but the visitador did not seem to notice in his response.
5. The news he actually brought back on this subject was in fact somewhat unclear. And of course, it turned out that they were not really going to be allowed to leave off all other forms of tribute duties.
6. Marcos is either reminding the father that there will be no money to pay them under this new system, or that local communal tasks (such as road repair) will be left undone, or possibly both.
7. The painter is remembering events that occurred in 1548–1549.
8. Such a thought was anathema to the Mexica. People owed duties to the state only when they attained full adulthood.
9. He went to assure the governor that his orders were to be complied with, that the leader of the church painters would acquiesce.
10. The exact translation is doubtful, but the meaning is clear.
11. The alcalde was the one who was going to have to enforce it, but he felt terrible and said it was not his fault. He wanted the father to think of a way to help.
12. These were old titles of authority—judges and executioners.
13. There was theoretically a one-year time limit for the governorship in the system the Spanish set up, but no one had ever paid that rule any attention.
14. This was the Spanish husband of doña Isabel, daughter of Moctezuma.
15. *Anales de Juan Bautista*, 318–319. The exact words about the feeling in the air at dawn were: *auh yno tlathuic yuhqui ne[n] ommoma[n] tlalli yc tlatequipacho*.
16. James Lockhart pointed out years ago that the nickname might have been in reference to the hallucinogenic qualities of some mushrooms, or their insubstantial nature (as if they were calling him a "paper tiger"); Lockhart, *The Nahuas after the Conquest* (Stanford: Stanford University Press, 1992), 118. I have only found the nickname used in documents dating to after the man's death.
17. The *Codex Aubin* tells us that he was buried in December of 1565.
18. *Anales de Juan Bautista*, 316–317. *auh mochi tlacatl quittac y[n] titehuan yhua[n] españolesme*.

19. For a summary of the images associated with Ehecatl, see Mary Miller and Karl Taube, *An Illustrated Dictionary of the Gods and Symbols of Ancient Mexico and the Maya* (New York: Thames & Hudson, 2011 [1993]), 84–85.
20. Older works include Luis González Obregón, *La Semblanza de Martín Cortés* (Mexico City: Fondo de Cultura Economica, 2005 [1906]); Lesley Byrd Simpson, *Many Mexicos* (Berkeley: University of California Press, 1963); Fernando Benítez, *The Century after Cortés* (Chicago: University of Chicago Press, 1965). More recent treatments include Victoria Anne Vincent, "The Avila-Cortés Conspiracy: Creole Aspirations and Royal Interests" (PhD dissertation, University of Nebraska, Lincoln, 1993); Anna Lanyon, *The New World of Martín Cortés* (Cambridge, MA: Da Capo, 2003); Donald Chipman, *Moctezuma's Children: Aztec Royalty under Spanish Rule, 1520-1700* (Austin: University of Texas Press, 2005). The best is Ethelia Ruiz Medrano, "Fighting Destiny: Nahua Nobles and Friars in the Sixteenth-Century Revolt of the Encomenderos against the King," in *Negotiation within Domination: New Spain's Indian Pueblos Confront the Spanish State*, edited by Ethelia Ruiz Medrano and Susan Kellogg (Boulder: University Press of Colorado, 2010).
21. Ruiz Medrano has developed this theme in "Fighting Destiny."
22. William Connell, *After Moctezuma: Indigenous Politics and Self-Government in Mexico City, 1524-1730* (Norman: University of Oklahoma Press, 2011) has emphasized class divisions within the indigenous urban community in this period, but he discusses no connection between the social tensions in their community and events within the Spanish community.
23. Luis Chávez Orozco, ed., *Códice Osuna accompañado de 158 páginas inéditas encontradas en el Archivo General de la Nación* (Mexico City: Instituto Indigenista Interamericano, 1947). The pictorial *Codex Osuna* is often studied on its own, but it is greatly illuminated by the legal proceedings for which it was prepared.
24. A facsimile with transcription is available in Walter Lehmann and Gerdt Kutscher, eds., *Geschichte der Azteken: Codex Aubin und verwandte Dokumente* (Berlin: Gebr. Mann, 1981). The British Library has also made the original available online. Internal textual evidence tells us this work also came from San Juan Moyotlan.
25. Rudolph van Zantwijk, *The Aztec Arrangement: The Social History of Pre-Spanish Mexico* (Norman: University of Oklahoma Press, 1985), especially chapter 4; Rebecca López Mora, "Entre dos mundos: Los indios de los barrios de la ciudad de México, 1550–1600," in *Los indios y las ciudades de Nueva España*, edited by Felipe Castro Gutiérrez (Mexico City: INAM, 2010).
26. For more on the early post-conquest political organization of the city, see Charles Gibson, *The Aztecs under Spanish Rule* (Stanford: Stanford University Press, 1964); Lockhart, *The Nahuas*; and Connell, *After Moctezuma*. The nature of the indigenous cabildo is discussed in depth in Robert Haskett, *Indigenous Rulers: An Ethnohistory of Town Government in Cuernavaca* (Albuquerque: University of New Mexico Press, 1991).
27. "Las informaciones de don Luis de Santa María, fue gobernador de México y ordenó mandamiento de amparo para tierras de su patrimonio, 1563," published in Luis Reyes García, et. al., eds., *Documentos nauas de la ciudad de México del siglo XVI* (Mexico City: CIESAS, 1996), 103–110.
28. *Anales de Juan Bautista*, 234–235.
29. Ibid., 194–195 and 198–199.

30. Ibid., 138–139.
31. Ibid., 304–305.
32. Luis Reyes García first noted this in his introduction to the *Anales de Juan Bautista*, 48.
33. Bernal Díaz del Castillo, *Historia verdadera de la conquista de la Nueva España* (Mexico City: Porrúa, 2000), 170. He referred to two other artists as well. Years later, in a segment of the manuscript where other errors are also found, Díaz referred to the same man as "Andrés de Aquino" (581), but this name is not in keeping with any other sources (see below.)
34. Gibson, *Aztecs*, 174, and *Documentos nahuas*, 103–110. Unlike their indigenous names, their Spanish surnames definitely were used as patronymics, and families did not tend to choose (or have chosen for them) names already in use by other leading families in the same town.
35. Because there is absolutely no contemporary evidence of the existence of anyone named Juan Diego, or indeed, of any apparition of the Virgin of Gaudalupe, scholars have been too quick to assume that there were no significant events at Tepeyac at all. Rodrigo Martínez Baracs has demonstrated that the place had a deep local religious history. See his "De Tepeaquilla a Tepeaca, 1528–1555," *Andes* no. 17 (2006).
36. The Franciscan provincial gave a sermon mentioning the painting by Marcos and accusing the secular hierarchy of egging on the Indians in their error in order to rack up converts. The archbishop therefore launched an investigation, beginning with the sermon itself. See Edmundo O'Gorman, *Destierro de sombras: Luz en el origen de la imagen y culta de Nuestra Señora de Guadalupe* (Mexico City: UNAM, 1986).
37. "Información que el arzobispo de México don fray Alonso de Montúfar mandó practicar de un sermón que en la fiesta de la natividad de nuestra Señora (8 de septiembre de 1556) predicó en la capilla de San José de Naturales del convento de San Francisco de México, el provincial fray Francisco de Bustamente acerca de la devoción y culto de nuestra Señora de Guadalupe," reprinted in Ernesto de la Torre Villar and Ramiro Navarro de Anda, eds., *Testimonios históricos Guadalupanos* (Mexico City: Fondo de Cultura Económica, 1982). See especially the testimony of Alonso Sánchez de Cisneros, 63. This should by no means be understood as tantamount to evidence for the story of Juan Diego. For those interested in the demolition of the claim that there is any early evidence for the Juan Diego story of the apparition, the most effective text probably remains the classic pamphlet by Joaquin García Icazbalceta, "Carta acerca del orígen de la imagen de Nuestra Señora de Guadalupe de México" (Mexico City, 1896). Readers should then turn to Stafford Poole, *The Guadalupan Controversies in Mexico* (Stanford: Stanford University Press, 2006).
38. Salvador Guilliem Arroyo, "The Discovery of the Caja de Agua of Tlatelolco: Mural Painting from the Dawn of New Spain," *Colonial Latin American Review* 22 (2013): 19–38. The beautifully painted water cistern was famous by the mid-1550s.
39. On the number of texts borrowing extensively from the *Aubin*, see Lehmann and Kutscher, *Geschichte der Azteken*. I argue that the writer did not move in the same circle as the writers of the *Anales de Juan Bautista* because they do not mention anyone of his surname. Nor did they share an artisanal craft.

40. See "Extract from the *Codex Aubin*," in *We People Here: Nahuatl Accounts of the Conquest of Mexico*, edited by James Lockhart (Los Angeles: University of California Press, 1993), 43.
41. Traditionally, the most common perspective taken by historians has been that of the viceroy, don Luis de Velasco. In fact, the visitador, Valderrama, was unsympathetically nicknamed "the scourge of the Indians" by posterity. However, two talented scholars who edited the latter's letters became so caught up in his own argumentation that they concluded he was a misunderstood, dedicated servant of the Crown. See France Scholes and Eleanor Adams, Prologue, in *Cartas de Valderrama* (Mexico City: José Porrúa, 1961). Scholars focusing on the indigenous in this affair have thus far tended to side with the governor.
42. See Camilla Townsend, "Glimpsing Native American Historiography: The Cellular Principle in Sixteenth-Century Nahuatl Annals," *Ethnohistory* 56, no. 4 (2009): 625–650.
43. Modesto Ulloa, *La hacienda real de Castilla en el reinado de Felipe II* (Madrid: Fundación Universitaria Español Seminario Cisneros, 1986).
44. This was in the wake of a new law passed in 1559. For both sides of the debate, see France Scholes and Eleanor Adams, eds., *Sobre el modo de tributar los indios de Nueva España a Su Majestad, 1561–1564* (Mexico City: José Porrúa, 1958).
45. *Cartas de Valderrama*, 65–66. "Todo esto que a los indios se les ha quitado y lo que a Vuestra Majestad se le ha acrecentado se consumía entre governadores y principales y frailes. Los gobernadores y principales se lo beben todo. Los frailes, creo yo que lo consumen en buenos usos y en sus iglesias y monasterios y plata y ornamentos de ellos, pero hacen malo en llevarlo contra voluntad de sus dueños."
46. Scholes and Adams, Prologue, *Cartas de Valderrama*.
47. *Cartas de Valderrama*, 0.39.
48. "Auto proveido por el Virrey, Visitador y Audiencia sobre el tasar los indios, 18 de enero de 1564," in *Sobre el Modo de tributar los indio*, 116–118. The number of pesos due was based on an assumption that a recent census taken in the city was accurate; Velasco continued to insist that it was inflated.
49. *Anales de Juan Bautista*, 184–185.
50. *Códice Osuna*, 13–16. There is no direct evidence that Valderrama's office was behind the lawsuit, but the charges would indicate that the indictment was largely the work of Spaniards, and in the *Anales de Juan Bautista*, Valderrama is quoted as making statements that indicate an acquaintance with the progress of the suit.
51. *Anales de Juan Bautista*, 196–197. James Lockhart discusses the succession of the governorship in this period in *The Nahuas after the Conquest* (Stanford: Stanford University Press, 1993), 34; as does Gibson in *Aztecs under Spanish Rule*, 169. It is possible that the young woman was instead the daughter of Huanitzin, who governed 1538–1541. See María Castañeda de Paz, "Historia de una casa real: Origen y ocaso del linaje gobernante en México-Tenochtitlan," *Nuevo Mundo Mundos Nuevos* (2011), https://nuevomundo.revues.org/. However, the writings of Chimalpahin render it virtually certain that she was the figurative daughter of Tehuetzquititzin, or more literally, his niece. See Arthur Anderson and Susan Schroeder, eds., *Codex Chimalpahin*, vol. 2 (Norman: University of Oklahoma Press, 1997), 119.

52. *Anales de Juan Bautista*, 198–199. At this point begins the time period covered in the selection that opens the chapter.
53. On the building of the tecpan and its symbolic importance, see Barbara Mundy, *The Death of Atec Tenochtitlan, the Life of Mexico City* (Austin: University of Texas Press, 2015), 108–110.
54. It seems that with Cuauhtemoc's defeat only forty years past, the people were still angry with him. They use the same verbal construction with regard to him as with regard to don Luis Cipac, at whom they are enraged. It is an unusual verb, *quitlanitoa*, not the usual *motlanitoa* or *tlatlanitoa*. I have found it only in one place: Molina's dictionary, p. 73, under *jugando*. By Chimalpahin's era, Moctezuma was known as the weakling and Cuauhtemoc as the strong one, but that does not seem to have been the case here, in the 1560s, among people who remembered both men.
55. The *Anales de Juan Bautista* are in agreement with Valderrama's own report in his *Cartas*,160.
56. *Códice Osuna*, 38 (*gente advenediza, bulliciosa y escandalosa*). The surrounding pages of the case give more details as to the background of Toribio Lucas Totococ.
57. See Camilla Townsend, "'What in the World Have You Done to Me, my Lover?': Sex, Servitude, and Politics among the Pre-conquest Nahuas as Seen in the *Cantares Mexicanos*," *The Americas* 62, no. 3 (2006): 349–389. Though the article uses the song to try to uncover women's experiences, it discusses the fact that the song was apparently primarily used by men to make a political statement about empire. See also chapter 4.
58. See Camilla Townsend, *Malintzin's Choices: An Indian Woman in the Conquest of Mexico* (Albuquerque: University of New Mexico Press, 2006).
59. *Cartas de Valderrama*, 11, 0.338
60. *Anales de Juan Bautista*, 218–219. One might assume that the "don Martín" mentioned was the marqués del Valle, except that the writer says specifically he was the alguacil mayor, and later (quite correctly), that he was temporarily taking the place of Juan de Sámano.
61. He is mentioned several times over the course of the next few pages, certainly more than his legitimate brother, the marqués.
62. These are Valderrama's words in a letter to the king, scoffing at the viceroy's weakness in regard to the Indians (*Cartas de Valderrama*, 161). However, it is likely that he represents the man's attitudes fairly, given his prior policies, and given the fact that the writer of the *Anales* says that a Spaniard recommended that they send a messenger straight to Velasco's bedside because he would almost certainly intercede.
63. María Justina Sarabia Viejo, *Don Luis de Velasco, virrey de Nueva España, 1550–1564* (Seville: Escuela de Estudios Hispano-Americanos, 1978), 470–471.
64. *Cartas de Valderrama*, 160–161. "Este alboroto de estos pocos indios no se puede creer que haya sido sin ser incitados a ellos, porque demás de ser ellos tan obedientes naturalmente, con la tasación se les ha hecho gran beneficio. . . . Y un animal sin razón entiende y conoce el bien que le hacen, cuanto más un hombre, aunque tenga poco. He hecho diligencia para entenderlos . . . y no se ha aclarado."
65. On Valderrama's bond with Ceynos, see *Cartas de Valderrama*, 51. On his moving into the Audiencia building in the wake of Velasco's death, see p. 155.
66. *Anales de Juan Bautista*, 278–279.

67. This is referenced in the *Anales de Juan Bautista*. Detailed treatment based on records related to the friars is found in Ruiz Medrano, "Fighting Destiny."
68. *Códice Osuna*, 32–37. They refrained from pointing out that the witnesses claiming that the tlatoque were illiterate representatives of a bygone age themselves could not sign their names, while they themselves had learned to.
69. Ibid., 37–38.
70. Ibid., 49–50.
71. Ibid., 76–77 and onward.
72. *Anales de Juan Bautista*, 254–255, 258–259.
73. Ibid., 238–239.
74. Ibid., 238–239.
75. Ibid., 288–289.
76. Ibid., 236–237.
77. Ibid., 242–243.
78. Ibid., 252–253, 258–259.
79. Ibid., 258–259.
80. Ibid., 246–247.
81. Ibid., 262–263.
82. Ibid., 250–251.
83. *Anales de Juan Bautista*, 248–249; and Lockhart, *The Nahuas*, 383. Lockhart was the first to translate this passage, and in doing so, he noted the use of the singular to express a sense of collectivity.
84. *Cartas de Valderrama*, 187. "Yo he dicho verdad en todo lo que he escrito, y Vuestra Majestad ha sido mal servido aquí antes que yo viniese y le tenían usurpada la jurisdicción y la hacienda y la tierra se gobernaba mal." His altered tone is noticeable throughout this period.
85. *Codex Aubin*, entry for Sunday, January 21, 1565.
86. *Anales de Juan Bautista*, 300–303.
87. A contemporary witness to the events described them in his 1589 manuscript. See Giorgio Perissinotto, ed., *Juan Suárez de la Peralta: Tratado del descubrimiento de las Indias y su conquista* (Madrid: Alianza, 1990). Large segments of the related trial transcripts were published by Manuel Orozco y Berra, *Noticia histórica de la conjuración del Marqués del Valle, 1565–68* (Mexico City: R. Rafael, 1853). Some of the originals are in the Library of Congress, but many are in the AGI, Patronato 208, 209, 210 and 211. The king was apparently never convinced that there had been any serious intent behind the rebellious talk, as he later forgave his boyhood companions.
88. This is recorded in both the *Códice Osuna* and the *Anales de Juan Bautista*.
89. *Códice Osuna*, 77–78.
90. *Anales de Juan Bautista*, 142–143. The writer says only that they were told at church on March 3 that she had died; he does not say how. However, the most likely explanation for a privileged young bride's death in a period when there was no epidemic would be related to pregnancy.
91. Ibid., 146–147.
92. For more on these events, see Townsend, *Malintzin's Choices*.
93. *Anales de Juan Bautista*, 148–149.
94. Ibid., 150–151; *Codex Aubin*, entries for Tuesday, July 16, and Saturday, July 3.
95. Ibid., 38–41. The men did continue the suit a few more months, until November, entirely futilely.

96. Ibid., 148–149.
97. *Códice Osuna*, 152–153.
98. *Anales de Juan Bautista*, 150–153.
99. Ibid., 154–157. For more on this subject, see Castañeda, "Historia de una casa real."
100. This becomes quickly evident by looking at a chart of Indian alcaldes in Tenochtitlan, 1555–1568, published by Charles Gibson in *Aztecs under Spanish Rule*, 174.
101. The written proceedings of don Martín's torture session were published by Orozco y Berra in *Noticia histórica*, 228–233. For more on the situation as a whole, see Townsend, *Malintzin's Choices*, 206–211.
102. *Codex Aubin*, entry for 1568. The translation of the entry is open to doubt. "To take ships from the sea" must have had an idiomatic meaning. What is clear is that by the time he wrote the entry, the author knew that those who were to die would not really be executed.
103. Juan García Totococ and Miguel García Ahuach took office, *Anales de Juan Bautista*, 172–173. These men's close connection to Toribio Lucas Totococ and Juan Ahuach is revealed earlier in the *Anales*, 139.
104. These items are noted in the *Anales de Juan Bautista*, the *Codex Aubin*, and other sets of annals.
105. *Anales de Juan Bautista*, 180–181.
106. Marcos Tlacuiloc said that he was, as previously noted. Other men mentioned in the *Anales* appear as witnesses in the *Códice Osuna* and likewise say they are in their fifties.
107. Townsend, "Glimpsing Native American Historiography."
108. Hernando Cortés, "Second Letter" in *Letters from Mexico*, edited by Anthony Pagden (New Haven, CT: Yale University Press, 1986), 84–85. On the "cellular principle," see Lockhart, *The Nahuas*.
109. The last words written by the copyist are "Mn de la Cruz Neccaltitlan." He could not have begun earlier than 1574, for in that year one "Juan Bautista" wrote out in another hand, in Spanish, that the notebook was to be used to collect the tribute of vagabond Indians who had not yet paid, and that he, Juan Bautista, had received his commission from His Excellency. Apparently not long after writing those words, Juan Bautista lost his notebook. It was later found by an indigenous person who put it to an alternative use. The copyist adds later entries beyond the main events, ending in 1582.
110. Other, more subtle but even more direct evidence that there was an original block of text that ran from 1566 through 1569, then backed up and covered 1564–1565, is found in the fact that both before and after that block we find brief bits of what I might call "nonsense material," clearly added long after by someone who did not fully grasp the agenda of the 1560s project. The material includes a few disjointed, unrelated entries about famous events (at the opening) or events of the later copyist's own decade (at the close). See *Anales de Juan Bautista*, 132–133, 330–331. The facsimile makes this even clearer than does the transcription, as the copyist who almost certainly introduced the unrelated material takes care to mark it off from the rest of the text with a horizontal line in each case.
111. López Mora, "Entre dos mundos," 61, 66. The author has mapped nearly all the barrios of the city in the mid-sixteenth century. In an earlier work, I had followed Luis Reyes García in assuming that Acatlan (mentioned briefly in the text) was

part of Moyotlan, but we were in error. It neighbored the Moyotlan barrios, but was administered by San Pablo.

Chapter 3

1. The original *Annals of Tecamachalco* manuscript is held by the University of Texas at Austin. A facsimile edition is Eustaquio Celestino Solís and Luis Reyes García, eds., *Anales de Tecamachalco, 1398–1590* (Mexico City: CIESAS, 1992). All citations will be to the latter, though my translations are independent.
2. This date is inserted in another hand. European dating continues in the margins, but will not be continued here until the main writer begins to include it in his own text.
3. Now called Tepeaca (as it will be in this chapter's discussion).
4. A prior tlatoani, Ce Olintzin, died the year before Cuetzpaltzin took the throne. Olin's granddaughter (literal or figurative) was also named as being important. So it was crucial that an emergent leader be accepted into this lineage in order to be envisioned as worthy of the chieftainship.
5. This undoubtedly marks a great ceremonial occasion.
6. Probably from these historical events came the idiom "to be one rabbited," meaning to starve and face decimation.
7. They asked for lands on which to grow crops for the Mexica. See below.
8. In the *Annals of Cuauhtitlan*, we learn that this same Chiyauhcoatl of Tepeaca had already been in power when Tepeaca launched a major war against Tecamachalco in 1442 (see above). So it was no wonder that the teller here relishes his destruction and repeats it twice.
9. See the discussion in this chapter.
10. This was the name of the lineage that produced Cuauhtitlan's kings, and hence was used as a title for the ruler. This is revealed later in the annals.
11. Legal documents demonstrate that the chosen godfather was an indigenous nobleman with extensive lands and the right to carry a sword.
12. Most likely a traditional title as opposed to a name.
13. A frequently mentioned cabildo member.
14. In-text references indicate that the writer probably meant his father-in-law and good friend, not the same man as above.
15. Saint Helena's finding (*inventio*, hence *yn vetio* in the text) of the cross was celebrated on May 3. If fray Juan was removed a few days after June 8, then the writer's "forty-one days" is correct.
16. This translation is not certain in its specific form, but it definitely conveys the sense of the situation. The author almost certainly witnessed hemorrhagic smallpox, an especially deadly form of the disease.
17. *Anales de Tecamachalco*, 48.
18. Ibid., 78.
19. Ibid., 78.
20. Ibid., 79. It is not often that don Mateo writes in the present tense, but the comet's appearance lasted for weeks.
21. The documented details of their connection will follow below.
22. When the friars established themselves in Tecamachalco in the early 1540s, Mateo (later don Mateo) became their student. He could not have been much younger than ten or much older than fifteen at the time. The birthdates of his

children are also in keeping with his having been born c. 1530. We know his father was not as highly ranked as a teuctli, for in his writings he refers twice to "our teuctli" when speaking of men with another surname.

23. The elder who gave don Mateo material for the section on the Spanish conquest reported on the hangings of the Cuauhtinchan nobles in a dire tone and with accurate detail. (See chapter 1 for more on the subject.) In the early years after the conquest, the narrator mentions events *ompa Tepeaca* ("there in Tepeaca") with great frequency, but ceases to do so after the friars establish themselves in Tecamachalco.

24. *Anales de Tecamachalco*, 27.

25. Eleanor Adams, *A Bio-Bibliography of Franciscan Authors in Colonial Central America* (Washington, DC: Academy of American Franciscan History, 1953), 78–79. France V. Scholes and Eleanor Adams, eds., *Don Diego Quijada, alcalde mayor de Yucatán, 1561–1565*, vol. 1 (Mexico City: Porrúa, 1938), xvii–xviii. At one time a number of historians repeated an assertion that Toral was born c. 1501, but the royal cédula naming him as bishop of Yucatán gives his age at that time (1560) as forty-five. He was therefore born c. 1515, a date which is in better keeping with the known events of his life.

26. "Fray Francisco de Toral a Felipe II, primero de marzo, 1563," published in Scholes and Adams, eds., *Don Diego Quijada*, 35. It is to be acknowledged that Toral was particularly disgusted with his peers at that moment, having just discovered the atrocities committed by fray Diego de Landa. See below.

27. Cited in Rosa Camelo Arredondo, Jorge Gurría Lacroic, and Constantino Reyes Valerio, *Juan Gerson: Tlacuilo de Tecamachalco* (Mexico City: INAH, 1964), 33.

28. Camelo et al. in *Juan Gerson* explore why Gerson's work was so influential among the Franciscans in Mexico that they would christen one of their acolytes in his honor. For the list of books present in the library at Tlatelolco, see "Comisión para tomar cuentas al mayordomo de Colegio de Tlatelolco," in Joaquín García Icazbalceta, ed., *Nueva colección de documentos para la historia de México* (Liechtenstein: Kraus Reprints, 1971 [1886]), vol. 3, 250–260.

29. In 1563 he confessed that his financial difficulties were due in part to "the expenses of ... some books that I bought for my studies," ("los gastos de ... unos libros que compré para mi estudio"); "Toral to Felipe II" in Schole and Adams, eds., *Don Diego Quijada*, vol. 2, 37.

30. These two figures make regular appearances in the *Annals of Tecamachalco*. It is impossible to determine with certainty exactly how they are related. They could have been brothers, but they were probably father and son, with Juan Gerson, counterintuitively, as the son. In 1544, one don Tomás Tlacochteuctli appears as a key nobleman in the community, one of the first to take a seat as alcalde on the newly organized cabildo. About the time that a talented student artist called "Juan Gerson" is first mentioned, a "don Tomás Gerson" appears as an important political player, and Tomás Tlacochteuctli ceases to be mentioned. Probably the father had adopted the surname that had been given to his notable son. That Tomás was the patriarch seems to be further evidenced by the fact that Tomás, but not Juan, appears frequently in legal documents from the area. In 1547, a witness in an unrelated case commented that he knew "Tomás, principal de Tecamachalco que en indio se llama Tlacustecotle" (quoted in Luis Reyes García, ed., *Documentos sobre tierras y señorío en Cuauhtinchan* [Mexico City: INAH, 1978], 58–59); and in 1555, one don Tomás Gerson asked for

permission to go about on horseback (AGN, Mercedes, vol. 4, folio 202v, cited by Celestino and Reyes, in *Annals of Tecamachalco*, 102). As of 1592, don Tomás was still politically active, his business appearing both in the annals and in mundane legal documents, and a Juan Gerson, *specifically identified as his legitimate son*, requested an estancia to keep livestock (AGN, Mercedes, vol. 18, folio 108v, cited by Celestino and Reyes, in *Annals of Tecamachalco*, 102). This Juan could, of course, have been another family member, not necessarily the same as the Juan Gerson mentioned here, but he probably was the same, as the Juan Gerson working for the church appears in the annals as late as 1585.

31. For more on this, see below, especially notes 43–46.
32. *Anales de Tecamachalco*, 28–29.
33. Ibid., 29.
34. Ibid., 31 and ensuing pages.
35. Ibid., 36–37.
36. The document is mentioned in the annals, but it is not extant, as far as we know.
37. *Anales de Tecamachalco*, 45. It is possible that the person who recopied the annals in about 1590 was himself a musician, and that it was he who welded the two accounts together. That seems unlikely, however, in that don Mateo's account is given pride of place and is clearly the dominant one, and in that it would have been extremely difficult for someone much younger, copying many years after the events, to have combined two accounts for the first time so seamlessly.
38. On musicians' connections with particular lineages, see Lidia Gómez García, "El testamento de don Lucas Quetzalcoatzin, indio cacique del pueblo de Santa María Atlihuetzian: El papel de los músicos indios en la construcción del nuevo orden novohispano," paper presented at the 54th International Congress of Americanists, Vienna, July 2012.
39. He mentions his mother's death in 1568; *Anales de Tecamachalco*, 56.
40. Toral was not the only one to bring these issues to his indigenous students' attention. The author of the *Codex Aubin* likewise noted the "golden number" of certain years. For more on indigenous uses made of European calendars, see David Tavárez, *The Invisible War: Indigenous Devotions, Discipline, and Dissent in Colonial Mexico* (Stanford: Stanford University Press, 2011), especially chapter 5.
41. A number of the era's European almanacs refer to golden numbers. See, for example, Andrés de Li, *Reportorio de los tiempos* (Zaragoza, 1495).The clearest explanation of the matter—the one I would guess most closely mirrored the classroom experience of Toral, and then of don Mateo—I found to be that presented in the first edition of the King James Bible in England, where Reformation thought encouraged direct explanations to a wider public. For more on the almanacs in general, readers might begin with Peter Whitfield, *The Mapping of the Heavens* (London: British Library, 1995).
42. *Anales de Tecamachalco*, 41, 43.
43. These paintings are still extant and visible. A published work reproducing them in full is *Juan Gerson: Pintor indígena del siglo XVI; símbolo del mestizaje* (Mexico City: Fondo Editorial de la Plástica Mexicana, 1972). For an excellent study comparing images from mid-sixteenth-century Bibles found in the Mexican National Library and their close parallels in Gerson's work, see Camelo et. al., *Juan Gerson*. We know that the paintings were done by the indigenous artist Juan Gerson because the Annals of Tecamachalco tell us

so. (See note 45.) Recently, some historians have argued that the text might be interpreted as meaning that Juan Gerson acted as scribe, not painter, at the time, the verb -ihcuiloa being ambiguous, but the full context of the surrounding sentences renders the translation clear beyond a shadow of a doubt: he was the painter.
44. Charles Dibble and Arthur J.O. Anderson, eds., *The Florentine Codex: General History of the Things of New Spain, by Bernardino de Sahagún* (Salt Lake City: University of Utah Press, 1950–1982), vol. 11, 29–30.
45. *Anales de Tecamachalco*, 44–45. He mentions the work twice, in 1561 and 1562, when it began and when it ended. This was typical Nahua style. See Sebastián van Doesburg, "Territory and Cultural Reproduction: Agrarian Conflict, Títulos and Pictorial Documents," paper presented at the 54th International Congress of Americanists, Vienna, July 2012.
46. It is remarkable that they carved Nahuatl words into the edifice, but not unheard of. See Van Doesburg, "Territory and Cultural Reproduction."
47. AGN, Mercedes, vol. 5–6, folio 213 (1561), cited in *Anales de Tecamachalco*, 44. Records indicate that it was common practice for cabildo members to be given such tangible rewards. This is the only time don Mateo seems to have benefited personally.
48. *Anales de Tecamachalco*, 44.
49. Ibid., 45.
50. These events have been well studied. See, for example, Inga Clendinnen, *Ambivalent Conquests: Maya and Spaniard in Yucatán, 1517–1570* (New York: Cambridge University Press, 1987).
51. *Anales de Tecamachalco*, 46.
52. Adams, *Bio-Bibliography*, 79. The full text of his letter appears in García Icazbalceta, *Nueva colección*, vol. 1, 254–259.
53. *Anales de Tecamachalco*, 50.
54. "Toral to Felipe II," in Schole and Adams, *Don Diego Quijada*, vol. 2, 36. "Tenían presos ciento y tantos principales en el monasterio de esta ciudad [de Mérida], y andaban prendiendo mas para hacer un auto y quemarlos a todos, cosa de gran atrevimeinto y libertad."
55. "Diego Rodríguez Bibanco, defensor de los indios, a Felipe II, 8 March 1563," published in *Cartas de Indias*, vol. 1 (Madrid: Biblioteca de Autores Españoles, 1974), 393. "Començaron el negoçio con gran riguridad e atroçidad, poniendo los yndios en grandes tormentos de cordeles e agua, y colgandolos en alto a manera de tormento de garrucha con piedras de dos y tres arrovas a los pies, y allí colgados dandoles muchas açotes, hasta que les corría a muchos de ellos sangre por las espaldas y piernas hasta el suelo; y sobre esto los pringavan, como se acostumbran hazer a negros esclavos, con candelas de çera ençendidas e derritiendo sobre sus carnes la çera dellas."
56. "Toral to Felipe II, 8 October, 1566," published in Stella María González Cicero, *Perspectiva religiosa en Yucatán, 1517–1571* (Mexico City: El Colegio de México, 1978), 229. "Soy mudo y sordo por no saber [la] lengua." Elsewhere Toral wrote savagely about the general inability of the Franciscans in Yucatán to understand anything the Indians said: "Toral to Felipe II, 18 July, 1566," published in ibid., 223.
57. *Anales de Tecamachalco*, 50.
58. Ibid., 54.

59. Ibid., 53, for the 1567 events. Ibid., 60, for the 1570 marriage of the young people. Ibid., 67, for Gerson's continuing dispute with the friars in 1573 about the role they had played in the decision made in 1567.
60. Ibid., 56. A recent study of these events is Nick Hazlewood, *The Queen's Slave Trader: John Hawkyns, Elizabeth I, and the Trafficking in Human Souls* (New York: Harper, 2005).
61. *Anales de Tecamachalco*, 59.
62. Ibid., 59.
63. "Indios gobernadores de varias provincias de Yucatán a Felipe II, 12 April, 1567," published in *Cartas de Indias*, vol. 1, 408. "Aunque nos sacó de la carçel y nos libró de la muerte y quitado los sant benitos, no nos a desagraviado en las ynfamias y testimonios que nos levantaron, diziendo que somos ydolatras, sacrificadores de hombres e que aviamos muerto muchos yndios; por que, al fin, es del hábito de los religiosos de Sant Françisco y haze por ellos." For more on this fascinating letter written by a collection of caciques to disown a prior letter that had been sent in their name by supporters of Landa, see Clendinnen, *Ambivalent Conquests*. For a study of Mayan responses to the Spaniards, including other letters and petitions, see Matthew Restall, *Maya Conquistador* (Boston: Beacon, 1998).
64. "Toral to Felipe II, 5 April, 1567," published in *Cartas de Indias*, vol. 1, 239. "Los naturales, temiendo perder sus tierras, an de usar de mill [sic] traiçiones y embustes, de arte, que todo a de cargar sobre Ud." The indigenous go-between held by Menéndez, don Luis Paquiquineo, did in fact turn on the Spaniards once they were in the Chesapeake. See Camilla Townsend, "Mutual Appraisals: The Shifting Paradigms of the English, Spanish, and Powhatans in Tsenacomoco, 1560–1622," in Douglas Bradburn and John C. Coombs, eds., *Early Modern Virginia: Reconsidering the Old Dominion* (Charlottesville: University of Virginia Press, 2011).
65. "Toral to Felipe II, 9 December, 1570," published in González, *Perspectiva Religiosa*, 250–251. "Como ya soy viejo, no he podido aprender la lengua de aquella tierra por lo cual he vivido con gran descontento por no poder predicar a mis ovejas. . . . Y si todavía Vuestra Majestad es servido que le sirva en este estado y dignidad, sea en tierra fría a donde pueda hacer mi oficio y que las ovejas oigan mi voz y yo las entienda. . . . Aunque más querría estar en un rincón libre de carga de ánimas."
66. *Anales de Tecamachalco*, 62. Some European sources report that he died in April, but that seems to have been the time of his funeral. The indigenous men seem to have heard the whole story from his interpreter, who was with him at the time. (See below.)
67. Ibid., 62.
68. AGN, General de Parte, 1579, exp. 379, folio 79, cited in *Anales de Tecamachalco*, 66.
69. *Anales de Tecamachalco*, 64.
70. Ibid., 71.
71. Ibid., 73.
72. Ibid., 75.
73. This number appears in several sets of annals from the region.
74. Ibid., 77–78
75. Ibid., 80.

76. Don Mateo was not merely imagining that the situation was deteriorating. Hildeberto Martínez has done a careful study of extant legal documents and has demonstrated that the region's Spanish population was gradually gaining control of local resources. See his *Codiciaban la Tierra: El despojo agrario en los señoríos de Tecamachalco y Quecholac (Puebla, 1520–1650)* (Mexico City: CIESAS, 1994).
77. *Anales de Tecamachalco*, 81.
78. See Luis Corteguera, *Death by Effigy: A Case from the Mexican Inquisition* (Philadelphia: University of Pennsylvania Press, 2012), 67–68. This book explores a 1578–1582 inquisition case as it unfolded in Tecamachalco. Indigenous people were not among the accused, but in 1581, a tiny handful believed to be literate were brought in to see if they recognized a particular handwriting. They did not.
79. *Anales de Tecamachalco*, 83. For the next few years, events are narrated from the perspective of Lucas Sánchez. He marries, experiences earthquakes, etc. Sadly, he died young, in the mid-1580s. Other relatives then took over the history for a few more years.
80. The letter was preserved by Sahagún and later sent back to Spain with a collection of his materials. They were later published in facsimile as the "Códice matritense del Real Palacio." See Francisco del Paso y Troncoso, ed., *Historia de las cosas de Nueva España*, vol. 7 (Madrid: Hauser y Menet, 1906), 41–42. The letter is folio 53 of the original. Though the letter bears no date, Miguel León Portilla has been able to date it to c. 1570 based on the address to which the letter was sent (as it is known where Sahagún lived when), combined with the place in his own materials where he stored it. See Léon Portilla, *Bernardino de Sahagún: First Anthropologist* (Norman: University of Oklahoma, 2002), 182–183. I would add that the shakiness of Sahagún's handwriting in his notations on the back also puts it to this date. A transcription and Spanish translation of the letter are to be found in Elena Díaz Rubio and Jesús Bustamente García, "Carta de Pedro de San Buenaventura a fray Bernardino de Sahagún," *Revista Española de Antropología Americana* 13 (1983): 109–120; I have a somewhat different translation.
81. For more on the elaborate style of Nahua letter writers, see Arthur J. O. Anderson, Frances Berdan, and James Lockhart, eds., *Beyond the Codices: The Nahua View of Colonial Mexico* (Berkeley: University of California Press, 1976), 196–203.
82. The solar year contained 360 days plus the unmarked five-day additional period. The *Florentine Codex* includes Nemontemi in Books 2 and 4, but it is clear that at the time of writing, Sahagún and his aides still did not fully understand the concept. (Note that the solar calendar was distinct from the ceremonial calendar of 260-day years. At any point, one was positioned within both calendars.)
83. Prologue, in fray Bernardino de Sahagún, *The Florentine Codex: General History of the Things of New Spain*, Introductory Volume, edited by Charles Dibble and Arthur J. O. Anderson (Santa Fe, NM: School of American Research and University of Utah, 1982), 55.
84. The friar's explanatory notes on the back of the letter are, like the letter itself, published in the facsimile *Códice matritense*, vol. 7, 42.
85. Prologues in *Florentine Codex*, Introductory Volume, 54.

86. For the best recent treatment of Valeriano and his context, see David Tavárez, "Nahua Intellectuals, Franciscan Scholars, and the *Devotio Moderna* in Colonial Mexico," *The Americas* 70 (2013): 203–235. For treatment of the Latin writings, see Andrew Laird, "Nahuas and Caesars: Classical Learning and Bilingualism in Post-Conquest Mexico; An Inventory of Latin Writings by Authors of the Native Nobility," *Classical Philology* 109.2 (2014): 150–169.
87. "Al prudente lector, 1564" facsimile and transcription published in Miguel León Portilla, *Coloquios y doctrina cristiana* (Mexico City: UNAM, 1986), 75.
88. Sahagún's comments and references within the letter both indicate that San Buenaventura was in Cuauhtitlan when he wrote to the friar.
89. Primo Feliciano Velázquez, the scholar who produced the invaluable facsimile through which we now know the work, the original having been lost, and Rafael Tena, the work's most recent editor, both assume that either San Buenaventura or Vegerano (Sahagún's other aide from Cuauhtitlan) must have produced the work, but have not offered evidence. See prefaces to Primo Feliciano Velázquez, ed., *Códice Chimalpopoca: Anales de Cuauhtitlan y Leyenda de los soles* (Mexico City: Imprenta Universitaria, 1945), x; and Rafael Tena, ed., *Anales de Cuauhtitlan*, 14–15.
90. That the extant version was once among the Ixtlilxochitl family papers is indicated by the fact that the Ixtlilxochitl genealogy is delineated on the endpapers. Close examination indicates that it may even have been in the hand of don Fernando de Alva, as Boturini asserted, or else of his brother, don Bartolomé de Alva, though small variations make positive identification uncertain. See Camilla Townsend, "Evolution of Alva Ixtlilxochitl's Scholarly Life," *Colonial Latin American Review* 23 (2014): 15. I believe that we are seeing San Buenaventura's own script in the letter itself, as it matches the signature at the bottom perfectly. León Portilla argues that it is the work of a scribe, because another signature, that of one Pedro González, also appears on the letter. But the latter signature is awkwardly scrawled in a strange place, and is more likely to have been an example of a later student practicing on whatever paper was available, or an aide of Sahagún's who was working on cataloguing the papers.
91. I worked with the Velázquez facsimile described in n. 89. It is customary with this text to refer to pages rather than folios, as the original is entirely lost and we are consulting photographs taken in 1945.
92. John Bierhorst notes that the *Florentine Codex* reveals that the lord Ometeuctli and the lady Omecihuatl inhabited the topmost of twelve layers. See his translation in his *History and Mythology of the Aztecs: The Codex Chimalpopoca* (Tucson: University of Arizona Press, 1992).
93. Bierhorst translates this as "a chamber that was hard to reach," and it may well be the best way.
94. The same word that I have translated elsewhere as "retainers" rather than "servants" is used, but in this instance, the point is to convey social inversion. He calls them "grandfathers" though it is they who serve him.
95. Again, we see polite social inversion.
96. I add "a bit" because the image of "sticking one's finger in" appears in other texts to express the idea of just going in for something to a very limited extent.
97. Bierhorst points out that this is probably a pun, as *huitztli* ("thorn") has a second meaning—pulque.
98. According to the *Florentine Codex*, taking a fifth draught is the sign of a drunkard.

99. The grammar is extraordinarily bizarre, with case endings reversed. It is a stylized song.
100. This term has political significance: she is a female of the noble line, either the one whose children would expect to rule an altepetl, or who was symbolically important in some other way. She is not necessarily literally his sister, but she certainly is one who should not be violated. See chapter 4.
101. Like many surviving Nahuatl songs (and indeed, like many modern songs), this piece is so stylized and ungrammatical as to be nearly untranslatable in a specific sense, although it is clearly a lament for a lost home. Both Bierhorst and Tena have made strong efforts to translate the song, but I cannot concur with either. There are simply too many unresolvable elements. Here, I have at least tried to give readers a sense of the lyrical quality, dividing the clauses line by line, so that one can recognize a certain rhythm in the words.
102. The final version was included in the *Florentine Codex*. See Arthur J. O Anderson and Charles Dibble, eds., *The Florentine Codex, Book 3: The Origin of the Gods* (Santa Fe, NM: School of American Research and University of Utah, 1952), 13–36.
103. The earliest draft, with marginal notes, is found in *Códices matritenses de Real Palacio*, folios 145–151, published in facsimile in Francisco del Paso y Troncoso, ed., *Historia de las Cosas de Nueva España*, vol. 7 (Madrid: Hauser y Menet, 1906), 235–250. Often it has been assumed that only Paso y Troncoso's volume 6 (only 6, 7, and 8 were ever published), later dubbed the "Primeros Memoriales," should be ascribed to the period in Tepepolco, and that all other materials known to us as the "Códices matritenses" belong to the period of making additions and changes in the ensuing years in Tlatelolco. However, the division was made by Paso y Troncoso, often, as he himself admitted, in great confusion. He took materials stored in the Real Palacio and in the Real Academia, both of Madrid, ripped them apart, and reordered them in new combinations. Studying the facsimiles he created, I conclude that we have to assume that far more than that which appears in what we now call the "Primeros Memoriales" originated in some form or other in Tepepolco. Just because the material is presented in a narrow central column does not indicate that it was the all-but-final version, as has been assumed, given Sahagún's final presentation in columns. The material sometimes is recorded this way in order to separate the clauses, for easier reading by a non-native speaker, or in order to place two Nahuatl versions side by side.
104. *Códices matritenses*, vol. 7, 215.
105. The marginal comments have become the first paragraphs of the chapters in *Florentine Codex* 3: 13–36, the first one appearing on p. 13, but with the comparison to Hercules omitted.
106. This significantly altered version is incorporated into a description of the Toltecs in *Florentine Codex* 10, 166–170. I cannot find this anywhere in the facsimile *Códices matritenses*, thus rendering it likely that this was a later writing.
107. Ibid., 169.
108. Bierhorst, ed., *History and Mythology of the Aztecs*, 40–41.
109. *Florentine Codex* 1, 39–40.
110. *Florentine Codex* 12, 5 and 9. There is a similar sentence at another mention of the conquest in another volume, 8, 21.

111. See Susan Gillespie, *The Aztec Kings: The Construction of Rulership in Mexica History* (Tucson: University of Arizona Press, 1989), 185–201; and Camilla Townsend, "Burying the White Gods: New Perspectives on the Conquest of Mexico," *American Historical Review* 108.3 (2003): 659–687. See also, for more in-depth treatment of the Spanish texts, Jacques Lafaye, *Quetzalcoatl and Guadalupe: The Formation of Mexican National Consciousness, 1531–1813* (Chicago: University of Chicago Press, 1974); and David Brading, *The First America: The Spanish Monarchy, Creole Patriots, and the Liberal State, 1492–1867* (Cambridge, UK: Cambridge University Press, 1991).
112. Chimalpahin and Ixtlilxochitl did read Gómara in later decades. Ixtlilxochitl's hero, Topiltzin, would travel toward the sea, to a place called Tlapallan, and he, too, would be burned at the time of his death. Only years later, after Ixtlilxochitl had had many discussions with Torquemada, would he elaborate on a purported prophecy of a return of Quetzalcoatl. See Townsend, "Evolution of Alva Ixtlilxochitl's Scholarly Life." For more on this, see chapter 4.
113. Reading the *Annals of Cuauhtitlan*, we are able to make sense, for example, of the garbled versions of Tetzcocan political history supplied by Torquemada or Ixtlilxochitl. See Camilla Townsend, "Polygyny and the Divided Altepetl: The Tetzcocan Key to Pre-conquest Nahua Politics," in *Texcoco: Prehispanic and Colonial Perspectives*, edited by Jongsoo Lee and Galen Brokaw (Boulder: University Press of Colorado, 2014).
114. In one of Chimalpahin's texts, the Cuernavaca noblewoman Miyahuaxihuitl similarly swallows a jeweled shaft shot over her compound wall by an invading Mexica enemy. For an analysis of the story, see Susan Schroeder, "The First American Valentine: Nahua Courtship and Other Aspects of Family Structuring in Mesoamerica," *Journal of Family History* 23, no. 4 (1998): 342–344.
115. On the complex politics of marriage and inheritance, see Camilla Townsend, "'What in the World Have You Done to Me, my Lover?' Sex, Servitude, and Politics among the Pre-Conquest Nahuas as seen in the *Cantares Mexicanos*," *The Americas* 62, no. 3 (2006): 349–389.
116. Bierhorst, *History and Mythology*, 137–138.
117. James Lockhart has pointed out the close correspondence between this segment of the *Annals of Cuauhtitlan* and chapter 2 in Book Twelve of the *Florentine Codex*. See his *We People Here: Nahuatl Accounts of the Conquest of Mexico* (Berkeley: University of California Press, 1993), 44.
118. Bierhorst, *History and Mythology*, 124–125.

Chapter 4

1. Chimalpahin produced many works, and the leading editions will be cited throughout. His magnum opus was the set of works now known as the *Ocho relaciones*. The original text is housed in the Bibliothèque Nationale de France, as Méxicain 74. A fine transcription and translation is Domingo Chimalpahin, *Las ocho relaciones y el memorial de Colhuacan*, edited by Rafael Tena (Mexico City: Consejo Nacional para la Cultura y las Artes, 1998). I worked with the latter edition, and all citations will be of it, although my translations are independent. Because the edition does not include a facsimile, and I wanted to examine the above segment in the original manuscript, David Tavárez was kind enough to lend me photographic images of those pages, which he possessed.

2. For the words of the song itself and a full analysis, see Camilla Townsend, ""What in the World Have You Done to Me, My Lover?": Sex, Servitude, and Politics among the Pre-Conquest Nahuas as Seen in the *Cantares Mexicanos*," *The Americas* 62 (2006): 349–389.
3. Literally "uttering a stone." This is an idiom unknown to me, but the general sense is clear.
4. Both of these items were used as money.
5. Chimalpahin records the details of his birth in his Seventh Relation, in *Las ocho relaciones*, vol. 1, 249. There he gives his name at the time of writing as I give it in this paragraph. Usually he also included "Muñón" as one of his *apellidos*, in honor of his patron (see below). An excellent brief summary of what we know of Chimalpahin's life appears in David Tavárez, "Reclaiming the Conquest," in *Chimalpahin's Conquest*, edited by Susan Schroeder, Anne J. Cruz, Cristián Roa-de-la-Carrera, and David Tavárez (Stanford, CA: Stanford University Press, 2010).
6. Susan Schroeder summarizes archaeological studies of the area in *Chimalpahin and the Kingdoms of Chalco* (Tucson: University of Arizona Press, 1991), 4.
7. "Memorial de Culhuacan," in *Las ocho relaciones*, vol. 1, 117.
8. The best study of Chalco's political organization and the Chimalpahin's place within it is Schroeder, *Chimalpahin and the Kingdoms of Chalco*.
9. "Eighth Relation," in *Las ocho relaciones*, vol. 2, 296–297.
10. "Seventh Relation," in *Las ocho relaciones*, vol. 2, 209.
11. Tomás Jalpa Flores, "Migrantes y extravagantes: Indios de la periferia en la ciudad de México durante los siglos XVI–XVII," in *Los indios y las ciudades de Nueva España*, edited by Felipe Castro Gutiérrez (Mexico City: UNAM, 2010).
12. *Annals of his Time*, edited by James Lockhart, Susan Schroeder, and Doris Namala (Stanford, CA: Stanford University Press, 2006), 39.
13. "Desde muy niño," Spanish introduction to "Eighth Relation" in *Las ocho relaciones*, vol. 2, 270. This is also where he tells us that his position was that of mayoral.
14. For a brief history of the church, see Rodrigo Martínez Baracs, "El Diario de Chimalpahin," *Estudios de cultura náhuatl* 38 (2007): 288–289.
15. *Annals of His Time*, 47.
16. Ibid., 53.
17. Ibid., 61.
18. Charles Dibble and Arthur J. O, Anderson, eds., *General History of the Things of New Spain*, Book 6: *Rhetoric and Moral Philosophy* (Salt Lake City: University of Utah Press, 1969), 35–36. I have amended the translation slightly.
19. *Annals of his Time*, 63. For more on the Tlaxcalans settling the north country, see Sean McEnroe, *From Colony to Nationhood in Mexico: Laying the Foundations, 1560–1840* (Cambridge, UK: Cambridge University Press, 2012).
20. *Annals of His Time*, 65.
21. Ibid., 89.
22. Ibid., 71.
23. Ibid., 75.
24. Ibid., 91.
25. Ibid., 101. For the full story of the drainage projects, see Vera Candiani, *Dreaming of Dry Land: Environmental Transformation in Colonial Mexico City* (Stanford, CA: Stanford University Press, 2014).

26. *Annals of his Time*, 103–107.
27. On the trading paths plied by canoes, see Richard Conway, "Lakes, Canoes and the Aquatic Communities of Xochimilco and Chalco, New Spain," *Ethnohistory* 59 (2012): 541–568.
28. *Annals of his Time*, 107.
29. Ibid., 111.
30. "Memorial de Culhuacan," in *Las ocho relaciones*, vol. 1, 162; "Sixth Relation," vol. 1, 435; "Seventh Relation," vol. 2, 21; "Eighth Relation," vol. 2, 272.
31. This paragraph summarizes the astute observations of Martínez Baracs in "El Diario de Chimalpahin."
32. "Eighth Relation," in *Las ocho relaciones*, vol. 2, 305–309 and 361.
33. Ibid., vol. 2, 317. Here I have a small but important disagreement with Rafael Tena regarding translation. He interprets the meaning to be that the group made a copy of some old written accounts, whereas I am certain that the sense is that they brought out presentations of old oral accounts (*quicenquixtihque y huehuetlahtolli*). This is important, for it means that Chimalpahin was reading a transcription of a rich verbal performance.
34. Ibid., vol. 2, 309.
35. Ibid., vol. 2, 347. For a complete list of the sources he mentions, see Schroeder, *Chimalpahin*, 18–19.
36. *Annals of his Time*, 303.
37. "Memorial de Culhuacan" and "Fifth Relation" in *Las ocho relaciones*, vol. 1, 87 and 353.
38. These documents are separate from the debated "Crónica mexicayotl" (see n. 39). A history of the Mexica in Spanish and another set of annals in Nahuatl found at the Bible Society in England in the 1980s are clearly entirely the work of Chimalpahin. They are published in Arthur J. O. Anderson and Susan Schroeder, eds., *Codex Chimalpahin*, vol. 1 (Norman: University of Oklahoma Press, 1997) and in Rafael Tena, ed., *Tres crónicas mexicanas: textos recopilados por Domingo Chimalpahin* (Mexico City: Cien de México, 2012).
39. This is the famous "Crónica mexicayotl." In-text evidence makes it clear that it was originally written or dictated by Tezozomoc, but the handwriting and location in the midst of Chimalpahin's papers render it equally clear that the only surviving version was copied out and perhaps edited by Chimalpahin. It is published in Anderson and Schroeder, eds., *Codex Chimalpahin*, and Tena, ed., *Tres crónicas*. On the debate over who should be considered "author" see Susan Schroeder, "The Truth about the Crónica Mexicayotl," *Colonial Latin American Review* 20 (2011): 233–247.
40. For transcriptions of various of these documents, see Anderson and Schroeder, eds., *Codex Chimalpahin*, vols. 1 and 2.
41. At least, copies of them survive to this day. In the early nineteenth century, Faustino Galicia Chimalpopoca copied as many as he could find, and José Fernando Ramírez, director of Mexico's Museo Nacional, later compiled them and several others into a collection that he labeled "Anales antiguos de México y sus contornos." That collection is now in the Biblioteca Nacional de Antropología e Historia in Mexico City. Many of the texts it preserves date to c. 1600. A few of these have been published. For example, some annals of Tlatelolco (1473–1521) appear in Jesús Monjarás Ruiz, Elena Limón, and María de la Cruz Paillés, eds., *Tlatelolco: Fuentes e Historia* (Mexico City: INAH, 1989), 185–198.

42. David Tavárez, "Nahua Intellectuals, Franciscan Scholars, and the *Devotio Moderna* in Colonial Mexico," *The Americas* 70 (2013): 208.
43. See his "translating out loud" of numbers in Nahuatl into numbers in Spanish; e.g., Fernando de Alva Ixtlilxochitl, *Obras históricas*, edited by Edmundo O'Gorman (Mexico City: UNAM, 1975–77), vol. 2, 284.
44. For a biographical study, see Camilla Townsend, "The Evolution of Alva Ixtlilxochitl's Scholarly Life," *Colonial Latin American Review* 23.1 (2014): 1–17. Important aspects of Ixtlilxochitl's life and work are treated by the various articles in this special issue. For instance, Peter Villella studies his use of the genre of indigenous noblemen's petitions to the crown, which had long been practiced by his own family, in "The Last Acolhua: Alva Ixtlilxochitl and Elite Native Historiography in Early New Spain," *Colonial Latin American Review* 23.1 (2014): 18–36. On Ixtlilxochitl as a nexus among collectors of indigenous materials, see Amber Brian, *Alva Ixtlilxochitl's Native Archive and the Circulation of Knowledge in Colonial Mexico* (Nashville, TN: Vanderbilt University Press, 2016).
45. See *Annals of his Time*, 83, 193, 305.
46. Ibid., 67, 73, 79, 165, 259. On Ixtlilxochitl's connections with Torquemada, see Townsend, "Evolution," 6–7.
47. For a detailed study of this problematic period in Ixtlilxochitl's life, see Bradley Benton, "The Outsider: Alva Ixtlilxochitl's Tenuous Ties to the City of Tetzcoco," *Colonial Latin American Review* 23.1 (2014): 37–52.
48. *Annals of his Time*, 12. On Sigüenza y Góngora's relationship to the inherited papers, see Amber Brian, "The Original Alva Ixtlilxochitl Manuscripts at Cambridge University," *Colonial Latin American Review* 23.1 (2014): 84–101.
49. On the former see Anderson and Schroeder, eds., *Codex Chimalpahin*, vol. 2; on the latter see Tavárez, "Reclaiming the Conquest," 21.
50. Martínez Baracs, "El Diario," 298.
51. Tavárez, "Reclaiming the Conquest," 27.
52. *Annals of his Time*, 75.
53. Ibid., 271
54. Ibid., 217–219.
55. Ibid., 263.
56. "First Relation," in *Las ocho relaciones*, 33 and throughout. He specifically comments on how Saint Augustine opens his work and what the purport of his Book I is.
57. Saint Augustine, *Confessions*, edited by R. S. Pine-Coffin (New York: Penguin, 1961), 33–34.
58. *Annals of His Time*, 259.
59. "Eighth Relation," in *Las ocho relaciones*, vol. 2, 273.
60. Rafael Tena included these inserts in his edited edition of *Las ocho relaciones*, 52–55 and 176–177.
61. José Rubén Romero Galván, "La historia según Chimalpahin," *Journal de la Société des Américanistes* 82.2 (1998): 183–195.
62. "Eighth Relation," in *Las ocho relaciones*, 295.
63. Valérie Benoist, "La construcción de una comunidad nahua/española en las *Relaciones* de Chimalpahin," *Estudios de Cultura Nahuatl* 34 (2003): 219–256; Rafael Tena, "La estructura textual de las relaciones primera y octava de Chimalpahin," *Estudios de Cultura Nahuatl* 28 (1998): 355–364.

64. Martin Nesvig, "The Epistemological Politics of Vernacular Scripture in Sixteenth-Century Mexico," *The Americas* 70 (2012): 165–201, reminds us that it was *all* vernacular literature, not just indigenous language texts, that was under assault by the 1570s. It was Spaniards, even conservative ones, who had their libraries inspected and some of their books confiscated.
65. Tavárez, "Reclaiming the Conquest," 29–30.
66. "Eighth Relation," in *Las ocho relaciones*, vol. 2, 361.
67. "Crónica mexicayotl," in *Codex Chimalpahin*, vol. 1, 69.
68. "Crónica Mexicana," in *Codex Chimalpahin*, vol. 1, 29.
69. Tavarez, "Reclaiming the Conquest," 28.
70. *Annals of his Time*, 249.
71. Ibid., 197. (The story is extensive, continuing from 195 to 201.)
72. Ibid., 181.
73. Ibid., 301.
74. "Seventh Relation," in *Las ocho relaciones*, vol. 2, 230–231.
75. The performance is summarized in Antonio de Ciudad Real, *Tratado curioso y doctor de las grandezas de la Nueva España* (Mexico City: UNAM, 1976 [1584]), vol. 1, 15.
76. Ixtlilxochitl, *Obras históricas*, vol. 1, 527.
77. "Eight Relation," in *Las ocho relaciones*, vol. 2, 347.
78. "First Relation," in *Las ocho relaciones*, vol. 1, 29.
79. "First Relation," in *Las ocho relaciones*, vol. 1, 47.
80. "First Relation," in *Las ocho relaciones*, vol. 1, 33.
81. "Second Relation," in *Las ocho relaciones*, vol. 1, 57.
82. "Second Relation," in *Las ocho relaciones*, vol. 1, 65.
83. For more on the Baltic crusades, see Roger Bartlett, *The Making of Europe: Conquest, Colonization and Cultural Change, 950–1350* (Princeton, NJ: Princeton University Press, 1993). For the suggestion made by Martínez, see Enrico Martínez, *Reportorio de los tiempos e historia natural de Nueva España* (Mexico City, 1606), 121. The latter asserts that the Baltic peoples were dark like the American indigenous.
84. "Second Relation," in *Las ocho relaciones*, 71. See Martínez, *Reportorio*, 119: "Excede esta parte del mundo a cualquiera de las otras tres en grandeza y en riqueza."
85. "Memorial de Culhuacan," in *Las ocho relaciones*, vol. 1, 97.
86. Ibid., 147.
87. Ibid., 169.
88. Ibid., 80–82, 175.
89. In his later work, Ixtlilxochitl incorporates a version of the Quetzalcoatl prophecy familiar to modern readers. On the increasing influence of Torquemada's work over Ixtlilxochitl's, see Townsend, "Evolution of Alva Ixtlilxochitl's Life."
90. "Third Relation," in *Las ocho relaciones*, vol. 1, 257.
91. "Fourth Relation," in *Las ocho relaciones*, vol. 1, 307.
92. "Fourth Relation," in *Las ocho relaciones*, vol. 1, 313.
93. Townsend, "What in the World Have You Done to Me, My Lover?"
94. "Eighth Relation," in *Las ocho relaciones*, vol. 2, 363–381.
95. "Seventh Relation," in *Las ocho relaciones*, vol. 2, 79.
96. *Chimalpahin's Conquest*, 162.
97. Ibid., 176.

98. Hernán Cortés, Second Letter, in *Letters from Mexico*, edited by Anthony Pagden (New Haven, CT: Yale University Press, 1986), 80.
99. *Chimalpahin's Conquest*, 177.
100. "Eighth Relation," in *Las ocho relaciones*, vol. 2, 331.
101. Ibid., vol. 2, 349.
102. "Memorial de Culhuacan," in *Las ocho relaciones*, vol. 1, 162. The family tree in Schroeder, *Chimalpahin*, is extremely helpful.
103. For a discussion of the places where the term is found in Chimalpahin, see Susan Schroeder, "Chimalpahin and Why Women Matter in History," in *Indigenous Intellectuals: Knowledge, Power, and Colonial Culture in Mexico and the Andes*, edited by Gabriela Ramos and Yanna Yannakakis (Durham, NC: Duke University Press, 2014), 115–117. For an example of the term's use in 1515, see the *Annals of Cuauhtitlan*, in *Codex Chimalpopoca: The Text in Nahuatl*, edited by John Bierhorst (Norman: University of Oklahoma Press, 1992), 75–76.
104. *Annals of his Time*, 75.
105. This would probably have been short for *tenenepil*, literally "somebody's tongue" but meaning "the tongue" as in "la lengua." See Tavarez, "Reclaiming the Conquest," 23 and 32. Chimalpahin could have seen Malinche referred to consistently and frequently as "la Lengua" in the work of Ixtlilxochitl.
106. *Codex Chimalpahin*, 119–123.
107. "Memorial de Culhuacan," in *Las ocho relaciones*, vol. 1, 162. The dramatic story of the sudden death of the church's current patron from violent stomach pains, and the ensuing battle over the inheritance of the church and its sudden closure are recounted in the diary of Bachiller Gregorio Martín del Guijo, and the segment is published in Günter Zimmermann, ed., *Die Relationen Chimalpahin's zur Geschichte México's* (Hamburg: Cram, de Gruyter, 1965), 146.

Chapter 5

1. This chapter primarily concerns the manuscript by don Juan Buenaventura Zapata y Mendoza which is located in the Bibliothèque Nationale, Paris, Méxicain 212. Though I have consulted the document in the original, I will refer in most cases to the published transcription by Luis Reyes García and Andrea Martínez Baracs, eds., *Historia cronológica de la noble ciudad de Tlaxcala por Don Juan Buenaventura Zapata y Mendoza* (Tlaxcala: Universidad Autónoma de Tlaxcala, 1995). The editors include a Spanish translation with which I am in accord in most places, but not all; thus readers will find my English translations to be independent.
2. The bridge across the Zahuatl was destroyed in flooding in September of the previous year, and they first started construction of new pilares on December 19. Then they must have taken a break for the holidays. Brad Skopyk has shown that the Zahuatl began to flood more seriously than ever before in the 1670s and 80s (and onward) because of changes in agricultural practices that snowballed in the 1660s—primarily, the sharply increased planting of erosion-causing maguey on people's fields away from their homes (that is, not on the callalli, but the more distant holdings). See Bradley Skopyk, "Undercurrents of Conquest: The Shifting Terrain of Indigenous Agriculture in Colonial Tlaxcala, Mexico," PhD dissertation, York University, 2010.

3. San Miguel is identified in numerous other references in Zapata as a settlement situated nearby, on the Ocotelolco side of the river (the same side as the traza of Tlaxcala).
4. The *other* side of the river was Quiyahuiztlan's territory, where the author Zapata was from, and therefore could elicit "our side" from him, even though there is ample in-text evidence that his main residence was in downtown Tlaxcala.
5. Josef de Alva is identified elsewhere as a Spaniard. The previous year, in the wake of public disturbances over taxation that had occurred the year before that, it was decided that the cabildo's receiver or collector of tribute would no longer be indigenous, but rather Spanish.
6. It could equally well be "They couldn't close it up at the edge."
7. The phrase is slightly ambiguous, but James Lockhart strongly agreed that this was the most probable meaning.
8. Again, there is uncertainty. He might mean that they had one sword with them.
9. Zapata probably meant "clothes," but the word he uses is literally "cloaks," a word often used for indigenous weavings in general.
10. San Silverio really was a pope, and he was tormented by Justinian and Theodora, but he wasn't martyred. Perhaps Zapata got carried away, knowing he was a sanctified pope and sandwiching a mention of him between San Juan Papa Mártir and San Pío Papa Mártir, both genuine martyrs.
11. The Nahuatl uses the suffix *-tzintli* only as a polite deprecation.
12. The day of San Apolinar Obispo Martir is July 23, and the day of Santiago Apostol is July 25. What it really says is that the feast day of Santiago was two days later, but the translation would be too awkward in that form.
13. This is a wooden frame holding fireworks to be set off sequentially, now called a *castillo*.
14. This is the most likely meaning, but it could have a more spiritual implication, that is, that they gave many thanks.
15. Zapata uses the term two other times: October 1662 and June 1665. Judging from the latter reference, a xochicalli seems to have allowed its maker great latitude, some being far more ornate than others. They were always temporary structures for festivals.
16. In the Nahuatl, both verbs *ilacatzoa* ("to spin") and *patla* ("to fly") combine with the embedded noun *quauhtli* ("stick, pole"). This ancient art is not lost.
17. Zapata has chosen to omit all references to a major crisis the people have had with the Spanish alcalde, don León de Arsa. Other Tlaxcalan annals tell us that the previous year, on the feast day of San Lorenzo, now celebrated on August 10, the indigenous people contended with him and he hired guards for protection. Now it seems that he is being replaced.
18. It seems likely that because of the political problems, some of the indigenous officeholders were steering clear for a while. Perhaps the Ocotelolco people were the ones who had staged the protest against Arsa the year before.
19. This is clearly the general meaning, but the original is extremely difficult to decipher. It seems to say *matalelu* and is probably a Spanish loan word twisted beyond recognition to us now.
20. This was don Manuel Santos y Salazar. See below for full discussion of the man and his edits.
21. Again the general sense is clear but the exact meaning is not certain. For *macero* the Diccionario de Autoridades has: *el que lleva la maza delante de los reyes o*

gobernadores, ciudades, villas, y otras comunidades. "*Seguían dos maceros, con sus mazas reales en los hombros, y luego dos reyes de armas, con sus cotas de insignias reales sobre damasco carmesí.*"

22. See, for instance, de la Cruz family papers, Gómez de Orozco collection 186, Archivo Histórico of the Instituto Nacional de Antropología e Historia, Mexico City. Together with Caterina Pizzigoni, I am embarked on a detailed study of these papers. The de la Cruz family lived in Tepemaxalco, in the Toluca region.
23. The classic work by Charles Gibson, *Tlaxcala in the Sixteenth Century* (New Haven: Yale University Press, 1952) and the important recent work by Andrea Martínez Baracs, *Un gobierno de indios: Tlaxcala, 1519–1750* (Mexico City: Fondo de Cultura Económica, 2008) both detail Tlaxcalan decisions in this era and the active steps the leadership took to protect Tlaxcalan interests.
24. Each teccalli is represented in the central image of the best-known version of the Lienzo de Tlaxcala, which dates from the middle of the sixteenth century and survives in tracings. See Mario de la Torre, Josefina García Quintana, and Carlos Martínez Marín, eds., *El Lienzo de Tlaxcala* (Mexico City: Cartón y Papel, 1983). For a full study of the Tlaxcalan conquest pictorials which we now call collectively the Lienzo of Tlaxcala, see Travis Kranz, "The Tlaxcalan Conquest Pictorials: The Role of Images in Influencing Colonial Policy in Sixteenth-Century Mexico," PhD dissertation, Department of Art History, University of California, Los Angeles, 2001.
25. James Lockhart, Frances Berdan, and Arthur J.O. Anderson, eds., *The Tlaxcalan Actas: A Compendium of the Records of the Cabildo of Tlaxcala, 1545–1627* (Salt Lake City: University of Utah Press, 1986). See especially "A Directory of Prominent Tlaxcalans in the Actas," 13, and discussion of the shifting surnames, 21. The records are complete only for 1545–1567.
26. Land transfer by doña Francisca de la Cerda Xicontencatl of Tizatlan, 27 octubre 1606, Archivo Histórico del Estado de Tlaxcala [AHET], Registro de Instrumentos Públicos [RIP], vol. 20, ff.319–320. The document refers to lands held by "Bentura Zapata y doña Magdalena de Mendoza su mujer."
27. Gibson, *Tlaxcala*, 96–98 and Appendix 5.
28. The vantage point of Zapata's text is clearly the center of the city. His granddaughter, who inherited the cacicazgo, lived on the Calle de los Arcos in what may well have been the family home for generations. Last will and testament of doña Agustina Rosa Zapata, 10 noviembre, 1755, AHET, RIP, vol. 211 ff.106v-109v.
29. Venta de tierras de doña Francisca Maxixcatzin Pimental y su esposo Diego Muñoz Camargo a Simón de Mesa, vecino, 28 abril, 1609, Parish Archive of Santa María Nativitas Atzatzacuala, reproduced in Luis Reyes García, ed., *La escritura pictográfica en Tlaxcala: Dos mil años de experiencia mesoamericana* (Tlaxcala: Universidad Autónoma de Tlaxcala, 1993), 250. At least two other surviving documents also refer to the lands held by Zapata's heirs, some being the family's own property and some pertaining to those held in trust as part of the cacicazgo. See his granddaughter's will (ibid.) as well as "Doña Phelipa Zapata y Mendoza y don Juan Zapata y Mendoza hermanos cassiques y principales contra don Juan Diego, maestro dorador," 22 febrero, 1713, AHET, Colonia 1713, caja 27, exp. 14, f.4v.
30. Reyes and Martínez, eds., *Historia cronológica*, 226. Reyes and Martínez say that this don Buenaventura Zapata could have been our Zapata's father

or grandfather, and ultimately lean toward father. However, he had to be the grandfather. Our Zapata says that his sister, doña María Magdalena Zapata y Mendoza, had her first child in 1661. That woman could not have been conceived in 1619 at the latest (the death date of the supposed father). Furthermore, a don Juan Zapata of Quiyahuiztlan who is said to be don Buenaventura's son and with whom our Zapata demonstrates ties of affection served as an officeholder in the late 1620s and 1630s before dying in 1641. (See n. 10.) On the nature of the indigenous cabildo and the positions that constituted it, see James Lockhart, *The Nahuas after the Conquest* (Stanford, CA: Stanford University Press, 1992).

31. On this don Juan Zapata serving as regidor, see Reyes and Martínez, *Historia cronológica*, 239–253; and as fiscal, 259. A careful reading of the entire decade of the 1630s reveals a much more detailed record of church affairs than is generally the case, suggesting that the record was made (or at least recalled) by someone who filled a church office. One open question is whether the two men are definitely the same, or whether there was a second "don Juan" who was our Juan's uncle or cousin. However, since we do not find any mention of don Juan Zapata of Quiyahuiztlan serving in the cabildo past 1631, and no record of his death until 1641, I think it is safe to assume that it was the same man entering a "second career." Even if they were actually two separate men, both would have served as role models for our figure.

32. On the role and high status of the indigenous fiscal in New Spain, see Lockhart, *The Nahuas*, 210–215.

33. "Solicitud del cabildo para nombrar como interprete a Juan de Coca, en lugar de Miguel de Parada," AHET, Colonia 1688, caja 95, exp. 5.

34. He is unmistakably referred to in this way in "Petición a don Carlos sobre pulque," AHET, Colonia 1681, caja 91, exp.12.

35. Reyes and Martínez, *Historia cronológica*, 270. His word *santopan* ("where the saints are") refers to any settlement large enough to have a communally owned image of a saint, ranging from a statue by the roadside to a church visited regularly by the clergy. It was by now archaic elsewhere in Mexico.

36. See Reyes and Martínez, *Historia cronológica*, 470 and 540, for Zapata's affectionate references to these sons. The baptism of Juan Gabriel Zapata on January 13, 1651 is recorded in the barrio of Tochitzin (cited in Reyes and Martínez, 17).

37. Ibid., 314.

38. On several occasions the text lists "don Juan Buenaventura Zapata y Mendoza" as alcalde, then several lines later, "don Juan Zapata" as regidor. The mystery is resolved in 1679, when Zapata was apparently ready to cut down on his activities somewhat. "For the first time became alcalde don Juan Zapata Younger Brother, and his regidores were don Juan Antonio de los Angeles, and don Juan Antonio of the same name" (Ibid., 567). We can recognize Zapata's brother-in-law in other lists because he lists him as the father in 1661 when his sister bears her first child (311).

39. Ibid., 604.

40. Ibid., 254 and 292.

41. On the ways in which the indigenous took European instruments and even performance styles and incorporated them into their own traditions, see Jonathan Truitt, "Adopted Pedagogies: Nahua Incorporation of European Music and Theater in Colonial Mexico City," *The Americas* 66, no. 3 (2010): 311–330.

42. An excellent study of this subject is Kelly McDonough, *The Learned Ones: Nahua Intellectuals in Postconquest Mexico*, (Tucson: University of Arizona Press, 2014), chapter 2, "Writing Tlaxcalan Memories that Matter: Don Juan Buenaventura Zapata y Mendoza."
43. Reyes and Martínez, *Historia cronológica*, 390.
44. Ibid., 422.
45. James Lockhart was the first to notice Zapata's ostentatious use of traditional forms, specifically mentioning his references to bridges (Lockhart, *The Nahuas*, 391–392). All that was left for me to do was seek instances within the text: Reyes and Martínez, *Historia cronológica*, 444, 524, 538, 584. Before his untimely death, David Webb continued the investigation of language use in Zapata's text, making some helpful observations regarding loan words in "The Construction of Nahua Identity in Seventeenth-Century Mexico: A Study of *La Historia Cronológica de la muy insigne, noble y leal ciudad de Tlaxcala.*" PhD dissertation, Department of Hispanic Languages and Literature, University of California, Los Angeles, 2005.
46. Reyes and Martínez, *Historia cronológica*, 394.
47. It is in the early 1660s that the entries become substantially more detailed, often moving month by month.
48. Frances Krug, "The Nahuatl Annals of the Tlaxcala-Puebla Region," an unfinished doctoral dissertation, Department of History, University of California, Los Angeles, under the directorship of James Lockhart. A health crisis prevented the completion of Krug's important work. For a summary of her contributions, see Frances Krug and Camilla Townsend, "The Tlaxcala-Puebla Family of Annals," in *Sources and Methods for the Study of Post-Conquest Mesoamerican Ethnohistory*, edited by James Lockhart, Lisa Sousa, and Stephanie Wood, electronic publication, 2007: http//whp.uoregon.edu/Lockhart/index.html.
49. Reyes and Martínez, *Historia cronológica*, 100.
50. Lockhart et al., eds., *The Tlaxcalan Actas*, 128–132.
51. "El Anónimo Mexicano," Bibliothèque Nationale, Paris, Méxicain 212, capítulo 5. On the evidence that don Manuel de los Santos Salazar authored this text, see below, this chapter. It is of course possible that don Manuel spoke figuratively, that he had no actual knowledge of a text authored by this Itzcacmacuextli, but that seems unlikely. There was almost certainly a real piece of paper at some point, given that we know the other men Zapata mentions actually existed. Someone named Tadeo de Niza, who served on the indigenous cabildo at the same time as the family of Lucas García, was known to have produced historical writings; Ixtlilxochitl (see chapter 4) cited them frequently.
52. Reyes and Martínez, *Historia cronológica*. 86.
53. Krug in "The Nahuatl Annals" (see note 48) first pointed out these parallels. A published transcription is available in Robert Barlow, "Anales de Tula, Hidalgo, 1361–1521," *Tlalocan* 3.1 (1949): 2–13.
54. Gibson, *Tlaxcala*, 28–33.
55. Reyes and Martínez, *Historia cronológica*, 96–100.
56. Ibid., 102–106. The central sentence actually has a singular subject: "A [pagan] adulterer, they killed him, still the way he was." The writer might have been referring to the last-named figure, a couple of lines above, or he might have been speaking of a generic pagan nobleman in the singular, representative of others.

That is the way I have interpreted the sentence. In either case, the narrator's objection remains the same.

57. Frances Krug did painstaking work to prove the existence of these genetic relationships. For a summary, see Krug and Townsend, "The Tlaxcala-Puebla Family of Annals." For a complete transcription of one set of annals, the content of which made it into the margins of Zapata's own work, and more on the subject of the mutual borrowings, see Camilla Townsend, *Here in This Year: Seventeenth-Century Nahuatl Annals of the Tlaxcala-Puebla Valley* (Stanford, CA: Stanford University Press, 2010).
58. For a full discussion, see Camilla Townsend, "Don Juan Buenaventura Zapata y Mendoza and the Notion of a Nahuatl Identity," in *The Conquest All Over Again: Nahuas and Zapotecs Thinking, Writing, and Painting Spanish Colonialism*, edited by Susan Schroeder (Eastbourne, UK: Sussex Academic Press, 2010).
59. Reyes and Martínez, *Historia cronológica*, 232.
60. Fray Alonso de la Mota, *Memoriales del Obispo de Tlaxcala* (Mexico City: Editorial Stylo, 1945), 107–108.
61. For a list of documented examples, see Luis Reyes García, ed., *Historia de Tlaxcala, por Diego Muñoz Camargo* (Tlaxcala: Universidad Autónoma de Tlaxcala, 1998), 18. For more on the man, see Charles Gibson, "The Identity of Diego Muñoz Camargo," *Hispanic American Historical Review* 30 (1950): 195–208.
62. See "Venta de Tierras" in Reyes, ed., *La escritura pictográfica*, 250.
63. Krug, "Nahuatl Annals," chapter 1, 32–35.
64. Reyes and Martínez, *Historia cronológica*, 212–214.
65. Ibid., 222–224.
66. See note 29 above.
67. Reyes and Martínez, *Historia cronológica*, 276, 282.
68. Ibid., 600. For more on don Manuel's contributions to the text, see below.
69. For more on this see Lockhart, *The Nahuas*, 109–111.
70. Reyes and Martínez, *Historia cronológica*, 384. For a more detailed study of Zapata's relations with others as evinced in his linguistic usages, see Camilla Townsend, "The Concept of the Nahua Historian: Don Juan Zapata's Scholarly Tradition," in *Indigenous Intellectuals: Knowledge, Power, and Colonial Culture in Mexico and the Andes*, edited by Gabriela Ramos and Yanna Yannakakis (Durham, NC: Duke University Press, 2014).
71. Reyes and Martínez, *Historia cronológica*, 350.
72. Ibid., 444. The last sentence literally says, "Your heart has granted things, has been generous." The phrase was used to express deep gratitude.
73. Ibid., 268, 336, 386 (twice), 458, 500, 520, 536, 554, 560, 600, 604, 632. Other uses in indigenous texts in Tlaxcala are extremely rare. It does appear in the cabildo minutes as early as 1552, when indigenous slaves were to be freed, in contrast to African ones. See Lockhart et al., eds., *Tlaxcalan Actas*, 77–78.
74. Reyes and Martínez, *Historia cronológica*, 510.
75. Ibid., 388.
76. Ibid., 462. For more on this important series of political events, see Townsend, "Don Juan Zapata and the Notion of a Nahua Identity," and Martínez Baracs, *Un gobierno de Indios*, 363–391.
77. Reyes and Martínez, *Historia cronológica*, 464.
78. Ibid., 478.

79. Ibid., 482.
80. Ibid., 486.
81. Ibid., 566.
82. Ibid., 638. Zapata must have died in 1688, because until then, the entries in the annals continue without interruption, and we continue to find his signature on cabildo documents. Then both of these cease.
83. There is no definite mention of this event. I have deduced it from the facts that come out in "Doña Phelipa Zapata y Mendoza y don Juan Zapata y Mendoza hermanos cassiques y principales contra don Juan Diego, maestro dorador," AHET, Colonial 1713, caja 27, 14. Doña María Jacoba, the daughter and legal heir of both don Juan Zapata and doña Petronilla de Paredes, had a baby when she was very young by a man who is never named. That baby, doña Antonia Sebastiana, carried the surname of her mother, Zapata y Mendoza. When she grew up, she did not marry outside the family as was customary but rather wed her uncle, don Salvador, younger son of don Juan Zapata. She, her uncle (now husband), and her mother all lived together in a house that was given to them by their maternal grandfather, don Juan de Paredes, on his deathbed. When doña Petronilla died, she referred to all her children by their proper full names, except for María Jacoba, whom she called, rather oddly, "María Jacoba de Paredes," leaving out the patronymic, almost as though she wished to hide that she and her granddaughter Antonia Sebastiana shared the same surname.
84. Ibid. The struggle over whether or not to refer to the defendant by the title "don" continues throughout the text. Eventually the Spanish court settled on "don Juan Diego alias Huehueton."
85. This couple had only two surviving children, both daughters, one of whom inherited the cacicazgo. See the last will and testament of the granddaughter, AHET, RIP, vol. 211, ff.106v–109v.
86. Reyes and Martínez, *Historia cronológica*, 630.
87. For more on the Tlaxcalan annals' revelation of the atrophying of the rotational system, see Townsend, Introduction, in *Here in This Year*, 27–28. The perorations of the aged were embedded in Nahua tradition; fragments of them were often recorded in wills. See Caterina Pizzigoni, ed., *Testaments of Toluca* (Stanford, CA: Stanford University Press, 2007), 21–22. Zapata's will does not seem to have survived.
88. Manuel Salazar, May 27, 1675, Libro de Informaciones de Novicios IV, Puebla de los Angeles Papers, John Carter Brown Library, Providence, Rhode Island.
89. Fray Luis de Garro to don Bernabé Antonio Salazar, October 23, 1675, Salazar Family Papers, Miscellaneous Manuscript Collections, Library of Congress, Washington, D.C., ff.4–5. Peter Villella made the immensely valuable discovery of the Salazar family papers at this unlikely site and was kind enough to share the material with me. For more on every aspect of this family's strategies, see Villella's "Indian Lords, Hispanic Gentlemen: The Salazars of Colonial Tlaxcala," *The Americas* 69, no. 1 (2012): 1–36.
90. Fray Luis de Garro to don Bernabé Antonio Salazar, April 15, 1676, Salazar Family Papers, f.6.
91. "Computo cronológico de los indios mexicanos," in *Documentos para la historia de México*, ser. 3, tomo 1 (Mexico City: Vicente García Torres, 1856), introduction. For a discussion of the attribution of this anonymous work to don Manuel, see below.

92. Villella, "Indian Lords," 18–19. Villella gleaned this information from the Bachiller of don Manuel, issued May 7, 1684; his Ordination in Puebla, October 1685; and a "Méritos" petition he submitted in 1707.
93. His mother's hometown is revealed in a petition to be given lands he inherited from his maternal great-grandmother, submitted September 29, 1695, included as an appendix in Reyes y Martínez, eds., *Historia Cronológica*, 684–687. The original is filed with Zapata's text in the Bibliothèque Nationale in Paris.
94. Reyes y Martínez, eds., *Historia Cronológica*, 616–618. Zapata does not explicitly mention Ocotelolco, but he repeats twice that the "only" indigenous people present were from the other three sub-altepetl.
95. Ibid., 682. Reyes followed don Manuel's signature on baptismal documents throughout his career until June of 1715. (He would die in August.) Don Manuel's placement at different churches is tracked in his 1707 "Méritos" petition, Salazar Family Papers, ff.47–48.
96. 1707 Méritos petition, Salazar Family Papers, f.48.
97. See, for example, some of the marginal comments in Zapata's manuscript. He could not abide mestizos.
98. Villella, "Indigenous Lords," 19–20.
99. The original is held by the John Carter Brown Library, Providence, Rhode Island, and has been made available online by that institution. The play ends with a note appended in Spanish on the final performance date, and instructions for the type of dancing to be done are included.
100. On the title page, he uses the verb *tecpanihcuiloa* ("to write down in an orderly manner") in reference to his own role.
101. "Colloquy of How the Fortunate Saint Helen..." in *Nahuatl Theater, Vol. 4: Nahua Christianity in Performance*, edited by Barry Sell and Louise Burkhart (Norman: University of Oklahoma Press, 2009), 286–287. Sell and Burkhart provide a complete transcription and English translation, as well as helpful introductory material and notes. Burkhart points out that there are interesting parallels between Tlaxcala's role in the conquest of New Spain and the wise pagan Constantine's role in the war in the play. Sell points out the subtle influence of Spanish in don Manuel's Nahuatl phrasing.
102. Sell and Burkhart, *Nahuatl Theater, Vol. 4*, 302–303. There are numerous jokes in the play.
103. For more on this, see Townsend, *Here in This Year*, as well as Villella, "Indigenous Lords."
104. Reyes y Martínez, eds., *Historia Cronológica*, 642. The note referring to the death of "my mother doña Petronilla" is in a new handwriting, evidently a son's.
105. Most of these additions have long been attributed to don Manuel. He added his name to the frontispiece, and thenceforward, his distinctive handwriting is recognizable. Scholars have generally worked with photocopies and microfilm of the original available in Mexico and the United States. Of course, the addition of the red and sometimes green ink can only be seen in consulting the original in Paris (see n. 1). I am certain the addition of the color was not Zapata's, because sometimes it actually obscures what Zapata wrote.
106. Don Manuel later elaborates on his intellectual debts and reveals his intellectual concerns in his introduction to "El Cómputo cronológico." On the attribution of the latter text to him, see n. 109.

107. "Anónimo Mexicano," Bibliothèque Nationale de France, Méxicain 254, f.1. We need no longer refer to the text as "anonymous": the handwriting appears to be don Manuel's, and the content is virtually identical to that in "El Cómputo cronológico." (On the latter's attribution to him, see n. 109.) Furthermore, the text of "Anónimo Mexicano" at one point includes a scribal rubric that closely resembles one that don Manuel or one of his aides occasionally used as he edited Zapata's work. (It does not resemble the one that he used to sign letters, and so is more likely to have been that of one of the brothers or nephews who worked for him.) A published edition of the text is Richley Crapo and Bonnie Glass-Coffin, eds., *Anónimo Mexicano* (Logan: Utah State University Press, 2005). There the editors argue that the text was a source for Torquemada, rather than the other way around. But except for the Tlaxcalan section (the fifth chapter) it bears little resemblance to other Nahuatl annals and instead sounds a great deal like European works on Nahua history. They note that the text includes additional specifics not included in Torquemada, which does not support the back-translation hypothesis. However, don Manuel, as we know, had access to plenty of other Nahuatl texts he could use in addition to Torquemada (whom we know he read from his explicit introductory comments in "El Cómputo cronológico").

108. Reyes and Martínez, *Historia Cronológica*, 37–48. The editors provide a line-by-line study of the two texts, discovering the common error and other elements that indicate either that the two texts share a common source, or else that one is drawn directly from the other. It is indeed possible that don Manuel and Zapata both worked from a common source, but since we know that don Manuel had Zapata's text in his keeping, that interpretation seems needlessly complex.

109. The copies that remain have no attribution, but the original was purchased by Lorenzo de Boturini, and he stated unequivocally that it was the work of don Manuel de los Santos Salazar. To this, Villella in "Indigenous Lords" adds the compelling argument that the work was dedicated to Saint Michael in the very period when don Manuel's patron, bishop Fernández de Santa Cruz, was making strong efforts to promote the veneration of that saint in the Tlaxcala region. Lastly, the fact that the text is in effect a Spanish translation of an account that stemmed partly from Zapata's work seems to me to render the attribution indisputable.

110. Villella, "Indigenous Lords," 22. Don Manuel mentions the work in his "Méritos" petition. Neither Villella nor I have been able to locate any extant copies thus far.

111. This was the comment of Juan de Balbuena, looking at the original in Boturini's collection. Cited in Gibson, *Tlaxcala*, 261. One might assume merely that don Manuel had grown old and tired, but the play on the Fortunate Saint Helen, copied out in the same era, still displays fine writing, and in some of his earlier work (such as some of his annotations of Zapata), when he was not making much of an effort, the same messiness reported by Balbuena was already evident. Alternatively, the variations could result from his employment of brothers and nephews.

112. An early version called the Revillagigedo copy is in the Archivo General de la Nación, Ramo de Historia, III, ff.22–41. This copy was used by Vicente García Torres in 1856 to print the copy I consulted on Google Books. It also generated a number of other surviving manuscript copies, outlined by Herbert

Bolton in *Guide to Materials for the History of the United States in the Principal Archives of Mexico* (Washington, DC: Carnegie Institution, 1913).
113. Villella, "Indigenous Lords," 21, 29.
114. For the family tree begun by don Manuel and continued by later relatives, see Villella, "Indigenous Lords." It is found in the Salazar Family papers, f.74.
115. The original no longer exists. A manuscript which we no longer have with us, now called "the Bartolache Annals," was excerpted by Josef Ignacio Bartolache in *Manifiesto satisfactorio anunciado en la Gazeta de México* (Mexico City, 1790). He saw it in the Real Pontífica Universidad in 1787 and copied the introductory paragraph written by "nehuatl Marcelo de Salazar" ("I, Marcelo de Salazar."), summarizing the rest. There are two copies of another slightly different original, also now lost, both of which reference Marcelo de Salazar as author. One was copied by J. J. Ramírez in "Anales de Puebla y Tlaxcala, no. 1, part I," in "Anales antiguos de México y sus contornos," an extensive collection of copied manuscripts in the BNAH; the other, by Federico Gómez de Orozco, is now in the BNAH, Colección Antigua 872, part 2.
116. This set is printed in its entirety in Townsend, *Here in This Year*. The original is also in the BNAH, Colección Antigua 872, part 1.
117. Villella, "Indigenous Lords," 34–35, carefully reconstructs the passage of don Manuel's materials through Boturini to the creole intellectuals of the late eighteenth century. Those figures are themselves studied by Jorge Cañizares Esguerra, *How To Write the History of the New World: Histories, Epistemologies, and Identities in the Eighteenth-Century Atlantic World* (Stanford, CA: Stanford University Press, 2001).

Epilogue

1. Doctor don Frutos Delgado, judge of the royal Audiencia.
2. This epilogue is based largely on a document named "The Annals of Puebla," Gómez Orozco 184 in the Archivo Histórico de la Biblioteca Nacional de Antropología e Historia, in Mexico City, recently removed to the national vault but still available onsite digitally. I have transcribed and translated the document in Camilla Townsend, *Here in This Year: Seventeenth-Century Nahuatl Annals of the Tlaxcala-Puebla Valley* (Stanford, CA: Stanford University Press, 2010). Readers who are interested in the full text of the Nahuatl will find it there, rather than in the appendix of this volume. In an introductory study, I have demonstrated that in-text references in this set of annals and another closely related colonial-era copy (see n. 11) prove that the author had to be one of the figures often mentioned, don Miguel de los Santos, an indigenous builder. In that volume, I allow for the possibility that the author was actually an extremely close connection of don Miguel's, perhaps a son or a nephew, but closer knowledge of the text at this point has convinced me that don Miguel himself was the author. Consider, for example, the author's close knowledge of the structure of the church that don Miguel helped to build (*Here in This Year*, 146). The introduction to that volume also details sources on the physical layout of sixteenth- and seventeenth-century Puebla.
3. See a still highly relevant classic work, Clarence Haring, *The Buccaneers in the West Indies in the XVII Century* (Hamden, CT: Archon, 1966 [1910]), as well

as the more current Kris Lane, *Pillaging the Empire: Piracy in the Americas, 1500–1750* (Armonk, NY: M. E. Sharpe, 1998); on this incident in particular see David Marley, *Sack of Veracruz: The Great Pirate Raid of 1683* (Windsor, Ontario: Netherlandic Press, 1993).

4. On these events, see José de Jesús Núñez y Domínguez, *Don Antonio de Benavides, el incognito "tapado"* (Mexico City: Ediciones Xochitl); and fray Cipriano de Utrera, "El Tapado de México" in *El tapado de México y el de Santo Domingo*, edited by José de Jesús Núñez y Domínguez (Trujillo, Dominican Republic: Tipográfica Franciscana, 1950). For broader commentary on this and similar phenomena, see Javier Villa Flores, "Wandering Swindlers: Imposture, Style and the Inquisition's Pedagogy of Fear in Colonial Mexico," *Colonial Latin American Review* 17 (2008): 251–272.

5. The text actually begins with the arrival of the Spaniards, but the entries become detailed and personal in the 1670s.

6. All but one of the annals from Puebla include verbatim quotes of the same material in a period of the sixteenth century, and this material is also found in several of the surviving Tlaxcalan manuscripts. See Townsend, *Here in This Year*, 16. For the general context of annals in the region being regularly borrowed and copied, see Frances Krug and Camilla Townsend, "The Tlaxcala-Puebla Family of Annals," in *Sources and Methods for the Study of Postconquest Mesoamerican Ethnohistory*, edited by James Lockhart, Lisa Sousa, and Stephanie Wood (electronic publication http:// whp.uoregon.edu/Lockhart/index/html).

7. For a classic work on the subject, see Manuel Toussaint, *La catedral y las iglesias de Puebla* (Mexico City: Porrúa, 1954).

8. See James Lockhart, "The Language of the Texts," appended to Townsend, *Here in This Year*.

9. Annals of Puebla in Townsend, *Here in This Year*, 128.

10. Ibid., 134. He experiences frustration in regard to the Spaniards in numerous other incidents as well, most notably in 1682 when the Spaniards declare that a small group of their fellows would hold monopoly rights over bread and tortilla making.

11. The original is actually now lost to us. We have two very closely related surviving copies: the version in the BNAH (see n. 1) and another in the Cathedral of Puebla, published in facsimile and transcription in Lidia Gómez García, Celia Salazar Exaire, and María Elena Stefanón López, eds. *Anales del barrio de San Juan del Río: Crónica indígena de la ciudad de Puebla, siglo XVII* (Puebla: Instituto de Ciencias Sociales y Humanidades, 2000). The first version is more complete in respect to alphabetic text, the latter in respect to images, but both definitely come from the same trunk version. At least four related versions are found in the nineteenth-century collection of copies entitled "Anales antiguos de México y sus contornos," in the BNAH. The closest copy found there is "Anales de Puebla y Tlaxcala no. 2 [1524-1674]," 802. Three closely related texts from the collection that have been published in facsimile and transcription are found in María Teresa Sepúlveda, ed., *Anales mexicanos: Puebla, Tepeaca, Cholula* (Mexico City: INAH, 1995).

12. This detail is mentioned not only in the annals here but also in Spanish chronicles. See Antonio Carrión, *Historia de la ciudad de Puebla de los Angeles* (Puebla: José M. Cajica, 1970 [1897]). For more on the crisis of 1691–1692, see the writings of the Mexican savant Carlos Sigüenza y Góngora (close friend of

Ixtlilxochitl's son and the preserver of Chimalpahin's manuscripts), "Alboroto y motín de los indios de la Ciudad de México," (1692) and R. Douglas Cope, *The Limits of Racial Domination: Plebeian Society in Colonial Mexico City* (Madison: University of Wisconsin Press, 1994).
13. There is a rich literature on the ways in which indigenous peoples of central Mexico remembered and used their history in the later colonial period. To begin, see Stephanie Wood, *Transcending Conquest: Nahua Views of Spanish Colonial Mexico* (Norman: University of Oklahoma Press, 2003), especially chapter 5; Robert Haskett, *Visions of Paradise: Primordial Titles and Mesoamerican History in Cuernavaca* (Norman: University of Oklahoma Press, 2005); and Ethelia Ruiz Medrano, *Mexico's Indigenous Communities: Their Lands and Histories, 1500–2010* (Boulder: University Press of Colorado, 2010), especially chapter 2. For a study of a specific text directly relevant to this book, see Rocío Cortés, *El "nahuatlato Alvarado" y el Tlalamatl Huauhquilpan: Mecanismos de la memoria colectiva de una comunidad indígena* (New York: Hispanic Seminary of Medieval Studies, 2011).
14. Annals of Puebla in Townsend, *Here in This Year*, 146.
15. Ibid., 152.
16. Ibid., 148.
17. For full treatment of this subject and the following see Camilla Townsend, "The View from San Juan del Río: Mexican Indigenous Annals and the History of the Wider World," *Medieval History Journal* 14, no. 2 (2011): 323–342.
18. Peter Gerhard, "Un censo de la diócesis de Puebla en 1681," *Historia Mexicana* 120 (1981): 530–560; Norma Castillo Palma and Susan Kellogg, "Conflict and Cohabitation between Afro-Mexicans and Nahuas in Central Mexico," in *Beyond Black and Red: African-Native Relations in Colonial Latin America*, edited by Matthew Restall (Albuquerque: University of New Mexico Press, 2005). A case study of an African woman in Puebla of the 1630s is Pablo Sierra Silva, "Maria de Terranova: A West African Woman and the Quest for Freedom in Colonial Meixco," *Journal of Pan-African Studies* 6, no. 1 (2013): 39–57.
19. Annals of Puebla in Townsend, *Here in This Year*, 130.
20. For more on this see Lockhart, "Language," in *Here in This Year*.
21. Zapata, Bibliothèque Nationale de France, Méxican 212, folio 2v. The story is actually told in the present tense, almost certainly being an allusion to an original performance.

Appendices

1. This was almost certainly a copying error.
2. The "ca" is found in the seventeenth-century iteration, not in the earlier one.
3. Rafael Tena has "yol mani." The segment is all but illegible. I believe it could as easily say "yoli nemini," and I cannot make sense of the sentence any other way. The seventeenth-century copyist, also confused, omitted the whole thing.
4. This is a reconstruction of which I am confident.
5. This is a reconstruction that is debatable.
6. Marginal gloss reads: "casa de quetzalcoatl."
7. The "l" is missing but obviously intended.
8. A corner is torn off. This and the following bracketed words are reconstructions.

BIBLIOGRAPHY

Adams, Eleanor. *A Bio-Bibliography of Franciscan Authors in Colonial Central America*. Washington, DC: Academy of American Franciscan History, 1953.
Alva Ixtlilxochitl, Fernando de. *Obras Históricas*. Edited by Edmundo O'Gorman. 2 vols. Mexico City: UNAM, 1977.
Altman, Ida. *The War for Mexico's West: Indians and Spaniards in New Galicia, 1524–1550*. Albuquerque: University of New Mexico Press, 2010.
Anderson, Arthur J. O., Frances Berdan, and James Lockhart, eds. *Beyond the Codices: The Nahua View of Colonial Mexico*. Berkeley: University of California Press, 1976.
Andrews, Richard. *An Introduction to Classical Nahuatl*. Norman: University of Oklahoma Press, 2004 [1975].
Arroyo, Salvador Guilliem. "The Discovery of the Caja de Agua of Tlatelolco: Mural Painting from the Dawn of New Spain." *Colonial Latin American Review* 22 (2013): 19–38.
Auerbach, Eric. *Mimesis*. Princeton, NJ: Princeton University Press, 1953 [1946].
Augustine, Saint. *Confessions*. Edited by R. S. Pine-Coffin. New York: Penguin, 1961.
Barlow, Robert. "Anales de Tula, Hidalgo, 1361–1521." *Tlalocan* 3, no. 1 (1949): 2–13.
Bartlett, Roger. *The Making of Europe: Conquest, Colonization and Cultural Change, 950–1350*. Princeton, NJ: Princeton University Press, 1993.
Benítez, Fernando. *The Century After Cortés*. Chicago: University of Chicago Press, 1965.
Benoist, Valérie. "La construcción de una comunidad nahua/española en las *Relaciones* de Chimalpahin." *Estudios de cultura náhuatl* 28 (1998): 355–364.
Benton, Bradley. "The Outsider: Alva Ixtlilxochitl's Tenuous Ties to the City of Tetzcoco." *Colonial Latin American Review* 23, no. 1 (2014): 37–52.
Bierhorst, John. *Cantares Mexicanos*. Stanford, CA: Stanford University Press, 1985.
Bierhorst, John, ed. *Codex Chimalpopoca: The Text in Nahuatl*. Norman: University of Oklahoma Press, 1992.
Bierhorst, John, ed. *History and Mythology of the Aztecs: The Codex Chimalpopoca*. Tucson: University of Arizona Press, 1992.
Bolton, Herbert. *Guide to Materials for the History of the United States in the Principal Archives of Mexico*. Washington, DC: Carnegie Institution, 1913.

Boone, Elizabeth Hill. *Cycles of Time and Meaning in the Mexican Books of Fate.* Austin: University of Texas Press, 2007.

Boone, Elizabeth Hill. "Ruptures and Unions: Graphic Complexity and Hybridity in Sixteenth-Century Mexico." In *Their Way of Writing: Scripts, Signs and Pictographies in Pre-Columbian America*, edited by E. H. Boone and Gary Urton. Washington, DC: Dumbarton Oaks, 2011, 197–225.

Boone, Elizabeth Hill. *Stories in Red and Black: Pictorial Histories of the Aztecs and Mixtecs.* Austin: University of Texas Press, 2000.

Brading, David. *The First America: The Spanish Monarchy, Creole Patriots, and the Liberal State, 1492–1867.* Cambridge, UK: Cambridge University Press, 1991.

Brian, Amber. *Alva Ixtlilxochitl's Native Archive and the Circulation of Knowledge in Colonial Mexico.* Nashville, TN: Vanderbilt University Press, 2016.

Brian, Amber. "The Original Alva Ixtlilxochitl Manuscripts at Cambridge University." *Colonial Latin American Review* 23.1 (2014): 84–101.

Brooks, Lisa. *The Common Pot: The Recovery of Native Space in the Northeast.* Minneapolis: University of Minnesota Press, 2008.

Burkhart, Louise. *The Slippery Earth: Nahua-Christian Moral Dialogue in Sixteenth-Century Mexico.* Tucson: University of Arizona Press, 1989.

Camelo Arredondo, Rosa, Jorge Gurría Lacroie, and Constantino Reyes Valerio. *Juan Gerson: Tlacuiloc de Tecamachalco.* Mexico City: INAH, 1964.

Candiani, Vera. *Dreaming of Dry Land: Environmental Transformations in Colonial Mexico City.* Stanford, CA: Stanford University Press, 2014.

Cañizares Esguerra, Jorge. *How to Write the History of the New World: Histories, Epistemologies and Identities in the Eighteenth-Century Atlantic World.* Stanford, CA: Stanford University Press, 2001.

Carochi, Horacio. *Grammar of the Mexican Language.* Edited by James Lockhart. Stanford, CA: Stanford Universit Press, 2001 [1645].

Carrasco, Davíd, and Scott Sessions, eds. *Cave, City, and Eagle's Nest: An Interpretive Journey through the Mapa de Cuauhtinchan No. 2.* Albuquerque: University of New Mexico Press, 2007.

Carrasco, Pedro. "Royal Marriages in Ancient Mexico." In *Explorations in Ethnohistory: The Indians of Central Mexico in the Sixteenth Century*, edited by H. R. Harvey and Hanns J. Premm. Albuquerque: University of New Mexico Press, 1984.

Carrión, Antonio. *Historia de la ciudad de Puebla de los Angeles.* Puebla: José C. Cajica, 1970 [1897].

Castañeda de Paz, María. "Historia de una casa real: Origen y ocaso del linaje gobernante en México-Tenochtitlan." *Nuevo Mundo Mundos Nuevos* (2011). https://nuevomundo.revues.org/60624.

Castillo Palma, Norma, and Susan Kellogg. "Conflict and Cohabitation between Afro-Mexicans and Nahuas in Central Mexico." In *Beyond Black and Red: African-Native Relations in Colonial Latin America*, edited by Matthew Restall. Albuquerque: University of New Mexico Press, 2005, 115–136.

Celestino Solís, Eustaquio, and Luis Reyes García, eds. *Anales de Tecamachalco, 1398–1590.* Mexico City: CIESAS, 1992.

Chávez Orozco, Luis, ed. *Códice Osuna acompañado de 158 páginas inéditas encontradas en el Archivo General de la Nación.* Mexico City: Instituto Indigenista Interamericano, 1947.

Chimalpahin Quauhtlehuanitzin, don Domingo de San Antón Muñón. *Annals of His Time*. Edited by James Lockhart, Susan Schroeder, and Doris Namala. Stanford, CA: Stanford University Press, 2006.

Chimalpahin Quauhtlehuanitzin, don Domingo de San Antón Muñón. *Codex Chimalpahin*. Edited by Arthur J. O. Anderson and Susan Schroeder. 2 vols. Norman: University of Oklahoma Press, 1997.

Chimalpahin Quauhtlehuanitzin, don Domingo de San Antón Muñón. *Las ocho relaciones y el memorial de Colhuacan*. Edited by Rafael Tena. Mexico City: Conaculta, 1998.

Chipman, Donald. *Moctezuma's Children: Aztec Royalty under Spanish Rule, 1520–1700*. Austin: University of Texas Press, 2005.

Ciudad Real, Antonio de. *Tratado curioso y doctor de las grandezas de la Nueva España*. Mexico City: UNAM, 1976 [1584].

Clendinnen, Inga. *Aztecs: An Interpretation*. New York: Cambridge University Press, 1991.

Clendennin, Inga. *Ambivalent Conquests: Maya and Spaniard in Yucatán, 1517–1570*. New York: Cambridge University Press, 1987.

Cline, Sarah. *Colonial Culhuacan*. Albuquerque: University of New Mexico Press, 1986.

Connell, William. *After Moctezuma: Indigenous Politics and Self-Government in Mexico City, 1524–1730*. Norman: University of Oklahoma Press, 2011.

Conway, Richard. "Lakes, Canoes and the Aquatic Communities of Xochimilco and Chalco, New Spain." *Ethnohistory* 59 (2012): 541–568.

Cope, R. Douglas. *The Limits of Racial Domination: Plebeian Society in Colonial Mexico City, 1660–1720*. Madison: University of Wisconsin Press, 1994.

Corteguera, Luis. *Death by Effigy: A Case from the Mexican Inquisition*. Philadelphia: University of Pennsylvania Press, 2012.

Cortés, Hernan. *Letters from Mexico*. Edited by Anthony Pagden. New Haven, CT: Yale University Press, 1986.

Cortés, Rocio. *El "nahuatlato Alvarado" y el Tlalamatl Huauhquilpan: Mecanismos de la memoria colectiva de una comunidad indígena*. New York: Hispanic Seminary of Medieval Studies, 2011.

Crapo, Richley, and Bonnie Glass-Coffin, eds. *Anónimo Mexicano*. Logan: Utah State University Press, 2005.

Curcio-Nagy, Linda. *The Great Festivals of Colonial Mexico City: Performing Power and Identity*. Albuquerque: University of New Mexico Press, 2004.

De la Torre, Mario, Josefina García Quintana, and Carlos Martínez Marín, eds. *El Lienzo de Tlaxcala*. Mexico City: Cartón y Papel, 1983.

De la Torre Villar, Ernesto, and Ramiro Navarro de Anda, eds. *Testimonios históricos Guadalupanos*. Mexico City: Fondo de Cultura Económica, 1982.

Díaz del Castillo, Bernal. *Historia verdadera de la conquista de la Nueva España*. Mexico City: Porrúa, 2000.

Díaz Rubio, Elena, and Jesús Bustamente García. "Carta de Pedro de San Buenaventura a fray Bernardino de Sahagún." *Revista Española de Antropología Americana* 13 (1983): 109–120.

Diel, Lori. *The Tira of Tepechpan: Negotiating Place under Aztec and Spanish Rule*. Austin: University of Texas Press, 2008.

Don, Patricia Lopes. *Bonfires of Culture: Franciscans, Indigenous Leaders, and Inquisition in Early Mexico, 1524–1540*. Norman: University of Oklahoma Press, 2010.

Durston, Alan. "Cristóbal Choquecasa and the Making of the Huarochirí Manuscript." In *Indigenous Intellectuals: Knowledge, Power, and Colonial Culture in Mexico and the Andes*, edited by Gabriela Ramos and Yanna Yannakakis. Durham, NC: Duke University Press, 2014, 151–172.

Durston, Alan. *Pastoral Quechua: The History of Translation in Colonial Peru, 1550–1650*. Notre Dame, IN: University of Notre Dame Press, 2007.

Edmonson, Munro. *The Book of the Year: Middle American Calendrical Systems*. Salt Lake City: University of Utah Press, 1988.

Escalante Gonzalbo, Pablo. "El patrocinio del arte indo-cristiano en el siglo XVI: La iniciativa de las autoridades indígenas en Tlaxcala y Cuauhtinchan." In *Patrocinio, colección y circulación de las artes*, edited by Gustavo Curiel. Mexico City: UNAM, 1997, 215–236.

Florescano, Enrique. *Memory, Myth and Time in Mexico: From the Aztecs to Independence*. Austin: University of Texas Press, 1994.

García Icazbalceta, Joaquín, ed. *Nueva colección de documentos para la historia de México*. Liechtenstein: Kraus Reprints, 1971 [1886].

García Torres, Vicente, ed. *Documentos para la historia de México*. Serie 3. Mexico City: Vicente García Torres, 1856.

Gibson, Charles. *The Aztecs under Spanish Rule*. Stanford, CA: Stanford University Press, 1964.

Gibson, Charles. "The Identity of Diego Muñoz Camargo." *Hispanic American Historical Review* 30 (1950): 195–208.

Gibson, Charles. *Tlaxcala in the Sixteenth Century*. New Haven, CT: Yale University Press, 1952.

Gibson, Charles, and John Glass. "A Census of Middle American Prose Manuscripts in the Native Historical Tradition." In *Handbook of Middle American Indians*, vol. 15. Austin: University of Texas Press, 1975.

Gillespie, Susan. *The Aztec Kings: The Construction of Rulership in Mexico History*. Tucson: University of Arizona Press, 1989.

Gómez García, Lidia. "El Testamento de don Lucas Quetzalcoatzin, indio cacique del pueblo de Santa María Atlihuetzian: El papel de los músicos indios en la construcción del Nuevo orden novohispano." Paper presented at the 54th International Congress of Americanists, Vienna, July 2012. http://ica2012.univie.ac.at/index.php?id=117124&no_cache=1&tx_univietablebrowser_pi1%5Bbackpid%5D=117123&tx_univietablebrowser_pi1%5Bfkey%5D=992&tx_univietablebrowser_pi1%5Buid%5D=11659.

Gómez García, Lidia, Celia Salazar Exaire, and María Elena Stefanón López, eds. *Anales del barrio de San Juan del Río: crónica indígena de la ciudad de Puebla, siglo XVII*. Puebla: Instituto de Ciencias Sociales y Humanidades, 2000.

González Cicero, Stella María, ed. *Perspectiva religiosa en Yucatán, 1517–1571*. Mexico City: El Colejio de México, 1978.

Gruzinski, Serge. *The Conquest of Mexico: The Incorporation of Indian Societies into the Western World*. London: Polity, 1993 [1988].

Haring, Clarence. *The Buccaneers in the West Indies in the XVII Century*. Hamden, CT: Archon, 1966 [1910].

Haskett, Robert. *Indigenous Rulers: An Ethnohistory of Town Government in Colonial Cuernavaca*. Albuquerque: University of New Mexico Press, 1991.
Haskett, Robert. *Visions of Paradise: Primordial Titles and Mesoamerican History in Cuernavaca*. Norman: University of Oklahoma Press, 2005.
Hassig, Ross. *Time, History and Belief in Aztec and Colonial Mexico*. Austin: University of Texas Press, 2001.
Hazlewood, Nick. *The Queen's Slave Trader: John Hawkins, Elizabeth I, and the Trafficking in Human Souls*. New York: Harper, 2005.
Himmerich y Valencia, Robert. *The Encomenderos of New Spain, 1521–1555*. Austin: University of Texas Press, 1991.
Horn, Rebecca. *Postconquest Coyoacan: Nahua-Spanish Relations in Central Mexico, 1519–1650*. Stanford, CA: Stanford University Press, 1997.
Jalapa Flores, Tomás. "Migrantes y extravagantes: Indios de la periferia en la ciudad de México durante los siglos XVI–XVII." In *Los indios y las ciudades de Nueva España*, edited by Felipe Castro Gutiérrez. Mexico City: UNAM, 2010, 79–104.
Juan Gerson, pintor indígena del siglo XVI: Símbolo del mestizaje. Mexico City: Fondo Editorial de la Plástica Mexicana, 1972.
Karttunen, Frances. *An Analytical Dictionary of Nahuatl*. Norman: University of Oklahoma Press, 1992 [1983].
Kirchoff, Paul, Lina Odena Güemes, and Luis Reyes García, eds. *Historia Tolteca Chichimeca*. Mexico City: INAH, 1976.
Kranz, Travis. "The Tlaxcalan Conquest Pictorials: The Role of Images in Influencing Colonial Policy in Sixteenth Century Mexico." PhD dissertation, Department of Art History, University of California, Los Angeles, 2001.
Krug, Frances, and Camilla Townsend. "The Tlaxala-Puebla Family of Annals." In *Sources and Methods for the Study of Post-Conquest Mesoamerican Ethnohistory*, edited by James Lockhart, Lisa Sousa, and Stephanie Wood. http//wph.uoregon.edu/Lockhart/index.html.
Lafaye, Jacques. *Quetzalcoatl and Guadalupe: The Formation of Mexican National Consciousness, 1531–1813*. Chicago: University of Chicago Press, 1974.
Laird, Andrew. "Nahuas and Caesars: Classical Learning and Bilingualism in Post-Conquest Mexico: An Inventory of Latin Writings by Authors of the Native Nobility." *Classical Philology* 109, no. 2 (2014): 150–169.
Lane, Kris. *Pillaging the Empire: Piracy in the Americas, 1500–1750*. Armonk, NY: M. E. Sharpe, 1998.
Lanyon, Anna. *The New World of Martín Cortés*. Cambridge, MA: Da Capo, 2003.
Lehmann, Walter, and Gerdt Kutscher, eds. *Geschichte der Azteken: Codex Aubin und verwandte Dokumente*. Berlin: Gebr. Mann, 1981.
Leibsohn, Dana. *Script and Glyph: Pre-Hispanic History, Colonial Bookmaking and the Historia Tolteca Chichimeca*. Washington, DC: Dumbarton Oaks, 2009.
León Portilla, Miguel. *Bernardino de Sahagún: First Anthropologist*. Norman: University of Oklahoma Press, 2002.
León Portilla, Miguel. *Coloquios y doctrina Cristiana*. Mexico City: UNAM, 1986.
León Portilla, Miguel. "Have We Really Translated the Mesoamerican 'Ancient Word'?" In *On the Translation of Native American Literatures*, edited by Brian Swann. Washington, DC: Smithsonian Institution Press, 1992, 313–338.

León Portilla, Miguel, and María del Carmen Aguilera García. *Mapa de México Tenochtitlan y sus contornos hacia 1550*. Mexico City: Celanese Mexicana, 1986.
Lockhart, James. "The Language of the Texts." In *Here in This Year*, edited by Camilla Townsend. Stanford: Stanford University Press, 2010, 45–65.
Lockhart, James. *The Nahuas after the Conquest*. Stanford, CA: Stanford University Press, 1992.
Lockhart, James. *Nahuas and Spaniards: Postconquest Central Mexican History and Philology*. Stanford, CA: Stanford University Press, 1991.
Lockhart, James, ed. *We People Here: Nahuatl Accounts of the Conquest of Mexico*. Berkeley: University of California Press, 1993.
Lockhart, James, Frances Berdan, and Aruthur J. O. Anderson, eds. *The Tlaxcalan Actas: A Compendium of the Records of the Cabildo of Tlaxcala, 1545–1627*. Salt Lake City: University of Utah Press, 1986.
López Austin, Alfredo. *Las razones del mito: La cosmovisión Mesoamericana*. Mexico City: Ediciones Era, 2015 [2008].
López Austin, Alfredo, and Luis Millones. *Los mitos y sus tiempos: Creencias y narraciones de Mesoamérica y los Andes*. Mexico City: Ediciones Era, 2015.
López Luján, Leonardo. *The Offerings of the Templo Mayor of Tenochtitlan*. Boulder: University Press of Colorado, 1994.
López Mora, Rebecca. "Entre dos mundos: Los indios de los barrios de la ciudad de México, 1550–1600." In *Los indios y las ciudades de Nueva España*, edited by Felipe Castro Gutiérrez. Mexico City: UNAM, 2010, 57–78.
Marcus, Joyce. *Mesoamerican Writing Systems: Propaganda, Myth and History in Four Ancient Civilizations*. Princeton, NJ: Princeton University Press, 1992.
Marley, David. *Sack of Veracruz: The Great Pirate Raid of 1683*. Windsor, Ontario: Netherlandic Press, 1993.
Martínez, Enrico. *Reportorio de los tiempos e historia natural de Nueva España*. Mexico City, 1606; reprinted, Mexico City: Novum, 1991.
Martínez, Hildeberto. *Codiciaban la Tierra: El despojo agrario en los señoríos de Tecamachalco y Quecholac (Puebla, 1520–1650)*. Mexico City: CIESAS, 1994.
Martínez Baracs, Andrea. *Un gobierno de indios: Tlaxcala, 1519–1750*. Mexico City: Fondo de Cultura Económica, 2008.
Martínez Baracs, Rodrigo. "De Tepeaquilla a Tepeaca, 1528–1555." *Andes* 17 (2006). http://www.redalyc.org/html/127/12701708/.
Martínez Baracs, Rodrigo. "El Diario de Chimalpahin." *Estudios de Cultura Náhuatl* 38 (2007). http://www.academia.edu/7974880/El_Diario_de_Chimalpahin.
McDonough, Kelly. *The Learned Ones: Nahua Intellectuals in Post-conquest Mexico*. Tucson: University of Arizona Press, 2014.
McEnroe, Sean. *From Colony to Nationhood in Mexico: Laying the Foundations, 1560–1840*. Cambridge, UK: Cambridge University Press, 2012.
Medina Lima, Constantino, ed. *Libro de los guardianes y gobernadores de Cuauhtinchan*. Mexico City: CIESAS, 1995.
Megged, Amos. *Social Memory in Ancient and Colonial Mesoamerica*. Cambridge, UK: Cambridge University Press, 2010.
Megged, Amos, and Stephanie Wood, eds. *Mesoamerican Memory: Enduring Systems of Remembrance*. Norman: University of Oklahoma Press, 2012.
Mendieta, fray Gerónimo. *Historia eclesiástica indiana*. Mexico City: Salvador Chávez Hayhoe, 1945.

Mengin, Ernst, ed. *Unos annales históricos de la nación mexicana*. Copenhagen: Einar Munksgaard, 1945.
Mignolo, Walter. "On the Colonization of Amerindian Languages and Memories: Renaissance Theories of Writing and the Discontinuity of the Classical Tradition." *Comparative Studies in Society and History* 34, no. 2 (1992): 301–330.
Mikulska Dabrowska, Katarzyna. "'Secret Language' in Oral and Graphic Form: Religious-Magic Discourse in Aztec Speeches and Manuscripts." *Oral Tradition* 25 (2010): 325–363.
Miller, Mary, and Barbara Mundy, eds. *Painting a Map of Sixteenth-Century Mexico City: Land, Writing, and Native Rule*. New Haven, CT: Beinecke Rare Book & Manuscript Library and Yale University Press, 2012.
Miller, Mary, and Karl Taube. *An Illustrated Dictionary of the Gods and Symbols of Ancient Mexico and the Maya*. New York: Thames and Hudson, 2011.
Molina, fray Alonso de. *Vocabulario en lengua castellana y mexicana y mexicana castellana*. Mexico City: Porrúa, 1970 [1571].
Monjarás Ruiz, Jesú, Elena Limón, and María de al Cruz Paillés, eds. *Tlatelcolco: Fuentes e Historia*. Mexico City: INAH, 1989.
Mota y Escobar, fray Alonso de la. *Memoriales del obispo de Tlaxcala*. Mexico City: Stylo, 1945 [1625].
Motolinía, fray Toribio de Benavente. *Historia de los indios de la Nueva España*. Madrid: Alianza, 1988.
Mundy, Barbara. *The Death of Aztec Tenochtitlan, the Life of Mexico City*. Austin: University of Texas Press, 2015.
Muñoz Camargo, Diego. *Historia de Tlaxcala*. Edited by Luis Reyes García. Tlaxcala: Universidad Autónoma de Tlaxcala, 1998.
Namala, Doris. "Chimalpahin in His Time: An Analysis of the Writings of a Nahua Annalist of Seventeenth-Century Mexico Concerning His Own Lifetime." PhD dissertation, Department of History, University of California, Los Angeles, 2002.
Navarrete Linares, Federico. *Los orígenes de los pueblos indígenas del valle de México: Los altepetl y sus historias*. Mexico City: UNAM, 2011.
Nesvig, Martin. "The Epistemological Politics of Vernacular Scripture in Sixteenth-Century Mexico." *The Americas* 70 (2012): 165–201.
Nesvig, Martin. "Spanish Men, Indigenous Language, and Informal Interpreters in Postcontact Mexico." *Ethnohistory* 19 (2012): 739–764.
Nicholson, H. B. "Pre-Hispanic Central Mexican Historiography." In *Investigaciones contemporáneas sobre historia de México*. Mexico City: UNAM, 1971, 38–81.
Núñez y Domínguez, José de Jesús, ed. *El tapado de México y el de Santo Domingo*. Trujillo, Dominican Republic: Tipográfica Franciscana, 1950.
O'Gorman, Edmundo. *Destierro de sombras: Luz en el orígen de la imagen y culta de Nuestra Señora de Guadalupe*. Mexico City: UNAM, 1986.
Olivier, Guilhem. *Mockeries and Metamorphoses of an Aztec God: Tezcatlipoca, "Lord of the Smoking Mirror."* Boulder: University Press of Colorado, 2003.
Olko, Justyna. *Insignia of Rank in the Nahua World*. Boulder: University Press of Colorado, 2014.
Orozco y Berra, Manuel. *Noticia histórica de la conjuración del marqués del Valle, 1565–68*. Mexico City: R. Rafael, 1853.

Osowski, Edward. *Indigenous Miracles: Nahua Authority in Colonial Mexico*. Tucson: University of Arizona Press, 2010.
Paso y Troncoso, Francisco del, ed. *Códice matritense del Real Palacio: Historia de las Cosas de Nueva España*. 3 vols. of projected 7. Madrid: Hauser y Menet, 1906–1908.
Pizzigoni, Caterina. *The Life Within: Local Indigenous Society in Mexico's Toluca Valley, 1650–1800*. Stanford, CA: Stanford University Press, 2013.
Pizzigoni, Caterina, ed. *Testaments of Toluca*. Stanford, CA: Stanford University Press, 2007.
Poole, Stafford. *The Guadalupan Controversies in Mexico*. Stanford: Stanford University Press, 2006.
Prescott, William. *History of the Conquest of Mexico*. 2 vols. New York: American Publishers, 1843.
Ramos, Gabriela, and Yanna Yannakakis, eds. *Indigenous Intellectuals: Knowledge, Power, and Colonial Culture in Mexico and the Andes*. Durham, NC: Duke University Press, 2014.
Rappaport, Joanne, and Thomas Cummins. *Beyond the Lettered City: Indigenous Literacies in the Andes*. Durham, NC: Duke University Press, 2014.
Restall, Matthew. *Maya Conquistador*. Boston: Beacon, 1998.
Restall, Matthew. *Seven Myths of the Spanish Conquest*. New York: Oxford University Press, 2003.
Reuter, Timothy, ed. *The Annals of Fulda*. Manchester, UK: Manchester University Press, 1992.
Reyes García, Luis. *Cuauhtinchan del Siglo XII al XVI*. Wiesbaden, Germany: Franz Steiner, 1977.
Reyes García, Luis. *La escritura pictográfica en Tlaxcala: Dos mil años de experiencia mesoamericana*. Tlaxcala: Universidad Autónoma de Tlaxcala, 1993.
Reyes García, Luis, ed. *¿Cómo te confundes? ¿Acaso no somos conquistados? Anales de Juan Bautista*. Mexico City: CIESAS, 2001.
Reyes García, Luis, ed. *Documentos nauas de la ciudad de México del siglo XVI*. Mexico City: CIESAS, 1996.
Reyes García, Luis, ed. *Documentos sobre tierras y señorios en Cuauhtinchan*. Mexico City: INAH, 1978.
Romero Galván, José Rubén. "La historia según Chimalpahin." *Journal de la Société des Américanistes* 82.2 (1998): 183–195.
Round, Philip. *Removable Type: Histories of the Book in Indian Country, 1663–1880*. Chapel Hill: University of North Carolina Press, 2010.
Ruiz de Alarcón, Hernando. *Treatise on the Heathen Superstitions that Today Live among the Indians Native to this New Spain, 1629*. Edited by Richard Andrews and Ross Hassig. Norman: University of Oklahoma Press, 1984.
Ruiz Medrano, Ethelia. "Fighting Destiny: Nahua Nobles and Friars in the Sixteenth-Century Revolt of the Encomenderos against the King." In *Negotiation within Domination: New Spain's Indian Pueblos Confront the Spanish State*, edited by Ethelia Ruiz Medrano and Susan Kellogg. Boulder: University Press of Colorado, 2010, 45–71.
Ruiz Medrano, Ethelia. *Mexico's Indigenous Communities: Their Lands and Histories, 1500–2010*. Boulder: University Press of Colorado, 2010.

Sahagún, Bernardino de. *The Florentine Codex: General History of the Things of New Spain*. Edited by Charles Dibble and Arthur J. O. Anderson. 12 vols. Salt Lake City: University of Utah Press, 1950–1982.
Salomon, Frank, and Mercedes Niño Murcía. *The Lettered Mountain: A Peruvian Village's Way with Writing*, Durham, NC: Duke University Press, 2011.
Sarabia Viejo, María Justina. *Don Luis de Velasco, virrey de Nueva España, 1550–1564*. Seville: Escuela de Estudios Hispano-Americanos, 1978.
Scholes, France V., and Eleanor B. Adams. *Don Diego Quijada, alcalde mayor de Yucatán, 1561–1565*. 2 vols. Mexico City: José Porrúa, 1938.
Scholes, France V., and Eleanor B. Adams. *Sobre el modo de tributar los indios de Nueva España a Su Majestad, 1561–1564*. Mexico City: José Porrúa, 1958.
Scholes, France V., and Eleanor B. Adams, eds. *Cartas de Valderrama*. Mexico City: José Porrúa, 1961.
Schroeder, Susan. *Chimalpahin and the Kingdoms of Chalco*, Tucson: University of Arizona Press, 1991.
Schroeder, Susan. "The First American Valentine: Nahua Courtship and Other Aspects of Family Structuring in Mesoamerica." *Journal of Family History* 23, no. 4 (1998): 343–348.
Schroeder, Susan. "The Truth about the Crónica Mexicayotl." *Colonial Latin American Review* 20 (2011): 233–247.
Schroeder, Susan, ed. *The Conquest All Over Again: Nahuas and Zapotecs Thinking, Writing, and Painting Spanish Colonialism*. Eastbourne, UK: Sussex Academic Press, 2010.
Sell, Barry, and Louise Burkhart, eds. *Nahuatl Theater, Vol. 4: Nahua Christianity in Performance*. Norman: University of Oklahoma Press, 2009.
Sepúlveda, María Teresa, ed. *Anales mexicanos: Puebla, Tepeaca, Cholula*. Mexico City: INAH, 1995.
Sierra Silva, Pablo. "María de Terranova: A West African Woman and the Quest for Freedom in Colonial Mexico." *Journal of Pan-African Studies* 6.1 (2013): 39–57.
Sigüenza y Góngora, Carlos. "Alboroto y motín de los indios de la Ciudad de México." In his *Seis Obras*. Caracas: Biblioteca Ayacucho, 1984.
Simpson, Lesley Byrd. *Many Mexicos*. Berkeley: University of California Press, 1963.
Skopyk, Bradley. "Undercurrents of Conquest: The Shifting Terrain of Indigenous Agriculture in Colonial Tlaxcala, Mexico." PhD dissertation, Department of History, York University, 2010.
Suárez de la Peralta, Juan. *Tratado del descubrimiento de las Indias y su conquista*. Madrid: Alianza, 1990.
Sullivan, John, ed. *Ytechcopa timoteilhuia yn tobicario*. Zapopan: El Colegio de Jalisco, 2003.
Swann, Brian, ed. *On the Translation of Native American Literatures*. Washington, DC: Smithsonian Institution Press, 1992.
Swanton, Michael. "El texto Popoloca de la Historia Tolteca Chichimeca." *Relaciones* 22.86 (2001): 117–140.
Tavárez, David. *The Invisible War: Indigenous Devotions, Discipline, and Dissent in Colonial Mexico*. Stanford, CA: Stanford University Press, 2011.

Tavárez, David. "Nahua Intellectuals, Franciscan Scholars, and the *Devotio Moderna* in Colonial Mexico." *The Americas* 70 (2013): 203–235.

Tavárez, David. "Reclaiming the Conquest." In *Chimalpahin's Conquest*, edited by Susan Schroeder, Ann J. Cruz, Cristián Roa-de-la-Carrera, and David Tavárez. Stanford, CA: Stanford University Press, 2010, 17–34.

Tedlock, Dennis, ed. *Two Thousand Years of Mayan Literature*. Berkeley: University of California Press, 2011.

Tena, Rafael, ed. *Anales de Cuauhtitlan*. Mexico City: Conaculta, 2011.

Tena, Rafael, ed. *Tres crónicas mexicanas: Textos recopilados por Domingo Chimalpahin*. Mexico City: Conaculta, 2012.

Tena, Rafael. "La estructura textual de las relaciones primera y octava de Chimalpahin." *Estudios de Cultura Náhuatl* 28 (1998): 355–364.

Tena, Rafael. *La religión mexica*. Mexico City: INAH, 1993.

Terraciano, Kevin. "Three Views of the Conquest of Mexico from the *Other Mexica*." In *The Conquest All Over Again: Nahuas and Zapotecs Thinking, Writing and Painting Spanish Colonialism*, edited by Susan Schroeder. Eastbourne, UK: Sussex Academic Press, 2010, 15–40.

Torquemada, fray Juan de. *Monarquía Indiana*. 3 vols. Mexico City: Porrúa, 1969.

Toussaint, Manuel. *La catedral y las iglesias de Puebla*. Mexico City: Porrúa, 1954.

Townsend, Camilla. "Burying the White Gods: New Perspectives on the Conquest of Mexico." *American Historical Review* 108, no. 3 (2003): 659–687.

Townsend, Camilla. "The Concept of the Nahua Historian: Don Juan Zapata's Scholarly Tradition." In *Indigenous Intellectuals: Knowledge, Power, and Colonial Culture in Mexico and the Andes*, edited by Gabriela Ramos and Yanna Yannakakis. Durham, NC: Duke University Press, 2014, 132–150.

Townsend, Camilla. "Don Juan Zapata y Mendoza and the Notion of a Nahua Identity." In *The Conquest All Over Again: Nahuas and Zapotecs Thinking, Writing and Painting Spanish Colonialism*, edited by Susan Schroeder. Eastbourne, UK: Sussex Academic Press, 2010, 144–180.

Townsend, Camilla. "The Evolution of Alva Ixtlilxochitl's Scholarly Life." *Colonial Latin American Review* 23, no. 1 (2014): 1–17.

Townsend, Camilla. "Glimpsing Native American Historiography: The Cellular Principle in Sixteenth-Century Nahuatl Annals." *Ethnohistory* 56 (2009): 625–650.

Townsend, Camilla. *Here in This Year: Seventeenth-Century Nahuatl Annals of the Tlaxcala-Puebla Valley*. Stanford, CA: Stanford Univesity Press, 2010.

Townsend, Camilla. *Malintzin's Choices: An Indian Woman in the Conquest of Mexico*. Albuquerque: University of New Mexico Press, 2006.

Townsend, Camilla. "Mutual Appraisals: The Shifting Paradigms of the English, Spanish and Powhatans in Tesenacomoco, 1560–1622." In *Early Modern Virginia: Reconsidering the Old Dominion*, edited by Douglas Bradburn and John C. Coombs. Charlottesville: University of Virginia Press, 2011, 57–89.

Townsend, Camilla. "Polygyny and the Divided Altepetl: The Tetzcocan Key to Pre-Conquest Nahua Politics." In *Texcoco: Prehispanic and Colonial Perspectives*, edited by Jongsoo Lee and Galen Brokaw. Boulder: University Press of Colorado, 2014, 93–116.

Townsend, Camilla. "The View from San Juan del Río: Mexican Indigenous Annals and the History of the Wider World." *Medieval History Journal* 14, no. 2 (2011): 323–342.

Townsend, Camilla. "'What in the World Have You Done to Me, My Lover?': Sex, Servitude and Politics among the Pre-Conquest Nahuas as seen in the Cantares Mexicanos." *The Americas* 63, no. 3 (2006): 349–389.

Truitt, Jonathan. "Adopted Pedagogies: Nahua Incorporation of European Music and Theater in Colonial Mexico City." *The Americas* 66, no. 3 (2010): 311–330.

Ulloa, Modesto. *La hacienda real de Castilla en el reinado de Felipe II*. Madrid: Fundación Universitaria Español Seminario Cisneros, 1986.

Van Doesburg, Sebastián. "Territory and Cultural Reproduction: Agrarian Conflict, Títulos and Pictorial Documents." Paper presented at the 54th International Congress of Americanists, Vienna, July 2012.

Van Zantwijk, Rudolph. *The Aztec Arrangement: The Social History of Pre-Spanish Mexico*. Norman: University of Oklahoma Press, 1985.

Velázquez, Primo Feliciano, ed. *Códice Chimalpopoca: Anales de Cuauhtitlan y leyenda de los soles*. Mexico City: Imprenta Universitaria, 1945.

Vetancurt, fray Agustín de. *Teatro Mexicano: Descripción breve de los sucesos ejemplares, históricos y religiosos del Nuevo Mundo de las Indias*. Mexico City: Porrúa, 1974 [1697].

Villa Flores, Javier. "Wandering Swindlers: Imposture, Style and the Inquisition's Pedagogy of Fear in Colonial Mexico." *Colonial Latin American Review* 17 (2008): 252–272.

Villella, Peter. "Indian Lords, Hispanic Gentlemen: The Salazars of Colonial Mexico." *The Americas* 69, no. 1 (2012): 1–36.

Villella, Peter. *Indigenous Elites and Creole Identity in Colonial Mexico, 1500–1800*. Cambridge, UK: Cambridge University Press, 2016.

Villella, Peter. "The Last Acolhua: Alva Ixtlilxochitl and Elite Native Historiography in Early New Spain." *Colonial Latin American Review* 23, no. 1 (2014): 18–36.

Vincent, Victoria Ann. "The Avila-Cortés Conspiracy: Creole Aspirations and Royal Interests." PhD dissertation, Department of History, University of Nebraska at Lincoln, 1993.

Wake, Eleanor. *Framing the Sacred: The Indian Churches of Colonial Mexico*. Norman: University of Oklahoma Press, 2010.

Wake, Eleanor. "Serpent Road: Iconic Encoding and the Historial Narrative of the Mapa de Cuauhtinchan No. 2." In *Cave, City and Eagle's Nest*, edited by Davíd Carrasco and Scott Sessions. Albuquerque: University of New Mexico Press, 2007, 205–254.

Webb, David. "The Construction of Nahua Identity in Seventeenth-Century Mexico: A Study of *La Historia cronológica de la muy insigne, noble y leal ciudad de Tlaxcala*." PhD dissertation, Department of Hispanic Languages and Literature, University of California, Los Angeles, 2005.

White, Hayden. *The Content of the Form: Narrative Discourse and Historical Representation*. Baltimore: Johns Hopkins University Press, 1987.

Whitfield, Peter. *The Mapping of the Heavens*. London: British Library, 1995.

Whittaker, Gordon. "The Principles of Nahuatl Writing." *Göttinger Beiträge zur Sprachwissenschaft* 16 (2009): 47–81.

Wood, Stephanie. "Nahuatl Terms Relating to Conquest." Paper presented at the American Historical Association, New York City, January 2015.

Wood, Stephanie. *Transcending Conquest: Nahua Views of Spanish Colonial Mexico*. Norman: University of Oklahoma Press, 2003.

Wyss, Hilary. *Writing Indians: Literacy, Christianity and Native Community in Early America*. Amherst: University of Massachusetts Press, 2000.

Yoneda, Keiko. "Glyphs and Messages in the Mapa de Cuauhtinchan No. 2." In *Cave, City and Eagle's Nest*, edited by Davíd Carrasco and Scott Sessions. Albuquerque: University of New Mexico Press, 2007, 161–204.

Zapata y Mendoza, don Juan Buenaventura. *Historia cronológica de la Noble Ciudad de Tlaxcala*. Edited by by Luis Reyes García and Andrea Martínez Baracs. Tlaxcala: Universidad Autónoma de Tlaxcala and CIESAS, 1995.

Zaragoza, Justo, et al. *Cartas de Indias*. Madrid: Biblioteca de Autores Españoles, 1974 [1877].

Zimmermann, Günter, ed. *Die Relationen Chimalpahin's zur Geschichte Mexico's*. Hamburg: Cram, de Gruyter, 1965.

INDEX

Acaçayol, Pedro (of Mexico City), 80–81
Adam (and Eve), 162, 164
Africans, 156, 213–14, 216, 222–23
alphabetic annals, 3–4, 151–52. *See also* xiuhpohualli
altepetl (concept of), 5, 17, 44, 55, 60, 79, 143, 175, 177, 217
Alva Ixtlilxochitl, don Fernando, *See* Ixtlilxochitl
Amaquemecan, 141–44
America (as continent), 165
amoxtli (as a term), 2, 31, 164
Amozoc, 22, 26
Angeles, don Juan de los (of Tecamachalco), 102, 116
annals (European), 6. *See also* xiuhpohualli
Annals of Cuauhtitlan, selection from, 124–33; main treatment of, 133–38
Annals of Juan Bautista, 13; selection from, 55–62; main treatment of, 91–96
Annals of Puebla, 14; selection from, 213–15; main treatment of, 218–23
Annals of Tecamachalco, selection from, 99–105; main treatment of, 110–20
Annals of Tlatelolco, 12; selection from, 37–41; main treatments of, 41–43, 46–49, 50–52
Annals of Tula, 188
Anónimo Mexicano, 296n107
anonymity, 8–9, 110–11
Aquinas, Saint Thomas, 164
Aquino, Tomás de (of Mexico City), 59, 68
arrows (symbolic), 49, 132, 166, 173
Arsa, don León de, 175–79

artisans, 66, 128–132. *See also* painters, featherwork
Asia, 148, 165, 207
Asunción, Santa María de, 177, 178, 183
Atzacualco, San Sebastián (barrio), 65, 73
Aubin, *See Codex Aubin*
Audiencia, 25, 30, 60, 186
Auerbach, Eric, 11
Augustine, Saint, 161, 164
Axayacatl (Mexica ruler), 141–43
Aztlan, 150, 161, 165. *See also* Seven Caves

Baltic peoples, 165, 167
baptism, 25, 190. *See also* Christianity
Bautista, Juan (of Mexico City), 59, 274n109
Benavente, fray Melchor de, 56–57
Benavides, don Antonio de, *See* el Tapado
bilingualism, 115, 117, 156, 183, 189, 218
birds (symbolic), 132, 163, 164
blacks, *See* Africans
Boone, Elizabeth Hill, 3
Boturini, Lorenzo, 210
bows, *See* arrows.
bread, 176, 179, 222
bullfighting, 179, 180
burning, death by, 38, 132, 142

Cabildo, foundations of, 66, 182–83, 190–91, 216; in times of crisis, 79, 106, 191. *See also* pipiltin
calendars, errors in, 193, 209; in Mesoamerican tradition, 4–5, 6, 33, 112, 121, 123, 132, 165; mixed usages of, 104, 149

Camaxtle (temple), 27
Cano, Juan, 59, 62. *See also* Moctezuma, Isabel de.
Casas, Bartolomé de las, 136
Castañeda, Alonso de (Spaniard), 25
Catañeda, Cristóbal de (male descendant), 28
Castañeda, don Alonso de (of Cuauhtinchan), 12, 21, 24–26, 29–31
Castañeda, María Ruiz de (female descendant), 37
Castillo, don Baltasar de (of Tecamachalco), 103, 105, 120
census, 86, 199, 213
Ceynos, Lic. Francisco, 78, 80–82, 87–88, 90
Chachalaca, Pedro (of Mexico City), 57, 58
"Chalca cihuacuicatl" (Chalca Woman's Song), 76–77, 141–43, 168
Chalchiuhtlicue (goddess), 144
Chalco, 141–43, 144–45, 149–50, 166–68
Chichimecacihuatl, doña Magdalena (of Mexico City), 73, 86
Chichimecs, 207. *See also Historia Tolteca Chichimeca*
Chicomoztoc. *See* Seven Caves
Chimalaxochitl (of the Mexica), 37, 38, 46
Chimalpahin, 8, 9, 13; selection from work, 141–43; life story of, 143–150, 173; as writer of annals, 150–54
Chimalpopoca (of Cuauhtinchan). *See* Castañeda, don Alonso de
Cholula, 23, 33, 45–46, 99
Christianity, as evangelical religion, 25, 148, 218; as church militant, 214. *See also* Adam (and Eve), baptism, priests
Cipac (as name). *See* Marcos; and Santa María, Luis de
clothing, 47, 126, 142–43, 171, 173, 176, 196
Codex Aubin, 13, 65, 68–70, 76, 90, 93
Codex Osuna, 13, 80, 86
Colloquy of How the Fortunate Saint Helen Found the Precious Revered Wooden Cross, 205
Columbus, Christopher, 167
comets, 106, 221–22
Cómputo cronológico de los indios mexicanos, 206, 208
Confessions of Saint Augustine, 157
Congregaciones, 21, 36, 102, 109
conquest. *See* Spaniards, arrival of
Cortés, Hernando, 91. *See also*, Spaniards, arrival of
Cortés, Martín (Marqués del Valle), 64, 70, 72, 87, 89, 90, 111

Cortés, Martín (son of la Malinche), 77, 87, 89, 90
Coxcoxtli (of Culhuacan), 37, 39, 40, 47, 50
coyotes, 167
crime, 176, 222
Cruz, Martín de la (of Mexico City), 92
Cruz, Sor Juana Inés de la, 203
crying. *See* weeping.
Cuauhtemoc (Mexica ruler), 61, 94
Cuauhtinchan, 21–22, 33. *See also Historia Tolteca Chichimeca*
Cuauhtli, Cristóbal (of Mexico City), 56, 92
Cuauhtli, Francisco (of Mexico City), 56, 59, 67
Cuernavaca, 173
Cuetlaxcohuapan. *See* Puebla
Cuitlahuac (Mexica ruler), 94
Culhuacan, 37, 39, 165. *See also* Coxcoxtli.
Cuneiform, 12

dancing. *See* music
death. *See* burning, disease, hanging
deer, 39, 58 (translated as "brute")
dependency (as woeful fate), 48–49, 51, 77
Desagüe, 149
dialogue, 6, 18, 95, 207, 223
Díaz, Bernal, 67
disease, as threat to social memory, 31, 221; in epidemics, 24, 29, 70, 101, 105, 108, 119, 147, 149–50, 183, 219; in individual suffering, 113, 118, 132, 183
Doctrina Cristiana, 108
Dominicans, 35, 78, 85, 88, 146
drought. *See* famine
drunkenness, 131, 133

eagle, landing and seizing item, 40, 52, 113; paired with jaguar, 28, 110
earthquake, 141
eclipse, 206, 219, 162
Ehecatl (god). *See* wind
Ejercicio quotidiano, 155
elder sister. *See* inhueltiuh
encomienda, 24
Eve (with Adam), 162, 164
Ezmallín, don Martín (of Mexico City), 59, 85, 95

Falces, marqués de (don Gaston de Peralta), 88–89, 115–16
famine, 132, 167, 219

INDEX

Faustino, don Diego Martín (of Tlaxcala), 175, 177
featherwork, 73, 128, 130
Fernández de Santa Cruz, Manuel (bishop of Puebla), 203, 204, 179
52 (as bundle of years), 5, 31, 133, 165
fire. *See* burning
fireworks, 177
flogging, 62, 76, 82, 114, 176
flooding, 149, 177, 219
Florescano, Enrique, 7
Franciscans, founding monasteries and churches, 21, 27, 102, 103–04, 107, 149, 215–16; defending their order, 35, 85, 103; defending Indians, 71, 81, 114; educating Indians, 3, 13, 68, 202; angering Indians, 74–75, 102, 117

Gallegos, Juan, 30
Gante, fray Pedro de, 67, 149, 189
García, Lucas (of Tlaxcala), 188
Gerson, Jean (French theologian), 108
Gerson, Juan (of Tecamachalco), 108, 110, 278nn43–46
Gerson, Tomás (of Tecamachalco), 105, 108, 116, 119
glyphs, 2–3, 31, 34, 69, 111, 206, 221
golden numbers, 101, 112
Gómara, Francisco López de, 136, 155, 161, 170
Grande, Juan, 154
Gruzinski, Serge, 7
Guadalupe, Santa María de, 68
Guzman, Nuño Beltran de, 25

hanging, death by, 27, 102, 190
Hawkins, John, 116
head-flying, 178
Hercules, 41, 134
historians (Nahua), 10–11, 13. *See also* xiuhpohualli, *and individual names or writers*
Historia Tolteca Chichimeca, 12, 31–32, 36, 94–95; selection from, 16–21; main treatment of, 41–49
Hojacastro, Martín de (bishop of Puebla), 102
horses, 179, 180, 214
Huanitzin, don Diego de Alvarado (ruler of the Mexica), 143, 153
Huemac, 18, 19, 50, 52, 134–35
huehuetlatolli. *See* rhetoric

Huexotzinco, 42, 50, 103, 167, 223
Huilacapitzin, don Tomás (of Cuauhtinchan), 26–27
Huitzilihuitl (of the Mexica), 37, 38, 47, 166
Huitzilopochtli (god), 52, 138
human sacrifice. *See* sacrifice
humor, 47, 156, 205, 224
hunting, 39, 49–50

Icxicouatl and Quetzalteueyac, 17–18, 19, 45, 95
idolatry (accusations of), 118, 176, 190, 204
indentured servitude, 76, 81, 116
indigenous intellectuals, 10. *See also* historians, Nahua; xiuhpohualli; *as well as individual names*
indio (as form of identity), 147, 161–62, 196–97, 201
inhueltiuh, 38, 131, 171–72
ink, 2. *See also* red-and-black
Inquisition, 117, 120 n.78.
Itzcacmacuextli, Benito (of Tlaxcala), 187–88, 189, 207
Itzcoatl (Mexica ruler), 170
Itzpapalotl (goddess), 126
Ixtlilxochitl, don Fernando de Alva, 154–55, 161, 162–63, 166

Jacobito, Martín, 122
jaguars, 146. *See also* eagles, paired with jaguars
Jesuits, 152
Jews, 167, 172, 205
Jiménez, Francisco (of Tecamachalco), 116, 118

land, 9, 51, 71, 100, 171
Landa, fray Diego de, 113–115
lawsuits, 30–31, 35, 73, 79–80, 118–19, 152
Leibsohn, Dana, 34
León Portilla, Miguel, 7
letters (written by Indians), 120
Libro de Guardianes, 26, 28, 37
literacy, 4, 120
logging, 159–50, 177
López (as author of *Codex Aubin*), 69

Macehualtin, in relations with pipiltin, 10, 25, 36, 55, 83; as those who suffer and work, 22, 37, 59, 61; meaning "Indians," 196–97
Malinche, 24–25

Mapas de Cuauhtinchan, 32
Marcos (called Marcos Tlacuiloc and Marcos Cipac), 56, 57–58, 67–68, 74, 80–81
marriage, politics of, 10, 41, 43–45, 169–70; of individual leaders, 45, 73
Matlalcueye, 180, 204
Martínez, Enrico, 150, 165
Martínez de Valdés, father Diego, 176, 177
Mary. *See* Guadalupe, Asunción
Mayas. *See* Yucatán
Mendieta, fray Gerónimo de, 35–36
Menéndez de Avila, Pedro, 117
mestizo (as subject of comment), 162, 198, 200
Mexica, and origin stories, 37–41, 45, 161; as dominant power, 23, 30, 32, 46, 49, 100, 145, 173; in crisis of 1560s, 62–76
Mexico City, 61–66, 141–43, 153–54
Mimesis, 4
mirrors, 129–30
Mixton War, 29
Miyahuaxihuitl (of Cuernavaca), 173
Moctezuma (Mexica ruler), 63, 138
Moctezuma, doña Isabel de, 162
Molina, fray Alonso de, 103
Momauhti, Martín (of Mexico City), 56, 59, 67
Montúfar, Alonso de (bishop of Mexico), 70
Monzón y Mujica, Felipe (of Puebla), 213
Mota, fray Alonso de la (bishop of Puebla), 192
Motolinía, 34, 136
Moyotlan, San Juan de (barrio), 55, 62–65, 73
Mulattoes, 213–14
Muñón, Sancho Sánchez de, 147–47, 148
Múñoz Camargo, Diego, 192–93
music (and dance), 20, 45, 61, 73, 102, 111, 131, 141–43, 180, 185, 205

Nahuatl (as subject of comment), 185–86, 193
Nauhecatl Tonatiuh (god), 137
Nicolás, Pedro (of Mexico City), 55–56, 57, 58, 59, 74, 91
nomadism, 126. *See also* Mexica, origin stories; arrows
Nonoualca, 17–19, 33, 52

Ocho relaciones, 150; selection from, 141–43; main treatment of, 163–69
Ocotelolco, 175, 178, 181, 204
Olmeca Xicallanca, 19–21, 48

Olmos, fray Andres de, 107
omens, 63, 138
Ome Tochtli (god), 160
Otomí, 26, 42, 160, 203

painters, church, 63, 55–56, 73–74
Paredes, Petronilla de (of Tlaxcala), 184
penance (auto-sacrifice), 127, 161
Pérez de Arteaga, Juan, 25
performance, of xiuhpohualli, 3, 22, 32–33, 63, 94, 95, 137; of music, 141–43, 168. *See also* theater
phoneticism, 2, 3–4, 12, 31, 32–33
pictorials, 3–4. *See also* glyphs
Pinome, 23, 26–27, 32, 45
pipiltin, in relations with macehualtin, 10, 83, 88; as those responsible for a larger entity, 55, 74, 180, 193–94, 195–96, 200–02; as those punished by Spaniards, 75, 113, 197–99; and the question of who constitutes, 144, 182, 195
piracy, 116, 221, 213
Plato, 161
polygamy, 26, 89, 184, 190
Popoloca, 35, 107
priests, indigenous as, 204–05; Spaniards as, 176–77. *See also* Christianity
processions, 45, 76, 177–78, 153, 180, 185, 221
Puebla, 102, 179, 181, 202–03, 213–15
pulque, 129–31

Quecholcohuatzin (of Chalco), 141–43, 168
Quetzalcoatl, as a god, 19, 52; in Annals of Cuauhtitlan, 125–33; transformed in texts, 133–36, 166.
Quilaztli (god), 126
Quiyahuiztlan, 175, 178, 179, 181, 184, 190, 196, 204

rabbits (symbolic), 100, 206
Ramírez, don Pascual (of Tlaxcala), 178, 201
red-and-black (in tlilli in tlapalli), 2, 4, 34, 84, 138, 159, 206
religion, ancient Nahua practice of, 27, 40, 51, 104, 127–28. *See also* baptism, Christianity, idolatry, penance, sacrifice
rhetoric, 55, 61, 85, 121, 147–48, 152, 157, 158
rioting, 61–62, 75–76, 78, 200, 219
Rivas, fray Juan de, 28, 102
Roman alphabet, 3, 12, 28. *See also* alphabetic annals, phoneticism

rotary draft labor, 59–60, 156. *See also* taxation
Ruiz, don Francisco (of Tlaxcala), 178, 179, 196

sacrifice, human, 18, 38, 129, 135, 166. *See also* penance.
Sahagún, fray Bernardino de, 37, 69, 119, 120–22, 155
Salazar, don Bernabe (of Tlaxcala), 184, 188, 194, 202–03
Salazar, don Manuel de los Santos, 14, 188, 194; life story of, 202–06, 209–20; as a writer, 206–09
Salazar, don Nicolás Simeón, 204, 209–10.
Salazar, Marcelo, 209
San Antonio Abad (church of), 144, 147, 173
San Buenaventura, Pedro de, 13; in relations with Sahagún, 120–23; as probable author of annals, 123–24, 133–36
Sánchez, Catarina de (first wife of Mateo), 103, 114
Sánchez, don Mateo, 13, 103, 105; life story of, 106–16; as saddened figure, 117–20
Sánchez, Lucas (son of Mateo), 103, 110, 120
Sánchez, Marta de (second wife of Mateo), 103, 106, 114, 119
San Francisco, church of (Mexico City), 155–56
San Josef de los Naturales, church of (Mexico City), 70, 146, 162
San Juan del Río, church of (Puebla), 215–16
San Pablo, don Pedro Dionisio de, 89
Santa Fe (New Mexico), 148
Santa María Cipac, don Luis de, 60–62, 70, 78–79, 82, 86
Santa María, Juan Bautista de (of Tecamachalco), 103
Santiago, don Diego de (of Tlaxcala), 178
Santos, don Manuel de los (*not* Salazar), 175, 178
Santos, don Miguel de los, 14; life story of, 215–19; as a writer, 218–19
Schroeder, Susan, 259n3
Sermonario en lengua Mexicana, 151
Seven Caves, 45, 150, 161
Sigüenza y Góngora, Carlos, 155, 208
slaves, Africans as, 156, 216, 221; women as, 18, 170–71, 221
snakes (symbolic), 38, 127–28, 134, 189
songs, 1, 168. *See also* music

sources (for annals), in *Historia Tolteca Chichimeca*, 33–34; in *Annals of Tecamachalco*, 110–12; in *Annals of Cuauhtitlan* 137–38; in Zapata, 187–94, in Chimalpahin, 151–53
Spaniards, arrival of, 24, 91, 93, 101, 137–38, 145, 166–67, 181, 189–90; as dominant group, 75, 85, 120, 161–62, 183, 218–19
stars, 132. *See also* comets
stones (symbolic), 125, 136, 142, 173
Suárez, fray Alonso, 102

Tapado, el ("the Covered One"), 214–15, 216–17
Tapia, Andrés de, 136
Tapia, Lorenzo de (of Puebla), 214
taxation, crises of, 1560s, 55–56, 71–72; 1570s, 118–19; 1670s, 199–200
teccalli, 181
Tecpan (of Mexico City), 59–60, 75–76, 84–85, 146
Teicniuh, Miguel (of Mexico City), 61, 84
Tena, Rafael, 259n3
teniente (role of), 177, 179, 194
Tenochtitlan. *See* Mexico City
teopantlaca (use of term), 29, 63
teotl (use of term), 137
Tepeaca, 25, 27, 29, 36, 99, 206
Tepepolco, 122–23, 133–34
Tepeticpac, 175, 178, 179, 181, 196, 204
Tepeyac (chapel of), 68
Tepeyacac. *See* Tepeaca
Teuhctlecozauhqui, 32, 44, 45–46
Tezcatlipoca (god), 18, 51, 129
Tezozomoc, don Hernando de Alvarado, 153, 160–61, 172
theater, indigenous, 163, 205
time, 159–60. *See also* calendars
tithes, 57, 194
títulos primordiales, 219–20
Tizaapan, 38
Tizatla, 175, 178, 179, 181, 204
Tizoc (Mexica ruler), 73
tlacuiloque. See painters
Tlalmanalco, 141–43, 144, 155
Tlapaltecatl, Antonio (of Mexico City), 55–56, 74, 84
Tlatelolco, altepetl of, 46, 65; school in, 28–29, 37, 68, 108, 122–23
tlatoani (role of), 5, 22, 24, 66, 73, 81, 100, 141–43, 171, 182, 190
tlatocapilli, 145, 171
tlatoque (as a term), 200–01

Tlaxcala, 14–15, 180–81; early history of, 42, 49–50, 99, 188–89; allied to Spaniards, 148, 190, 217–18, 221; in written record, 175–80, 191–92
Tollan (idealized place), in *Historia Tolteca Chichimeca*, 17–21, 33, in *Annals of Cuauhtitlan*, 124–25, 130
Toral, fray Francisco de, 102–03, 107–09, 112–18, 122
Torquemada, fray Juan de, 154, 161
Totococ, Toribio Lucas, 76, 80, 86, 88, 90
traza (concept of), 66, 216, 219
tribute, *See* taxation.
Tripartito del cristianísimo doctor Juan Gerson, 108
Tula. *See* Tollan
turquoise, 126–28, 142–43, 173
Tzaqualtitlan Tenanco, 144

University (of Mexico City), 156, 194, 203–04

Valderrama, Lic. Jerónimo de, 56, 70, 71–72, 78, 85, 87
Valeriano, Alonso, 122
Velasco, don Luis de, 64, 70, 71–73, 77, 109
Veracruz, 213–14, 216
Vetancurt, fray Agustín de, 202–03, 206–07
villainy (as concept), 50, 61
Virgin Mary. *See* Guadalupe, Asunción
vultures, 167. *See also* birds

warfare, 22, 25, 32, 37, 40, 41–42, 46, 99. *See also* weapons, women
weapons, 20–21, 49, 62, 176, 214

weeping, 19, 20, 38, 49, 84, 131–32
whipping. *See* flogging
wind, 63, 100, 146, 213
women, as royalty (or bearers of royal line), 126, 133, 169, 171–72, 192; in pre-conquest wars, 18, 27, 37, 46–47, 76–77, 141–43, 170–71; as sufferers under Spanish rule, 27, 82, 84–85, 102, 146, 184, 213; as sympathetic figures, 172, 214, 221

Xinmamal, Francisco (of Mexico City), 56, 57
xiuhpohualli, defined and explained, 1–6; question of authorship of, 8–10; durability of, 180–81, 217–18, 220–22; disappearance of genre of, 224–25. *See also individual texts by title*
Xiuhtlacuiloxochitzin (of Cuauhtitlan), 126–27
Xochimilco, 39–40, 154

Yucatán, 113–17

Zahuatl River, 175, 177
Zapata y Mendoza, don Juan Buenaventura, 14; selection from text of, 175–80; life story of, 181–87, 201–2; as writer of annals, 186–93; as named office holder, 176–77, 184, 196
Zapata, don Juan Buenaventura (son of Zapata), 184, 201
Zapata, don Salvador Mateo (son of Zapata), 201
Zimmermann, Gunter, 8
Zumárraga, fray Juan de, 101, 108

www.ingramcontent.com/pod-product-compliance
Ingram Content Group UK Ltd.
Pitfield, Milton Keynes, MK11 3LW, UK
UKHW041307180426
11947UKWH00009B/739